THE NEW AMERICAN HOUSE 2

**Innovations in Residential Design
and Construction**

30 Case Studies

1

THE NEW AMERICAN HOUSE 2

Innovations in Residential Design and Construction

30 Case Studies

Edited by
OSCAR RIERA OJEDA

Whitney Library of Design
an imprint of
Watson-Guptill Publications/New York

HALF-TITLE PAGE: *Paulk Residence, James Cutler Architects.*
Photography: Timothy Hursley.
TITLE PAGE: *Mosley House and Studio, Architrope.*
Photography: Paul Warchol.

Senior Editor: Ziva Freiman
Editor: Micaela Porta
Designer: Abigail Sturges
Production Manager: Hector Campbell

Copyright © 1997 by Oscar Riera Ojeda

Published in the United States in 1997 by Whitney Library of
Design, an imprint of Watson-Guptill Publications, a division of
BPI Communications, Inc., 1515 Broadway, New York, NY 10036.

Library of Congress Cataloging-in-Publication Data

The new American house 2: innovations in residential design and
construction: 30 case studies/edited by Oscar Riera Ojeda.
   p. cm.
   Includes index.
   ISBN 0-8230-3164-0
   1. Architecture, Domestic--United States--Case studies.
2. Architecture, Modern--20th century--United States--Case studies. 3. Architecture--United States--Case studies. I. Riera Ojeda,
Oscar.
   NA7208.N45 1997
   728'.0973—dc20   97-23273
                                                           CIP

Manufactured in China
First printing, 1997

1 2 3 4 5 6 7 8 9 / 02 01 00 99 98 97

*I would like to dedicate this book to my father, Oscar
Luciano Riera Ojeda, with whom I recently recovered con-
tact after eight years of painful separation; to my aunt,
Marta Guerrero, and my uncle, Félix Juan Testone; and in
memory of my uncle Mateo Testone, whom I remember
vividly for his great heart and joyfulness.*

Oscar Riera Ojeda

Contents

Foreword

FACING PAGE: *The Bach Residence, Frank Lupo and Daniel Rowen, Architects. Photography: Michael Moran.*

BELOW: *Type/Variant House, Vincent James Associates. Photography:Dont F. Wong Photography.*
BOTTOM: *Paulk Residence, James Cutler Architects. Photography: Timothy Hursley.*

Houses have come a long way from the simple child's sketch depicting a box, triangle roof, two windows, and door. The great residential designs of today seek to incorporate what being at home has always meant to us—that is, feeling welcome, safe, and comfortable—while consciously pushing the boundaries to adapt to our contemporary lifestyles. The houses included in this volume illustrate how our notions of "home" can be reverted or employed beyond their conventional definitions. For instance, in the Miller O'Herlihy Residence designed by Lorcan O'Herlihy, a wall dematerializes into a flow of directional energy; a floor becomes a ceiling in Alfredo De Vido's Moore House; and a ceiling can even become a wall, as in the Golden Beach Residence's beachfront "casita" designed by Carlos Zapata.

As we find ourselves perched on the threshold of a new millennium, the pursuit of change chronicled in these pages is also defined by the architects' desire to explore new media and horizons. East meets West in Peter Gluck's Mies House Pavilions, architecture becomes sculpture in Vincent James' Type/Variant House and Simon Ungers and Tom Kinslow's T-House, distinctions between inside and outside are blurred in Schweitzer BIM's The Monument, and the natural and man-made fuse in James Cutler's design for the Paulk Residence. Dispelling the image of the house as a single volume, the Bach House by Frank Lupo and Daniel Rowen shows how two houses can be one, just as the Mosley House and Studio by Architrope illustrates that one house can be two. In response to the growing number of people choosing to work from home, many of these structures have had to accommodate two vastly different pursuits under one roof. The Elm Court House by Lake/Flato Architects serves as an example of a residence, workshop, and gallery that seamlessly coexist. Robert Luchetti Associates, in a ranch in Lake County, California, incorporated a greater spatial richness and quality of exterior spaces amid typical rural village constructions. All these variables refer to the multifaceted solutions characteristic of today's cutting-edge residential design.

In their attempt to reinterpret the very structure of the house, the examples shown in *The New American House 2* essentially redefine the factors that condition design. Many of these houses show a great respect for the environment, albeit from totally opposing viewpoints. In the Paulk Residence in Seabeck, Washington, client and architect showed their reverence of the site by suspending the house within a dense forest that was completely protected, allowing an intimate, uninterrupted relationship with nature. Such care was also given to the interior

in that the materials speak for themselves, left exposed to reveal their innate characteristics. Alfredo DeVido and Emilio Ambasz also made minimal site disturbance a priority. In Lakeville, Connecticut, the Moore House is entangled with the earth in an organic play of horizontal planes while the interior reflects the palette of the landscape. In a private estate that he designed in Montana, Emilio Ambasz brought the idea of harmony with nature to a poetic extreme; over time, the facade will be overgrown with ivy, causing the house to virtually disappear from its site. In Dean/Wolf's design for the Spiro House in Armonk, New York, the site's inherent contradictions establish the characteristics of the design itself. Even after part of the solid granite dome from which the house rises was leveled, the final effect pays homage to the site through a sculptural entrance patio made from the remains of the granite formation. For Schweitzer BIM, the connection with the site was established by a strong respect for its rock formations. Outside, the design echoes the rocks, and inside each aperture frames changing still lifes of rocks and sky. Interior and exterior spaces serve the principal protagonist—the landscape—and the unity here reaches a grade of near-complete integrity.

Projection toward the landscape is a theme that characterizes several of these houses. In many of them this disposition is expressed in plan. The Tennessee River House designed by Mockbee/Coker Architects is a sort of anticipated revelation, after parading through the totality of the various spatial alternatives discovered while descending toward the landscape. In the Miller O'Herlihy Residence in Malibu, California, transparent perimeter walls project the interior activity toward the ocean and roof terraces. Similarly, Wendell Burnette's house and studio in Sunnyslope, Arizona, maximizes the perception of the space as it fills with natural light and images of the changing landscape. A fragmented vision at different levels characterizes the Von Stein Residence designed by Fernau & Hartman in Sonoma County, California, as opposed to the panoramic view visible from Smith-Miller + Hawkinson's MAXmin House in Damascus, Pennsylvania.

Four houses—the Jimenez House designed by Carlos Jimenez, the Essex Residence by Wheeler Kearns, the WorkHouse by Guthrie+Buresh, and the MAXmin House—represent possible residential prototypes. The Essex Residence successfully addresses how multiple programmatic constrictions can engender practical and original systems of construction without sacrific-

BELOW: *Tarzana Residence, Daly, Genik. Photography: J. Scott Smith*

ing aesthetic aspirations. The Jimenez House's simplicity, clarity, and economy provide a viable solution for housing in depressed neighborhoods, just as the WorkHouse, although more experimental, serves as a point of reference for urban dwellings of the future. The MAXmin House, intimately tied to the culture of the mobile home, would not be difficult to imagine in diverse versions throughout various rural settings.

The benefit of life in the open air, in those sites where the climate allows it, has generated innovative versions of patios and intermediate and exterior spaces. One of the more interesting is Darryl Ohlenbusch's screened corner room in a house he built for his mother in San Antonio, Texas. An interior patio and a series of galleries that extend from interior to exterior and vice-versa diversify the possible uses of space in this small and humble residence. The same plurality of uses runs through the Von Stein House, allowing its residents to alternate throughout the day among the various qualities of its exterior spaces. In the Elm Court Residence, patios act as determinants of the spirit that reigns within its adjacent spaces: peace and tranquillity next to the art gallery, and vitality adjacent to the master bedroom and work studio.

But the collection of houses featured here is not limited to new construction, as several projects address the extension and remodeling of existing houses in distinctly different ways. Peter Gluck and Partners' design for the Mies House Pavilions and Second Addition in Weston, Connecticut, remains contextual without degenerating into mimicry. For Daly, Genik, in the Tarzana Residence in Tarzana, California, remodeling demanded an improvement of the definition of the interior spaces, and this was achieved (after demolishing almost all interior walls) through the use of freestanding sculpted objects. Audacity and dynamism were the premises for the Golden Beach Residence in Miami, to the point where few would believe the limitations that once constrained the existing building.

To achieve practicality, programmatic flexibility, and greater amplitude in spaces are common goals in each house. Peter Forbes, in the Norberg House in Surry, Maine, incorporated these qualities in the very genesis of the project by allowing the directing geometry to locate service functions at the perimeters, thereby liberating the space. In his flexible design with shared amenities, Eric J. Cobb responded to the need for a more relaxed lifestyle of his clients, his parents. Creating a sense of transition from public to private realms in the small transversal space of the Meadow House designed by

Olson Sundberg in King County, Washington, has not been an obstacle to maintaining the spatial fluidity from the spectacular and captivating vistas of the southeast to the serenity of the north court. The Root House interior in Ormond Beach, Florida, designed by Pasanella Klein Stolzman Berg Architects, and the New York townhouse by Tod Williams and Billie Tsien use monumental elements (an interior bridge in the first case, and a wall containing the vertical circulation in the second) to command attention and define the sense of movement.

The demand for houses will surely continue unfettered, just as architects and designers—as well as their clients—will continue to demand newer amenities, more flexible programs, and more innovative designs. While the necessity to grow and improve is so basic as to be practically instinctive, it takes fantastic creativity and hard work to rise above the crowd. These thirty examples are proof that many architects have assumed, with talent and professionalism, that difficult responsibility.

THE NEW AMERICAN HOUSE 2

Innovations in Residential Design and Construction

30 Case Studies

Paulk Residence *1994*
JAMES CUTLER ARCHITECTS

Owner: Elinor and John Paulk
Architect: James Cutler Architects, Bainbridge Island, Washington
Design Team: James Cutler, FAIA, Bruce Anderson, AIA
Engineer: Ratti Swenson Perbix (structural)
Consultant: General Testing Laboratories, Inc. (geology)
General Contractor: Pleasant Beach Construction
Photography: Art Grice

Site: Seabeck, Washington
Program: Residence and garage/workshop/guest house including living room, dining room, kitchen, half bathroom, laundry, master bedroom, bathroom, 2 bedrooms, den, storage, garage, workshop.
Square Footage: 2100 in residence, 1400 in garage/guest house
Structural System: Douglas fir post-and-beam frame, 2 x 12 floor joists and rafters, 2 x 4 stud framing
Mechanical System: Propane forced air heating unit, CFC-free
Major Exterior Materials: 1 x 6 bevel tight-knot cedar siding, galvanized corrugated metal (roof)
Major Interior Materials: 1 x 6 tongue and groove pine paneling with light white stain, maple, carpeting
Furnishings and Storage: Dining room table designed by James Cutler Architects, built by Art Grice
Doors and Hardware: Douglas fir frames and rails; Schlage
Windows: Douglas fir windows custom by Northwest Window Works.
Fixtures: Lighting designed by James Cutler Architects, fabricated by John Paulk.
Appliances and Equipment: White, Westinghouse, GE
Cost: Withheld at owner's request.

Site
Perched on a 200-foot waterfront bluff on the east side of the Hood Canal in Washington State, the Paulk residence commands a striking view of the Olympic Mountains. The land is wooded with a second growth cedar thicket in the center, tapering to young red alder with salal and evergreen huckleberry at the margins of the bluff.

Design
The owners wanted a residence and garage/workshop/guest house that would both provide beautiful views of the Olympic Mountains and comply with mandatory eighty-foot setbacks from the edge of the bluff. Nestled into the forest on the remnants of an old logging road, the house is anchored to the ground at its south end, and rises to fifteen feet above the sloping ground at the north. The entrance is accessed by a 130-foot ramp that rises from the east, passes through the building, and ends at a belvedere on the west edge of the bluff. The ramp not only provides access to the building but also preserves the forest floor while allowing an opportunity

TOP: *Southeast entrance detail*
MIDDLE: *Access bridge*
BOTTOM: *Northeast section sketch*
FACING PAGE: *Southeast façade*

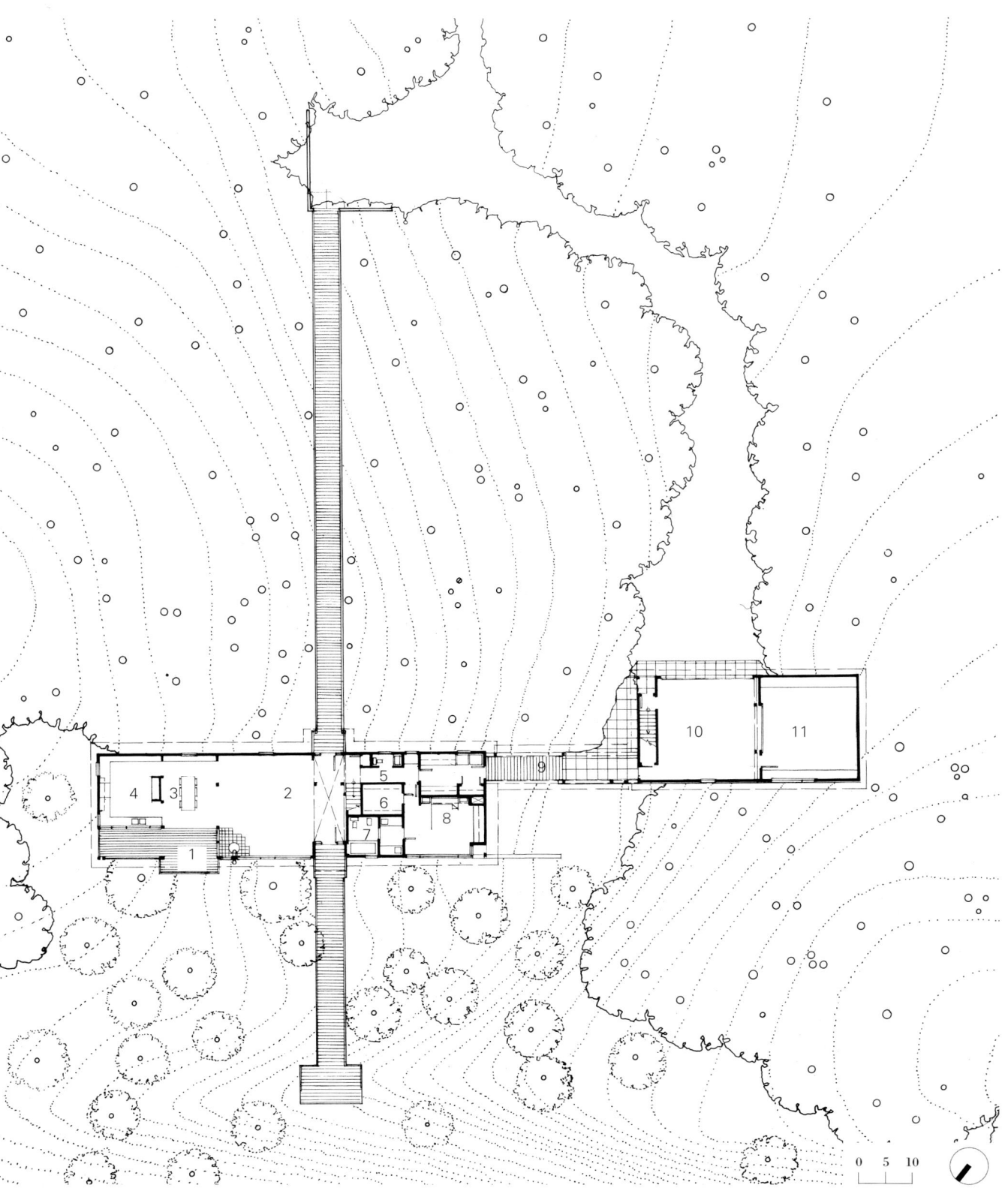

First level floor plan

to intimately experience nature. Inside, a glass-gridded wall measuring twenty feet in height connects the interior to the outdoors.

Construction

Construction was coordinated to minimize disturbance of the land: footings were dug by hand, vegetation was replaced, and only three trees were felled in the entire process.

With the intention of making the house as "true" as possible, the architect lets materials speak for themselves, leaving them exposed to reveal their innate characteristics. The house's form and "ornament" flashings directly respond to views, sun, wind, and rain. On the inside, the ceiling is pulled back in places, framing in the foyer is exposed, and floor joists are cut at random lengths. In places, sheet metal is screwed into place as soffits or wall panels.

1. GUEST ENTRY
2. LIVING ROOM
3. DINING ROOM
4. KITCHEN
5. HALF BATHROOM
6. LAUNDRY
7. BATHROOM
8. MASTER BEDROOM
9. BREEZEWAY
10. GARAGE
11. WORKSHOP
12. GUEST BEDROOM
13. BEDROOM
14. DEN
15. STORAGE

Roof details

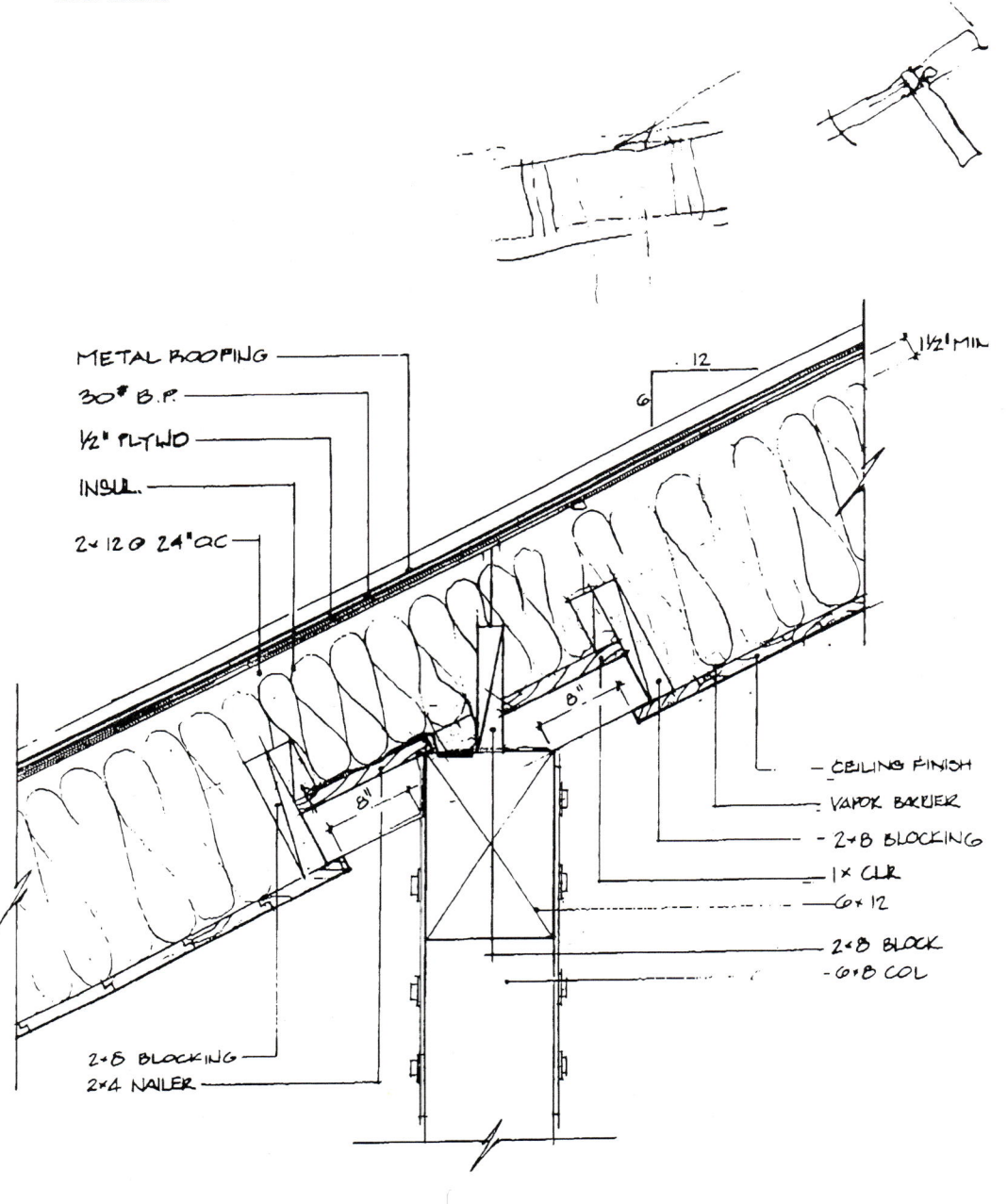

METAL ROOFING
30# B.P.
½" PLYWD
INSUL.
2×12 @ 24"OC

12
6
1½"MIN

8"
8"

2×8 BLOCKING
2×4 NAILER

CEILING FINISH
VAPOR BARRIER
2×8 BLOCKING
1× CLR
6×12
2×8 BLOCK
6×8 COL

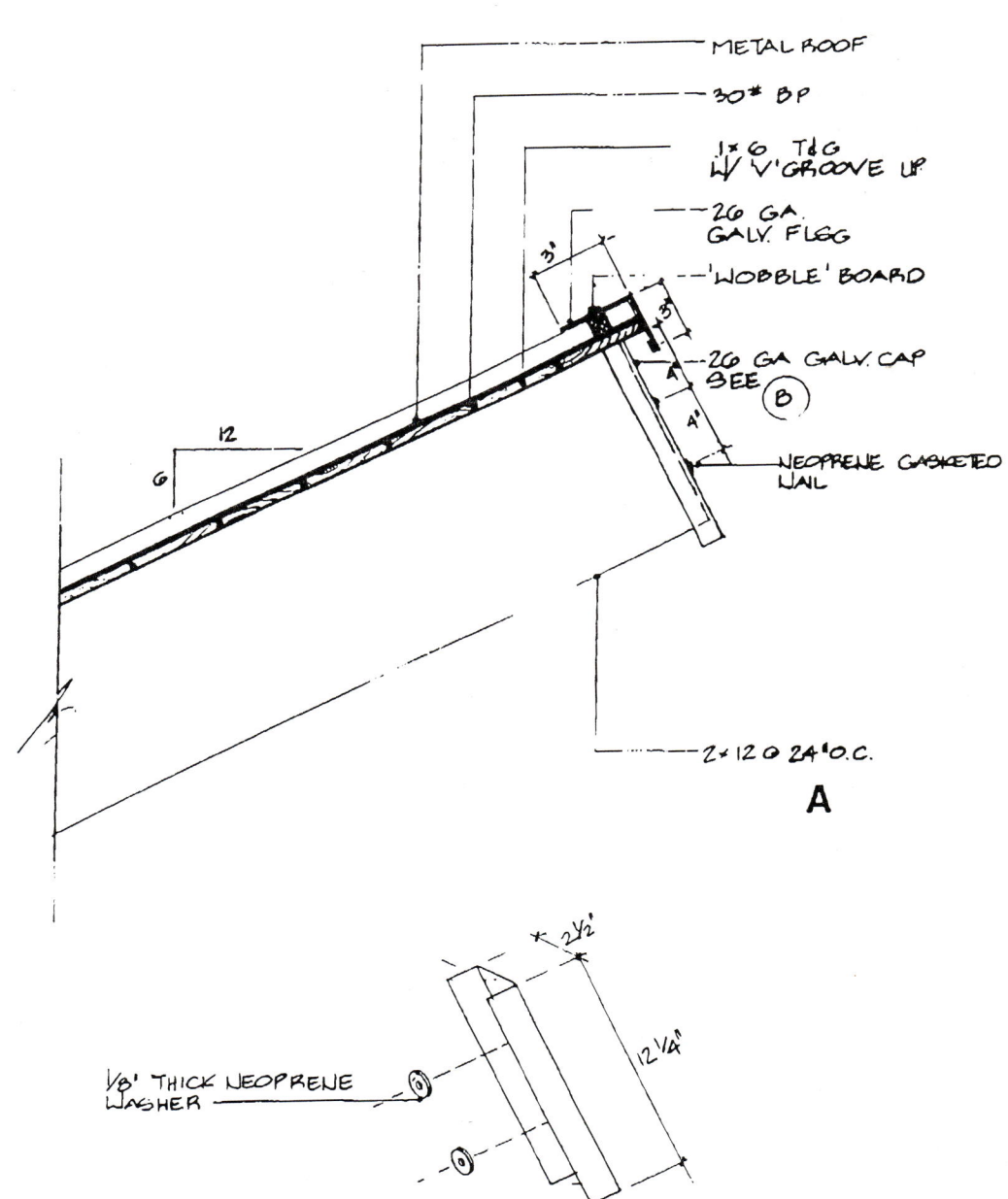

METAL ROOF
30# BP
1×6 T&G
W/ V'GROOVE UP
26 GA.
GALV. FLSG
'WOBBLE' BOARD
26 GA GALV. CAP
SEE (B)
NEOPRENE GASKETED
NAIL

3'
5'
4'
4'

12
6

2×12 @ 24" O.C.

A

⅛" THICK NEOPRENE
WASHER
2½"
12¼"

LEFT AND BOTTOM: *Views of entrance hall*
FACING PAGE: *View of living room and dining room*

Southwest section

Access bridge to terrace detail

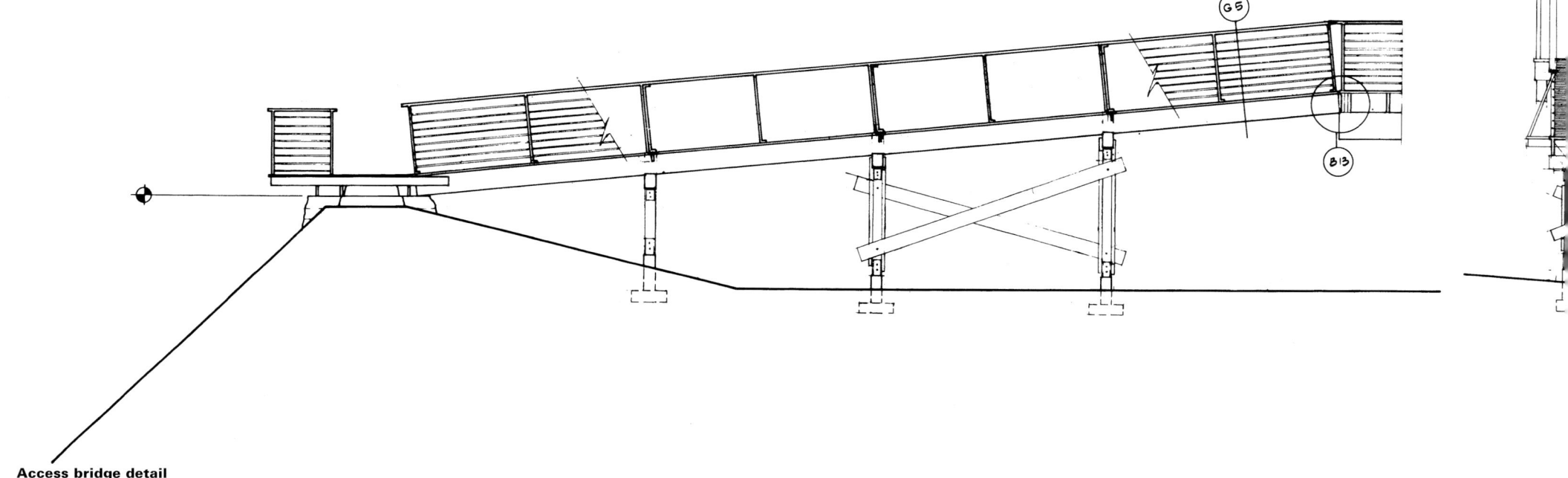

G5

B13

Access bridge detail

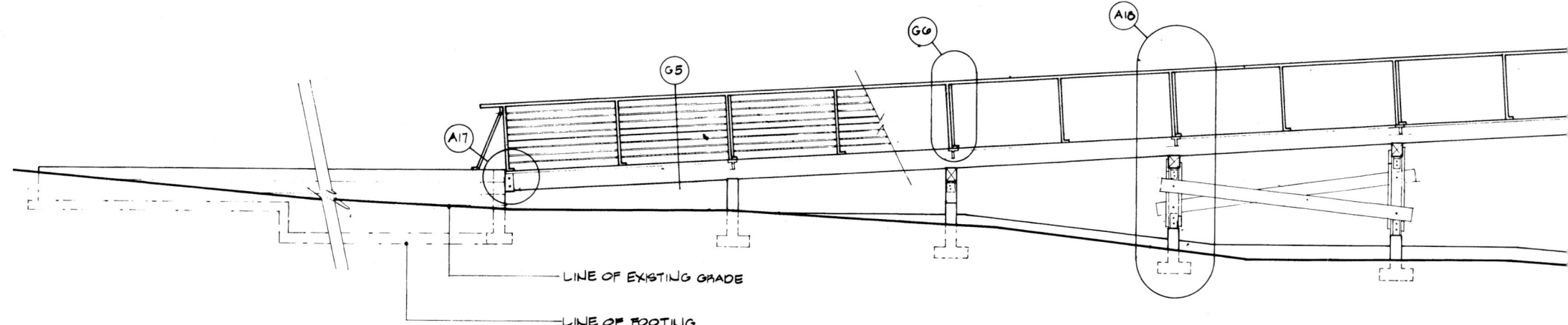

A18

G6

G5

A17

LINE OF EXISTING GRADE

LINE OF FOOTING

FAR LEFT: *View of access bridge*
LEFT: *Access bridge at entrance*

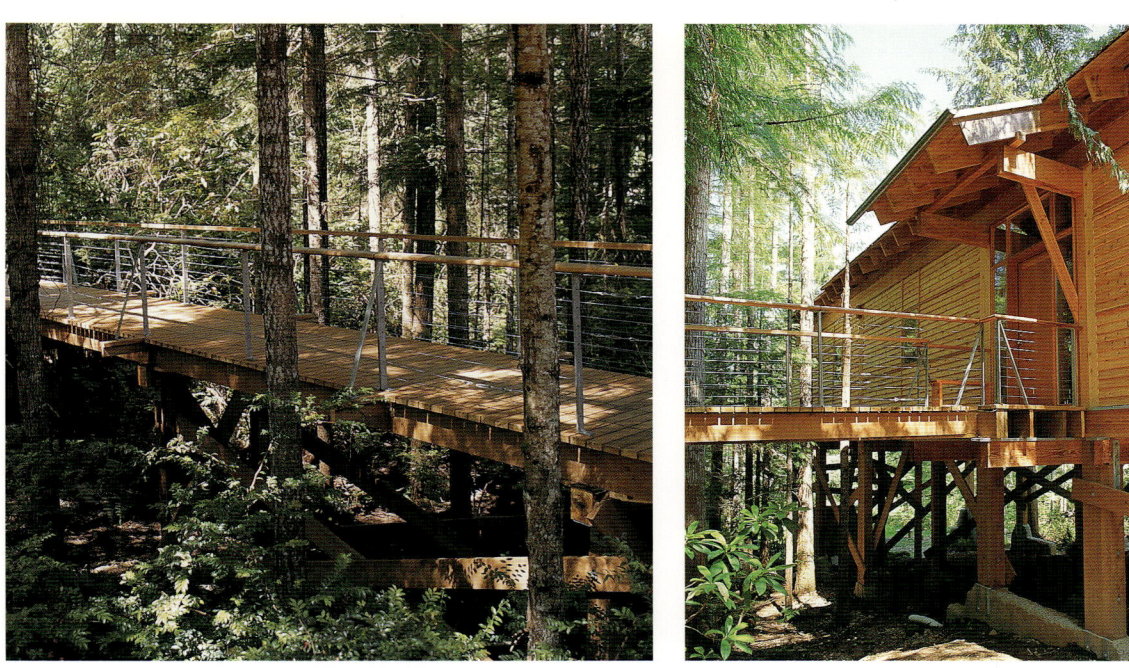

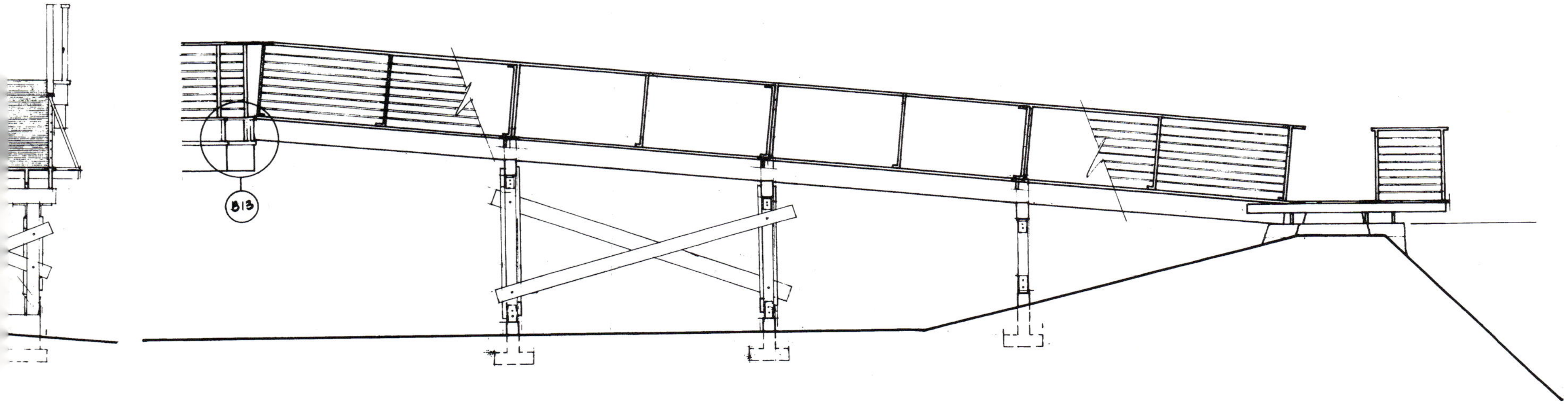
B13

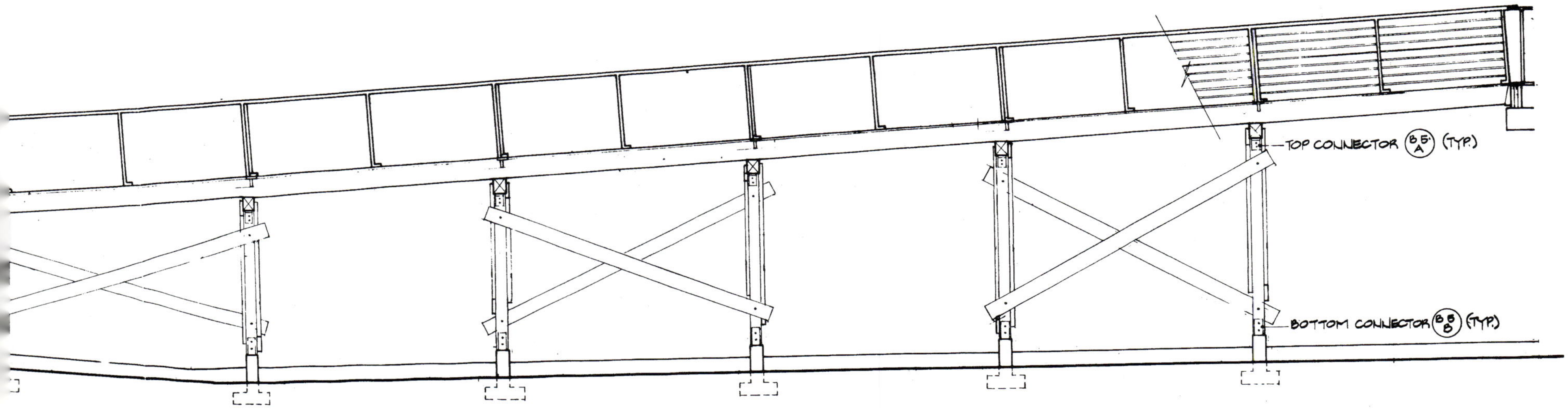
TOP CONNECTOR B5 A (TYP.)
BOTTOM CONNECTOR B5 B (TYP.)

The Meadow House *1992*
OLSON SUNDBERG ARCHITECTS

Owner: Name withheld at owner's request.
Architect: Olson Sundberg Architects, Seattle, Washington
Design Team: Tom Kundig (principal architect), Jim Olson (design critic), Marc Brown, Bill Sleeth.
Engineer: Ratti Perbix Swenson Clark (structural)
General Contractor: John Brown Builder
Photography: Michael Shopenn

Site: Finn Hill, King County, Washington
Program: House for a family of four including living room, dining room, kitchen, family room, laundry, half bathroom, master bedroom and bathroom, 2 bedrooms, bathroom, garage.
Square Footage: 5000
Structural System: Wood frame construction with architectural cast-in-place and tilt-up concrete.
Mechanical System: Forced air heating and cooling
Major Exterior Materials: Marine plywood (soffits), cedar (siding), standing seam metal (roof), architectural cast-in-place and tilt-up concrete, galvanized steel (details).
Major Interior Materials: Maple (flooring), concrete (columns), painted gypsum board (walls and ceilings), glass (relites).
Furnishings and Storage: Provided by owner; custom cabinetry and interior architecture by architect.
Doors and Hardware: Wood doors with commercial hardware
Windows: Quantum wood
Fixtures: Columbia billboard lighting
Appliances and Equipment: Sub-Zero (refrigerator/freezer), Thermador (oven), Lightolier (lighting).
Cost: $135 per square foot

Site

Situated at the edge of a high, forested plateau in a south sloping meadow, the house overlooks an adjacent lake, distant mountains, and nearby cities. The clients' family life and desire for privacy, combined with the site's natural beauty and views, led to the decision to strongly state the concepts of "refuge" and "prospect." By depressing the private spaces into the landscape on the north for privacy, and running the public spaces along the crest of the hill to take advantage of the tremendous views and the natural setting, the house satisfies both ends of the clients' program while maximizing the site.

Design

Public and private spaces are divided, with private spaces aligned perpendicular to the crest of the hill, and the public spaces sited parallel to the hill's contours. The north end of the house, which contains the private spaces, is depressed slightly into the hillside, hugging the earth and providing physical and visual relief from the wide-open expanses of the meadow and distant vistas. Landscaping on the north side of the house takes the form of a berm that naturally extends the meadow, rolling onto the roof of the garage and children's

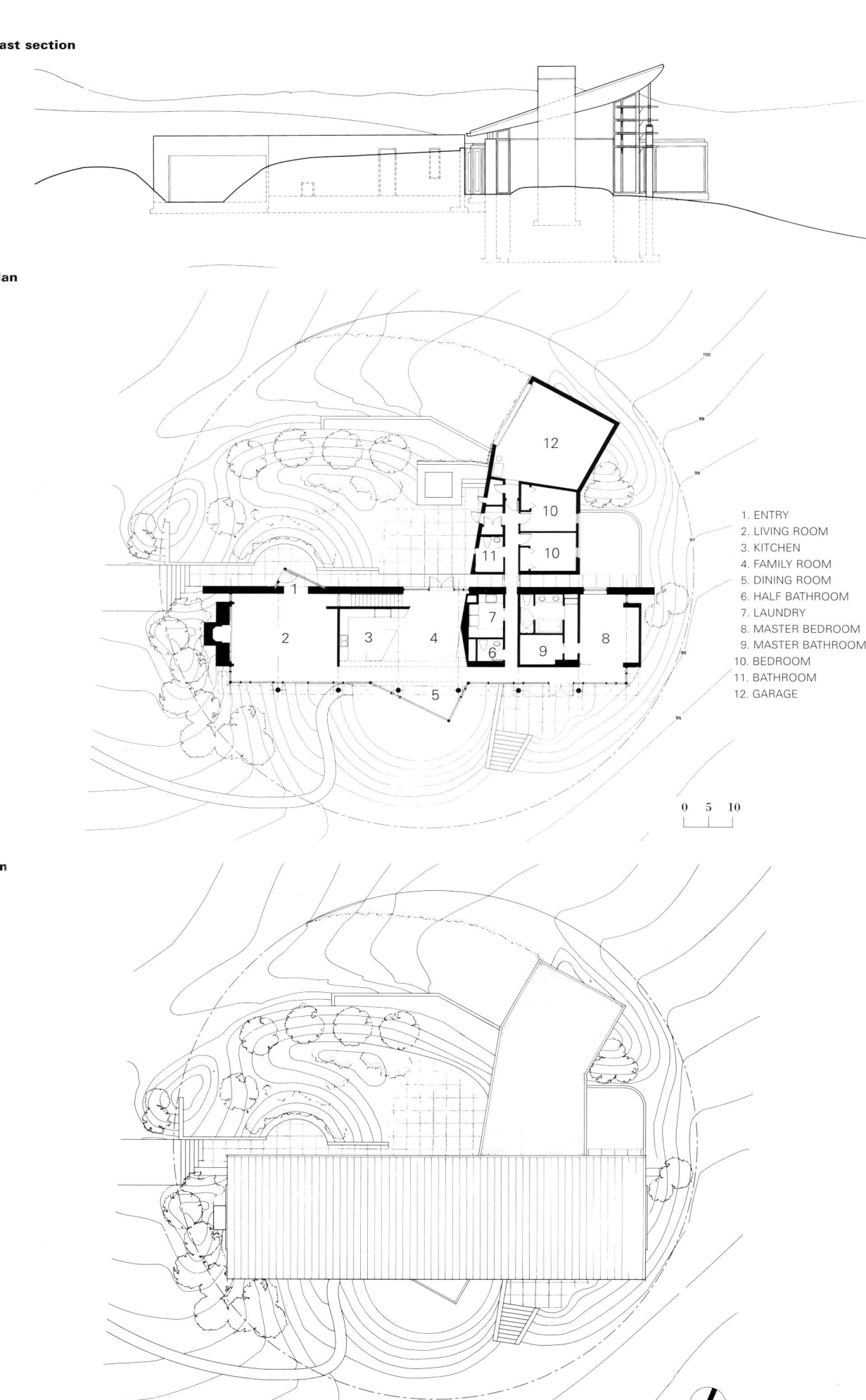

Southeast section

Floor plan

1. ENTRY
2. LIVING ROOM
3. KITCHEN
4. FAMILY ROOM
5. DINING ROOM
6. HALF BATHROOM
7. LAUNDRY
8. MASTER BEDROOM
9. MASTER BATHROOM
10. BEDROOM
11. BATHROOM
12. GARAGE

0 5 10

Site plan

bedrooms, allowing nature to reinforce the ideas of refuge and security. A hollow channel created between the berm and the house serves both as a secluded point of entry and an enclosed private garden.

As the house crests the hill, it emerges from the site, opening up the views of the meadow and beyond. Leaving the earthbound protected refuge, the house opens horizontally and vertically to the south to become a platform and terrace that hover over the ground. This space contains the public areas—kitchen, dining room, and living room—and is covered by an upwardly sloping ceiling that functions as both a luminaire and roof. The south edge of the house is a window wall that runs the entire length of the house to maximize the intake of light and views. A galley separates the window wall from activity areas and buffers the living spaces from direct light. A small articulated nook projects out into space from the window wall, providing the house's ultimate point of prospect.

Works of art are an important component of the architect's design as well. Jeffrey Bishop painted a pair of wall murals in the lower level living room that, while nominally representative of fire and water, evoke the deep, dark blues of timeless, endless space. Before each mural is a thematically-linked glass sculpture by Nancy Mee that builds upon the ideas of the mural. The rainbow created by Walter White's prismatic skylight contributes to the theme of transcendence by mixing ideas of time and space. Glass is used in a variety of ways to express illusion both through expanding and reflecting space. The kitchen backsplash is made of mirrored glass panels by artist Ann Gardner. These panels, backed by mirrors and impregnated with metal, enliven the relatively low level of light in the kitchen.

Construction

Materials were selected to conceptually augment the house's program. Heavy, low-tech materials such as concrete, and low 8'6" ceilings in the beamed portion of the house reinforce the feeling of sanctuary. As one moves into the pavilion, light colored woods, metal, and glass take over, visually lightening the space and connecting it to the airy views.

The spiritual spaces are enhanced through abstractions of form such as knife-edged light shelves with diffuse concealed uplites, glass walls that allow space to flow freely, and art integrated directly into the architecture. Changing ceiling heights are used for dramatic effect, creating spaces that appear to be free of the perimeter window walls.

RIGHT: *Building under construction*
FAR RIGHT: *Southeast façade and entrance*

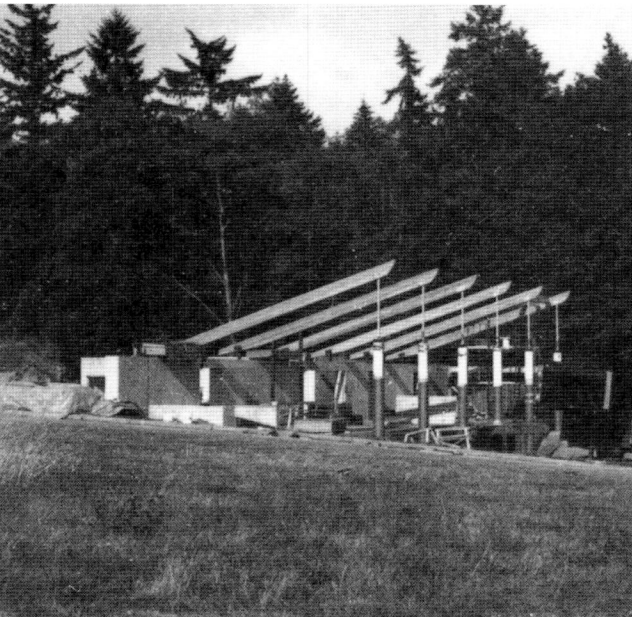

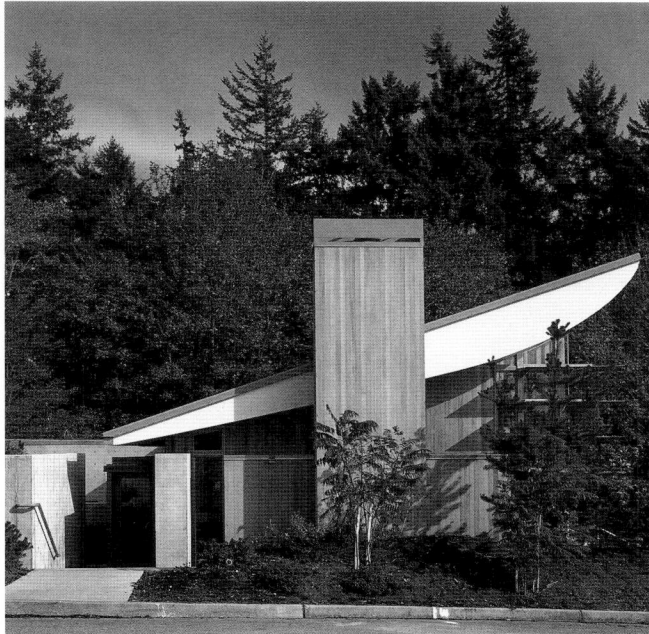

Axonometric

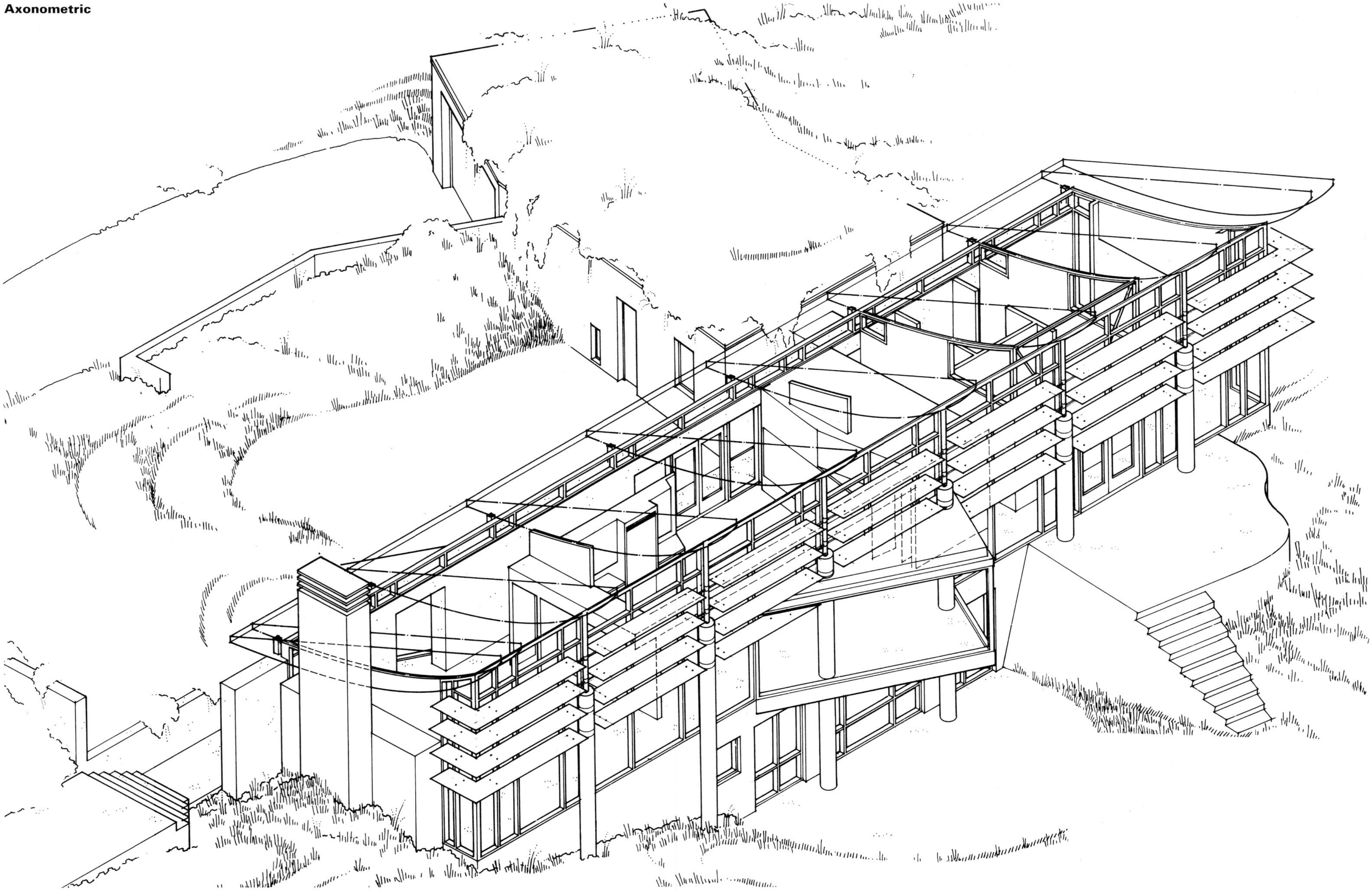

CLOCKWISE FROM TOP LEFT:
Living room; corridor from master bedroom to public areas; entrance; private garden; kitchen
FACING PAGE: *View of kitchen toward breakfast nook*

RIGHT: *View of living room*

Concrete column and sunscreen details

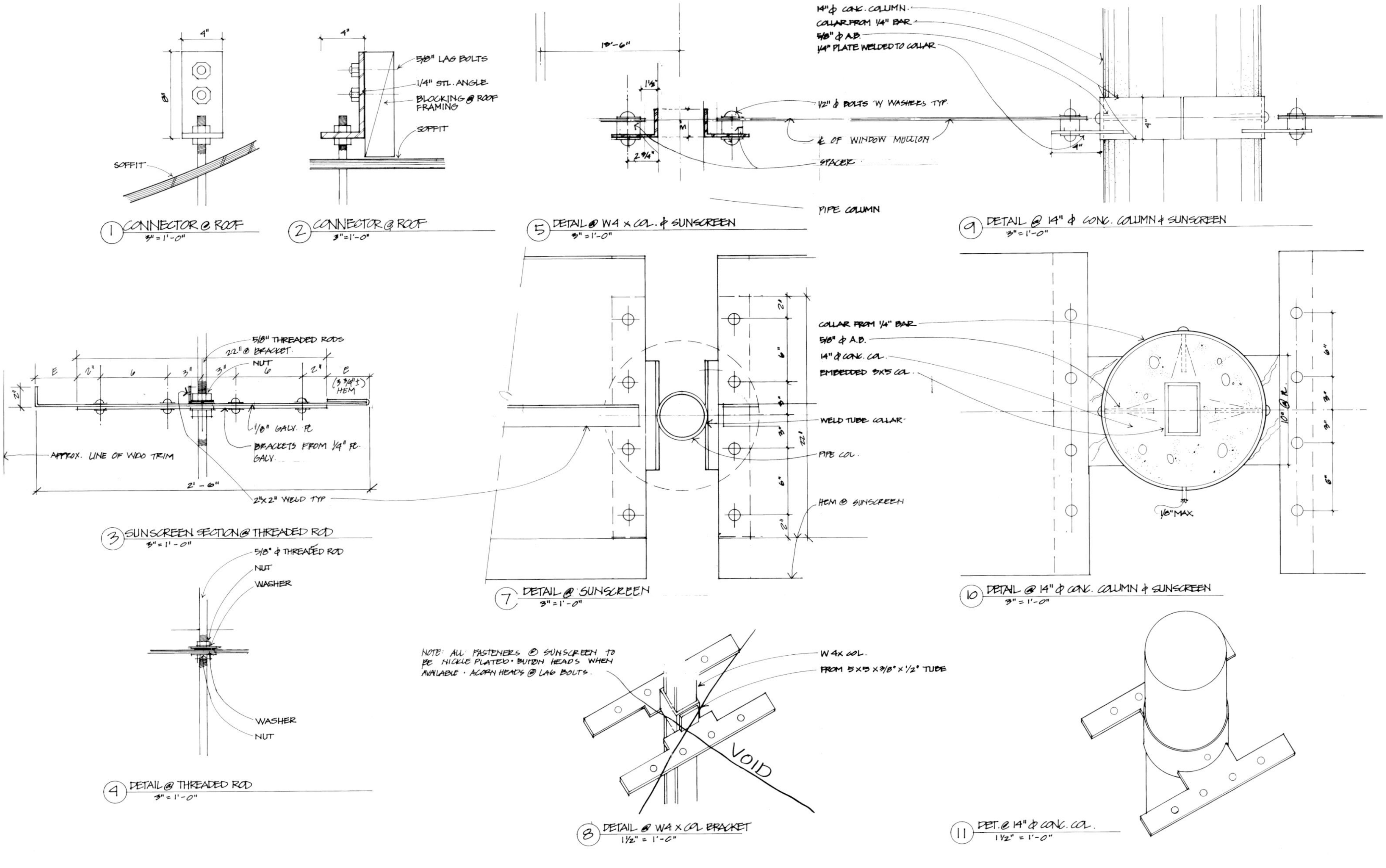

5/8" LAG BOLTS
1/4" STL. ANGLE
BLOCKING @ ROOF FRAMING
SOFFIT

SOFFIT

① CONNECTOR @ ROOF
3"=1'-0"

② CONNECTOR @ ROOF
3"=1'-0"

14"ø CONC. COLUMN
COLLAR FROM 1/4" BAR
5/8" ø A.B.
1/4" PLATE WELDED TO COLLAR

1/2"ø BOLTS 'W WASHERS TYP.

₵ OF WINDOW MULLION

SPACER

PIPE COLUMN

⑤ DETAIL @ W4 X COL. & SUNSCREEN
3"=1'-0"

⑨ DETAIL @ 14"ø CONC. COLUMN & SUNSCREEN
3"=1'-0"

5/8" THREADED RODS
21/2"ø BRACKET.
NUT
1/8" GALV. PL.
BRACKETS FROM 1/4" PL. GALV.
APPROX. LINE OF WDO. TRIM
2'-6"
2"X 2" WELD TYP

③ SUNSCREEN SECTION @ THREADED ROD
3"=1'-0"

5/8"ø THREADED ROD
NUT
WASHER

WASHER
NUT

④ DETAIL @ THREADED ROD
3"=1'-0"

COLLAR FROM 1/4" BAR
5/8" ø A.B.
14"ø CONC. COL.
EMBEDDED 5X5 COL.

WELD TUBE COLLAR
PIPE COL.

HEM @ SUNSCREEN

⑦ DETAIL @ SUNSCREEN
3"=1'-0"

1/8" MAX

⑩ DETAIL @ 14"ø CONC. COLUMN & SUNSCREEN
3"=1'-0"

NOTE: ALL FASTENERS @ SUNSCREEN TO BE NICKLE PLATED. BUTTON HEADS WHEN AVAILABLE. ACORN HEADS @ LAG BOLTS.

W 4X COL.
FROM 5 X 5 X 3/8" X 1/2" TUBE

VOID

⑧ DETAIL @ W4 X COL BRACKET
1½"=1'-0"

⑪ DET. @ 14"ø CONC. COL.
1½"=1'-0"

RIGHT: *Bris-soleil detail*

Galvanized steel fin details

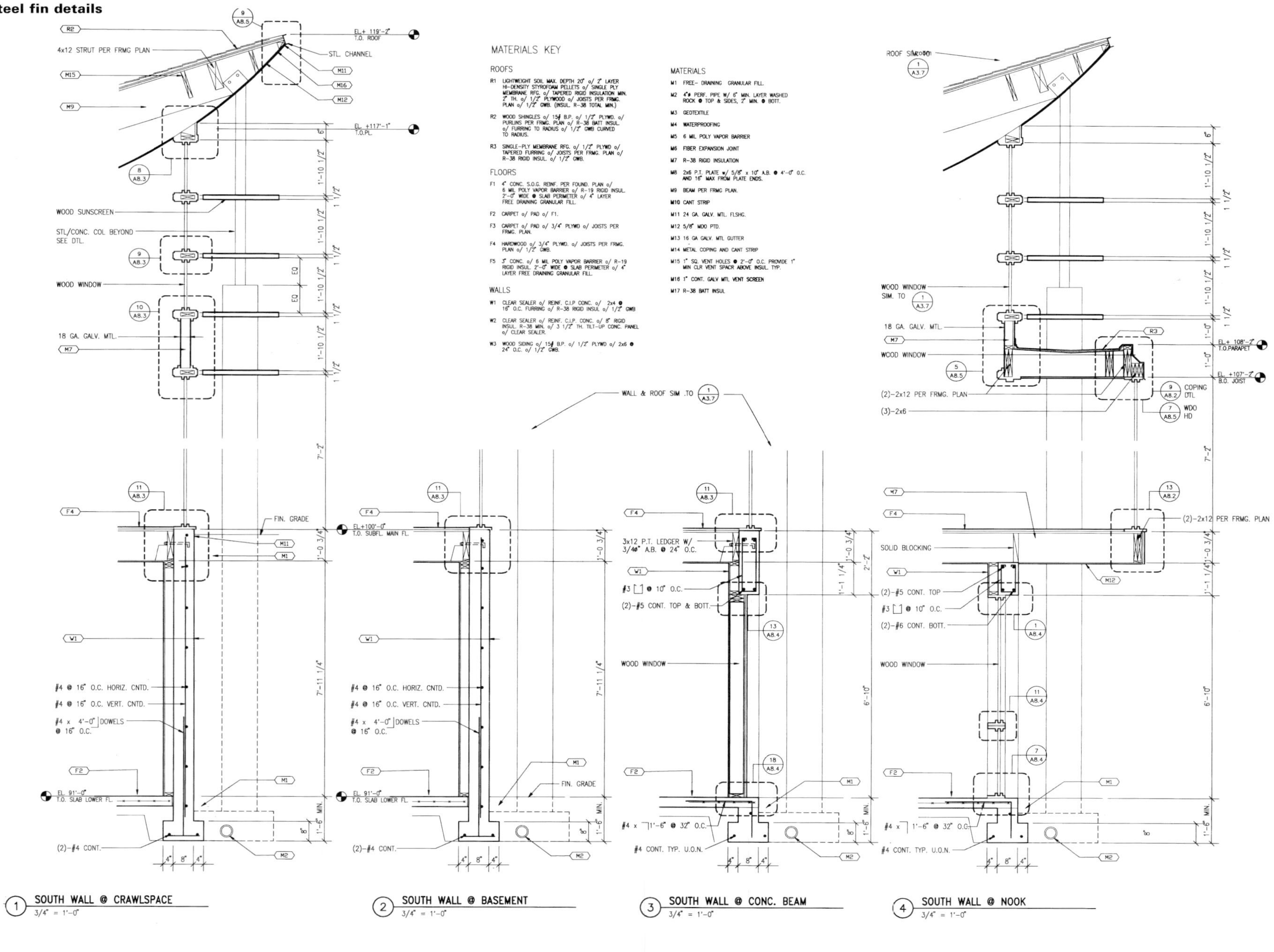

MATERIALS KEY

ROOFS

R1 LIGHTWEIGHT SOIL MAX. DEPTH 20" o/ 2" LAYER
HI-DENSITY STYROFOAM PELLETS o/ SINGLE PLY
MEMBRANE RFG. o/ TAPERED RIGID INSULATION MIN.
2" TH. o/ 1/2" PLYWOOD o/ JOISTS PER FRMG.
PLAN o/ 1/2" GWB. (INSUL. R-38 TOTAL MIN.)

R2 WOOD SHINGLES o/ 15# B.P. o/ 1/2" PLYWD. o/
PURLINS PER FRMG. PLAN o/ R-38 BATT INSUL.
o/ FURRING TO RADIUS o/ 1/2" GWB CURVED o/
TO RADIUS.

R3 SINGLE-PLY MEMBRANE RFG. o/ 1/2" PLYWD o/
TAPERED FURRING o/ JOISTS PER FRMG. PLAN o/
R-38 RIGID INSUL. o/ 1/2" GWB.

FLOORS

F1 4" CONC. S.O.G. REINF. PER FOUND. PLAN o/
6 MIL POLY VAPOR BARRIER o/ R-19 RIGID INSUL.
2'-0" WIDE @ SLAB PERIMETER o/ 4" LAYER
FREE DRAINING GRANULAR FILL.

F2 CARPET o/ PAD o/ F1.

F3 CARPET o/ PAD o/ 3/4" PLYWD. o/ JOISTS PER
FRMG. PLAN.

F4 HARDWOOD o/ 3/4" PLYWD. o/ JOISTS PER FRMG.
PLAN o/ 1/2" GWB.

F5 5" CONC. o/ 6 MIL POLY VAPOR BARRIER o/ R-19
RIGID INSUL. 2'-0" WIDE @ SLAB PERIMETER o/ 4"
LAYER FREE DRAINING GRANULAR FILL.

WALLS

W1 CLEAR SEALER o/ REINF. C.I.P CONC. o/ 2x4 @
16" O.C. FURRING o/ R-38 RIGID INSUL o/ 1/2" GWB.

W2 CLEAR SEALER o/ REINF. C.I.P CONC. o/ 8" RIGID
INSUL. R-38, MIN. o/ 3 1/2" TH. TILT-UP CONC. PANEL
o/ CLEAR SEALER.

W3 WOOD SIDING o/ 15# B.P. o/ 1/2" PLYWD o/ 2x6 @
24" O.C. o/ 1/2" GWB.

MATERIALS

M1 FREE- DRAINING GRANULAR FILL.

M2 4" PERF. PIPE W/ 6" MIN. LAYER WASHED
ROCK @ TOP & SIDES, 2" MIN. @ BOTT.

M3 GEOTEXTILE

M4 WATERPROOFING

M5 6 MIL POLY VAPOR BARRIER

M6 FIBER EXPANSION JOINT

M7 R-38 RIGID INSULATION

M8 2x6 P.T. PLATE w/ 5/8" x 10" A.B. @ 4'-0" O.C.
AND 16" MAX FROM PLATE ENDS.

M9 BEAM PER FRMG. PLAN.

M10 CANT STRIP

M11 24 GA. GALV. MTL. FLSHG.

M12 5/8" WOOD PTD.

M13 16 GA GALV. MTL. GUTTER

M14 METAL COPING AND CANT STRIP

M15 1" SQ. VENT HOLES @ 2'-0" O.C. PROVIDE 1"
MIN CLR VENT SPACE ABOVE INSUL. TYP.

M16 1" CONT. GALV. MTL. VENT SCREEN

M17 R-38 BATT INSUL

---

(1) SOUTH WALL @ CRAWLSPACE
3/4" = 1'-0"

(2) SOUTH WALL @ BASEMENT
3/4" = 1'-0"

(3) SOUTH WALL @ CONC. BEAM
3/4" = 1'-0"

(4) SOUTH WALL @ NOOK
3/4" = 1'-0"

Cobb House *1996*

ERIC J. COBB, ARCHITECT

Owner: Else and Leonard Cobb
Architect: Eric J. Cobb, Architect, Seattle, Washington
Design Team: Eric Cobb (project architect and manager), Kirsten Mercer
Engineers: Gary MacKenzie, Swenson Say Faget (structural), Carstel Corporation (mechanical)
Consultant: Glenn Carter, Advanced Building Consultants
Photography: Paul Warchol

Site: Seattle, Washington
Program: Modest, informal residence for the architect's parents including living room, dining room, kitchen, elevator, terrace, pantry/laundry, 2 bathrooms, study/bedroom, studio/media room, bedroom, roof deck.
Square Footage: 2880 interior, 1570 exterior
Structural System: Concrete foundation and retaining walls, manufactured wood framing, steel moment frame and pipe columns.
Mechanical System: Gas fired, forced air heating
Major Exterior Materials: Clear cedar tongue and groove siding, galvanized steel, aluminum, painted steel, stainless steel.
Major Interior Materials: Clear maple (flooring and cabinetry), smooth wall sheetrock, lacquered plate steel (rails and risers), stainless steel (countertops).
Furnishings and Storage: Provided by owner; custom by architect.
Doors and Hardware: Painted solid core wood doors, Schlage hardware
Windows: Milgard Manufacturing
Fixtures: Kohler (plumbing), Lightolier and Juno (lighting)
Appliances and Equipment: Inclinator (elevator), GE, Maytag, Amana.
Cost: $380,000

Site

The site is a steep south-facing slope in central Seattle. The neighborhood's character is unusual for its park-like setting of dense trees and varied terrain, yet located only ten minutes from downtown Seattle. For this reason, the neighborhood has become increasingly urban in nature, with larger lots divided into smaller sites for economic gain. The house expresses the boundary pressures of the site, and selectively opens itself to the assets of adjacent properties by "borrowing" trees, light, shade, and views.

A tight 5000-square-foot site and an extreme slope in the rear dictated a compressed relationship with the street. In addition, the primary light and view exposures are both to the south. This required a highly organized and coordinated southern elevation, with entry, parking, and views negotiated on a single surface of the building.

Design

Having lived nearby for thirty-two years in a classical 1920s house surrounded by gardens, the couple found their house too formal, requiring too much maintenance,

TOP: *Front balcony detail*
BOTTOM: *View of south façade*
FACING PAGE: *South façade*

and generally not well suited to their post-retirement lifestyle. The living spaces of the new house were to be relaxed, open, and light-filled. All spaces were to be used in their daily lives, with two rooms flexible enough to accommodate guests, office space, or studios as needed. The architect's parents also wanted a deck and a roof garden with potted plants instead of a planted yard.

Responding to site conditions, the body of the house is elevated and shielded on three sides with a wood shell, with the south side left as open as possible. The shell contains two interlocking promenades, one public and the other private, which explore the varying light and view conditions offered by the site. The paths themselves are the interior and exterior linked spaces of the house that widen, narrow, and climb to create a loose, flexible fit for the program. Shorter spurs and loops depart from the two promenades and lead to smaller, "discovered" spaces.

The "guest path" begins at the sidewalk, rises to the entry, moves past the living spaces, and slowly ascends to the roof garden. The "domestic path" begins at the street, turns through the driveway and carport, climbs to the kitchen, through dining and living spaces, and up to the bedroom.

Interior spaces share amenities. Each is considered in terms of its own occupation as well at its impact on and from adjacent spaces. For example, the flush kitchen cabinetry appears as a maple surface when viewed from the living area, and the living area "wall slot" is a light source when viewed from the stair.

The structure is conceived as an abstract assembly of selected materials: glass, wood, metal, stone, and wallboard. Instead of focusing on familiar architectural elements such as "the window," the architect viewed each element as an assembly of materials, joined and positioned according to specific use and necessity. For example, the fifty-foot "window," made of repeated glass and aluminum members, breaks down the assembly into a rhythm of parts as opposed to a single unit. Similarly, the terrace rail is made of metal and glass, but glass panels are held off the metal frame, exposing material thickness and edge detail.

Construction

Severe topography, slide-prone soils, and a modest budget mandated a lightweight structure with minimal earth disturbance. The structure is framed with manufactured wood components and a steel moment frame on the south elevation. Soil and trees in the steepest areas could not be disturbed, and fifteen cast auger piles were necessary to shore the hillside during construction.

Unusual design elements like the strip window, aluminum sunscreen, angled stairs, and seismic frame were researched and detailed early in the process so that they could be built with standard methods and materials. Complex construction assemblies were directed to shop facilities. Repetitive industrial elements like aluminum grating, flat bar railings, and the exterior metal stair offered precision, economy, and detail to the project.

Site study

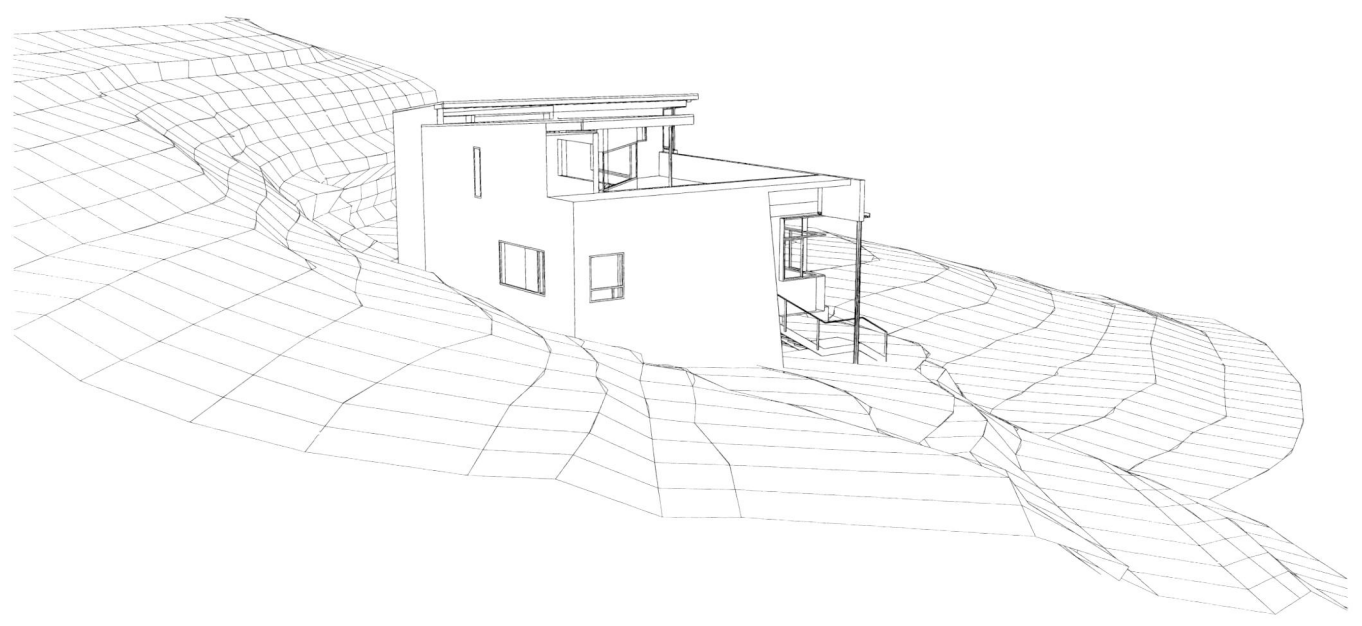

Site plan

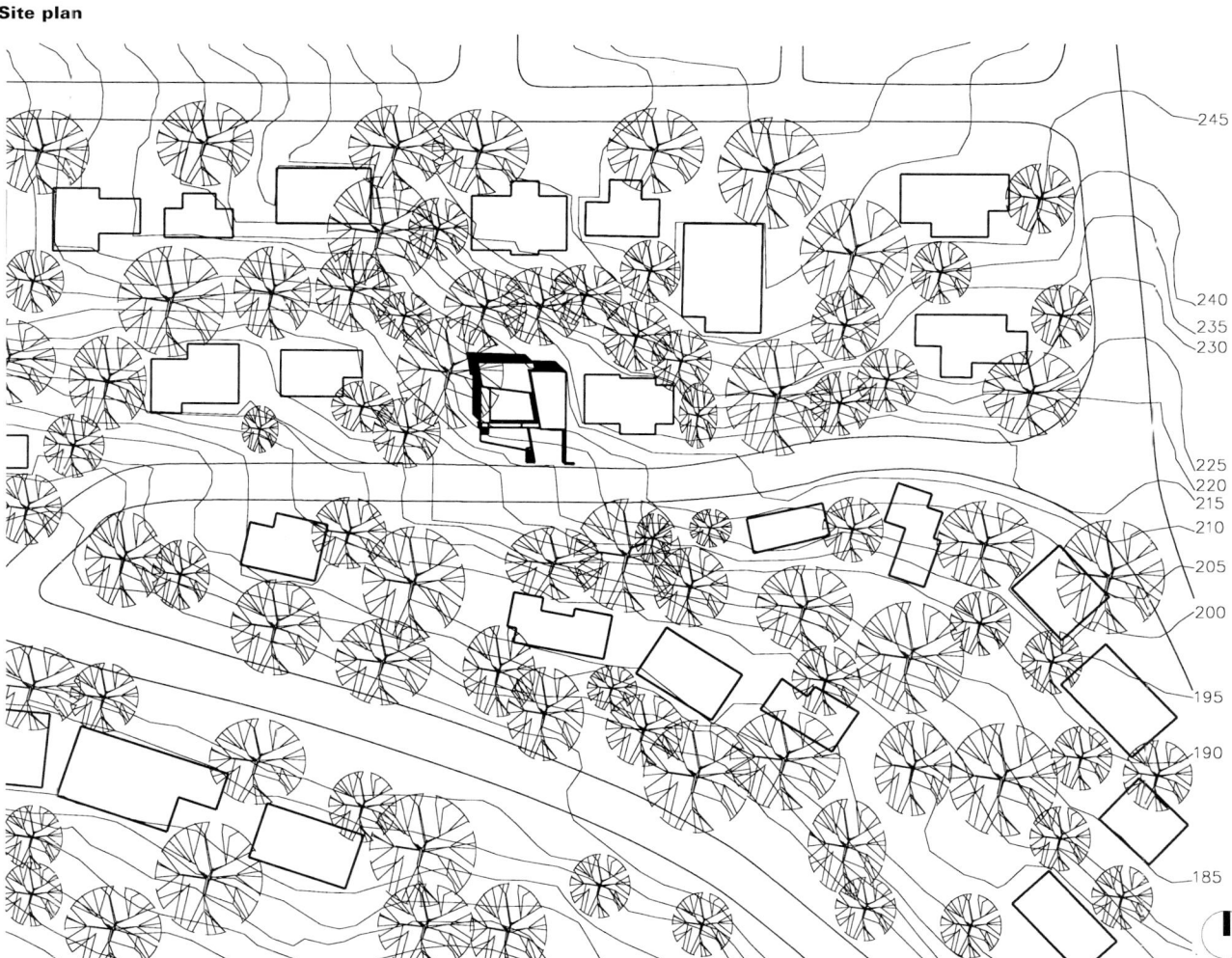

Second level floor plan

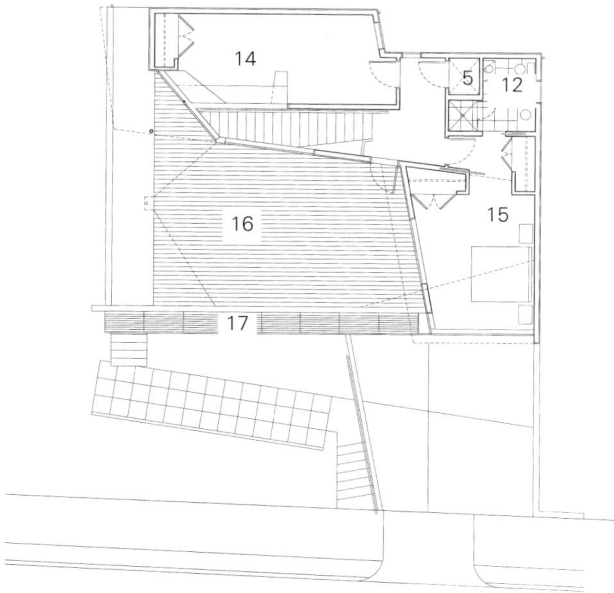

South elevation

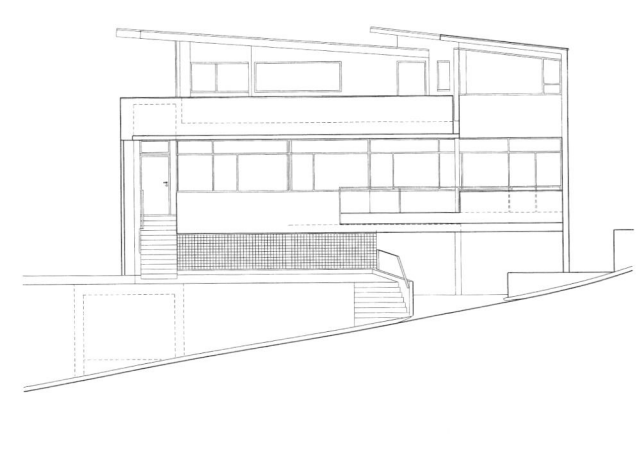

First level floor plan

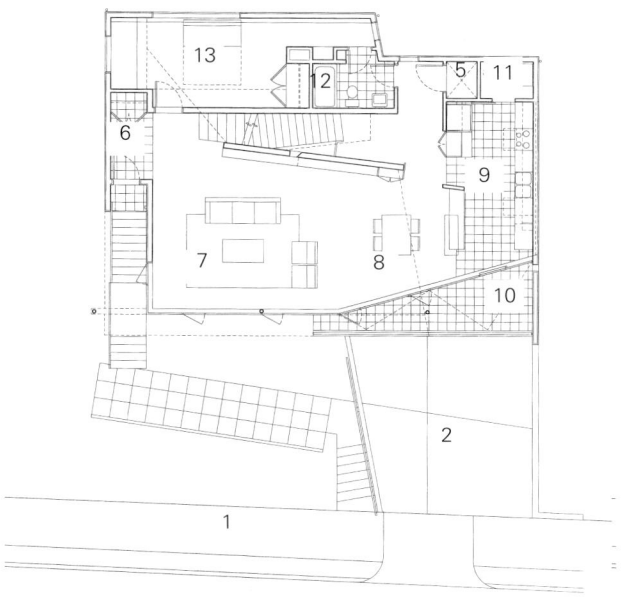

Section looking north

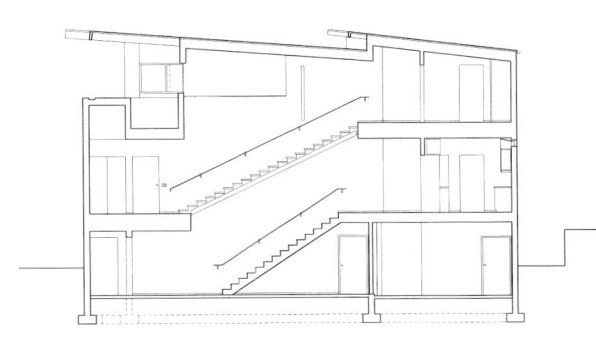

Lower level floor plan

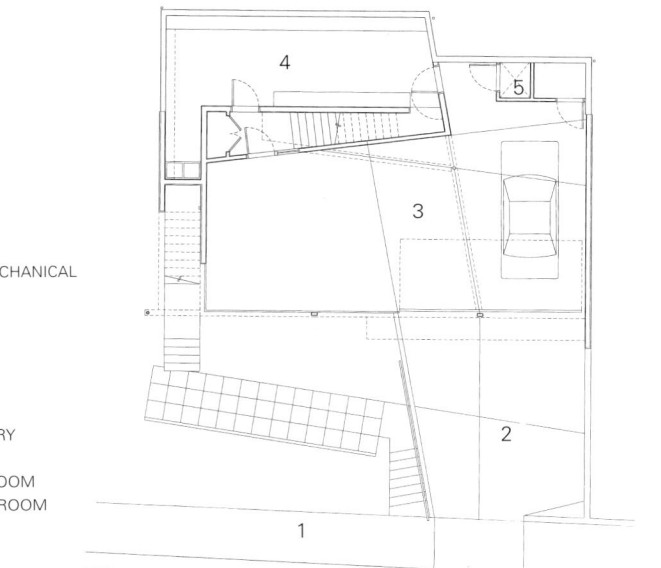

1. SIDEWALK
2. DRIVEWAY
3. CARPORT
4. WORKSHOP/MECHANICAL
5. ELEVATOR
6. ENTRY
7. LIVING ROOM
8. DINING ROOM
9. KITCHEN
10. TERRACE
11. PANTRY/LAUNDRY
12. BATHROOM
13. STUDY/GUESTROOM
14. STUDIO/MEDIA ROOM
15. BEDROOM
16. ROOF DECK
17. SUNSCREEN

Section looking east

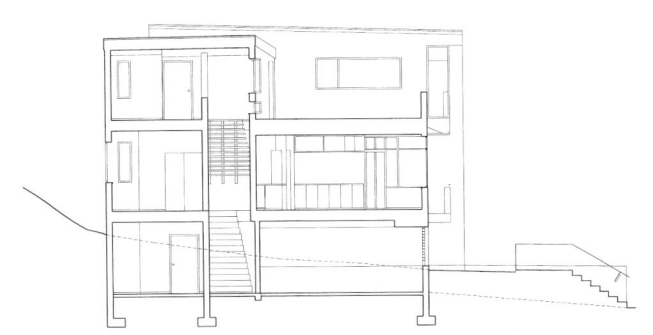

0   5   10

LEFT: *View of dining room toward kitchen*
BOTTOM: *Stair descending to first floor*
FACING PAGE: *View of living room from kitchen*

Window details

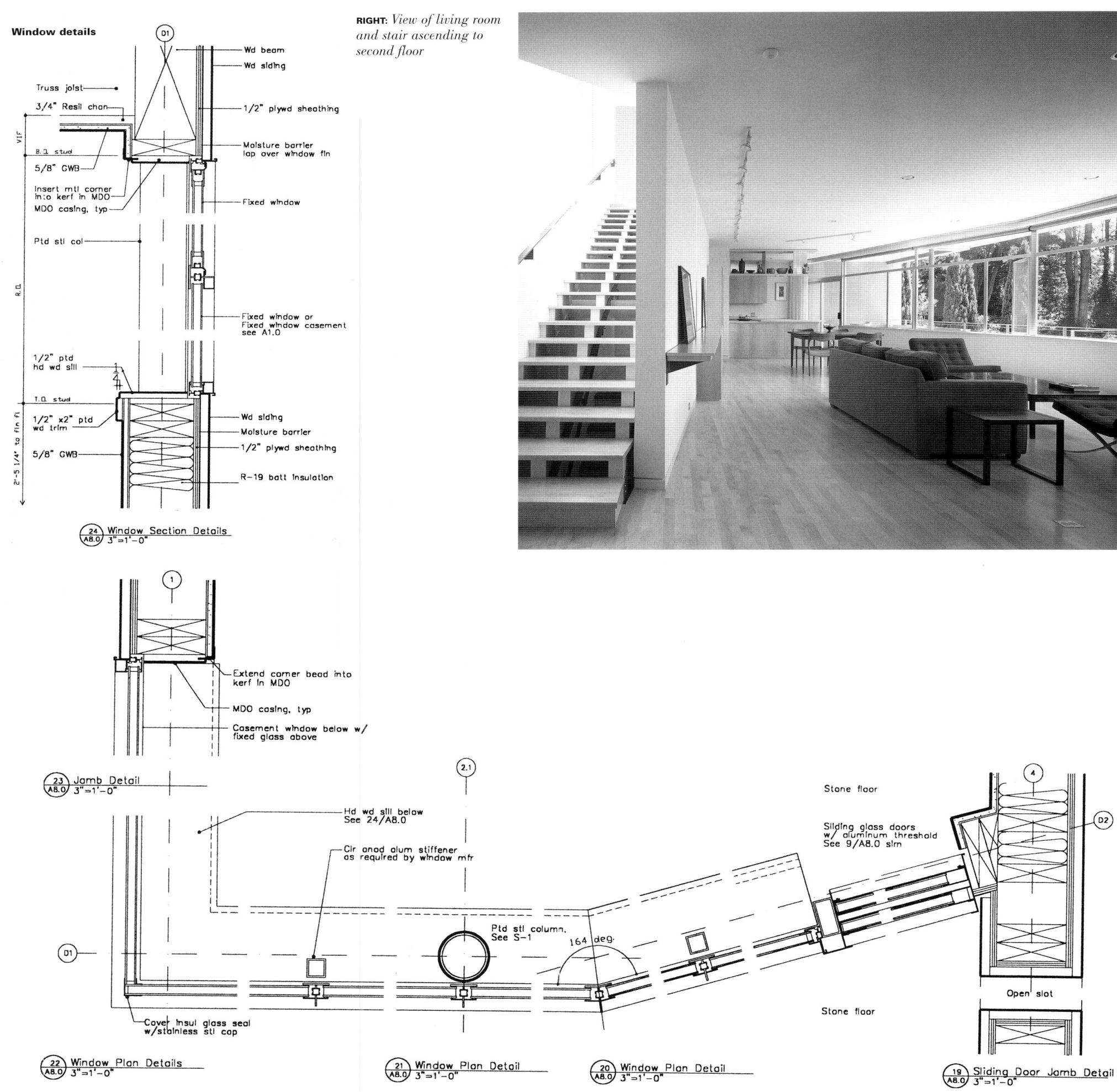

D1

- Wd beam
- Wd siding
- Truss joist
- 3/4" Resil chan
- 1/2" plywd sheathing
- Moisture barrier lap over window fin
- B.O. stud
- 5/8" GWB
- Insert mtl corner into kerf in MDO
- MDO casing, typ
- Fixed window
- Ptd stl col
- Fixed window or Fixed window casement see A1.0
- 1/2" ptd hd wd sill
- T.O. stud
- 1/2" x2" ptd wd trim
- 5/8" GWB
- Wd siding
- Moisture barrier
- 1/2" plywd sheathing
- R-19 batt insulation

VIF
R.O.
2'-5 1/4" to Fin Fl

24 Window Section Details
A8.0   3"=1'-0"

1

- Extend corner bead into kerf in MDO
- MDO casing, typ
- Casement window below w/ fixed glass above

23 Jamb Detail
A8.0   3"=1'-0"

RIGHT: *View of living room and stair ascending to second floor*

2.1

- Hd wd sill below See 24/A8.0
- Clr anod alum stiffener as required by window mfr
- Ptd stl column. See S-1
- 164 deg.

D1

- Cover insul glass seal w/stainless stl cap

22 Window Plan Details
A8.0   3"=1'-0"

21 Window Plan Detail
A8.0   3"=1'-0"

20 Window Plan Detail
A8.0   3"=1'-0"

- Stone floor
- Sliding glass doors w/ aluminum threshold See 9/A8.0 sim
- **4**
- **D2**
- Open slot
- Stone floor

19 Sliding Door Jamb Detail
A8.0   3"=1'-0"

Wall section

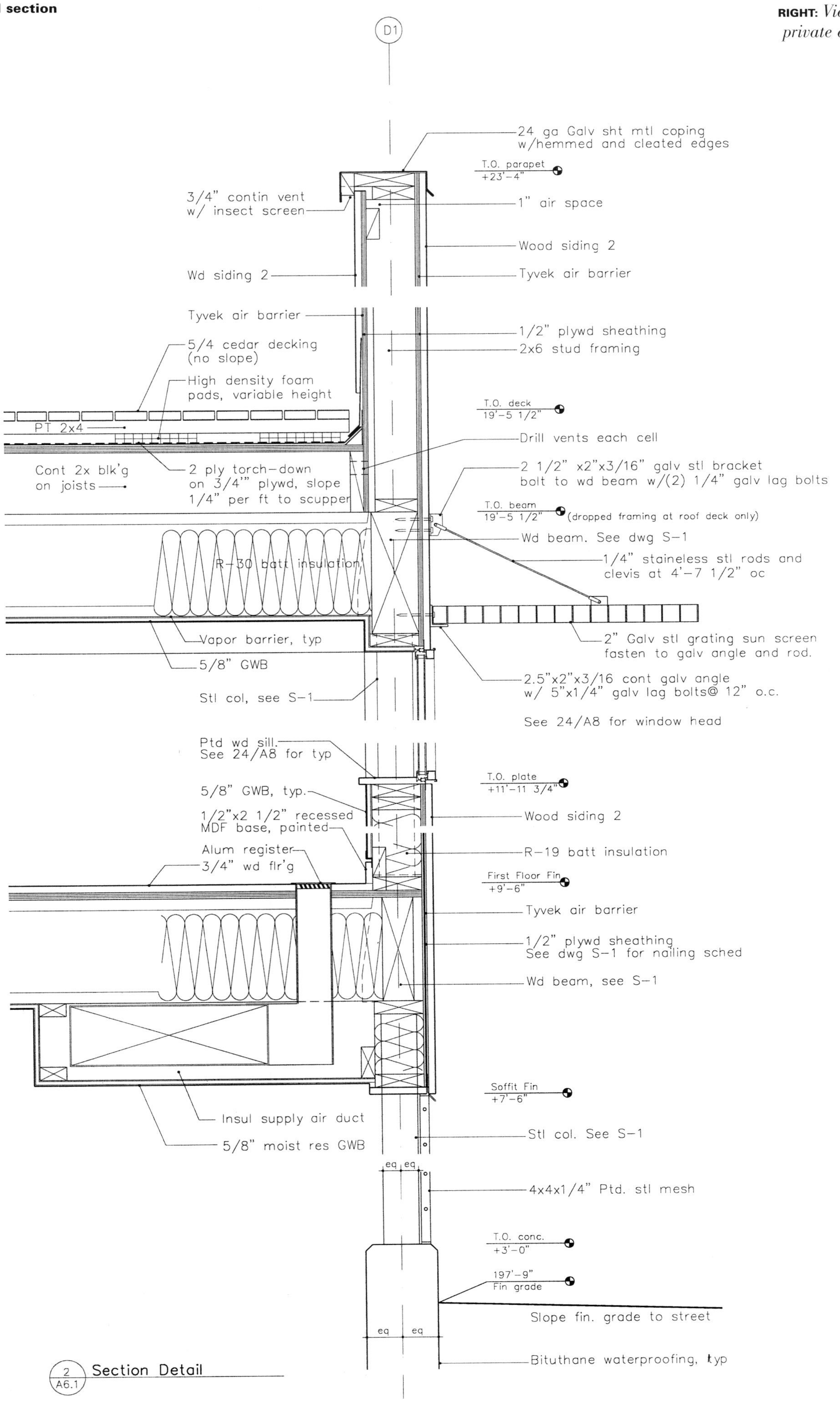
D1
24 ga Galv sht mtl coping w/hemmed and cleated edges
T.O. parapet +23'-4"
3/4" contin vent w/ insect screen
1" air space
Wood siding 2
Wd siding 2
Tyvek air barrier
Tyvek air barrier
5/4 cedar decking (no slope)
1/2" plywd sheathing
2x6 stud framing
High density foam pads, variable height
T.O. deck 19'-5 1/2"
PT 2x4
Drill vents each cell
Cont 2x blk'g on joists
2 ply torch-down on 3/4" plywd, slope 1/4" per ft to scupper
2 1/2" x2"x3/16" galv stl bracket bolt to wd beam w/(2) 1/4" galv lag bolts
T.O. beam 19'-5 1/2" (dropped framing at roof deck only)
Wd beam. See dwg S-1
R-30 batt insulation
1/4" staineless stl rods and clevis at 4'-7 1/2" oc
Vapor barrier, typ
2" Galv stl grating sun screen fasten to galv angle and rod.
5/8" GWB
2.5"x2"x3/16 cont galv angle w/ 5"x1/4" galv lag bolts@ 12" o.c.
Stl col, see S-1
See 24/A8 for window head
Ptd wd sill. See 24/A8 for typ
T.O. plate +11'-11 3/4"
5/8" GWB, typ.
Wood siding 2
1/2"x2 1/2" recessed MDF base, painted
Alum register
R-19 batt insulation
3/4" wd flr'g
First Floor Fin +9'-6"
Tyvek air barrier
1/2" plywd sheathing See dwg S-1 for nailing sched
Wd beam, see S-1
Soffit Fin +7'-6"
Insul supply air duct
Stl col. See S-1
5/8" moist res GWB
eq eq
4x4x1/4" Ptd. stl mesh
T.O. conc. +3'-0"
197'-9" Fin grade
Slope fin. grade to street
eq eq
Bituthane waterproofing, typ
2 A6.1 Section Detail

RIGHT: *View of private entrance*

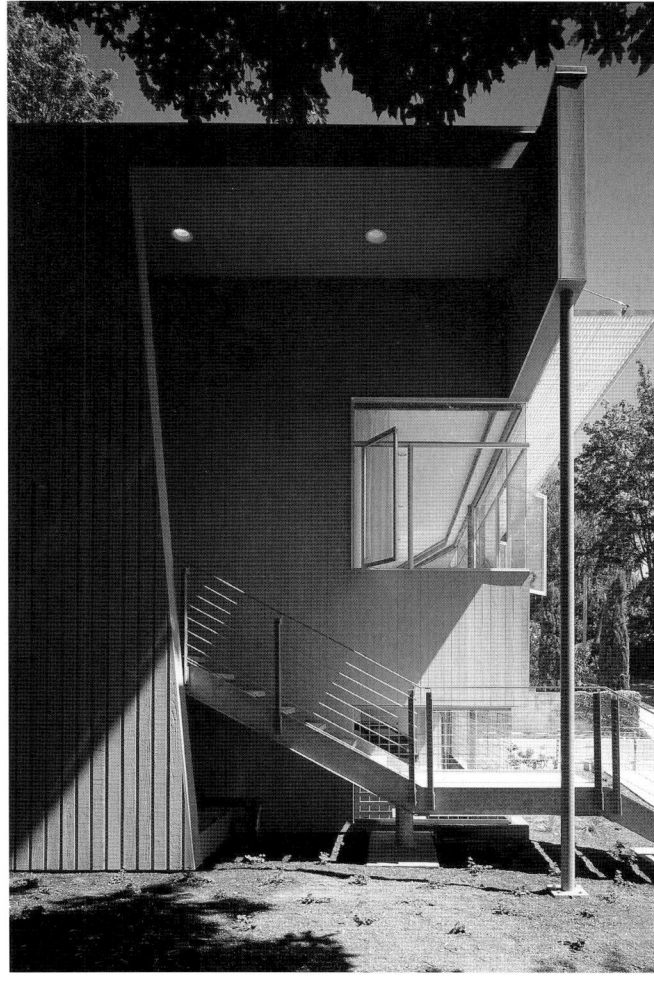

Von Stein House *1990-1992*
FERNAU & HARTMAN ARCHITECTS

Owner: Werner and Sigrid von Stein
Architect: Fernau & Hartman Architects, Berkeley, California
Design Team: Richard Fernau and Laura Hartman (principals-in-charge); Timothy Gray, Beth Piatnitza, Anni Tilt; Emily Stussi, Kimberly Moses, Sarah De Vito, Geof Gainer, Susan Stoltz, Hugo Marrack (project team).
Engineers: Lawrence Fowler and Associates (structural), Lefler and Associates and Warm Zone (mechanical), O'Mahony & Myer (electrical).
Consultant: John Britton Associates, BEC (energy)
General Contractor: Fine Carpentry Inc.
Photography: Richard Barnes, Cesar Rubio

Site: Sonoma County, California
Program: Living room, dining room, kitchen, innenhof, patio, 2 bathrooms, half bathroom, master bedroom and bathroom, bedroom, guest bedroom, carport.
Square Footage: 2400
Structural System: Wood frame on poured-in-place concrete foundation
Mechanical System: Radiant slab heating
Major Exterior Materials: Concrete base, stucco, redwood bevel siding, board and batten, tern-coated stainless steel.
Major Interior Materials: Douglas fir, stained concrete, painted gypsum board, stained channel-rustic siding.
Furnishings and Storage: Purchased by owner; built in by architect.
Doors and Hardware: Vertical grain Douglas fir with "Fin-Ply" door facing (living room)
Windows: Aluminum
Fixtures: Purchased by owner.
Appliances and Equipment: Sullivan (awnings), Thermador (cooktop), Brown (range hood), Dacor (oven), Sub-Zero (refrigerator and freezer), Kitchen-Aid (dishwasher), Whirlpool (washer and dryer).

Site
The Sonoma county site of the von Stein house slopes steeply to the southwest and overlooks the vineyards of the Valley of the Moon, where the sun can be brilliant, even harsh. With the exception of several small California live oaks principally located at the upper edge of the site, the property is covered with dry wax-wood brush. There are protected natural views to the east; however, the primary vista is the south, into and across the valley.

Design
The owners are northern Europeans captivated by California's wine country. They wanted to spend as much time outdoors as indoors, and desired a house that engaged its site and context. Inspired by early northern-European modern architecture, and the work of Alvar Aalto in particular, the house digresses from the dominant discourse of orthodox modernism to find connection with site and circumstance.

FACING PAGE: *View of house from bottom of hill*

Site plan

The program required accomadations for visiting family and guests, while still providing a maximum of privacy. A wall that runs with the slope slices through the site, shielding occupants from the road and adjacent buildings. The wall also serves as a spine that organizes the circulation and structures a series of alternating indoor and outdoor rooms that step up the hill. A garden pavilion brackets this progression of rooms at the top of the site, while a carport holds the place at the bottom.

Each of the outdoor rooms has its own character determined by the degree of architectural definition, the amount of sun protection, and the type of planting. At the bottom of the site is a sunny court with native planting and a lone California live oak, and at the top is a shady moss garden. At the center of the progression is an *innenhof*, an outdoor room for living and dining. Wrapped around the *innenhof* is a butterfly-roofed form extruded along the front wall that houses the main living spaces and the master bedroom loft.

Two towers punctuate the scheme. The taller one forms an entry gate through which the primary circulation is threaded. This tower commands the best view of the site, and contains a bedroom/study and an observation/sleeping platform. The smaller of the two towers, rising from among the trees as in a walled "philosopher's" garden, occupies the corner at the highest point of the site. Located for views, privacy, and breezes, this structure serves as a guest house. A combination of fixed metal sunshades, operable awnings, and wooden trellises keep the sun at bay. The occupants of the house gravitate from room to room, indoors and out, as the sun moves across the site.

Construction

A poured-in-place concrete foundation steps up the hill and supports a standard 2 x 6 wood frame. Rafters and decking in the main building are left exposed (with rigid insulation above). The loft in the living room is minimally supported by a steel beam and slender steel column. Trellises are a mixture of 4x and 2x redwood. Steel is used in the sunshades and at the exterior stair.

Longitudinal section

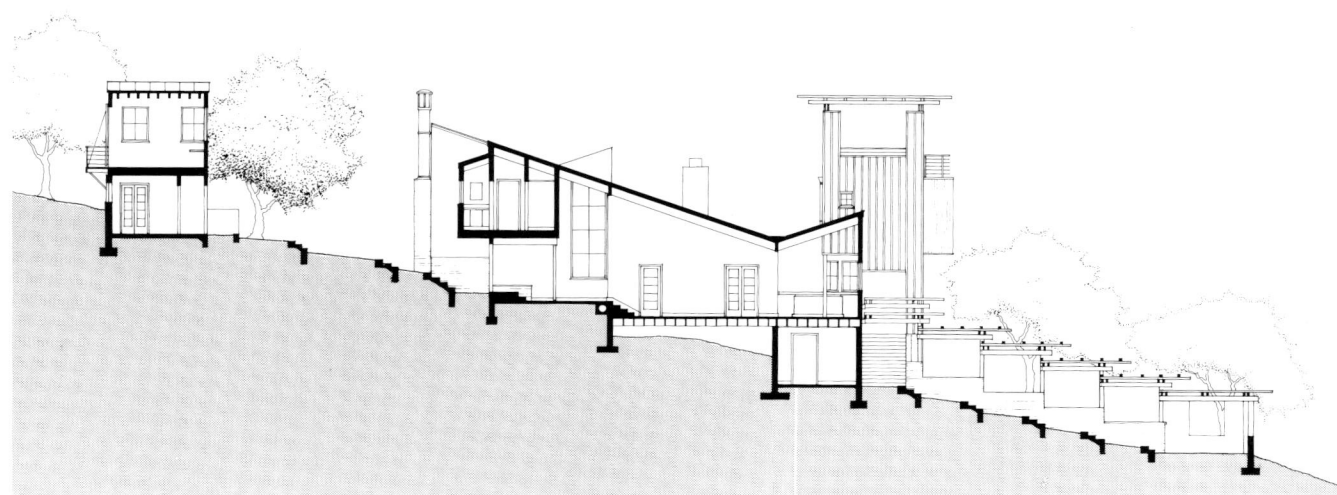

Second level floor plan

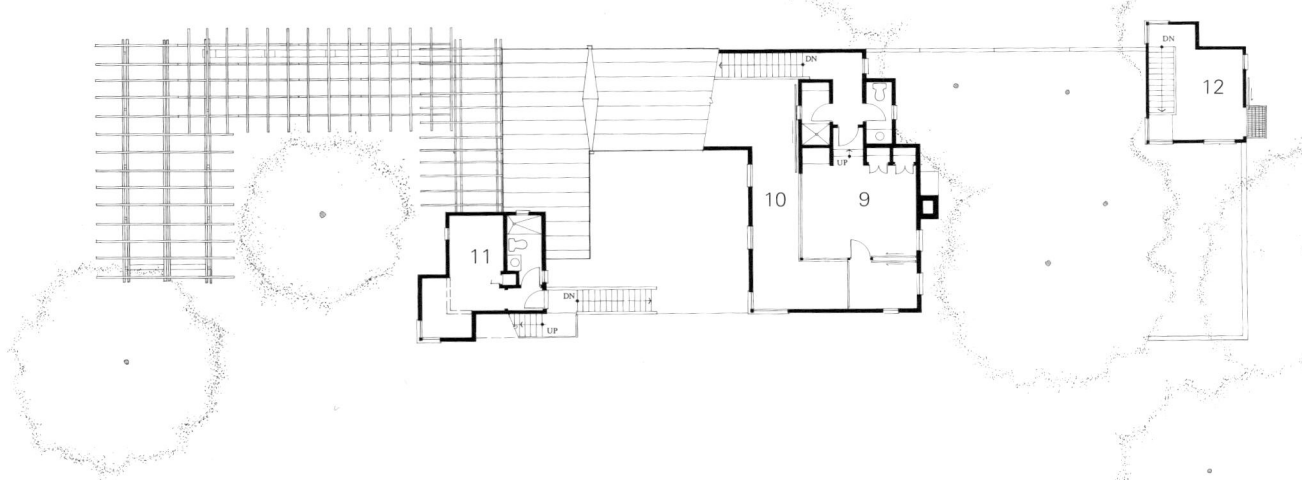

ABOVE: *Inner court*

First level floor plan

1. INNENHOF
2. LIVING ROOM
3. KITCHEN
4. DINING ROOM
5. PATIO
6. BATHROOM
7. CARPORT
8. ENTRY TERRACE
9. MASTER BEDROOM
10. OPEN TO BELOW
11. BEDROOM
12. GUEST BEDROOM

0 5 10

ABOVE: *Master bedroom*
ABOVE RIGHT: *View of master bedroom open to living room below*

CLOCKWISE FROM TOP LEFT:
Dining room; living room; kitchen

Bookshelf details

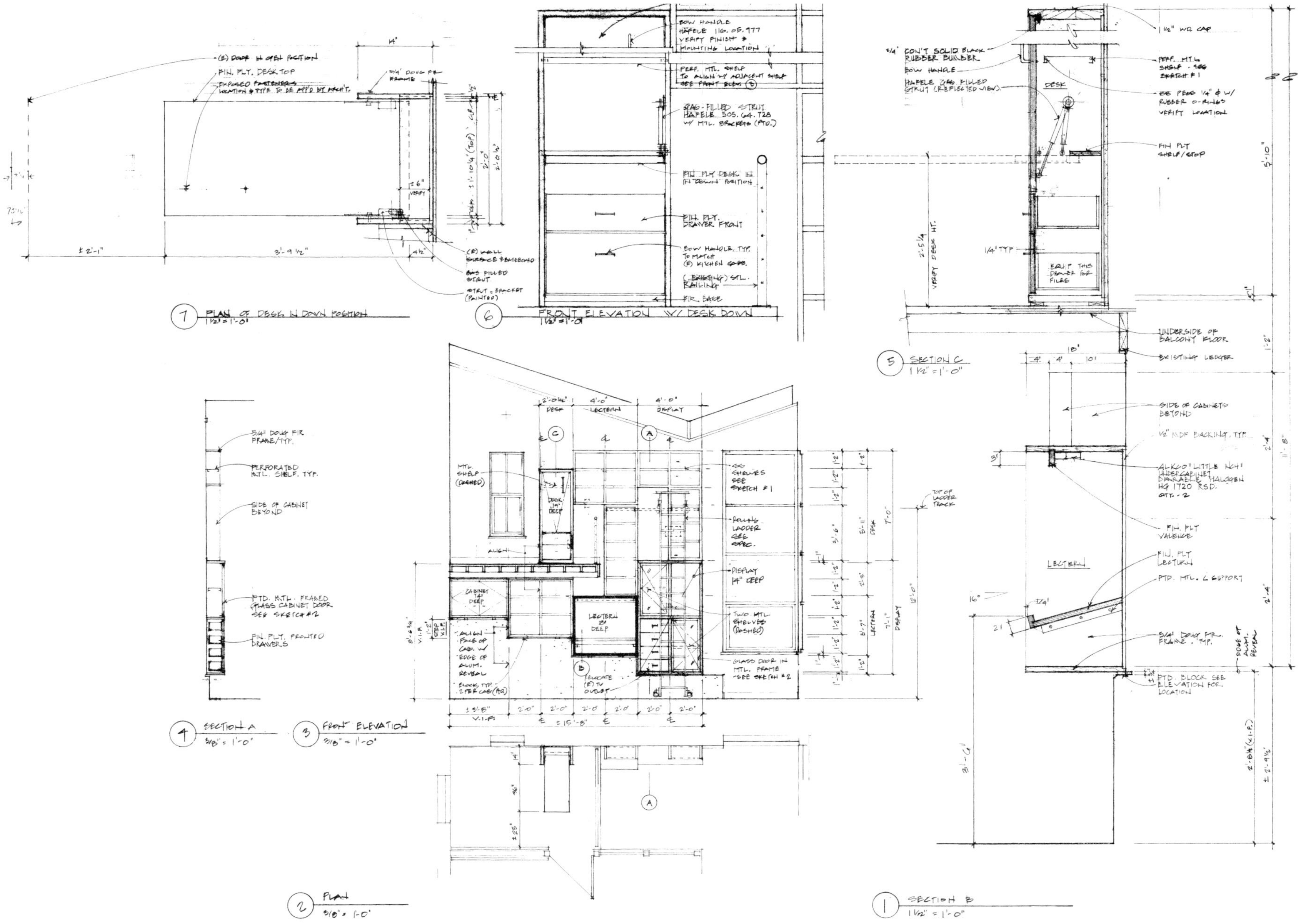

Sunshade section and plan details

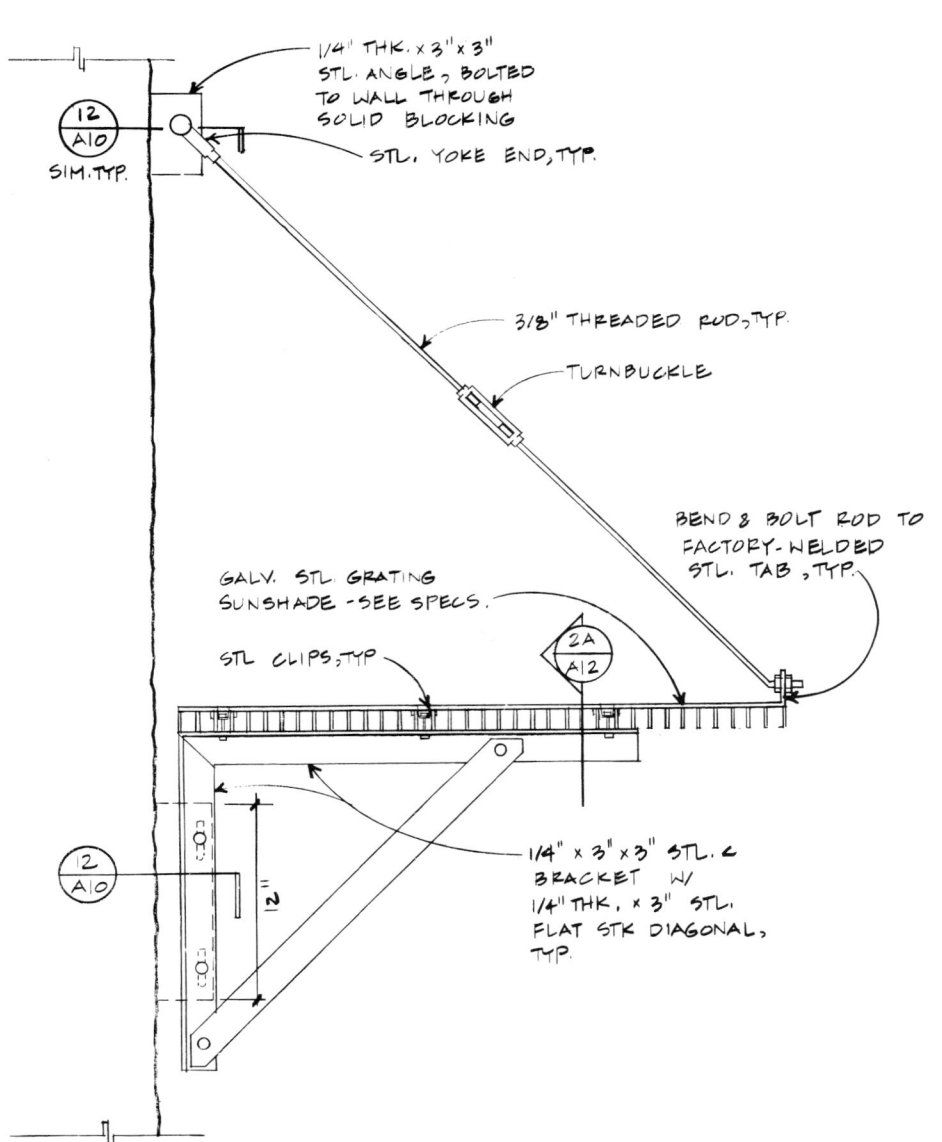

12/A10 SIM.TYP.

1/4" THK. x 3" x 3" STL. ANGLE, BOLTED TO WALL THROUGH SOLID BLOCKING

STL. YOKE END, TYP.

3/8" THREADED ROD, TYP.

TURNBUCKLE

BEND & BOLT ROD TO FACTORY-WELDED STL. TAB, TYP.

GALV. STL. GRATING SUNSHADE - SEE SPECS.

STL. CLIPS, TYP

2A/A12

12/A10

2"

1/4" x 3" x 3" STL. L BRACKET W/ 1/4" THK. x 3" STL. FLAT STK DIAGONAL, TYP.

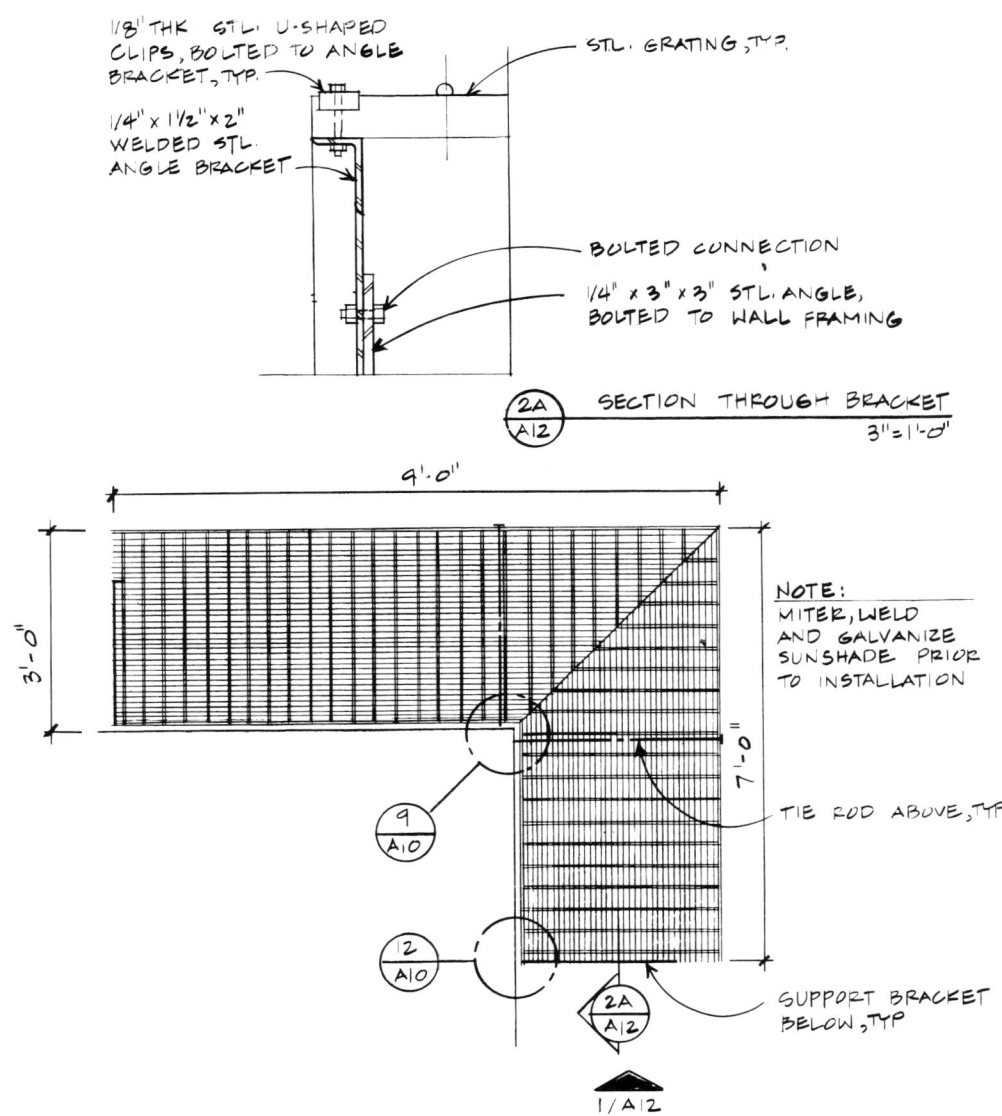

1/8" THK. STL. U-SHAPED CLIPS, BOLTED TO ANGLE BRACKET, TYP.

1/4" x 1 1/2" x 2" WELDED STL. ANGLE BRACKET

STL. GRATING, TYP.

BOLTED CONNECTION

1/4" x 3" x 3" STL. ANGLE, BOLTED TO WALL FRAMING

2A/A12 SECTION THROUGH BRACKET
3"=1'-0"

9'-0"

3'-0"

7'-0"

NOTE: MITER, WELD AND GALVANIZE SUNSHADE PRIOR TO INSTALLATION

9/A10

12/A10

2A/A12

TIE ROD ABOVE, TYP

SUPPORT BRACKET BELOW, TYP

1/A12

WorkHouse *1994-1996*
GUTHRIE + BURESH ARCHITECTS

Owner: Danelle Guthrie and Tom Buresh
Architect: Guthrie + Buresh Architects, Los Angeles, California
Design Team: Danelle Guthrie, Tom Buresh, Mike Fergeson, Adam Woltag, Josh Coggeshall.
Engineer: Dave Maynard (structural)
General Contractor: RAC Construction (concrete and framing), Thomasson and Associates (shell enclosure), Guthrie + Buresh with Josh Coggeshall, Chris Waight, Kenny Hooper, David Ketch, and Adam Woltag (finish).
Photography: Tom Bonner, Guthrie + Buresh

Site: West Hollywood, California
Program: Live/work studio including carport for two automobiles on ground level and combined living room/dining room/kitchen; upper levels contain studio, 2 bedrooms, and 2 bathrooms.
Square Footage: 1850
Structural System: Wood frame bearing wall, wood wall truss on concrete foundation, stem walls and floor slab.
Mechanical System: Electric heat pump
Major Exterior Materials: Cement plaster, extruded polycarbonate, concrete.
Major Interior Materials: Concrete (floor), plywood (floors and walls), gypsum board (walls and ceiling), Douglas fir (exposed framing and trim).
Furnishings and Storage: Built in by architect.
Doors and Hardware: Custom by Alpine Door & Trim; Baldwin
Windows: Milgard (aluminum)
Fixtures: Kohler
Appliances and Equipment: Amana (refrigerator), Maytag (oven, dishwasher, washer/dryer)
Cost: Withheld at owner's request.

Site

Accessed by a busy commuter boulevard, a 40' x 115' residential lot in West Hollywood is the location for this combination studio/residence. Prior to beginning the WorkHouse, Guthrie + Bouresh contributed to *re: American Dream,* a collection of proposals for increasing the housing density in Los Angeles. The architects envisioned a fabric of three distinct street types—hybrid, private, and open—defined by the current use of the street and multiple combinations of densities of living and working spaces. They began on WorkHouse by implementing the strategy of the hybrid street, whereby the noise and activity from the boulevard is buffered by positioning a smaller building at the front, leaving the rear of the lot for the larger WorkHouse. The WorkHouse is now complete; a smaller building with a studio and one-bedroom apartment will be built in the future.

RIGHT: *North view*
BOTTOM: *Street façade*
FACING PAGE: *Front façade*

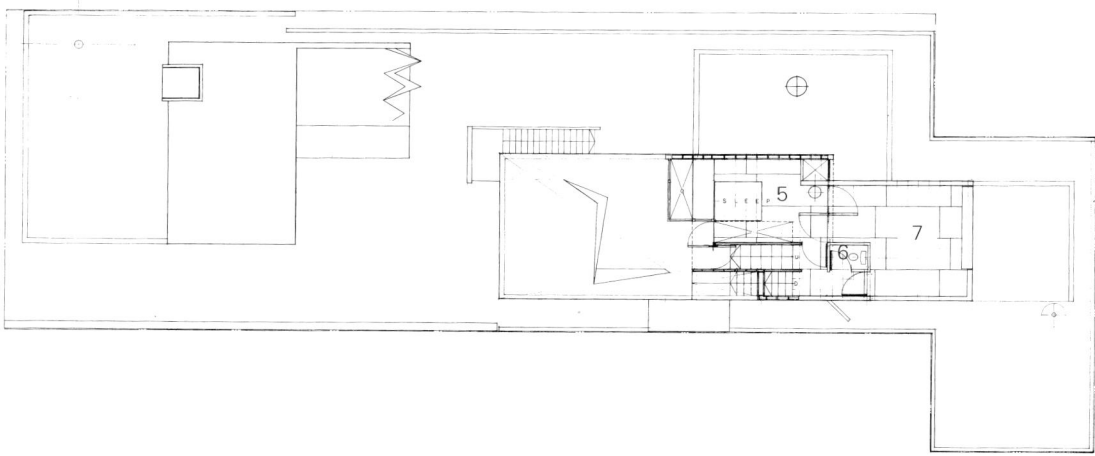

Design

The development of contained exterior space and its extension to the interior was studied through a series of axonometric drawings and partial models. Employing elements of space and shape in conjunction with material and light studies, the architects established a spatial fabric of interlocking orthogonally formed spaces in simultaneous and multiple containment and release.

Breaches in the normative spatial and boundary distinctions in the WorkHouse—between the collective and the individual in general and working and living in particular—were forged through the strategic positioning of the program and the visual characteristics of the materials selected. Friction occurs when site and program positioning conflict. One way this is resolved here is through the deployment of opaque plywood sheeting of the interior slipping behind the translucent membrane at the studio. Shared space between adjacent buildings threatens to encroach on the WorkHouse, yet the translucent membrane of the side elevations preserves both privacy and a sense of openness.

Ocular transgression proceeds to the interior where sectional shifts and various screening devices configure the space. Through a window to the street, the mezzanine shower reintroduces the most private spaces to the adjacent spaces—simultaneously deep/shallow, up/down, and protruding from the structure only at the view from the studio to the street.

Construction

Materials were specified for their experiential characteristics and ability to contribute to the multiple spatial understanding of the project. While the visual properties of opacity and transparency are understood and certain, translucency occupies the curious territory between the two, where spatial boundary or extension change with the light and the position of the observer.

Second level floor plan

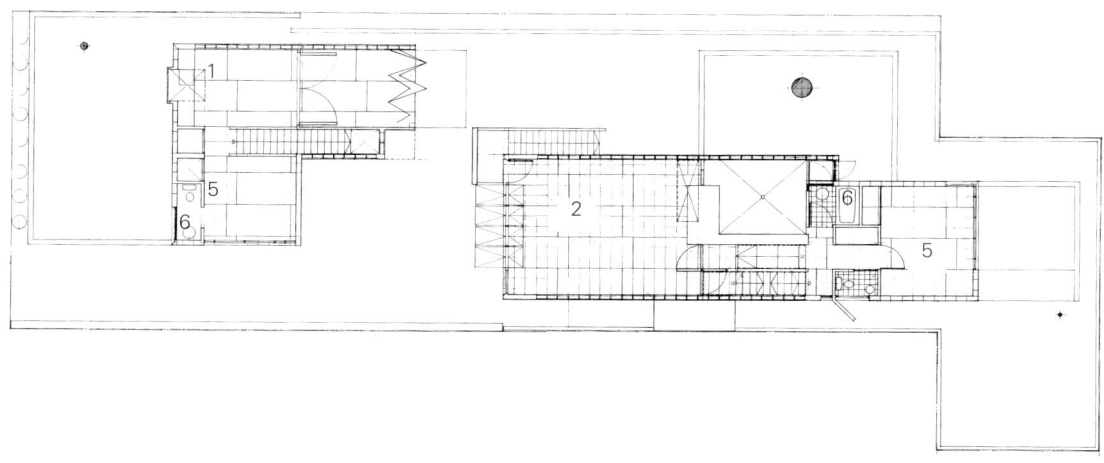

First level floor plan

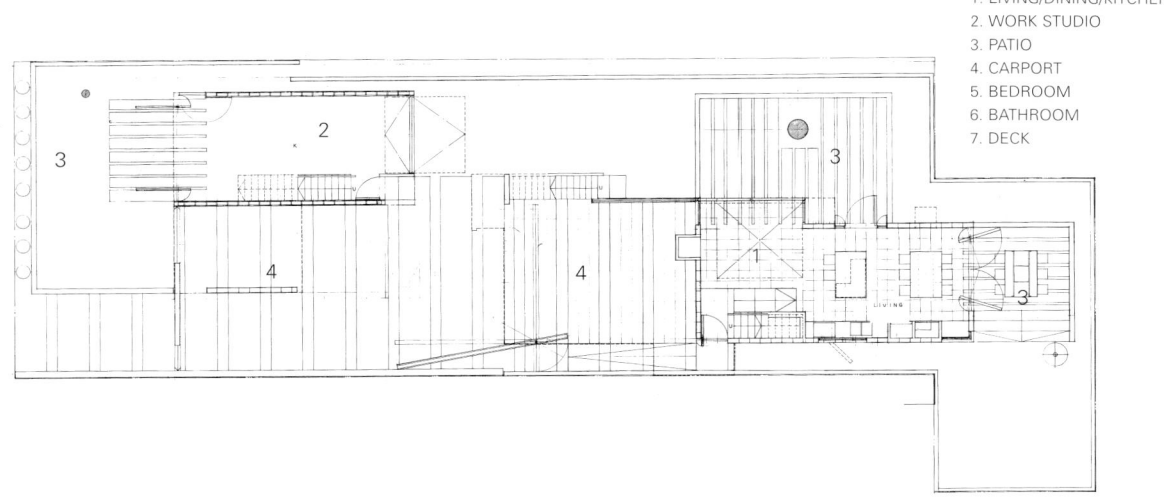

1. LIVING/DINING/KITCHEN
2. WORK STUDIO
3. PATIO
4. CARPORT
5. BEDROOM
6. BATHROOM
7. DECK

0   5   10

South elevation

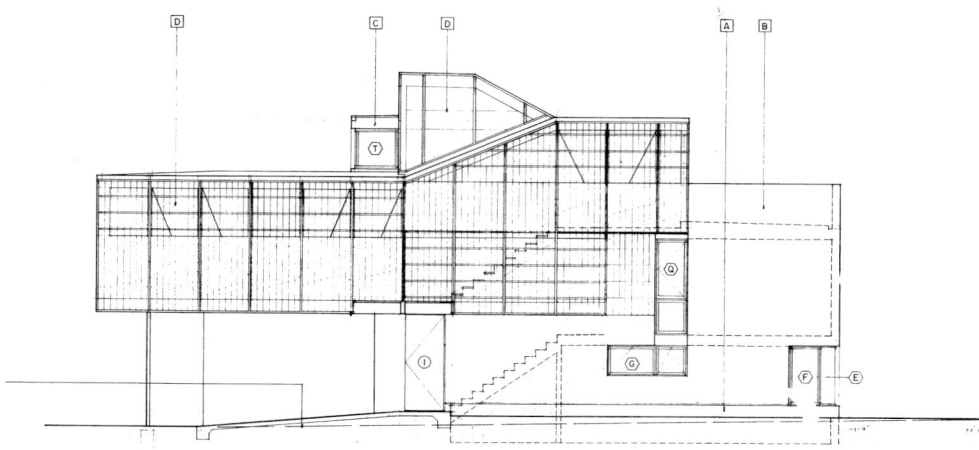

North elevation

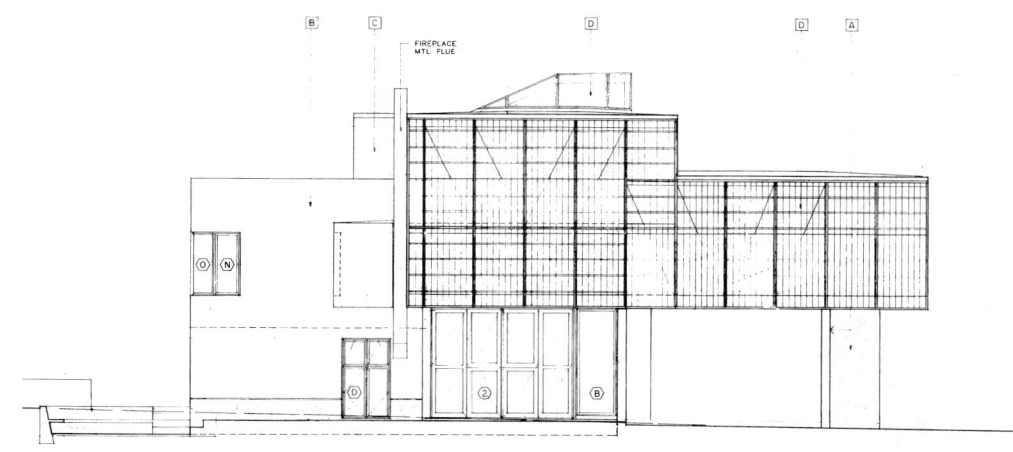

Section

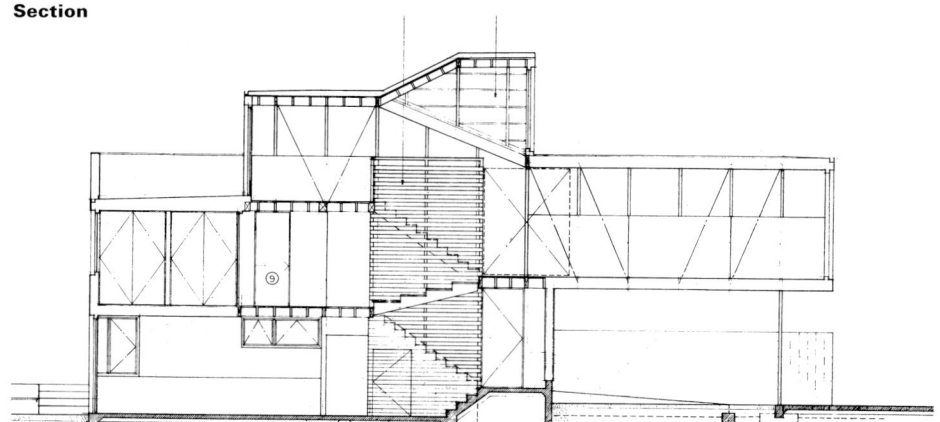

Section

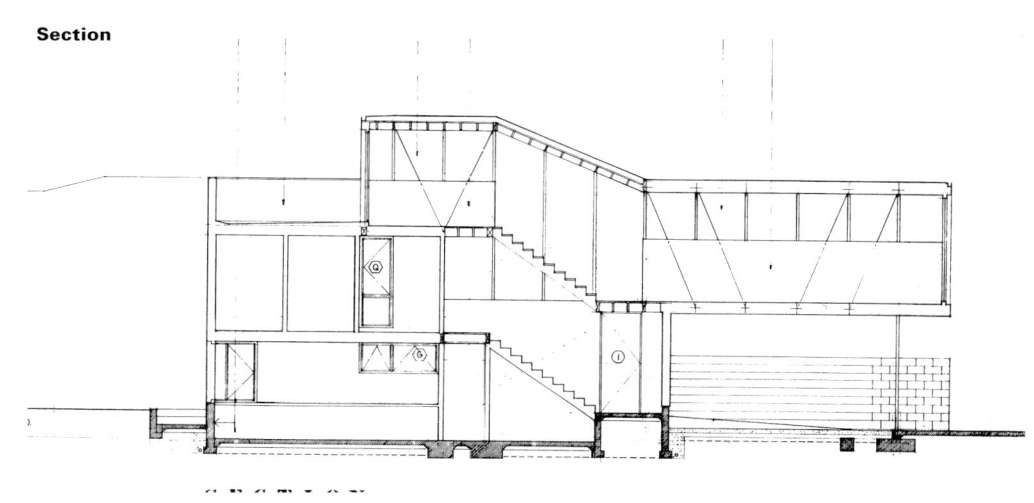

Volumetric studies

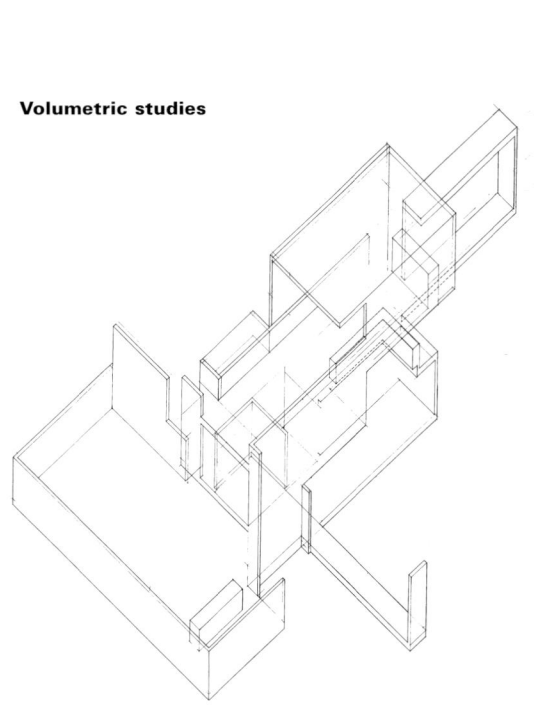
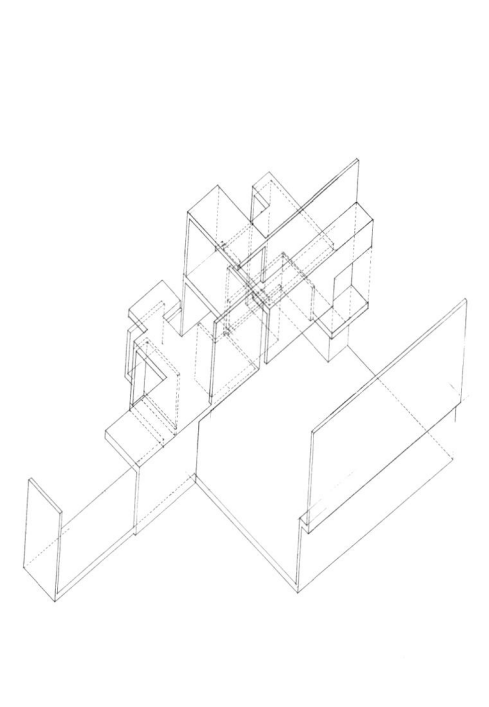
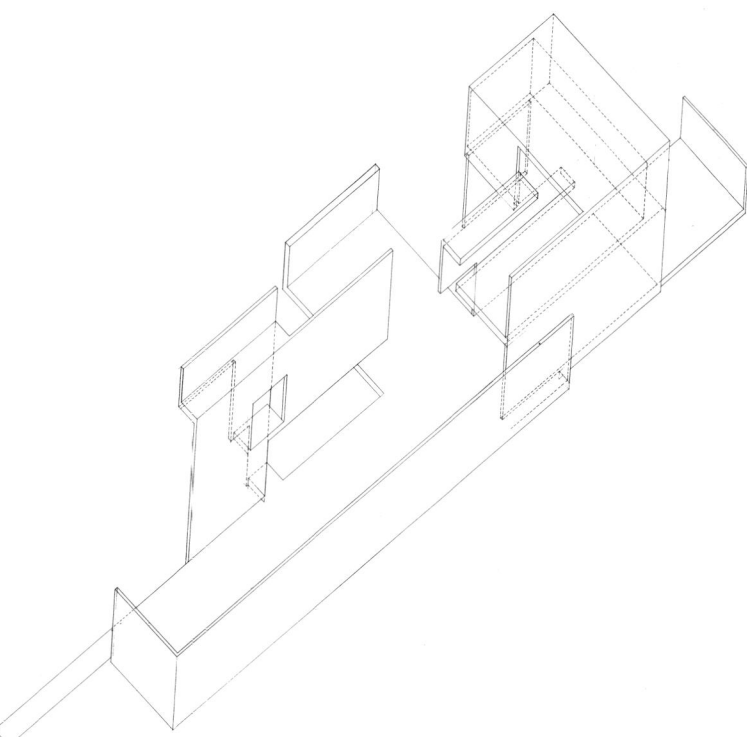

LEFT: *Living Room*
BOTTOM: *Stair to bedroom*
FACING PAGE: *Studio*

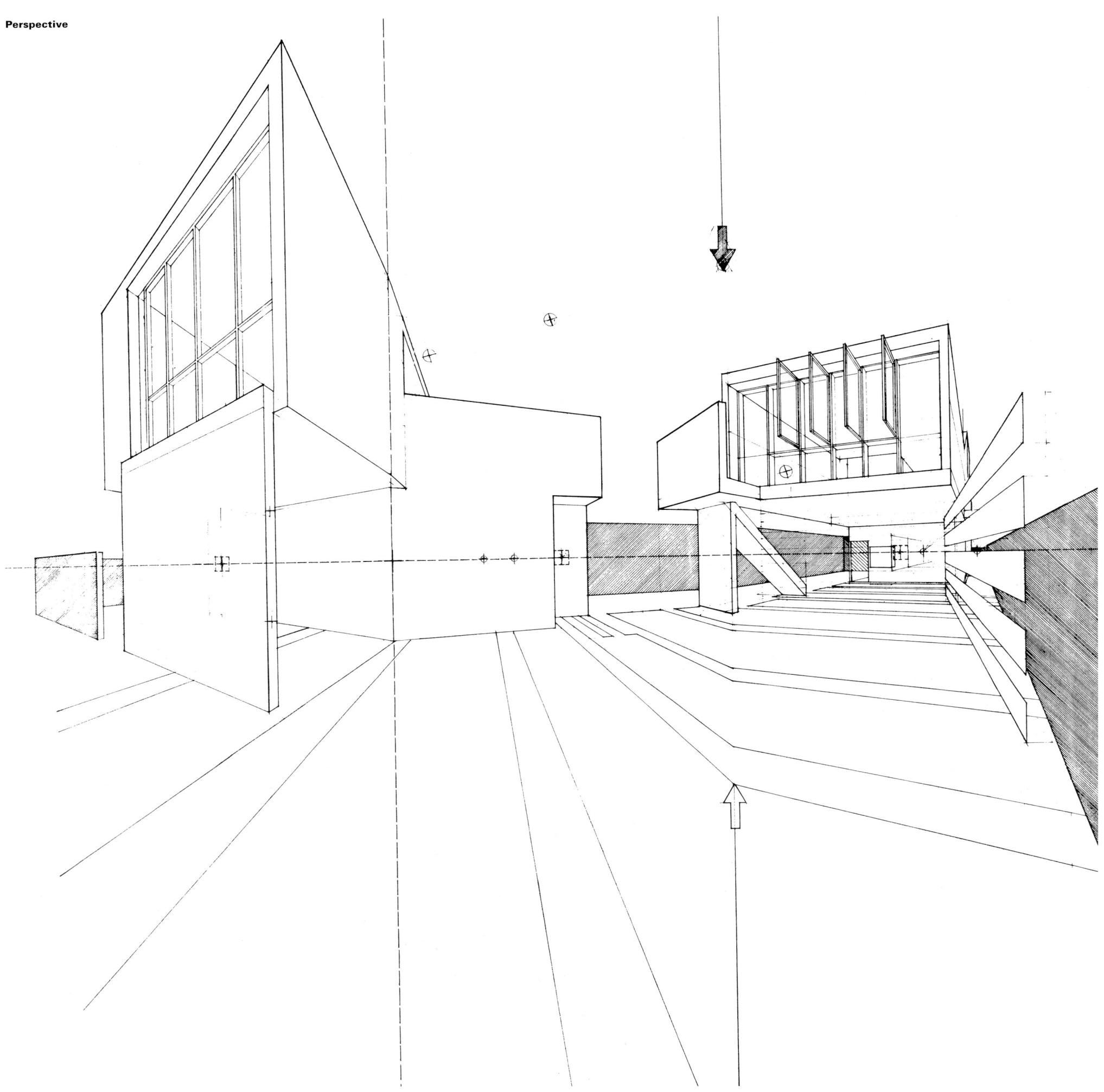

Wall section details

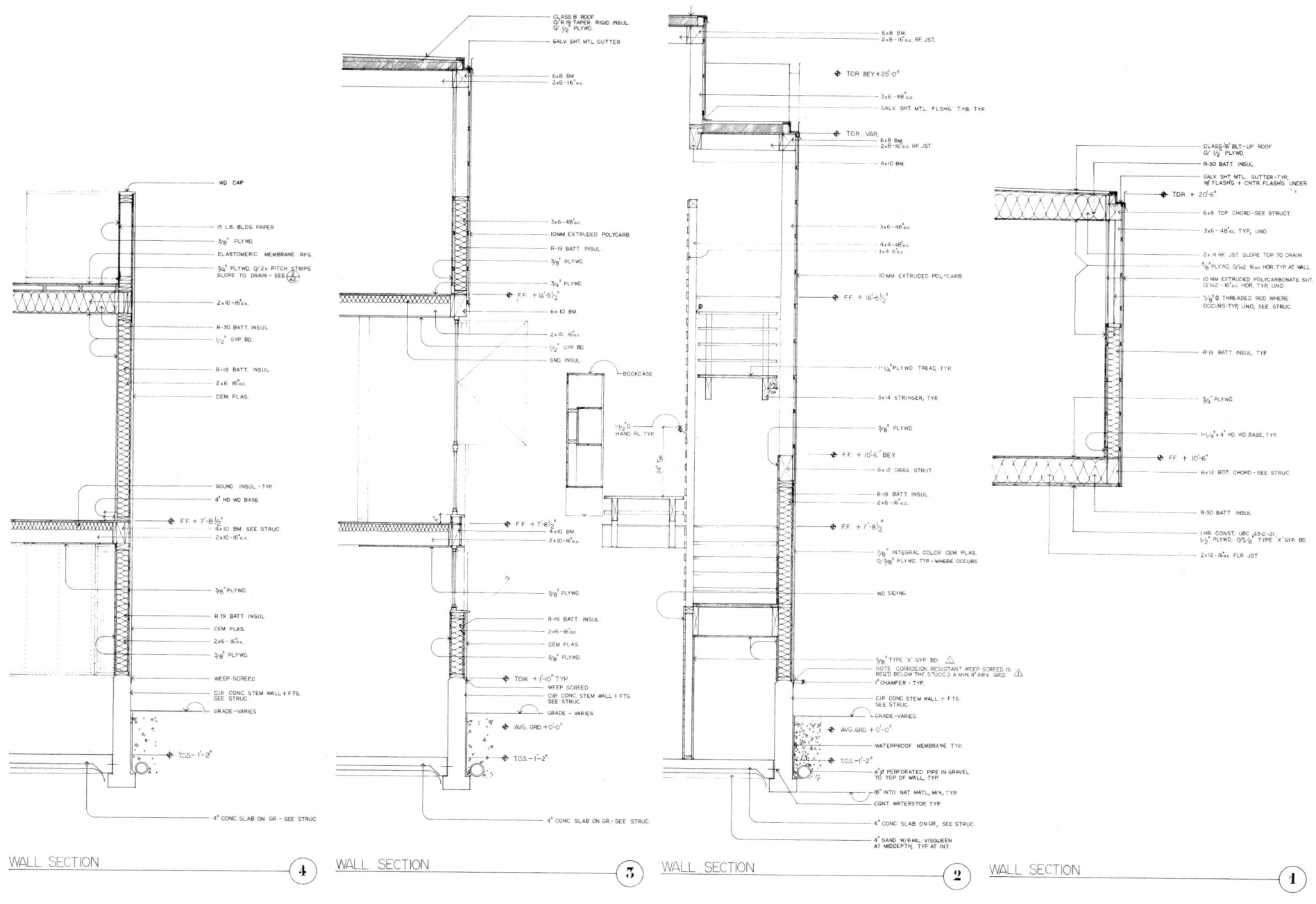

WALL SECTION ④

WALL SECTION ③

WALL SECTION ②

WALL SECTION ①

51

Coyote Valley Ranch House

1993-1995

ROBERT LUCHETTI ASSOCIATES, INC.

Owner: Lawrence and Petra Luchetti
Architect: Robert Luchetti Associates, Inc., Cambridge, Massachusetts
Design Team: Robert Luchetti (principal), Michael Tongeley (project architect), Ellen Fortin, William Cromar, Saul McDonnez.
Engineer: Cuarves Cuaroff Engineers, Boston, Massachusetts (structural)
Consultant: Jeffrey Lumetti, Mudstate Construction, Petaluma, California (construction manager)
General Contractor: Head Construction, Middletown, Massachusetts
Photography: Richard Barnes

Site: Coyote Valley, Middletown, Lake County, California
Program: 4 bedroom suites with private bathrooms and individual outdoor decks, second-level open sleeping loft, third-level open study, kitchen, dining room, living room, freestanding double-sided fireplace, TV/family room, screened porch, sun deck, guest bathroom, mud room, laundry room.
Square Footage: 4200
Structural System: Balloon and platform wood framing, nailed
Mechanical System: Gas fired forced air heating, electrical forced air cooling, ceiling fans
Major Exterior Materials: Pre-finished v. crimp sheet steel roofing and flashing, rough sawn redwood plywood, redwood battens and trim, MDO plywood, 2x Douglas fir framing, redwood decking, bonderized galvanized steel sheet flashing.
Major Interior Materials: Douglas fir 2x framing, Hemlock roof decking, gypsum wall board, painted pine trim, white pine (floors), plastic laminate and stained MDF (cabinets), slate and tile (floors).
Furnishings and Storage: Custom by architect (cabinets, bookcases, tables).
Doors and Hardware: Exterior sliding glass doors by Millore, interior painted birch doors by Sound Core
Windows: Millore
Fixtures: Delta, American Standard, Just
Appliances and Equipment: GE (refrigerators and gas hub cooktop), Jenn-Air (ovens), Kitchen Aid (dishwasher).
Cost: $95 per square foot

Site

Located on a 600-acre working cattle ranch in Northern California, this house serves both as a country retreat for a retired couple and a comfortable, flexible gathering place for their large extended family. Two existing barns on the property, classic examples of indigenous lightweight balloon-framed vernacular building, provided the architectural inspiration for the project.

Design

The new house references the authentic simplicity and elegance of the existing structures, particularly in terms of their form, materials, and construction. Organized according to several geometries, the design reflects the dynamic views and dramatic force generated by its site.

RIGHT: *South façade*

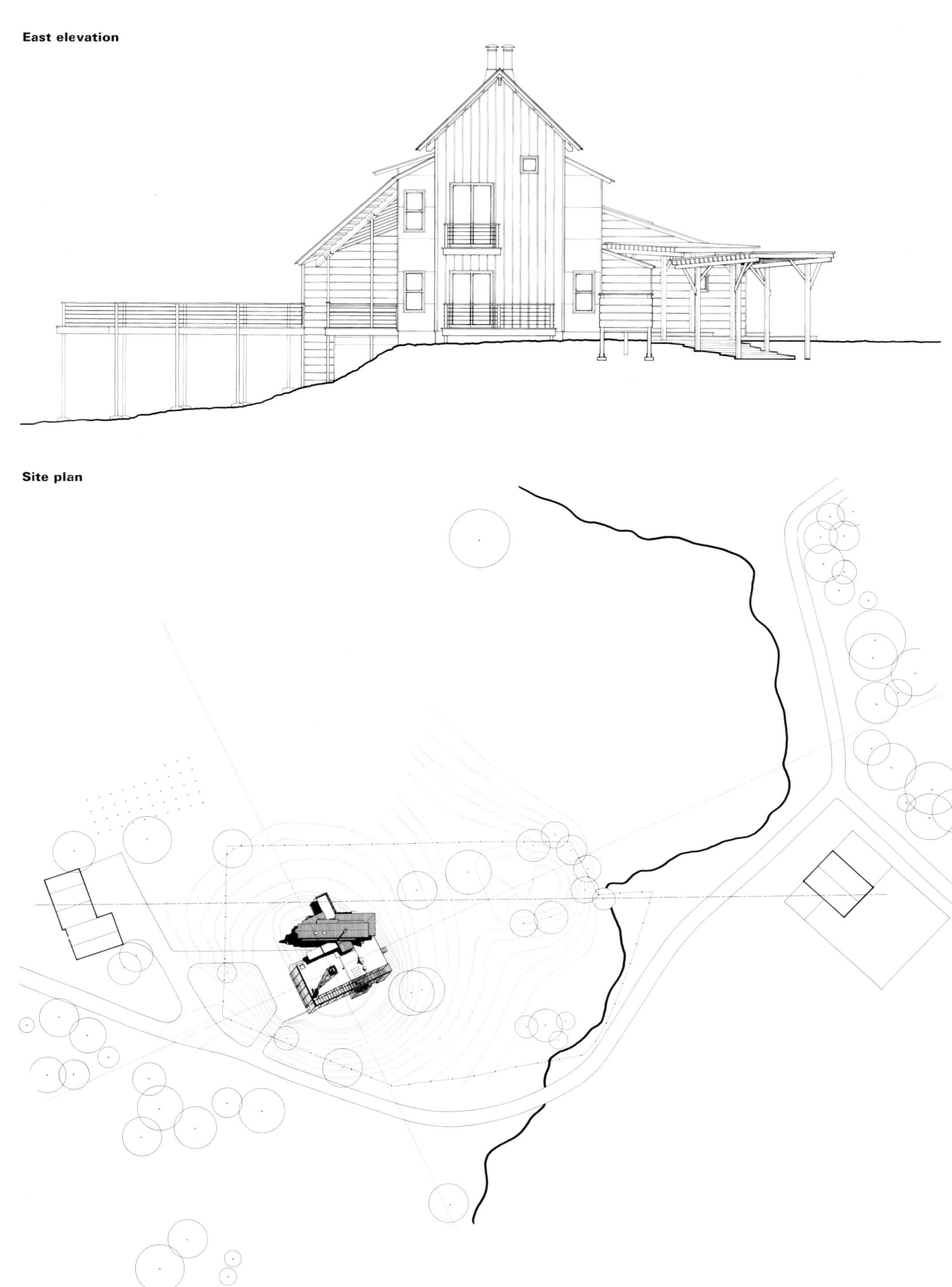

One large, tall, linear volume—the main living space—is articulated with an exposed structural frame composed of a series of simple sandwiched 2x framing members. Ancillary functions are housed in open shed-like additions at the perimeter of the living volume and overlooking the loft spaces. Located at the other end of the house are quiet, private areas, including four bedroom suites on two floors, each with its own private bathroom and small outdoor deck.

An acute awareness of the natural and historical context is demonstrated in the sensitive integration of the house with the landscape. Traditional energy conservation design features were employed such as an east-west orientation of the primary building axis, large overhangs, and a screened porch to the south and west to shield the house from the afternoon sun; orientation to catch the cooling prevailing breezes; minimal fenestraton; and super insulation. To the north, a large outdoor terraced "room,"oriented to the cardinal points of the compass, extends the living spaces into the landscape. Defined spatially by the house, a wooden pergola, the rectangular lawn, and planting beds, this "room" serves multiple functions—as a shaded outdoor area for gathering in the summer heat, as a garden area for growing vegetables and herbs in small raised beds, and as an outdoor cooking and dining area. A freestanding outdoor brick oven, two barbecue grills, and a large granite slab table are aligned on axis with the kitchen and dining spaces inside the house.

Interior and exterior colors and finishes were selected to capture and complement the surrounding natural landscape. Simple laminate cabinets in the kitchen are faced with solid colors that refer to the local tree-covered hills. Similarly, the exposed interior structure, wood floor, and ceiling are stained a variety of gray-green colors. Warm interior stains and wall paints, carpets, and furniture colors complement this primary palette.

Construction

The balloon-frame structure is exposed internally wherever possible and detailed to reflect indigenous vernacular building techniques. Except at the floor tie-downs, all structural joints are made with nailed connections; no bolts were used in the structural framing of the entire house. Other details have contextual references as well. The stairs and railings, for example, designed with open wood framing, stained plywood panels, and galvanized cables, are reminiscent of the steel and wire structure of an existing windmill located on the property.

Third level floor plan

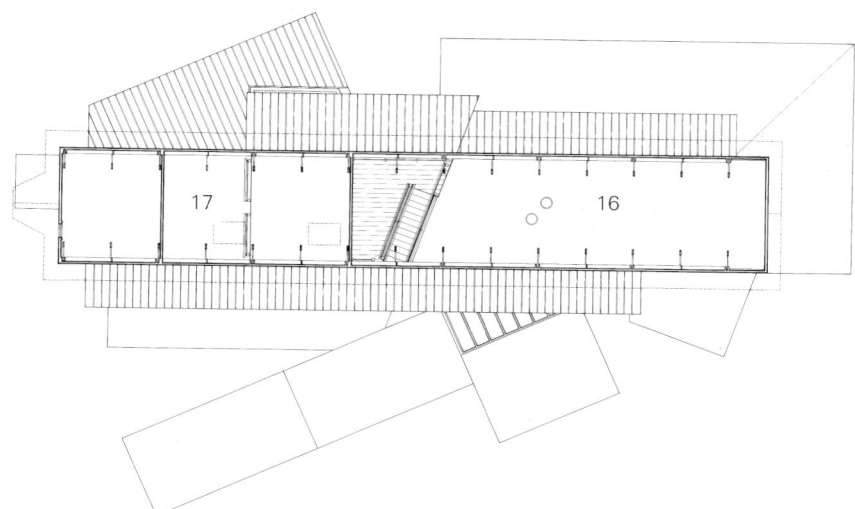

Second level floor plan

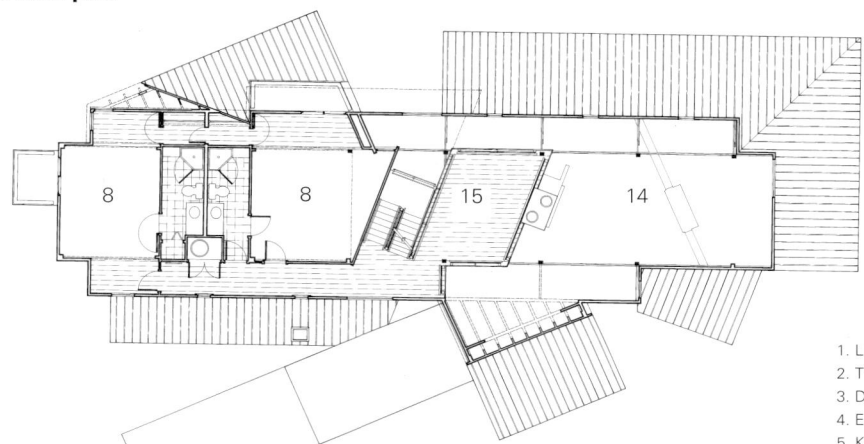

1. LIVING ROOM
2. TV LOUNGE
3. DINING ROOM
4. ENTRY HALL
5. KITCHEN
6. SCREENED PORCH
7. SUN DECK
8. BEDROOM WITH DECK
9. MUD ROOM
10. GUEST BATHROOM
11. LAUNDRY
12. ENTRY PERGOLA
13. HILLTOP PATIO,
OVEN/GRILL
14. OPEN TO BELOW
15. SLEEPING LOFT/LOUNGE

First level floor plan

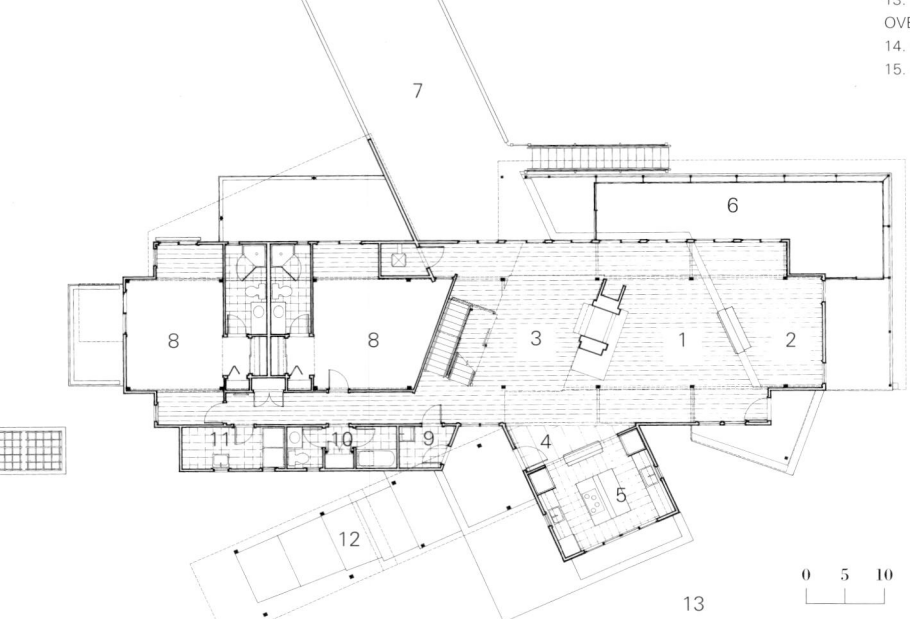

0   5   10

Longitudinal section

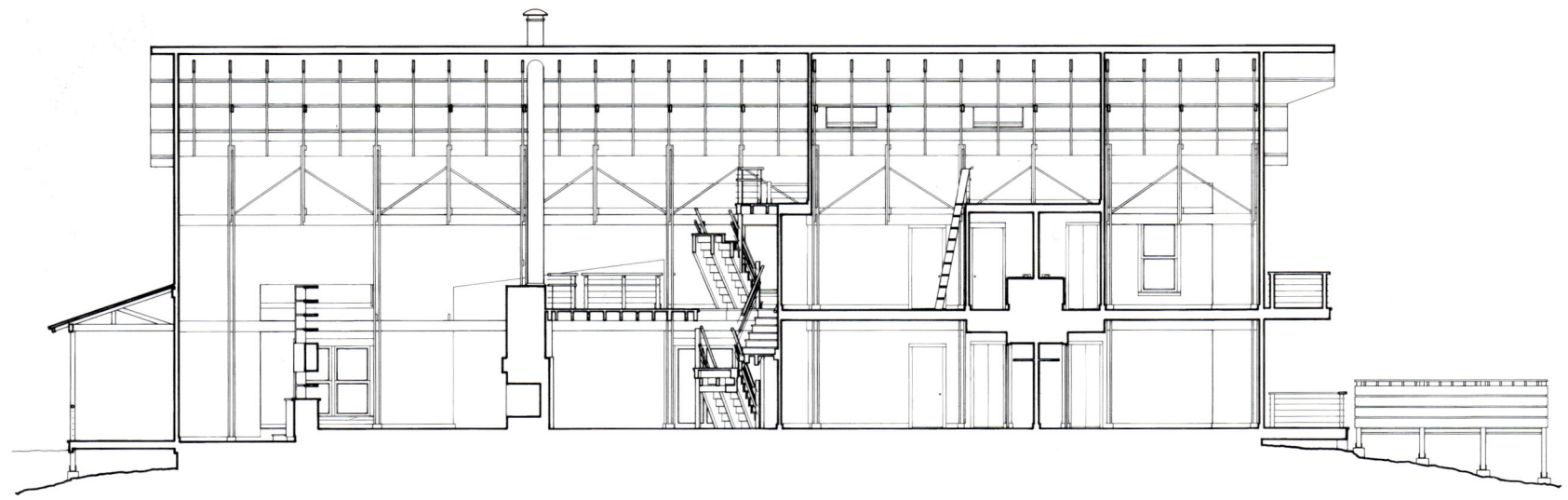

ABOVE: *Kitchen*
LEFT: *Stair to office loft*
FACING PAGE, LEFT: *Exposed framing at loft/lounge*
FACING PAGE, RIGHT: *Living room*

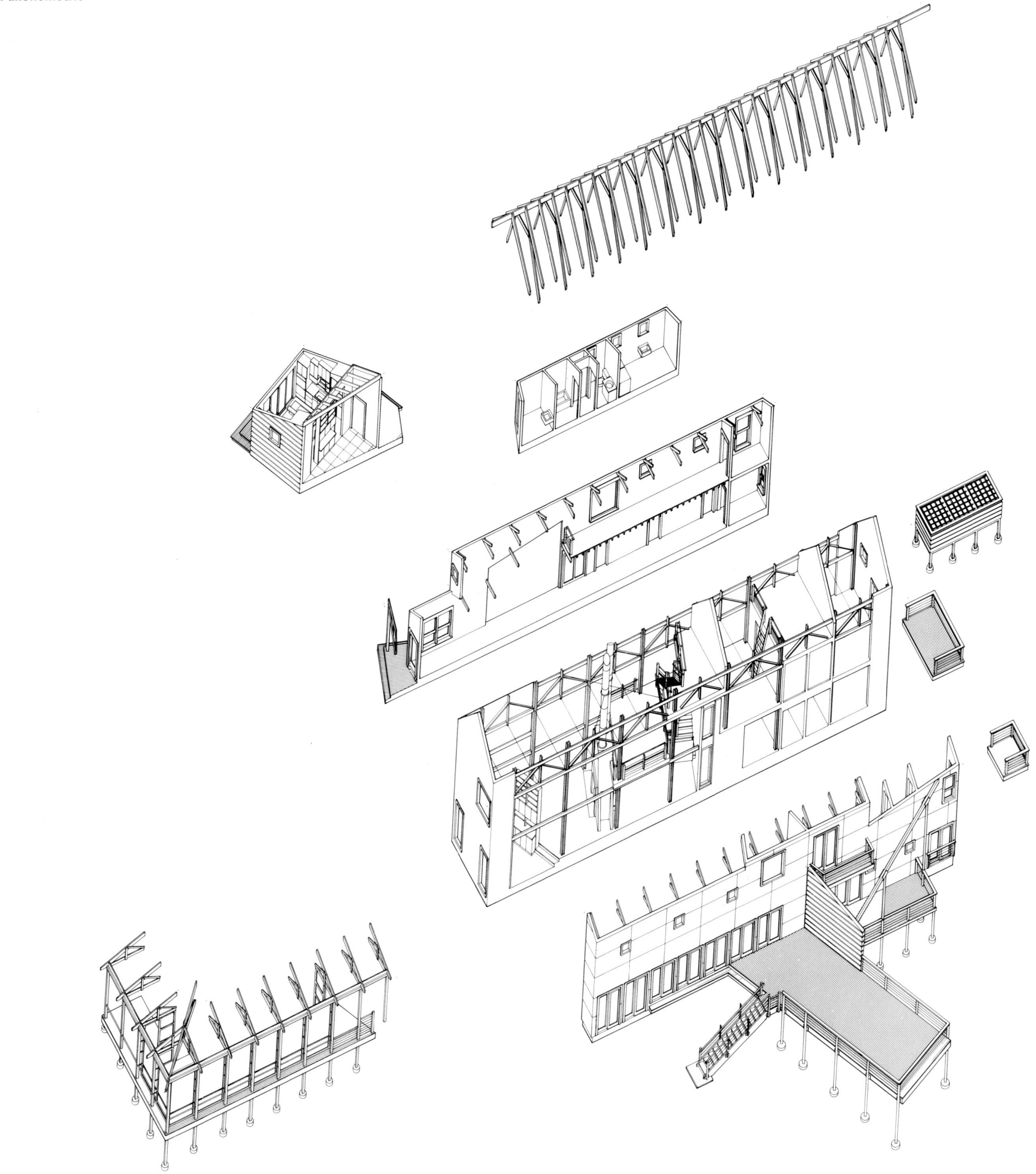

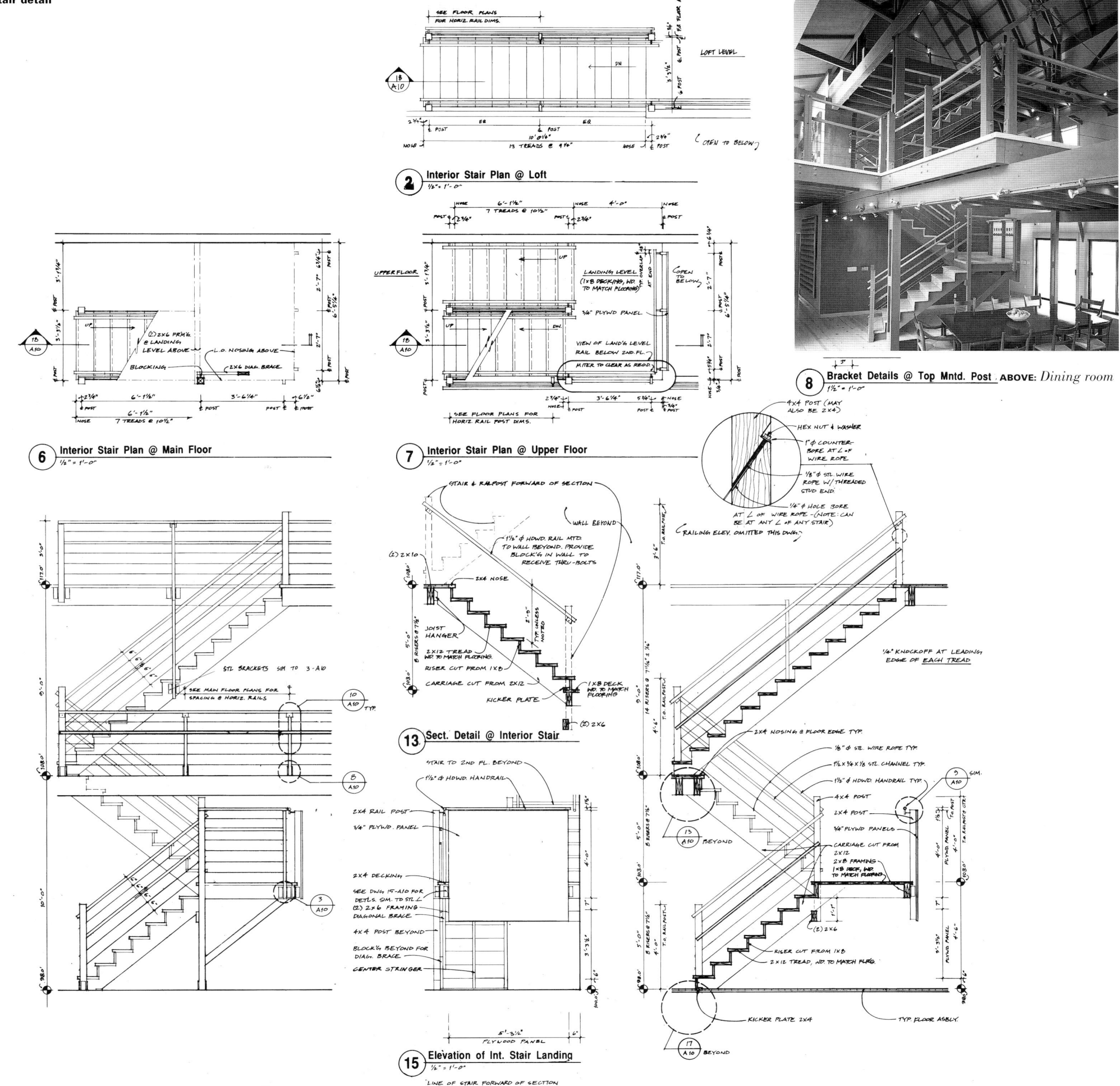

2 Interior Stair Plan @ Loft
½" = 1'-0"

6 Interior Stair Plan @ Main Floor
½" = 1'-0"

7 Interior Stair Plan @ Upper Floor
½" = 1'-0"

8 Bracket Details @ Top Mntd. Post   ABOVE: *Dining room*
1½" = 1'-0"

13 Sect. Detail @ Interior Stair

15 Elevation of Int. Stair Landing
½" = 1'-0"

Miller-O'Herlihy Residence

1993

LORCAN O'HERLIHY ARCHITECTS

Owner: Mike Miller and Patricia O'Herlihy Miller
Architect: Lorcan O'Herlihy Architects, Venice, California
Design Team: Lorcan O'Herlihy, Richard Warner
Engineer: William Koh (structural)
Consultant: Tim Cambell (CAD)
General Contractor: Fred Hammond, Pat Smith
Photography: Tom Bonner

Site: Malibu, California
Program: A residence and guest house for married couple with two children including living/dining room, kitchen, powder room, 2 bedrooms, bathroom, lower and upper studios, master bedroom and bathroom, study, roof deck.
Square Footage: 5800
Structural System: Steel moment frame and wood platform framing on poured concrete foundation.
Mechanical System: Gas-fired central forced air heating
Major Exterior Materials: Channel Glass, cement stucco, aluminum (window system), painted steel (railings), painted aluminum sheet metal.
Major Interior Materials: Skim coat plaster, birch plywood (flooring), birch (cabinetry), Eternit (countertops and walls).
Furnishings and Storage: Built-in cabinets by architect.
Doors and Hardware: Aluminum curtain wall system; Douglas fir doors
Fixtures: Speakman, Kohler, Porcher
Appliances and Equipment: Sub-Zero (refrigerator), Thermador
Cost: $165 per square foot

Site

The house sits on a 50' x 160' steeply sloping lot facing the Pacific Ocean.

Design

Roof terraces and maximized views to the ocean were among the clients' main requests. The deep vertical section of the site and its relation to wonderful views suggested the building's stereometric staggering of volumes along the steep slope of the site. Given the slope and its relation to views and structure, volume and light were used as the root to the architectural solution.

The silhouette of the house echoes the slope. Working with proportion and light, the living spaces are broken into a series of volumes supported by a structural steel frame. In section, the house is a layering of trays from the lowermost garage through the reception zones to the master suite above; a freestanding elliptical pavilion is sited at the high end of the lot, and is intended as an independent unit for guests. The house was conceived as both shelter and outlook. The steel frame lifts the ocean-side end high in the air to be enclosed by clear and translucent channel glass. Further, it enables the

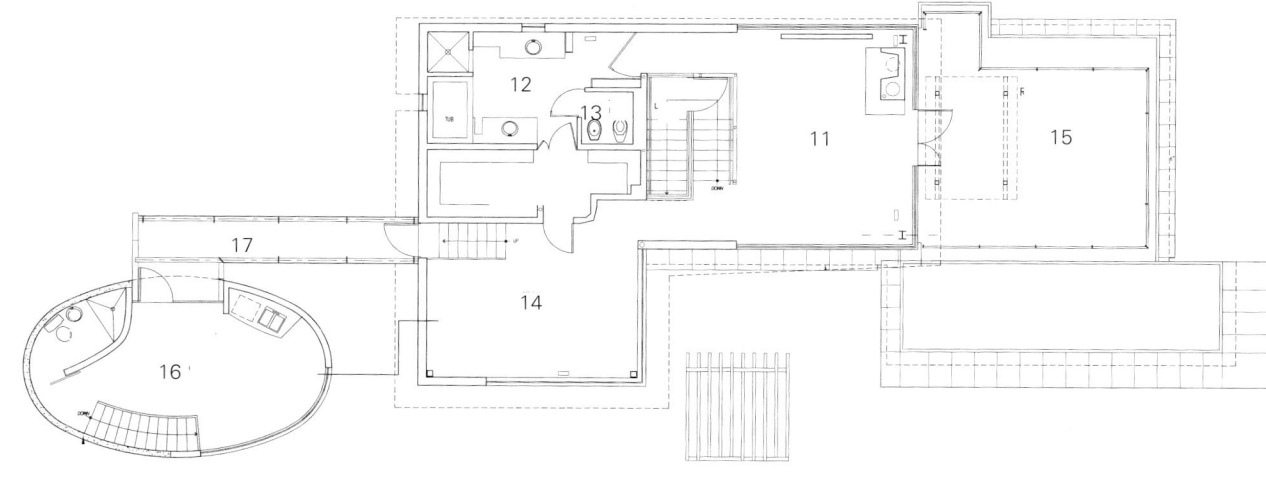

breaking down of the constituent parts of the building: the interior life of the house is activated by extending itself to the exterior via the transparent walls.

Construction

The base construction is poured in-situ concrete "shelving" that runs both vertically and in lateral shifts up the site so that the pieces of the house lock into the land. The front part of the building is a steel moment frame that "frees" up the skin in order to allow as much transparency as possible to take advantage of the ocean vista. Translucent channel glass on the east and west façades provides light as well as visual privacy from the neighboring houses.

First level floor plan

1. ENTRY
2. LIVING/DINING ROOM
3. KITCHEN
4. POWDER ROOM
5. LANDING
6. EXTERIOR DECK
7. BEDROOM
8. BATHROOM
9. BRIDGE OVERHEAD
10. LOWER STUDIO
11. MASTER BEDROOM
12. MASTER BATHROOM
13. TOILET
14. STUDY
15. ROOF DECK
16. UPPER STUDIO
17. BRIDGE

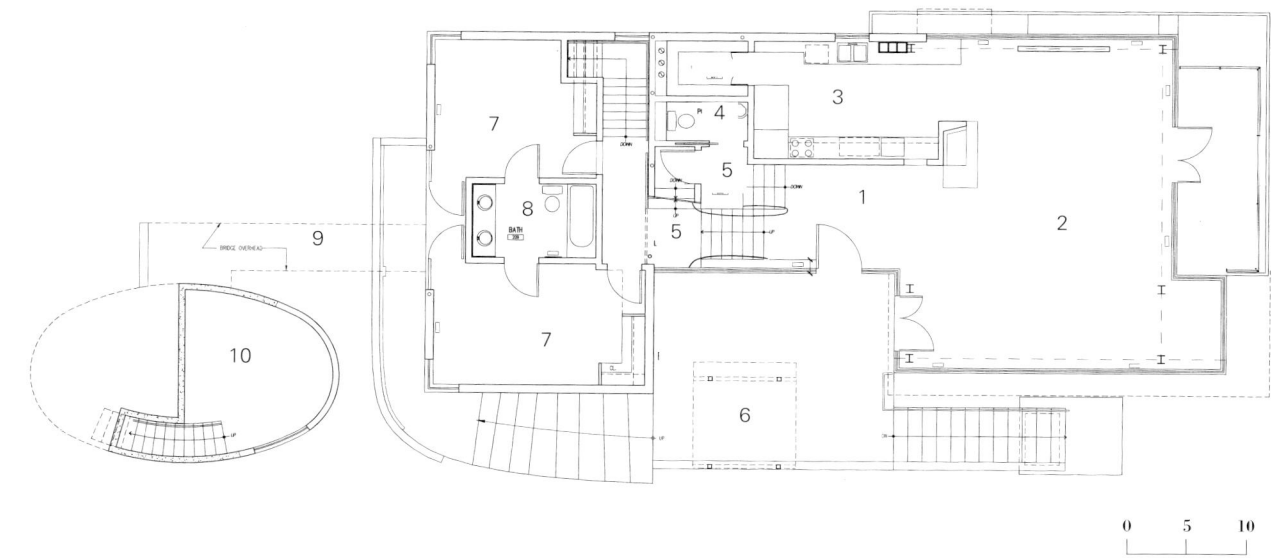

Site plan

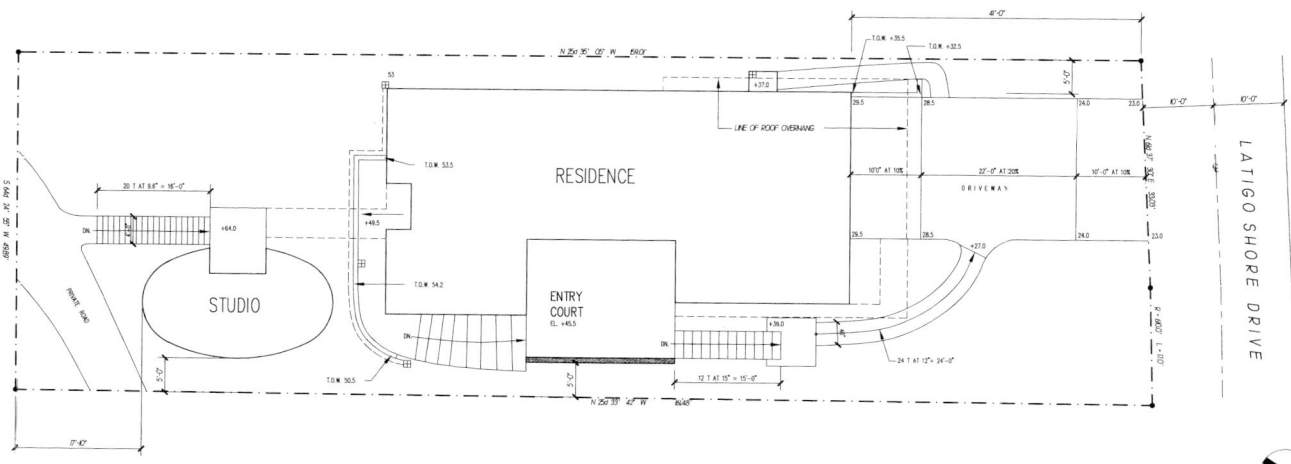

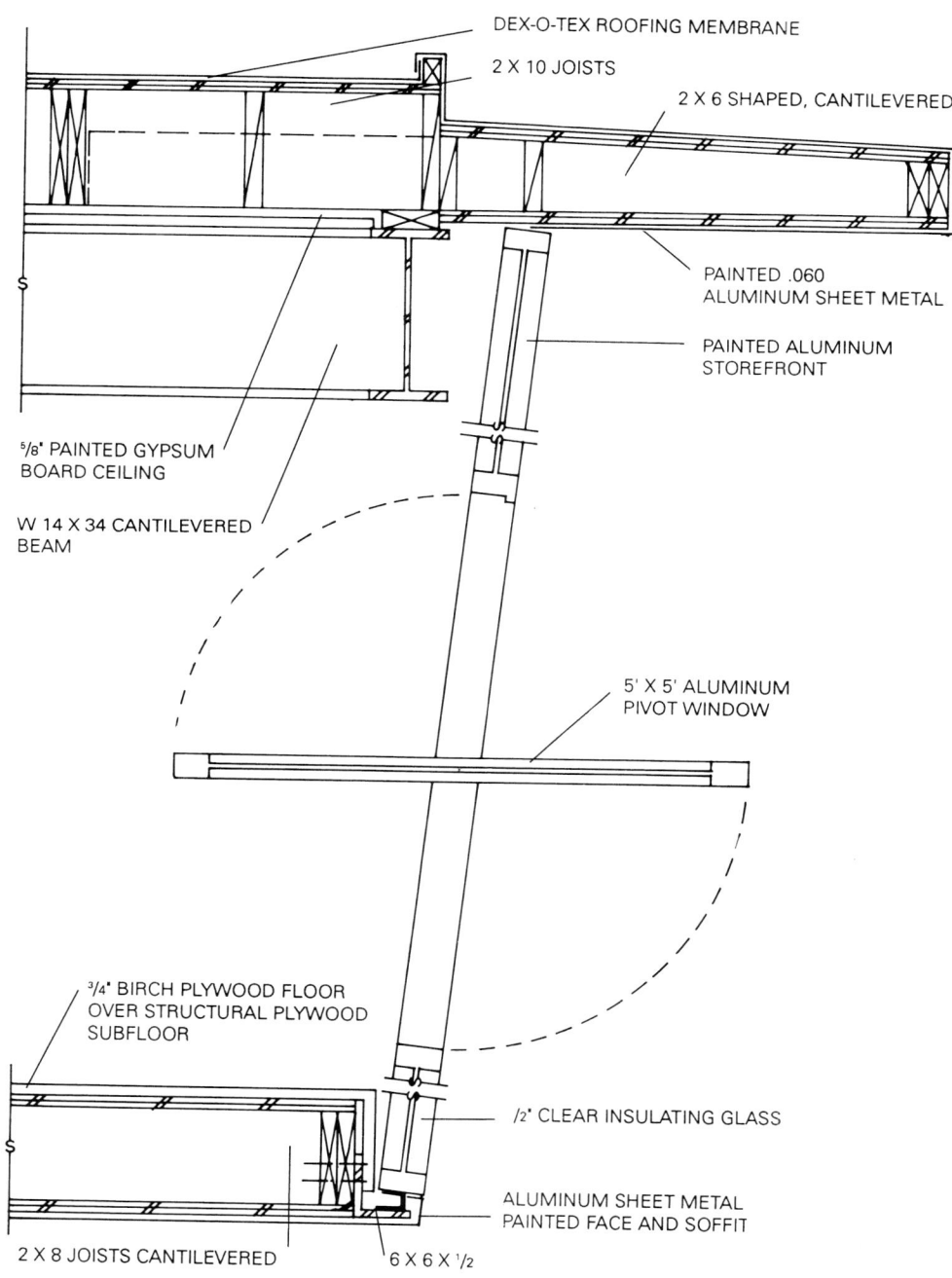

DEX-O-TEX ROOFING MEMBRANE

2 X 10 JOISTS

2 X 6 SHAPED, CANTILEVERED

PAINTED .060
ALUMINUM SHEET METAL

PAINTED ALUMINUM
STOREFRONT

⁵/₈" PAINTED GYPSUM
BOARD CEILING

W 14 X 34 CANTILEVERED
BEAM

5' X 5' ALUMINUM
PIVOT WINDOW

³/₄" BIRCH PLYWOOD FLOOR
OVER STRUCTURAL PLYWOOD
SUBFLOOR

/2" CLEAR INSULATING GLASS

ALUMINUM SHEET METAL
PAINTED FACE AND SOFFIT

2 X 8 JOISTS CANTILEVERED

6 X 6 X ¹/2

SLOPED GLASS WALL AT LIVING ROOM – DETAILS 2,3

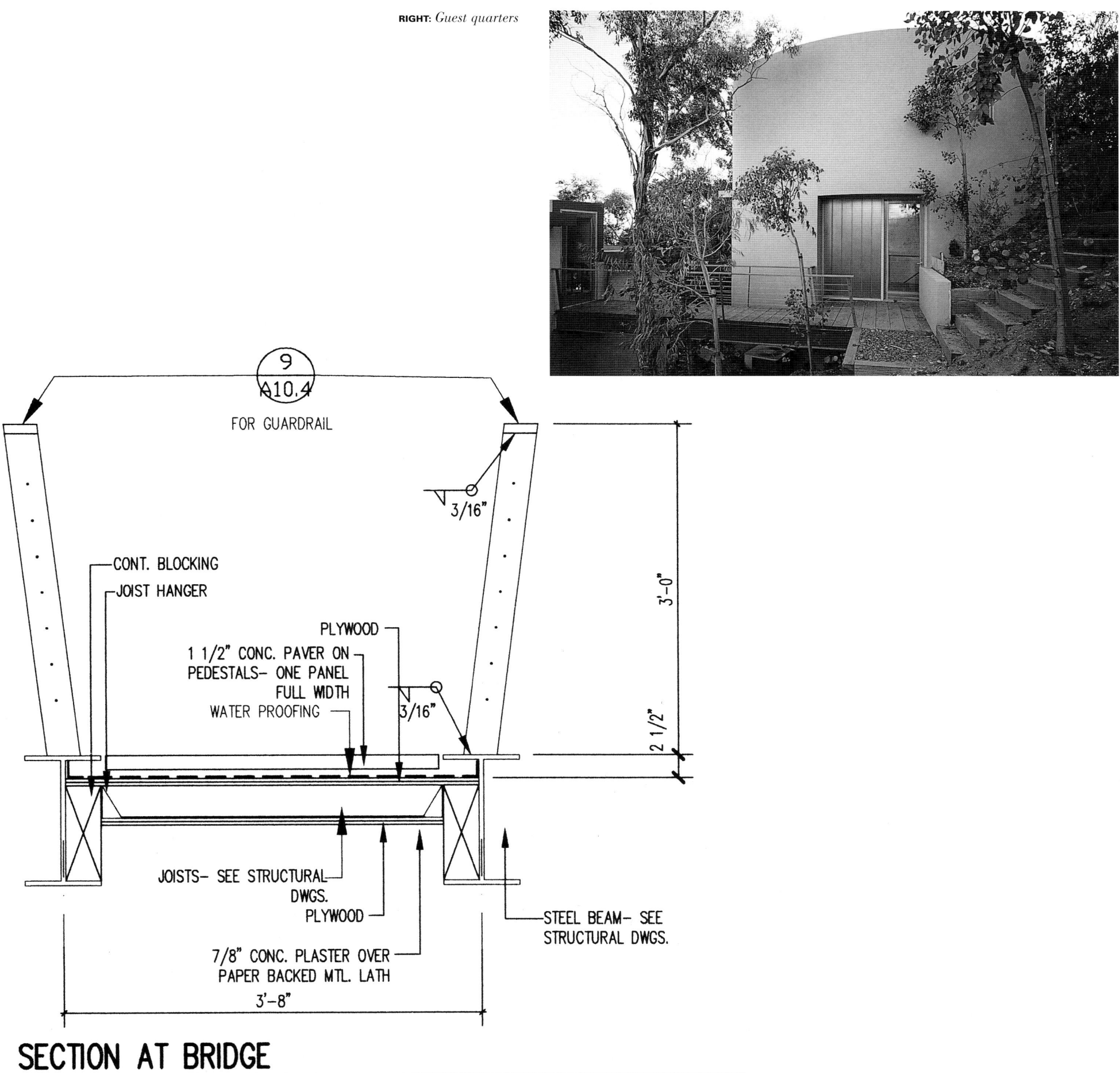

9
A10.4

FOR GUARDRAIL

3/16"

3'-0"

CONT. BLOCKING
JOIST HANGER

PLYWOOD

1 1/2" CONC. PAVER ON
PEDESTALS— ONE PANEL
FULL WIDTH
WATER PROOFING

3/16"

2 1/2"

JOISTS— SEE STRUCTURAL
DWGS.
PLYWOOD

STEEL BEAM— SEE
STRUCTURAL DWGS.

7/8" CONC. PLASTER OVER
PAPER BACKED MTL. LATH
3'-8"

SECTION AT BRIDGE

Tarzana Residence *1994*
DALY, GENIK

Owner: Name withheld at owner's request.
Architect: Daly, Genik, Santa Monica, California
Design Team: Kevin Daly, Christopher Genik, Jacki Hah, Janet Simon, Padraic Cassidy.
Engineer: Parker, Resnick (structural)
Consultant: Melinda Taylor (landscape)
General Contractor: Sanfilipo Construction
Photography: Dominique Vorillon, © J. Scott Smith

Site: Tarzana, California
Program: Renovation of existing house and addition of canopied exterior area.
Square Footage: 3300 existing, 100 in addition
Structural System: Wood frame, moment frame at clerestory addition
Mechanical System: Forced air heat and air conditioning
Major Exterior Materials: Plaster, steel-troweled plaster, galvanized steel (sunshade).
Major Interior Materials: Birch (flooring), unalloyed aluminum, Douglas fir plywood (cabinets), slate (floors), sitka spruce (pivoting screen).
Furnishings and Storage: Dining room table, glass screen, living room bench, and family room coffee table custom by architect.
Doors and Hardware: Aluminum storefront and storefront door by Animal Fronts.
Windows: Clear anodized casement and awning windows by Metal Window Corp.
Fixtures: Kohler
Appliances and Equipment: Sub-Zero (refrigerator/freezer), Kitchen Aid (ovens, warming drawer, twin dishwashers)
Cost: $350,300

Site

Situated in a Los Angeles suburb close to the Santa Monica Mountains, the project was developed from a 1968 tract house occupying the majority of a large lot.

Design

The owners, a couple whose grown children have moved out, wanted a house that would more effectively address their personal needs and interests—larger living area, ample storage, and a studio in which to create and display the wife's artwork. In order to spatially restructure the family home, the architects expanded the interior by demolishing most of the house to its perimeter walls.

At the main entry, a central core opened to become a fluid, loft-like space, one encounters freestanding sculpted objects that serve to define and partition the social wings of the house. The most striking among these freestanding objects is an aluminum clad fireplace. The once-mundane, traditional stone and brick face was wrapped in distressed aluminum to become a dynamic and centrally positioned volume. Punctuated by rivets, the fireplace's texture appears as silvered fabric, coolly

Transversal section

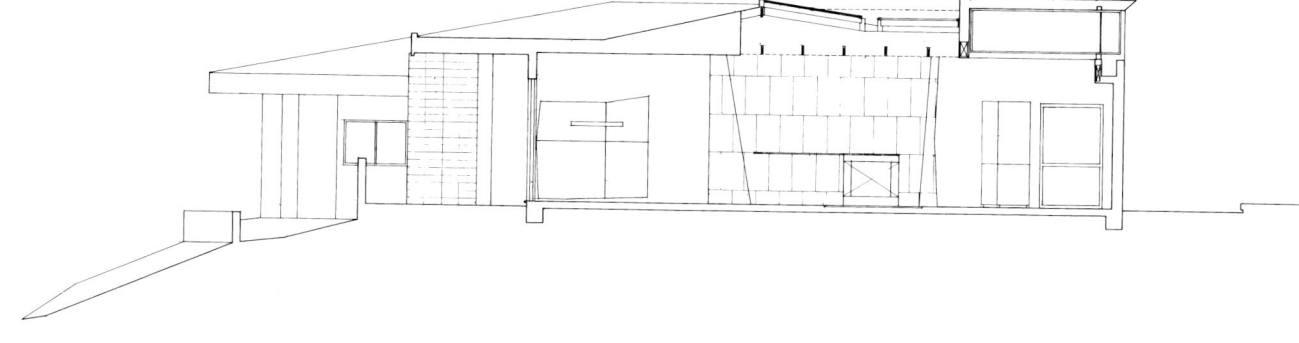

complementing the blond wood flooring. The angular entry screen is hinged to allow the dining room to expand into the living room. Adjacent to the dining room, a faceted cabinet centers the room and demarcates the boundaries of dining room and family room. The warm tones of spruce and Douglas fir offset the metallic gleam of the fireplace. The variegated, high-texture palette extends to the private rooms, with their modular storage cabinets, and to the iridescent hues of the guest bathroom.

On the exterior, the front façade respects the introspective characteristics of the surrounding houses. The rear façade is more playful, where subtle elements were introduced to expand and enhance the quality of the social areas. A galvanized steel canopy filters and diffuses sunlight, and a clerestory added to the raised roof draws in light that is prismatically reflected by the fireplace. A large window projecting from the rear provides views of the fireplace and living room, thereby linking the interior and exterior.

Construction

A program of interior renovation was developed that retains much of the existing exterior and the introspective nature of the site. The roof was raised to enlarge the space, and a clerestory inserted to maximize the absorption of light. Custom furnishings and storage units designed by the architect further add to the house's uniqueness.

Longitudinal section

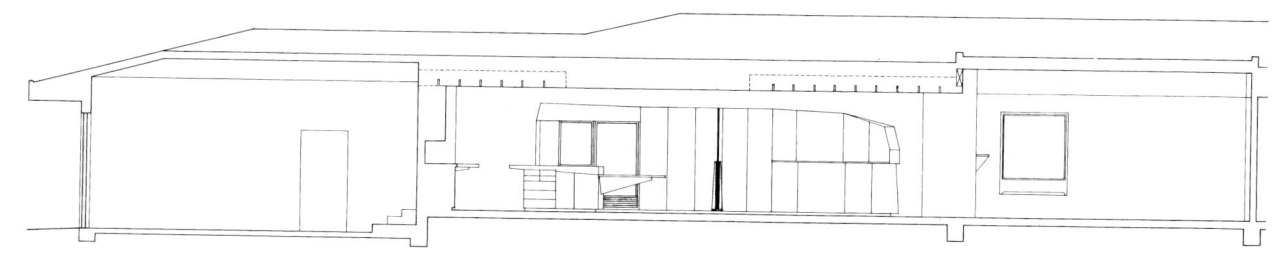

Floor plan

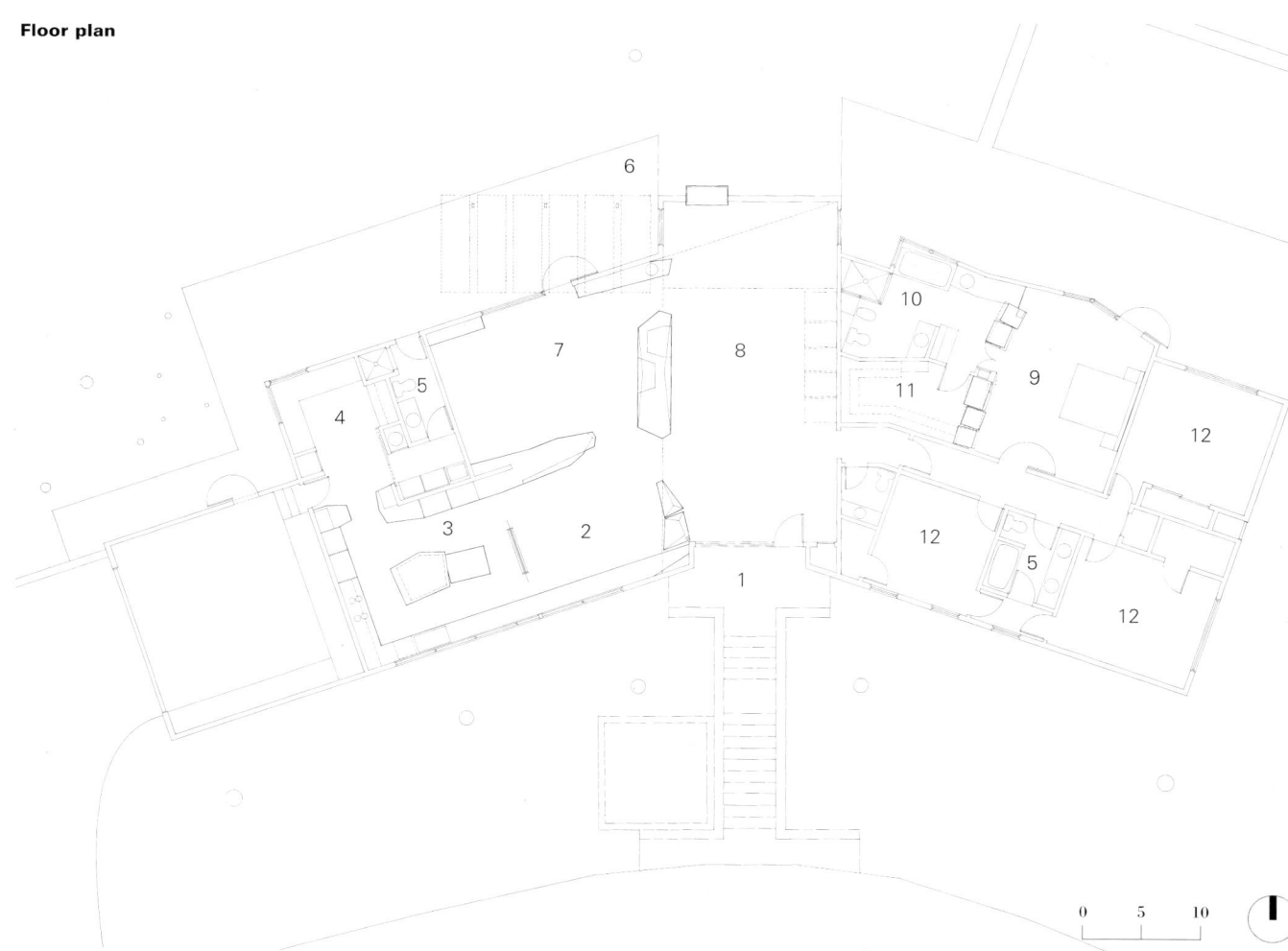

1. ENTRY
2. DINING ROOM
3. KITCHEN
4. STUDY
5. BATHROOM
6. SUNSCREEN/CANOPY
7. MUSIC/VIDEO ROOM
8. MAIN SPACE
9. MASTER BEDROOM
10. MASTER BATHROOM
11. DRESSING/STORAGE
12. BEDROOM

0   5   10

Canopy detail

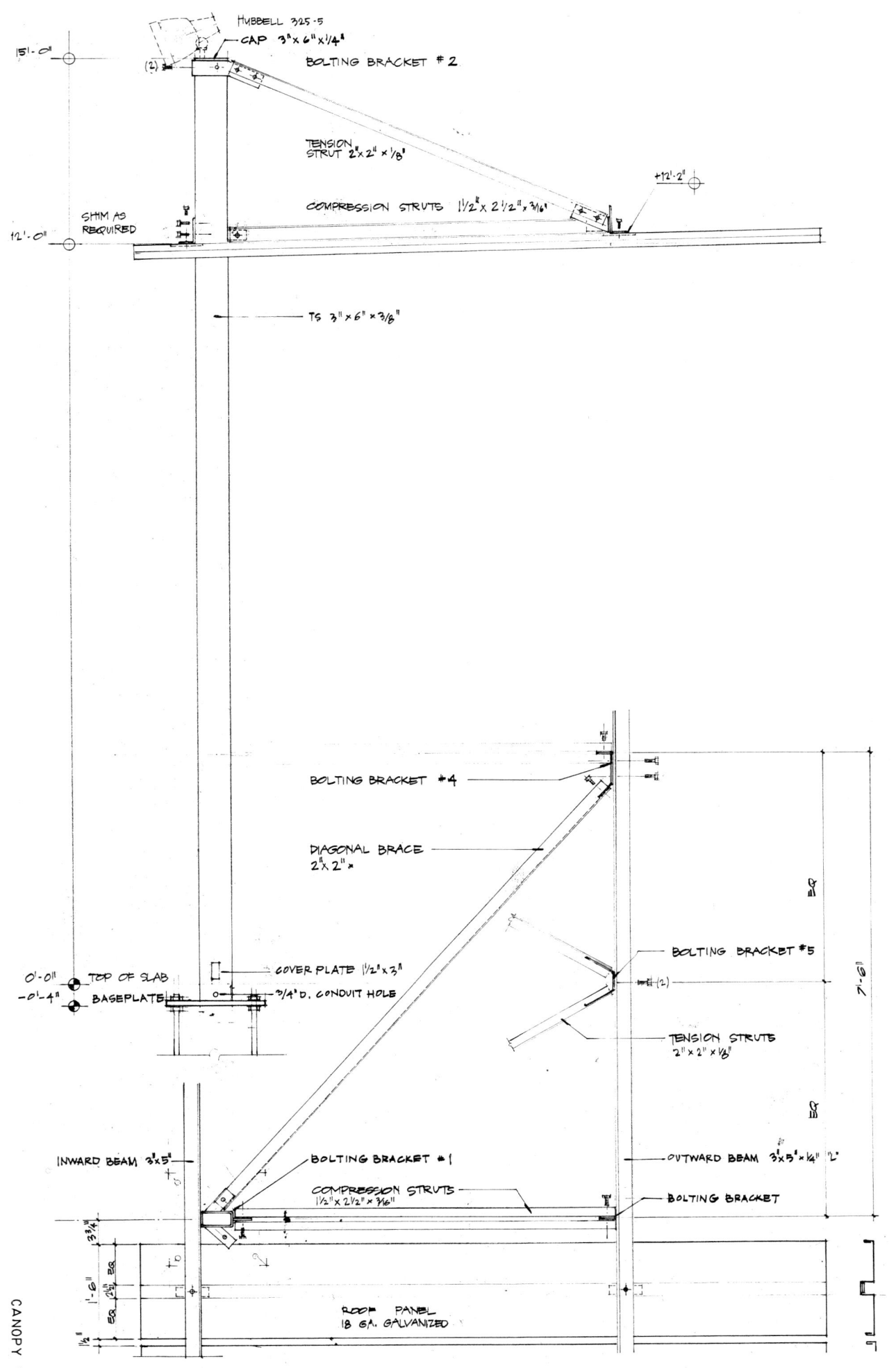

HUBBELL 325·5
15'-0" CAP 3" × 6" × 1/4"
(2) BOLTING BRACKET #2

TENSION
STRUT 2" × 2" × 1/8"

+12'-2"
SHIM AS
REQUIRED   COMPRESSION STRUTS 1½" × 2½" × 3/16"

12'-0"

TS 3" × 6" × 3/8"

BOLTING BRACKET #4

DIAGONAL BRACE
2" × 2" ×

BOLTING BRACKET #5
(2)

0'-0" TOP OF SLAB   COVER PLATE 1½" × 3"
-0'-4" BASEPLATE   3/4" D. CONDUIT HOLE

TENSION STRUTS
2" × 2" × 1/8"

INWARD BEAM 3" × 5"   BOLTING BRACKET #1   OUTWARD BEAM 3" × 5" × 1/4" '2'

COMPRESSION STRUTS   BOLTING BRACKET
1½" × 2½" × 3/16"

ROOF PANEL
18 GA. GALVANIZED

CANOPY 7

71

RIGHT: *View of dining room toward living room*
MIDDLE: *Dining room*
BOTTOM: *Master bedroom*
FACING PAGE: *Living room*

RIGHT: *Dining room table, custom by architect*

Cabinetry details

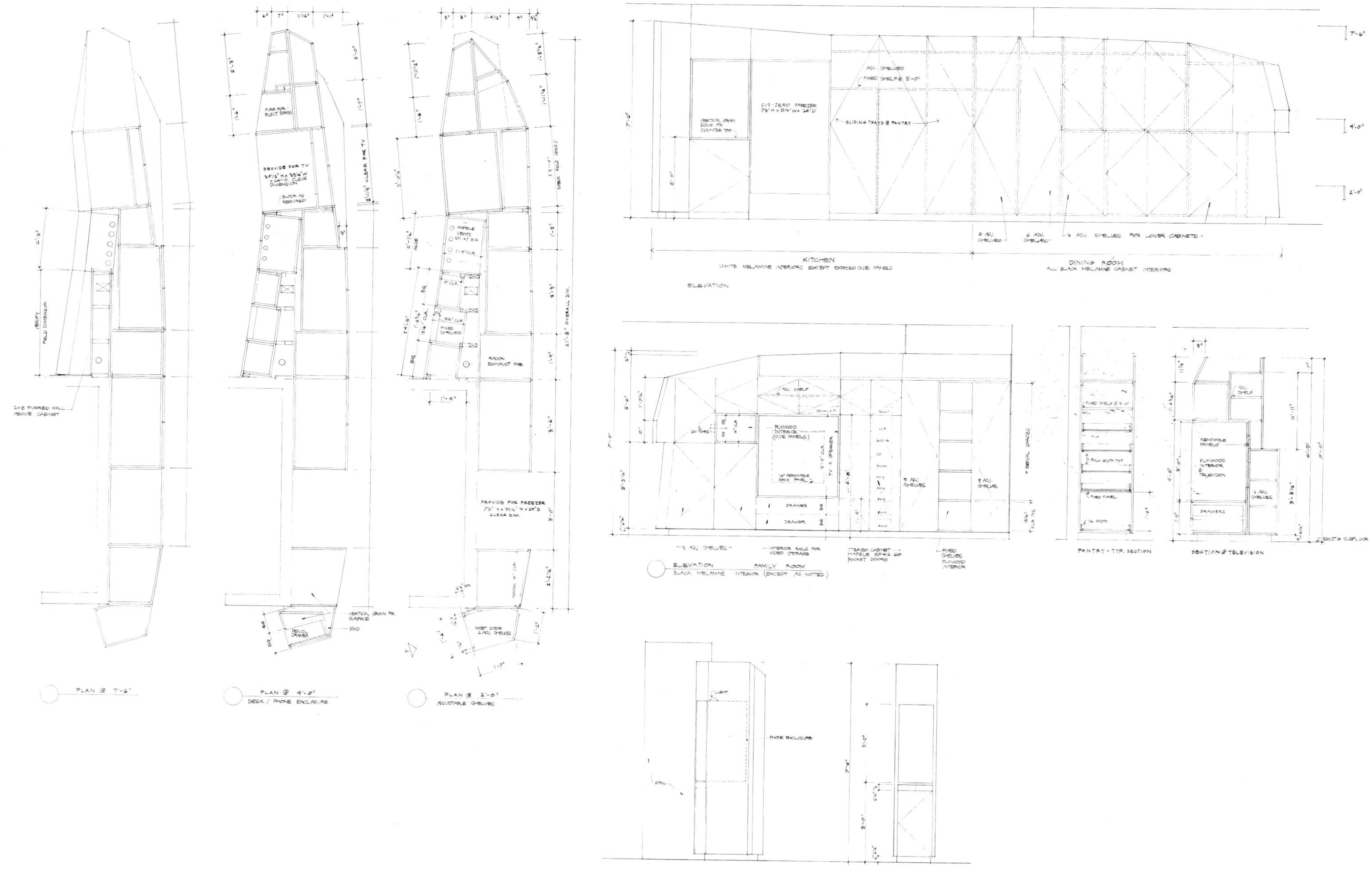

Table details

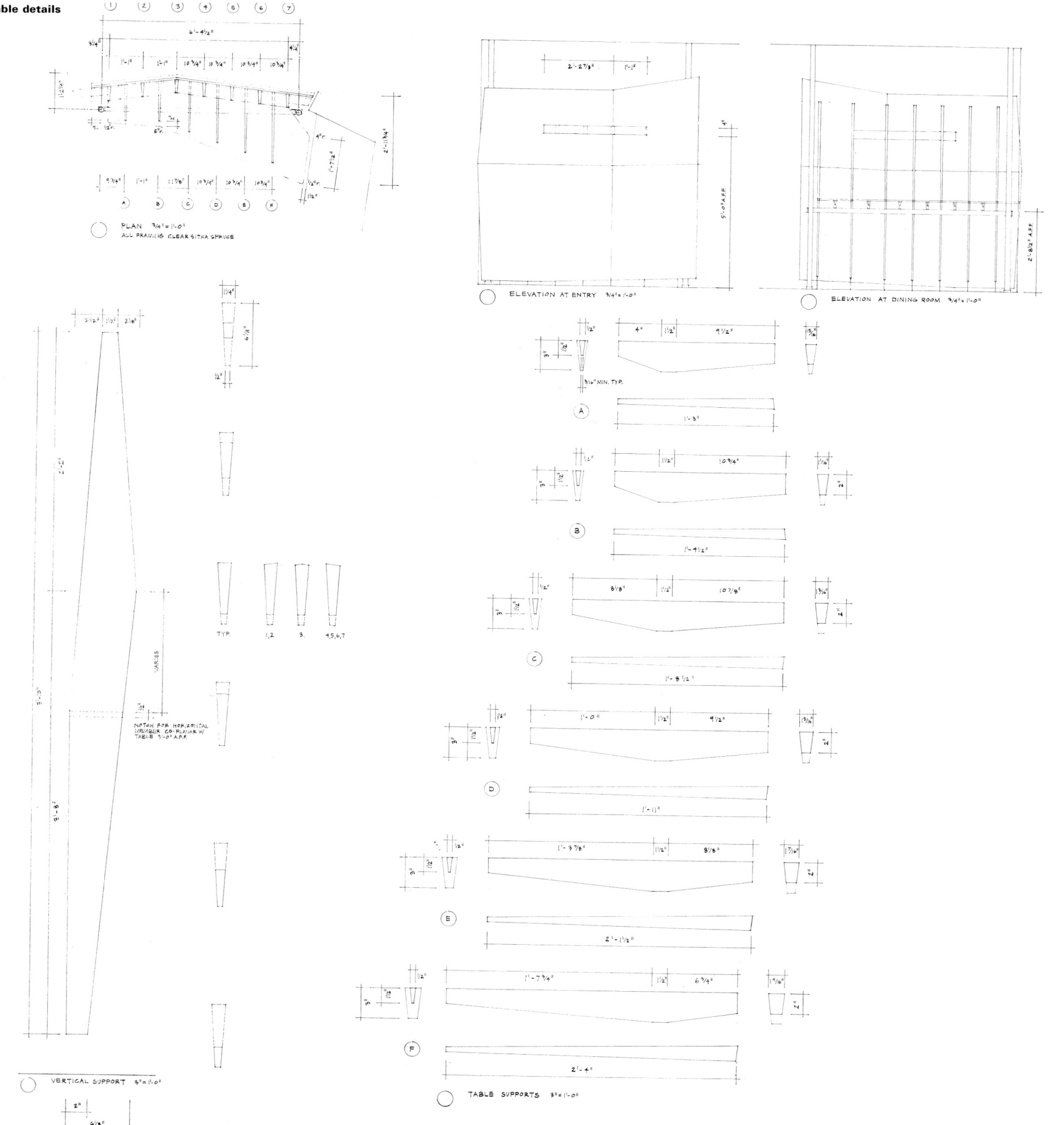

PLAN 3/4" = 1'-0"
ALL FRAMING CLEAR SITKA SPRUCE

ELEVATION AT ENTRY 3/4"=1'-0"

ELEVATION AT DINING ROOM 3/4"=1'-0"

TYP.   1,2   3.   4,5,6,7

NOTCH FOR HORIZONTAL
MEMBER CO-PLANAR W/
TABLE 3'-0" A.F.F.

VERTICAL SUPPORT 3"=1'-0"

A

B

C

D

E

F

TABLE SUPPORTS 3"=1'-0"

Private Residence *1989-1995*
CENTRAL OFFICE OF ARCHITECTURE

Owner: Name withheld at owner's request.
Architect: Central Office of Architecture, Los Angeles, California
Design Team: Ron Golan, Eric A. Kahn, Russell N. Thomsen
Engineer: Miguel Castillo (structural)
General Contractor: Surfside Construction
Photography: Benny Chan, COA

Site: Laguna Beach, California
Program: Addition to existing single-family residence including master bedroom and bathroom, office, and pool house.
Square Footage: 1100
Structural System: Steel column, wood frame, concrete slab
Mechanical System: Hydronic radiant slab
Major Exterior Materials: Fiber cement panels, stainless steel, glass, terrazzo, plaster.
Major Interior Materials: Fiber cement panels, terrazzo, white oak (casework), black granite, plaster.
Furnishings and Storage: Built-in storage units and custom furniture by architect. Chairs by Le Corbusier with Charlotte Perriand and Pierre Jeanneret (Grand Confort) and Mies van der Rohe (Barcelona).
Doors and Hardware: Custom by architect.
Windows: Marvin Windows
Fixtures: American Standard, Kroin
Appliances and Equipment: U-Line (refrigerator)
Cost: $150,000.

Site

The hilltop site consists of four contiguous parcels directly overlooking the Pacific Ocean to the south and west. The strategy reorganizes the site into two distinct domains, one public and the other entirely private. On the public side of this division is a neighboring residence and a driveway used to approach the house. On the opposing side is the domain of the existing house with a pool and promenade deck area which had the potential to become an outdoor living space in the Southern California Case Study House tradition.

Design

The intervention clearly distinguishes public from private space through the use of a primary wall element. Constructed of fiber cement panels, the high wall organizes the program of the addition into closed or open spaces. The master bedroom is connected both literally and visually to the outdoors by three full-height pivoting glazed doors. Enhancing clarity and awareness of the site, the wall also demarcates the differential between the open and closed conditions on either side. The building volumes reflect this Janus-faced relationship in both the scale and definition of their respective openings and boundaries. Further, the wall connects the existing house to the addition, delineating an interior circulation path that is illuminated by natural light from a small

FACING PAGE: *View of master bedroom with pool house at left*

outdoor space resulting from the angled placement of the buildings' volumes.

The entry sequence, characterized by movement between the public and private zones, results in an extended threshold of space between the volumes, effectively contrasting the closed quality of the initial entry to the expansiveness of the sea and horizon beyond. After passing through a perforated metal gate one experiences a compressed passage between the bedroom wing on the one side and the new poolhouse on the other, which culminates in a panoramic view of the Pacific. In this way the architecture permits greater understanding of the relationship of building to environment that can be effected through tectonic clarity, sequence, and order.

Construction
The primary construction system is wood frame wall and roof. Walls are clad with either stucco or fiber cement panels. A single steel column supports the roof at the edge of the swimming pool. Floors are poured-in-place terrazzo with an in-slab radiant heating system.

Floor plan

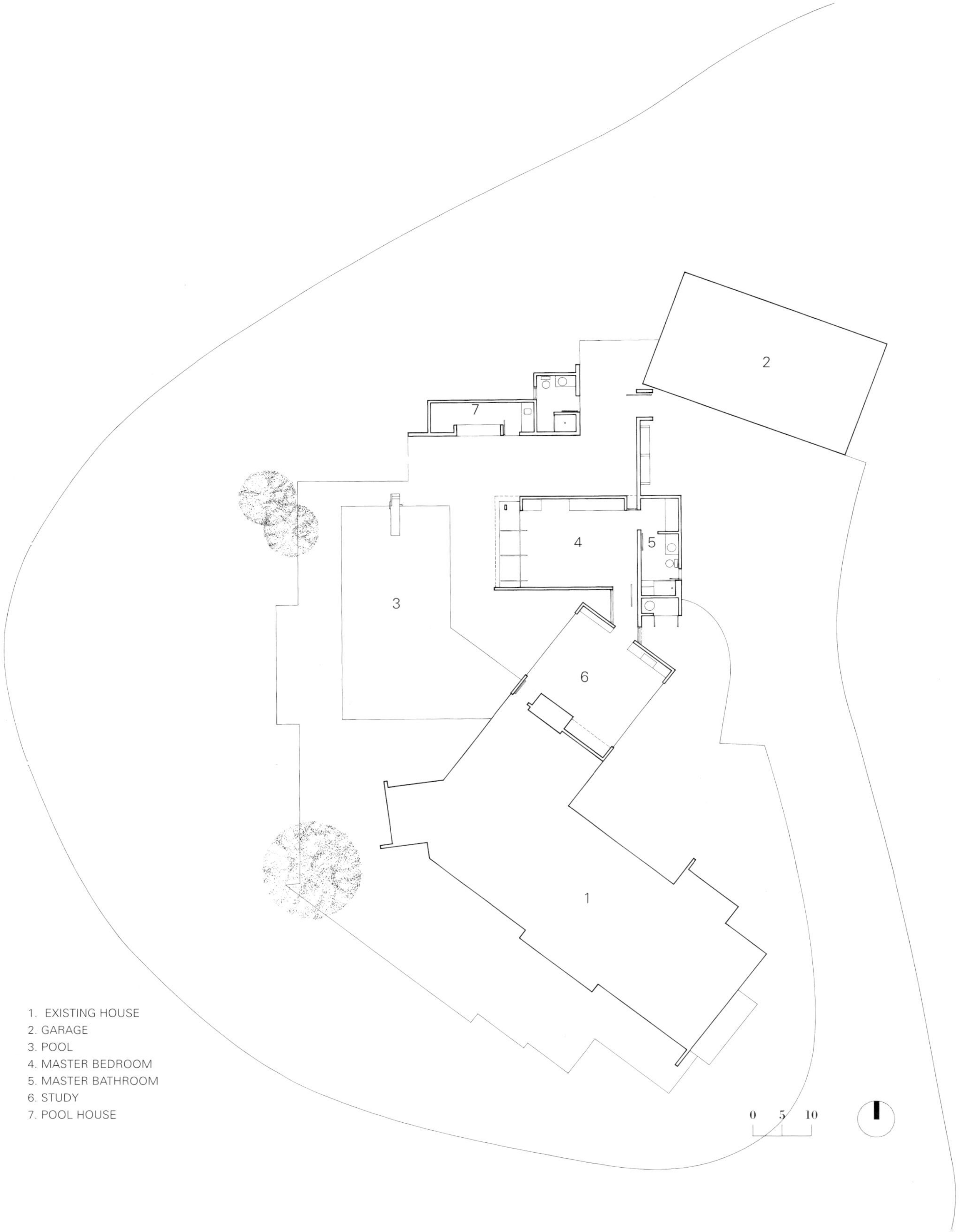

1. EXISTING HOUSE
2. GARAGE
3. POOL
4. MASTER BEDROOM
5. MASTER BATHROOM
6. STUDY
7. POOL HOUSE

0   5   10

LEFT: *Pool house*

South elevation

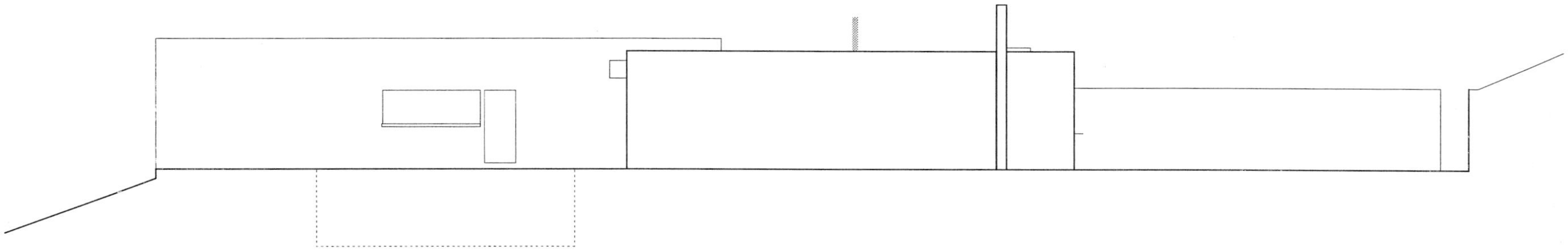

West elevation

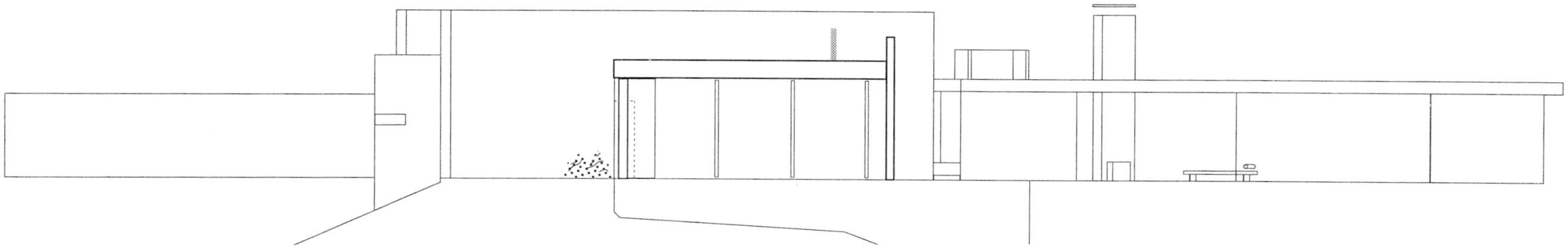

North elevation

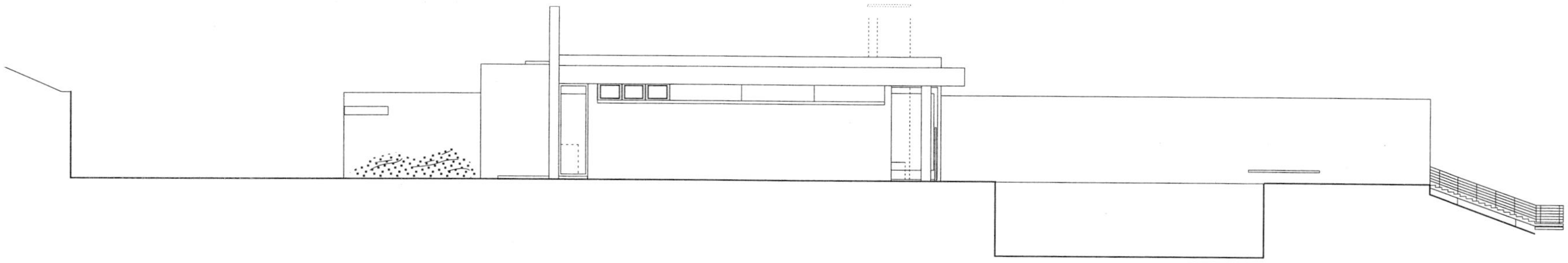

East elevation

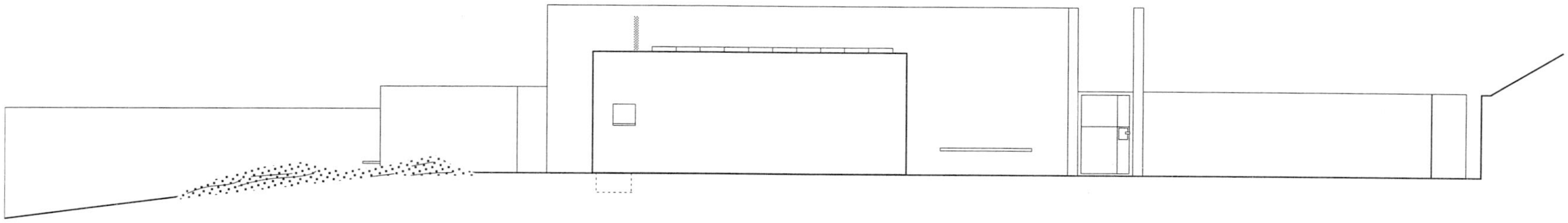

79

Wall section

Wall section

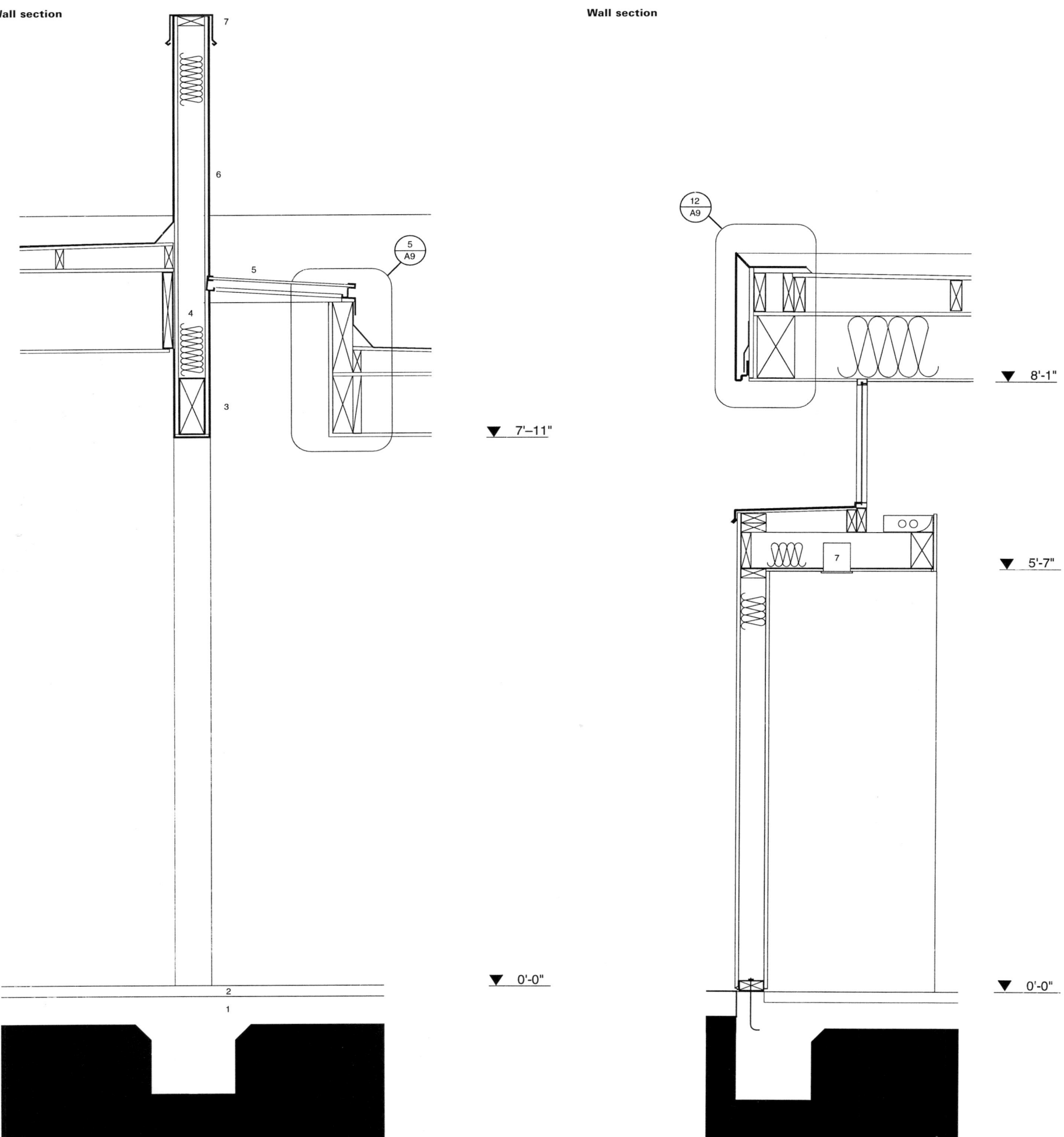

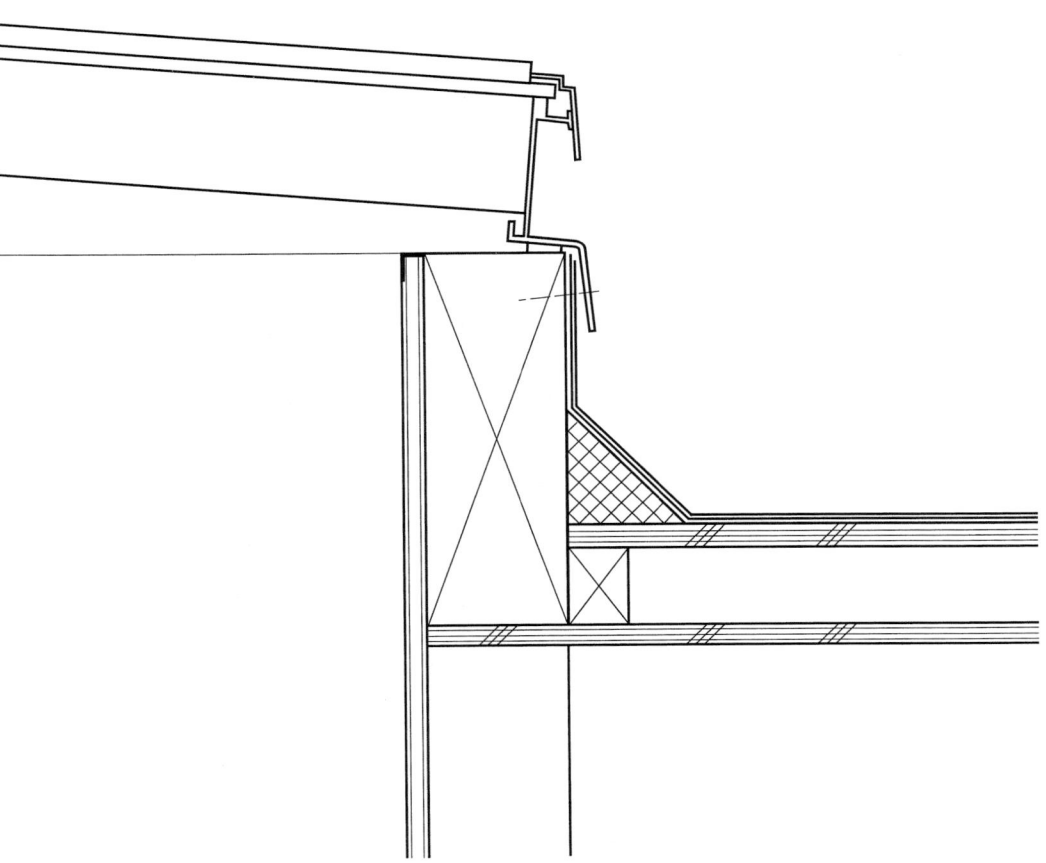

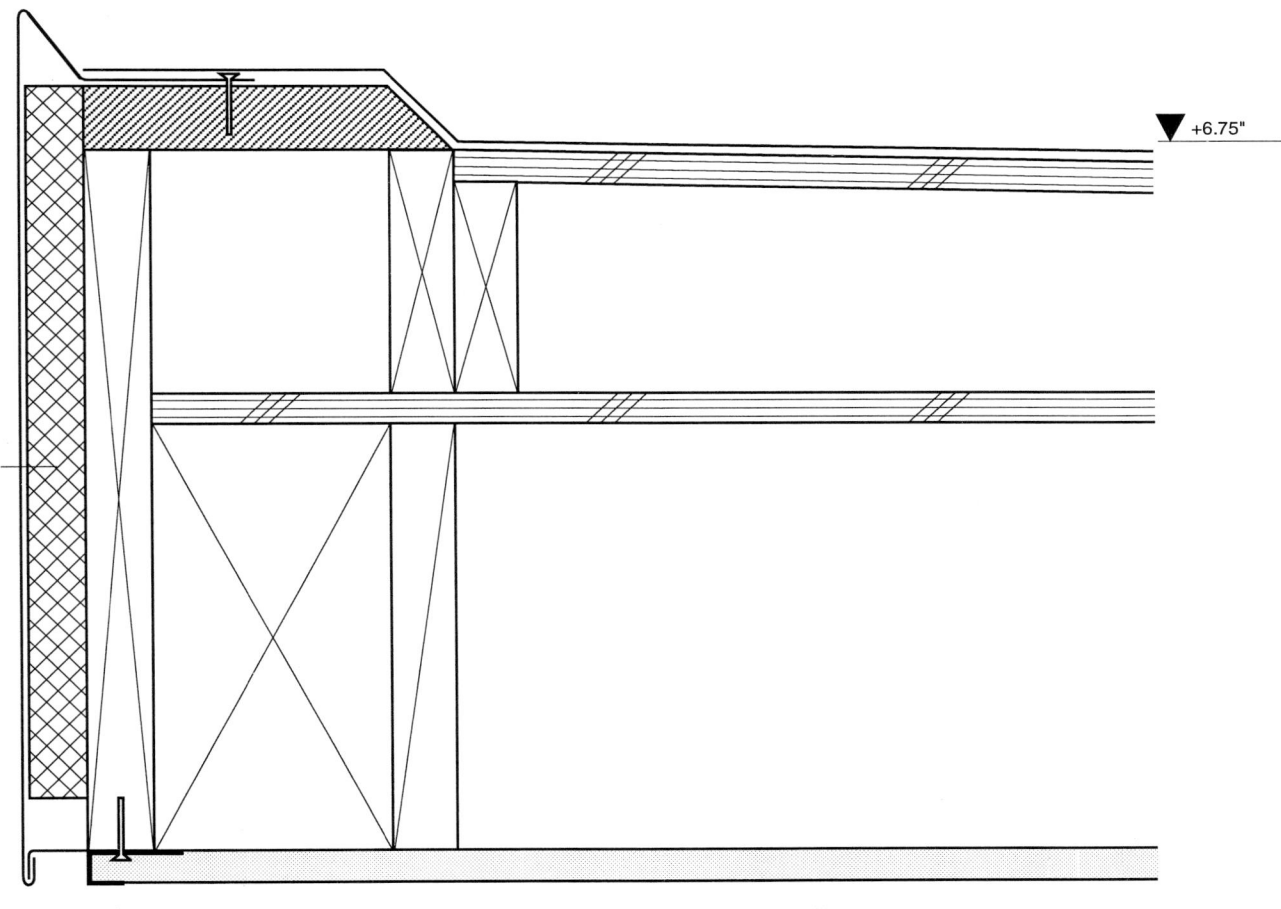

▼ +6.75"

10

The Monument *1990*

SCHWEITZER BIM, INCORPORATED

Owner: Name withheld at owner's request.
Architect: Schweitzer BIM, Incorporated, Los Angeles, California
Design Team: Josh Schweitzer, Scott Prentice, Pat Ousey, Marywether Felt.
Engineers: Comeau Engineers (mechanical), Davis-Fejes Design (structural)
General Contractor: Silverstrand Partnership
Photography: Tim Street-Porter

Site: Joshua Tree, California
Program: Weekend and vacation retreat for three couples including living space, dining space, kitchen, bathroom, bedroom, 2 sleeping lofts.
Square Footage: 950
Structural System: Slab on grade with wood framing
Mechanical System: Rooftop mounted package unit
Major Exterior Materials: Exterior cement plaster
Major Interior Materials: Exposed aggregate concrete slab (flooring), gypsum board (walls), painted wood (cabinets).
Furnishings and Storage: Built in by architect.
Doors and Hardware: Custom by architect.
Windows: Custom by architect.
Fixtures: Speakman, Delta
Cost: $165,000

FACING PAGE: *View of house*

Site

Located three hours outside of Los Angeles, the Joshua Tree National Monument is unlike other national parks. Devoid of leafy trees, green grass, and large bodies of water, it stretches across the high desert, an expanse of sand carpeted with giant boulders and interspersed with cacti, thorny brush, yucca plants, and Joshua trees. One mile outside the park is the Monument, a unique weekend and vacation house sited on ten acres of desert scrubland. Built on one of the site's few flat areas, the structures are surrounded by huge boulders. In turn, the Monument's monolithic forms echo the shapes of the rocks.

Design

Composed of simple geometric forms, this 950-square-foot house is not so much a container for living as a series of rooms that supplements the primary space—the landscape. Used as a retreat by architect Josh Schweitzer and five friends, the house is actually an assemblage of one-room buildings, each of which contains a separate function.

An outside porch-like structure painted a rich burnt orange provides shaded outdoor space during the day, as well as a vantage point for beautiful sunsets over a distant ridge. The living room is enclosed by twenty-four-foot-high olive-green walls punctured by irregular openings to fractured views of rocks and sky. An

Section looking west

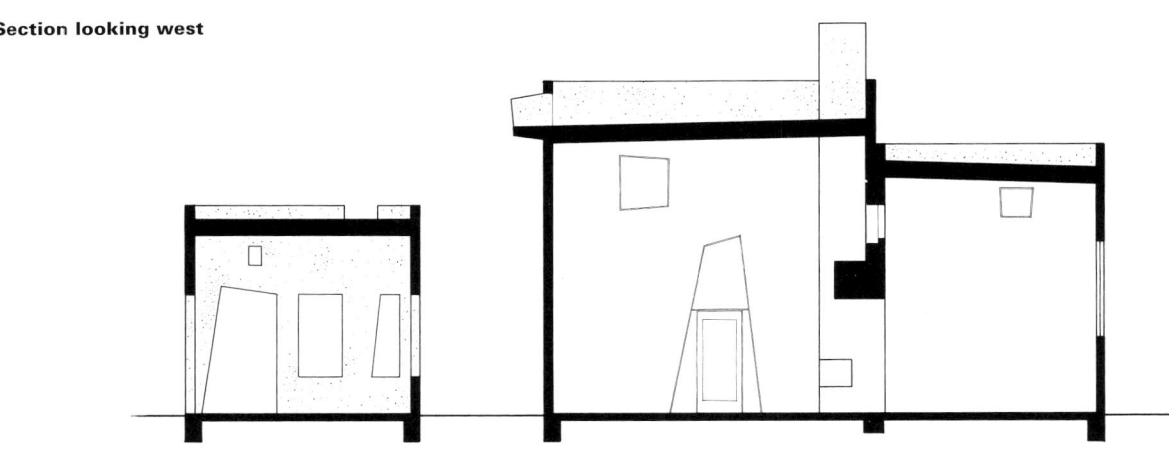

L-shaped volume, painted purple-blue, contains in one leg a small dining area and a kitchen with sleeping lofts overhead, and in the other, the bathroom and single bedroom.

Construction

The house is constructed of such simple materials as painted stucco walls, exposed aggregate concrete floors, and windows framed with redwood. Colors were carefully selected to mirror the natural surroundings: orange of desert flowers, blue of distant ridges, olive of cacti and yucca. Interior colors are subtle variations of the exterior, enhancing the space's relationship to the landscape. The architects sought to achieve simplicity of form—not the perfection or purification of it—and to create a symbiotic relationship with the desert. Here, the building and the land are read as one living space, keeping alive R.M. Schindler's ideal of the house as a "permanent camp."

Section looking north

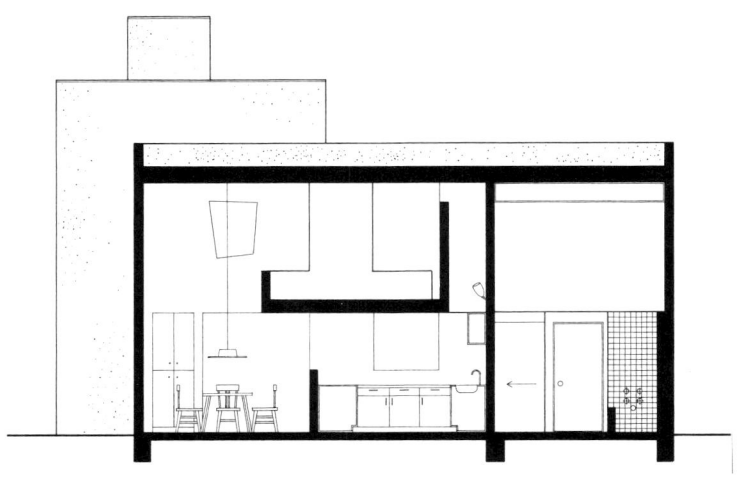

Floor plan

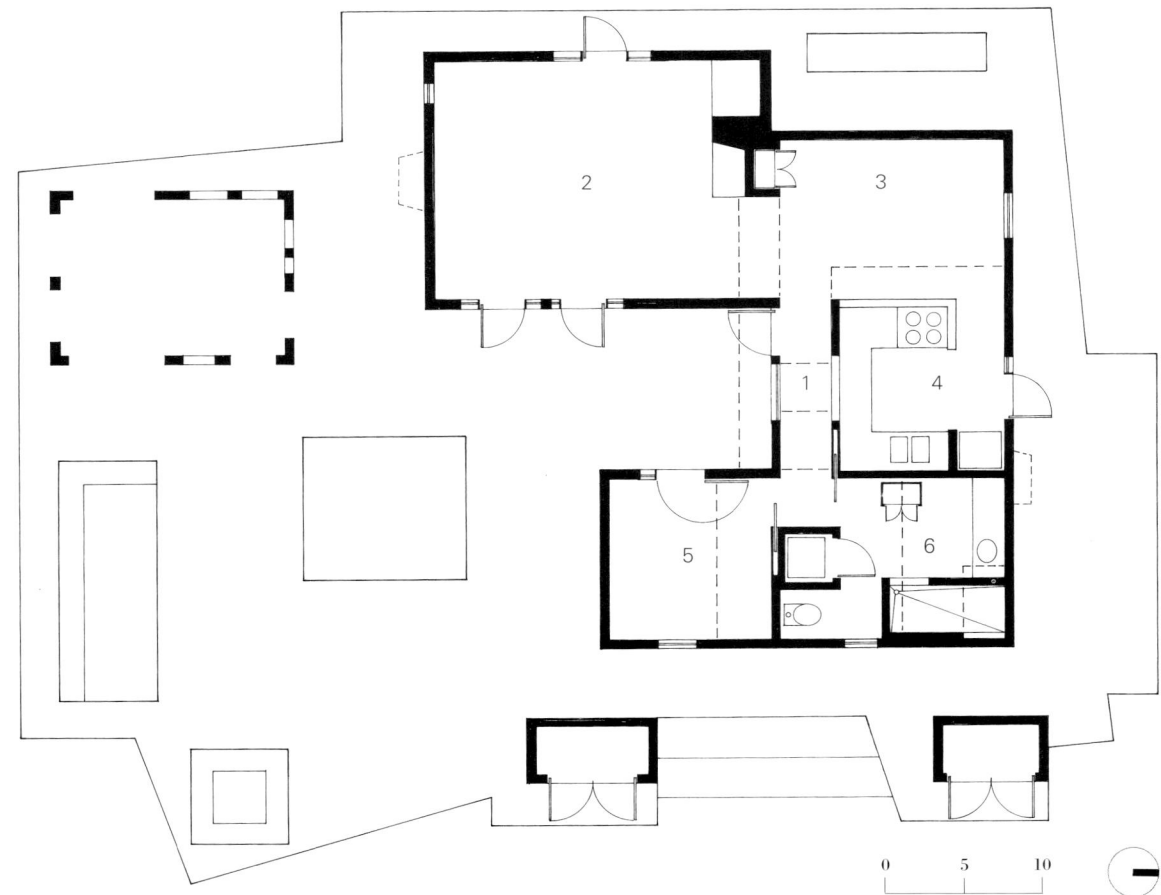

1. ENTRY
2. LIVING ROOM
3. DINING ROOM
4. KITCHEN
5. BEDROOM
6. BATHROOM

0   5   10

Axonometric

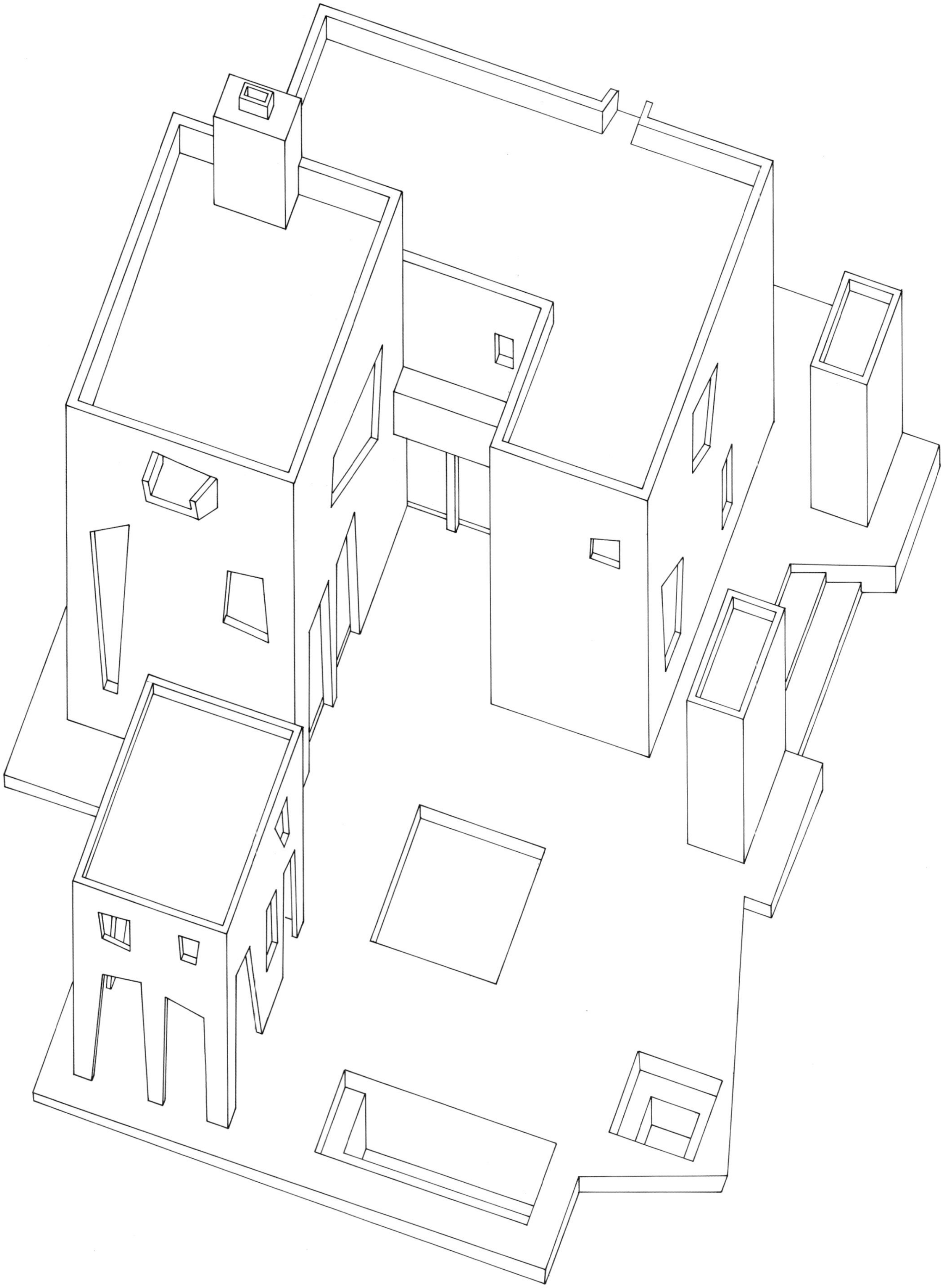

RIGHT: *North façade*

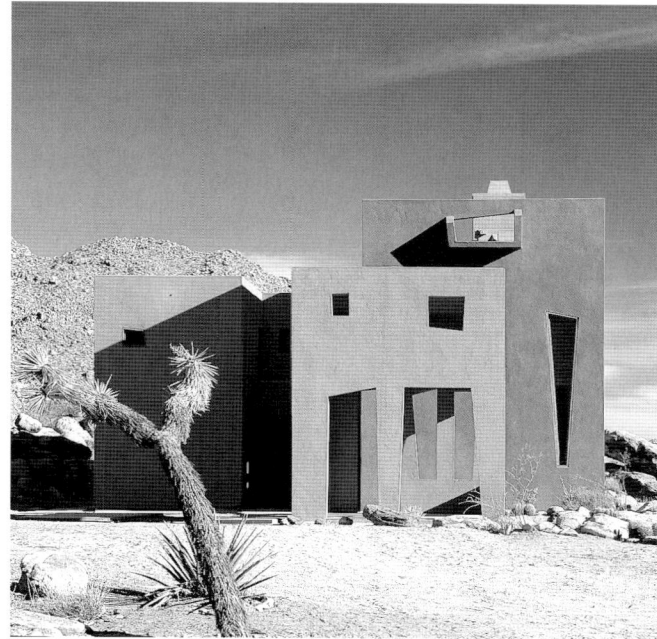

ABOVE: *Dining room*
ABOVE, RIGHT: *Bedroom*
FACING PAGE: *Living room*

Window details

ROOF SCUPPER / OVERFLOW -
FLASH AS REQ.

EXT. CEM. PLASTER -
PAINTED - SEE PLASTER
NOTES (TYP.)

¼" CLR. PLT. GLASS
SET IN WD. FRAME
(TYP.)

OPEN

(2) 2x6'S

(2) 2x6'S

(2) 2x6'S

(2) 2x6'S

L

¼" CLR.
PLT. GLASS
SET IN WD.
FRAME

K

N

O

3'-0"

2'-0"

2"

1'-8"

3'-6"

4"

3"

4"

3'-0"

1'-4"

6x6 HEADER

1'-6" 1'-6"

2'-0" 2'-0"

8'-0"

10'-0"

10'-2"

A

M

2'-6"

1'-6" 9" 9" 1'-0"

3'-0"

¼" CLR TEMP GLASS
IN REDWOOD FRAME (PAINT)
(TYP)

4'-0" 1'-0"

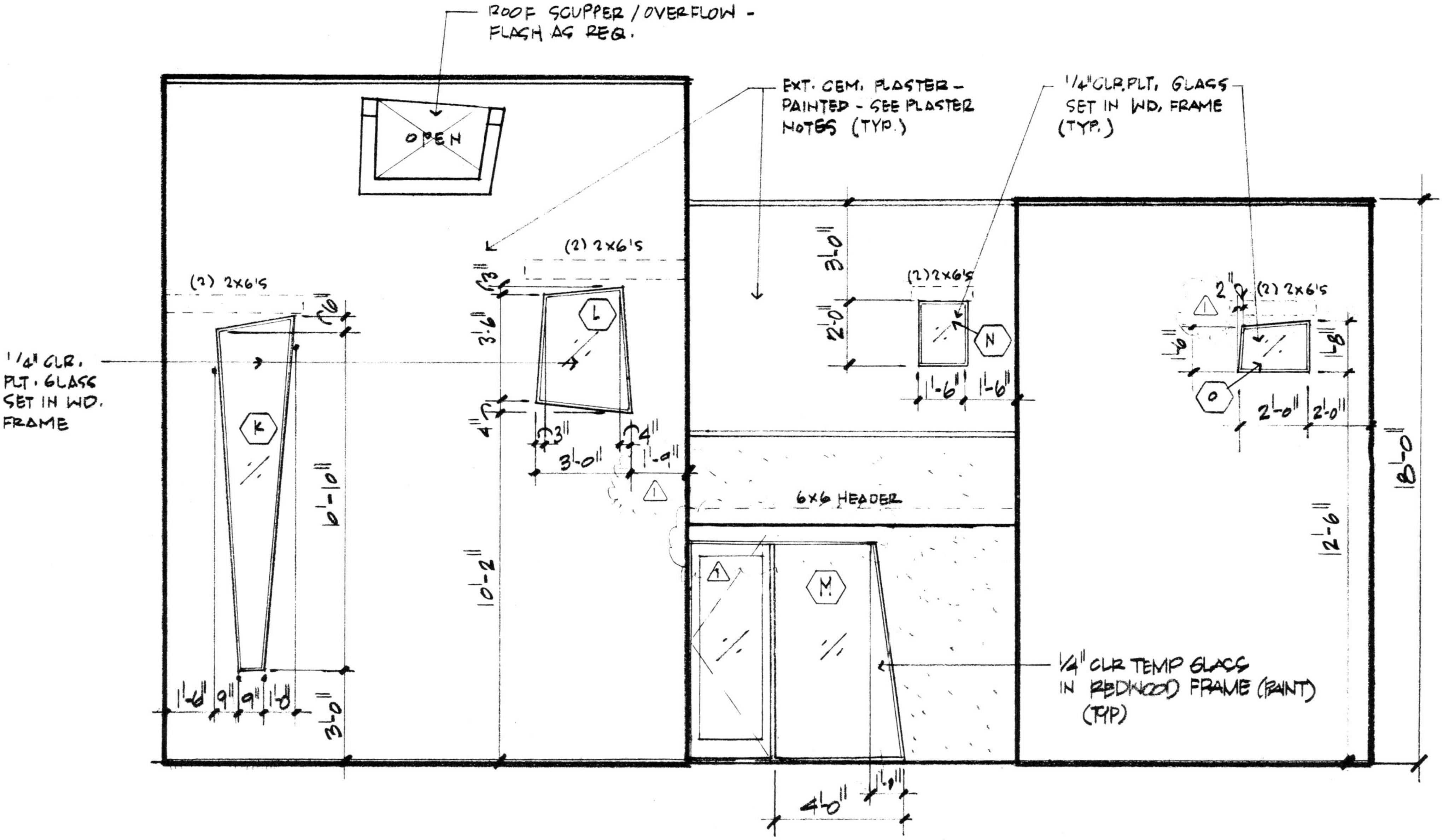

RIGHT: *Door at living room*

Window details

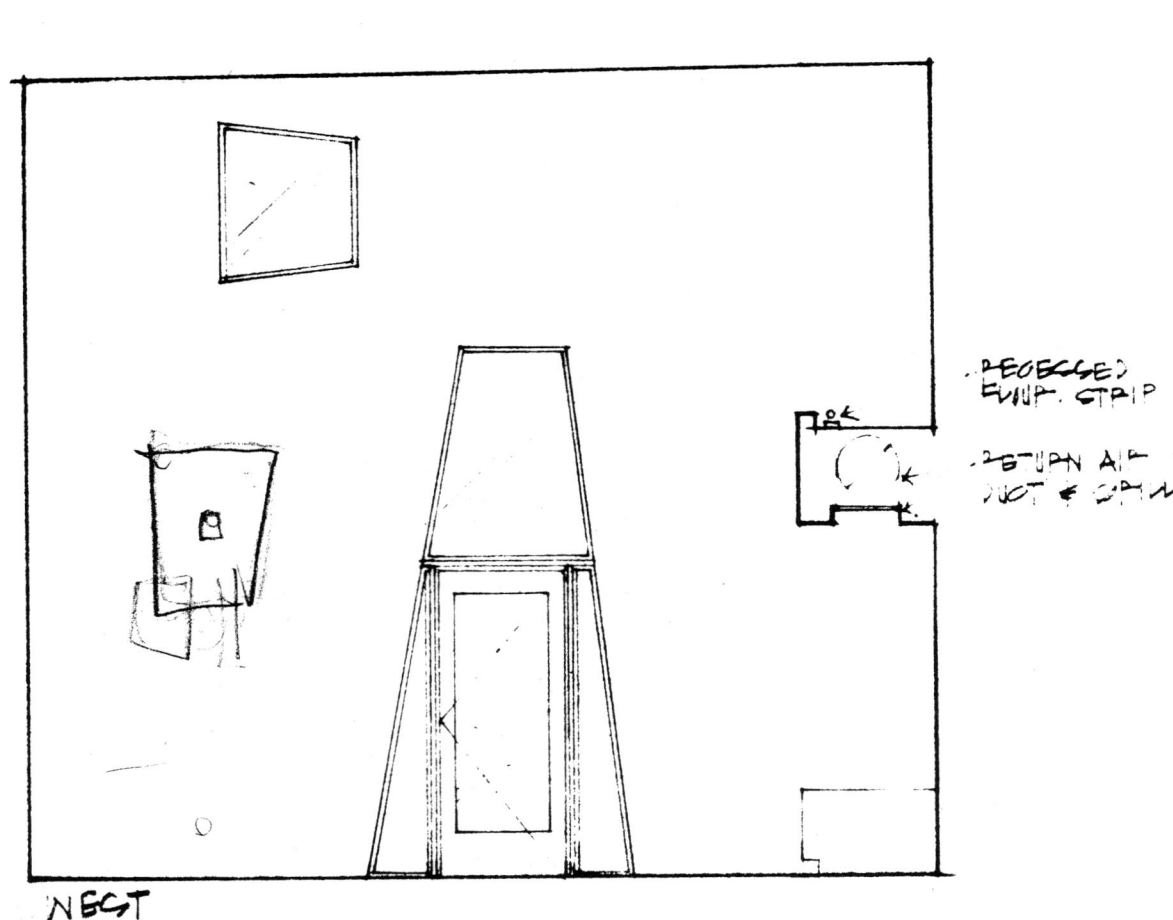

NEST

· RECESSED
  EVAP. STRIP

· RETURN AIR
  DUCT & GRILE

SOUTH

Convent Avenue Studios

1995-1996

RICK JOY ARCHITECT

TOP: *General view of house*
BOTTOM: *Corner view*
FACING PAGE: *Access*

Owner: R.J. Brezer
Architect: Rick Joy Architect
Design Team: Rick Joy (principal), Holly Damerell (intern architect), Franz Bühler (construction supervisor).
Engineers: M.R. Behnejad, P.E. Southwest Structural Engineers, Inc. (structural), Roy T. Otterbein, P.E. (mechanical and plumbing)
Consultants: Rocky Brittain Architect (adobe), Alex Kimmelman (historic)
General Contractor: Rick Joy Architect (construction management), Quentin Branch, Rammed Earth Solar Homes, Inc. (walls and foundations), Franz Bühler (carpentry), Tony Guzman (adobe restoration and plastering), Steve Lambach Electric, Benchmark Concrete (floors and showers), Bud Brown Plumbing (site).
Photography: Bill Timmerman

Site: Tucson, Arizona
Program: Renovation and new construction. House profiled includes kitchen, dining room, living/work area, bedroom, bathroom.
Square Footage: 1000 (each new house), 520 (existing house), 250 (laundry/storage).
Structural System: Rammed earth, cast-in-place concrete, wood frame roof.
Mechanical System: Heat pump
Major Exterior Materials: Exposed rammed earth, weathered steel
Major Interior Materials: Exposed rammed earth, weathered steel (stairs, hardware), Douglas fir (beams, ceilings, doors, windows), uniform red birch (cabinets), white imperial plaster, integrally colored concrete (main floor), elm (loft floor).
Furnishings and Storage: Max Gottschaulk (Pretzel chairs, "K"bar stool, "K"dining chairs), Georgo Bellolli (black leather sling chairs), custom cabinets by architect, fabricated by Bob Mick, fountains and steel stair custom by architect, fabricated by Desert Metal Works.
Doors and Hardware: Custom doors and hardware by architect, fabricated by Franz Bühler (doors) and Desert Metal Works (hardware), gates custom by architect, fabricated by Desert Metal Works.
Windows: Custom windows by architect, fabricated by Franz Bühler.
Fixtures: Grohe, American Standard, Elkay, Delta.
Appliances and Equipment: U-Line (refrigerators and freezers), GE Monogram (cooktops and ovens).
Cost: $90 per square foot

Site

Located in the heart of Barrio Historico—one of the oldest neighborhoods in Tucson—this long and narrow site laid vacant for more than forty years while the mud adobe walls of the original houses dissolved into the ground. All that remained was a portion of a row house on the southwest corner and a twelve-foot-high streetfront adobe wall that was once the common front wall of three row houses. There were once a total of seven houses on this site.

Listed in the National Register of Historic Places, Barrio Historico is a dense urban neighborhood that occupies approximately twenty blocks just south of downtown Tucson. First settled in the mid-1980s, the area is rich in Hispanic culture. Today the residents enjoy a surprising diversity of ethnic and economic backgrounds.

The site's long axis aligns east/west with Convent Avenue on the west end and Rubio Alley on the east. It is surrounded by tightly clustered courtyard residences that share common walls and outside spaces.

Design

An organic program was developed to restore the existing building on the southwest corner as well as the front wall, and to build three new houses beyond. In order to avoid having a theme park-like atmosphere, the architects avoided copying the style of the older buildings and instead allowed the new studios to be independent of the historic structures. The three new houses are simple elongated shed-roofed forms that were abstracted from a common building type in the neighborhood. The wedge-shaped plan was developed by simply placing the smaller rooms to one end of the building and the larger living or work areas on the other. This configuration not only leaves courtyard spaces for each unit, but helps to resolve many of the encroachment and sun access issues for the neighbors.

By not placing the houses on the property lines, north- and south-facing windows and larger, more private courtyards for each house were made possible. One feels a sense of mystery along the streetscape as passersby can glimpse through the historic front wall into courtyards with fountains and new extra-large mesquite trees.

Construction

While the houses were constructed of earthen materials in much the same way the original settlers built, the techniques used were more true to our time. The structure of the new buildings comprises eighteen inches of unreinforced exposed rammed earth walls on concrete stem walls, spread footings, and a variety of custom imbedded structural steel components. The rammed earth is cast monolithically into standard concrete slip forms in ten-inch lifts and compacted to five inches (approximately ninety-five percent compaction). The earth mix on this project combined soils from three different sources in the Tucson area. They were chosen for their color and structural integrity and blended with a small amount of red pigment and three percent portland cement. Each building weighs approximately 180 tons.

Plaster was stripped from all existing adobe walls, new stone foundations were built underneath, and then replastered with traditional lime plaster. The adobe house was completely restructured and all new services installed along with a new bathroom and kitchen. Rough sawn Douglas fir was used for the heavy roof, floor timbers, doors, ceilings, and windows. Cabinets are uniform red birch veneer.

RIGHT: *Building in context*

Site plan

1. ENTRY
2. RESTORED HOUSE
3. NEW HOUSE
4. COURTYARD
5. LAUNDRY
6. STORAGE
7. PARKING
8. FUTURE HOUSE
9. NEIGHBOR ACCESS

Longitudinal section

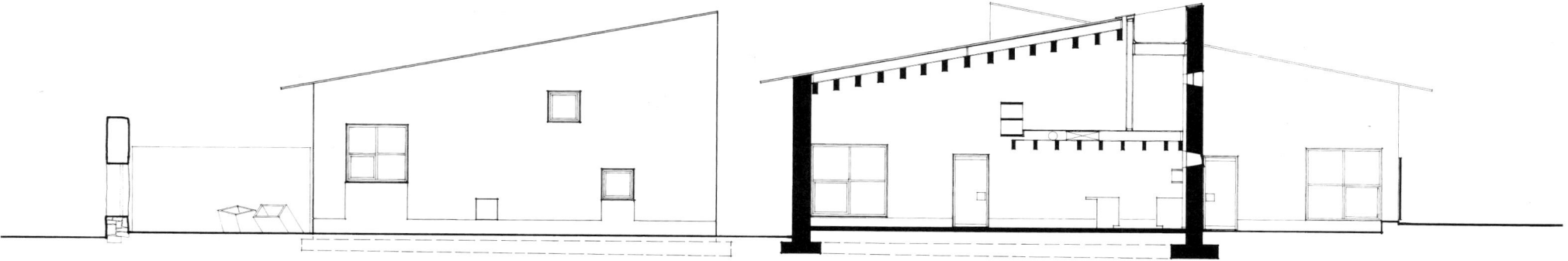

Second level floor plan

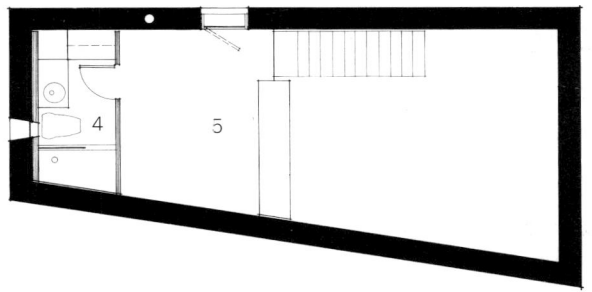

1. KITCHEN
2. DINING ROOM
3. LIVING/WORK AREA
4. BATHROOM
5. BEDROOM

First level floor plan

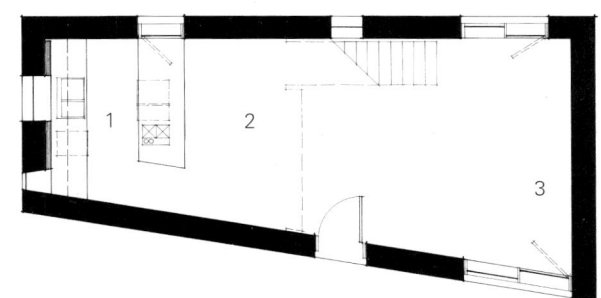

0   5   10

ROWS ABOVE: *Textures
and details*
RIGHT: *Kitchen*
FACING PAGE: *Living room*

Framing and section details

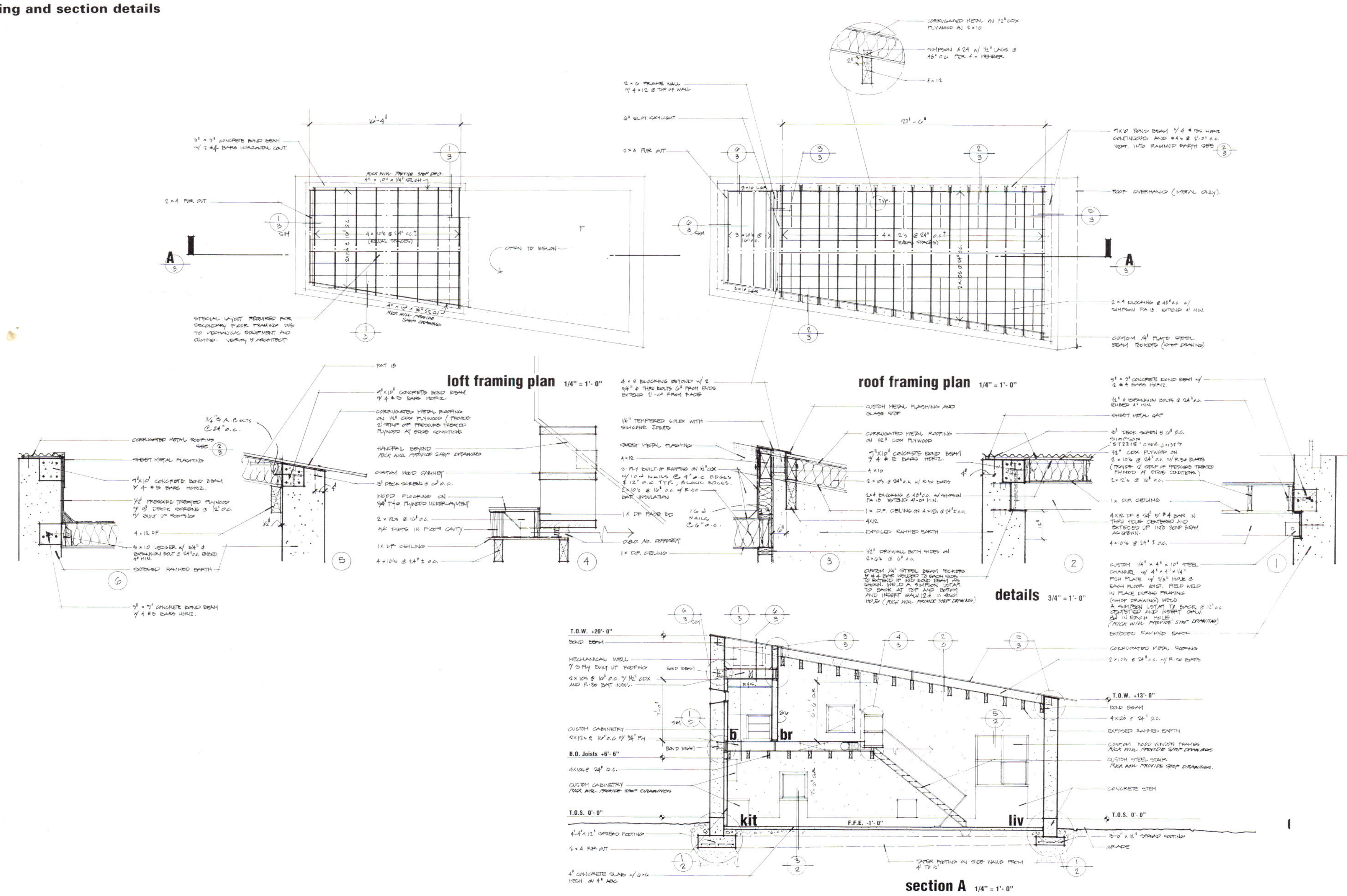

loft framing plan 1/4" = 1'-0"

roof framing plan 1/4" = 1'-0"

details 3/4" = 1'-0"

section A 1/4" = 1'-0"

FACING PAGE, FAR LEFT: *View of living room toward kitchen and mezzanine*
FACING PAGE, LEFT: *Mezzanine*
RIGHT: *Courtyard*

Footing and plan details

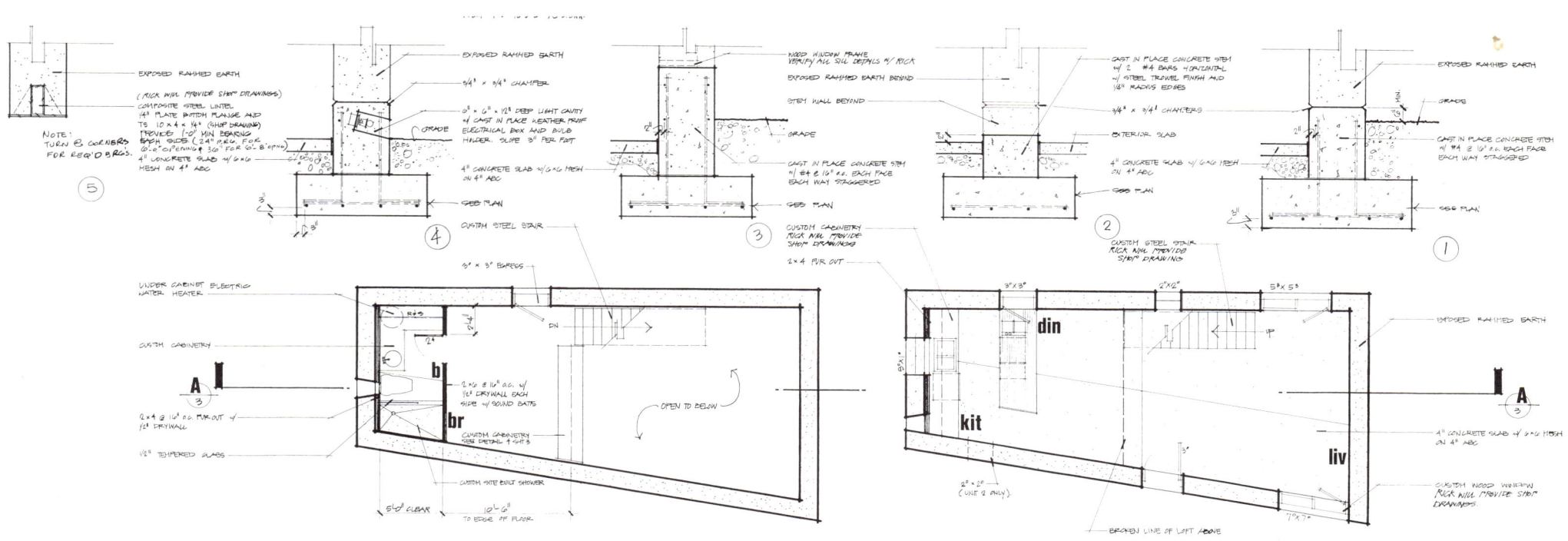

Single-Family Studio Residence *1988-1995*
WENDELL E. BURNETTE

Owner: Wendell E. Burnette
Architect: Wendell E. Burnette, Phoenix, Arizona
Engineer: Paul Scott, Caruso Turley and Scott Consulting Structural Engineers, Roy Otterbein, Otterbein Engineering (mechanical), Charles Avery, CA Energy Designs (electrical).
Consultant: Debra Burnette, Burnette Landscape Design
General Contractor: Wendell E. Burnette
Photography: Bill Timmerman

Site: Sunnyslope, Arizona
Program: Entry court, evaporative pool, carport, studio, kitchen, living room, half bathroom, master bedroom and bathroom, 1 bedroom with bathroom.
Square Footage: 1160
Structural System: Post-tensioned cantilevered masonry with in-situ concrete slabs between floor and roof
Mechanical System: High-efficiency heat pumps, shaded evaporative pool
Major Exterior Materials: Masonry, glass
Major Interior Materials: Masonry, in-situ concrete (floors and ceiling), semi-translucent glass (north–south partitions), MDO plywood on Abacus cable system (east–west partitions).
Furnishings and Storage: Built in by architect.
Doors and Hardware: Custom by architect.
Windows: 1" insulated glass with low-E on surface 3, Solex exterior light.
Fixtures: Grohe, Kohler
Appliances and Equipment: Sub-Zero (under-counter refrigerator and freezer), Gaggenau (oven), Kenmore (cooktop).
Cost: $120,000

Site

Occupying one-quarter acre of virgin Sonoran desert, the project site came with an existing ten-foot-wide scar that essentially sliced the desert site in half. A dense neighborhood of late 1950s to early 1970s arid ranch style houses surrounds the site along the west border of the Phoenix Mountain Preserve. Seventeenth street defines the east boundary, where the east-facing slope rises twenty feet to the west, affording distant vistas to the central and west Phoenix valley.

Design

The design acts as a band-aid for the scar by drawing attention to the view through a man-made canyon. This makes the surrounding neighborhood less visible and creates a sense of isolation, reorienting the views toward the desert mountains to the east. An internal court allows natural light to penetrate the ninety-two-foot-long bar, providing a moment of focus, or pause, within the canyon.

A series of cantilevered translucent glass walls form an entry corridor and court by day and a primary-colored sculpture by night. From the auto and pedestrian entry, one ascends to the internal garden, an oasis of light, shade, and water. Cast-in-place concrete stairs lead to

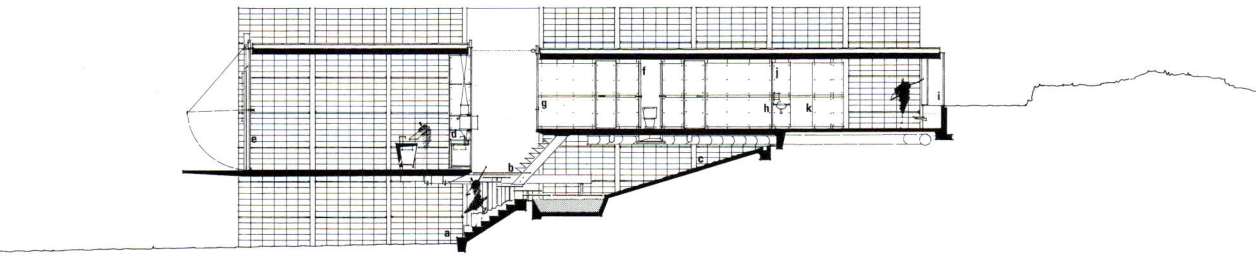

the house's discrete interior volumes and outdoor living spaces above and below. This vertical movement culminates in a clear acrylic plunge pool. Suspended in mid-air by stainless steel cables, the pool washes the court with refracted light, imbuing the space with a constantly changing sense of drama. A sky-bridge connects the ocean liner-like roof terraces, from which 360-degree views of sunrise and sunset and the nighttime grid of city lights are visible.

The design's innovation extends to the mechanical system as well. A fully shaded evaporative pool below the studio floor emits water via a trough, similar to a desert canyon seep, down the natural slope of the site. This strategy creates a micro-climate in the internal court that enhances cross ventilation through the plan. The interior volumes are heated, and natural convection "pulls" cool air from the exterior court. High efficiency heat pumps provide for heating and cooling to moderate the desert's extreme temperature fluctuations.

Construction

Parallel rows of post-tensioned cantilevered masonry monoliths act as stilts, allowing the in-situ concrete slabs to span the house's sixteen-foot width and float above the natural slope, minimizing costly mountain-site excavation. The R-28 monoliths are separated by vertical six-inch-wide glass slots. Eight-foot-wide monoliths are utilized on the south façade, minimizing penetration of south light into the interior. In contrast, the north façade utilizes four-foot-wide monoliths, creating a strikingly more porous massing that allows maximum penetration of north light.

Inside, the multi-function zone articulated by the north wall creates symmetrical and asymmetrical relationships with the more numerous north slots. The primary circulation is along the opposite south wall through which light filters and creates "tracks" across the floor.

Wood is used primarily as a mold and is "recycled" back into the house as an interior finish. All east-west partitions are suspended panels of MDO plywood on an abacus cable system that minimizes overall partition thickness (three inches total) and also allows light to extend across the concrete floor, ceiling, and at sitting height to maximize the perception of space. A water-based non-toxic form release agent was used on the Kraft paper form surface. This particular agent was selected because it was known to naturally render the formwork a deep reddish-brown color. Panels were first cleaned, edged, and banded with Alder, then clear sealed with a water-based non-toxic product and buffed to a reflective finish similar to hundred-year-old saddle leather. The panels document the construction process as minor imperfections were left evident, such as a rebar chair indention in the formwork. All north-south partitions are semi-translucent glass that permit the sunrise and sunset to penetrate the full length of the house. To ensure privacy, auto-tint film technology coats the windows without compromising views of the desert or mountain ridge beyond.

Second/main level floor plan

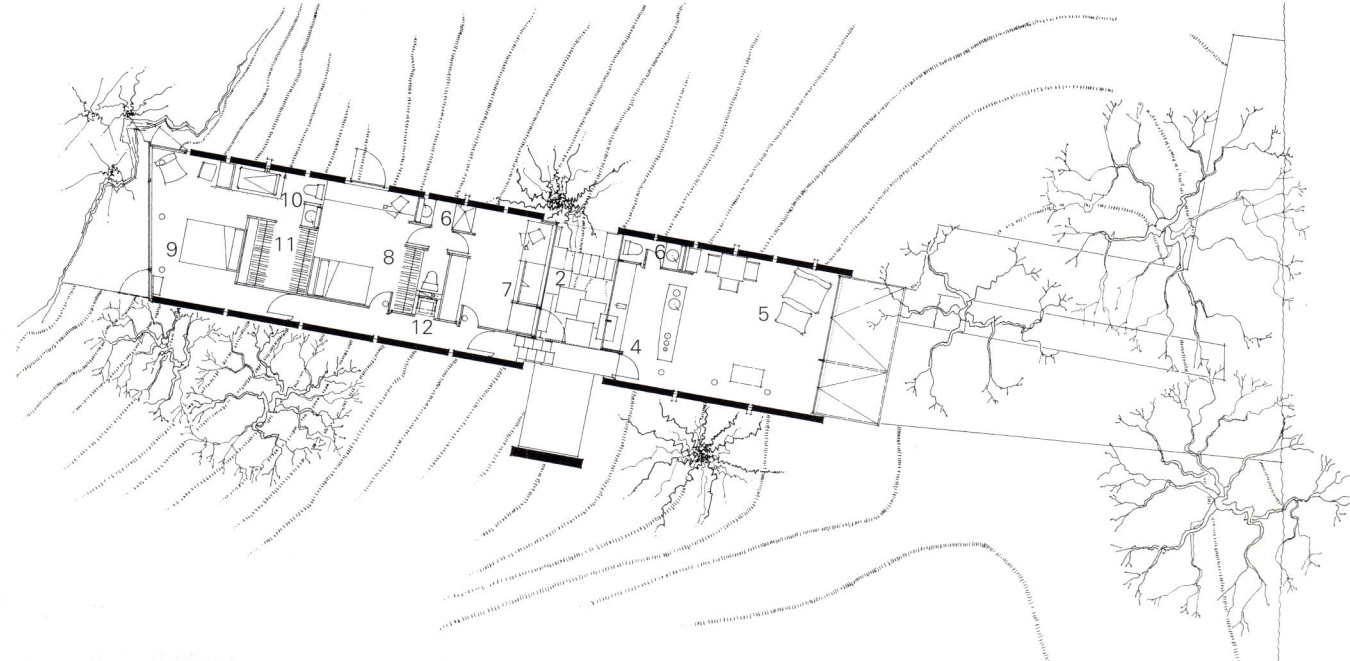

First/ground level floor plan

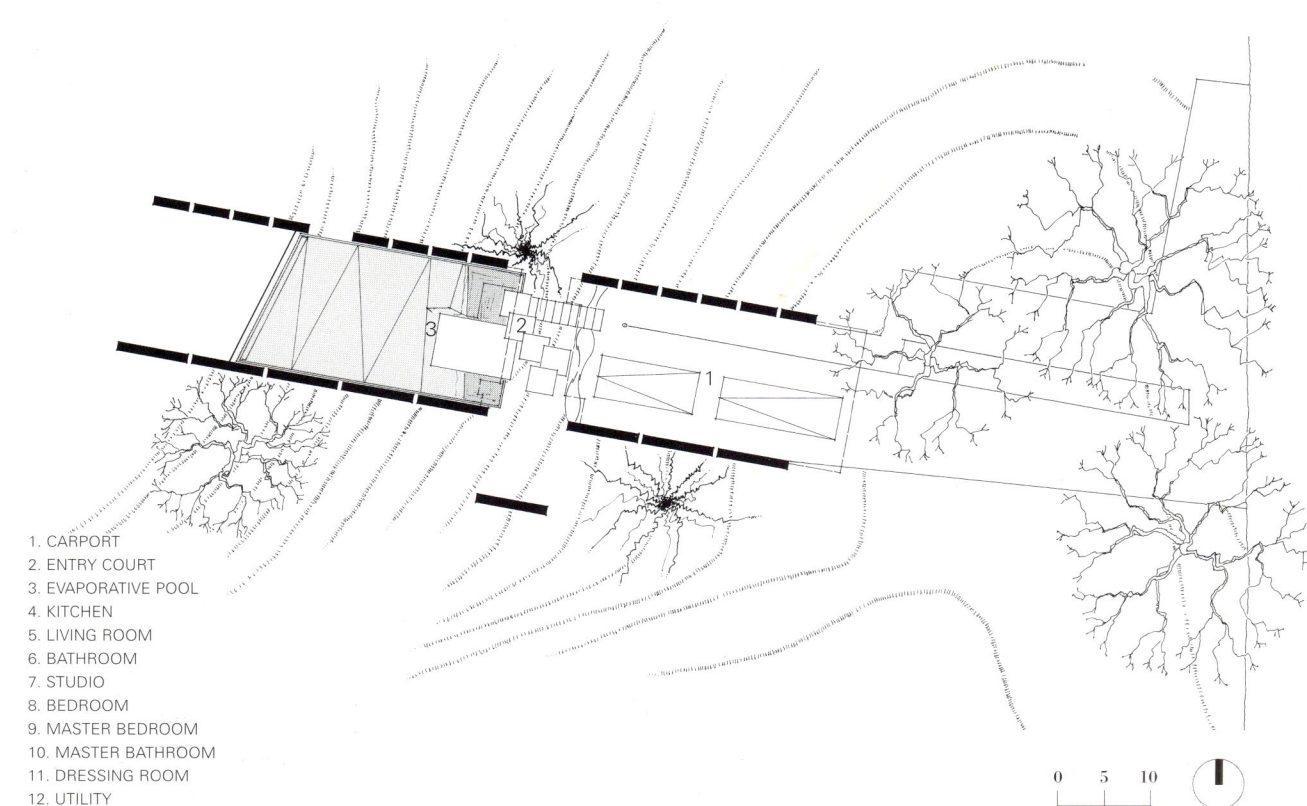

1. CARPORT
2. ENTRY COURT
3. EVAPORATIVE POOL
4. KITCHEN
5. LIVING ROOM
6. BATHROOM
7. STUDIO
8. BEDROOM
9. MASTER BEDROOM
10. MASTER BATHROOM
11. DRESSING ROOM
12. UTILITY

0 5 10

CLOCKWISE FROM TOP LEFT:
*Terrace over entry court;
kitchen; master bedroom*
FACING PAGE: *Living room*

LEFT: *Rear façade*

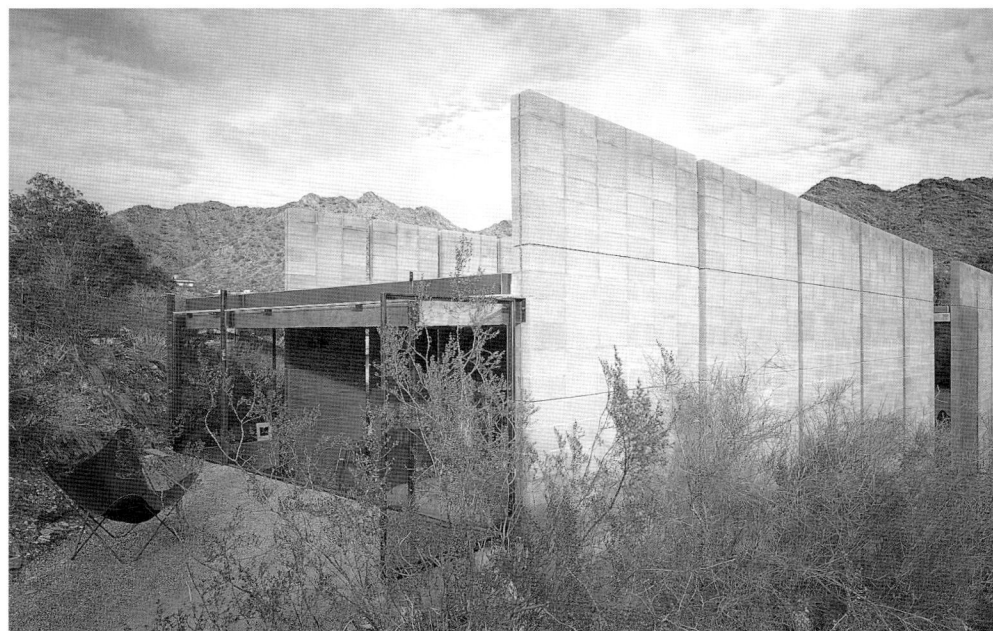

Longitudinal section details

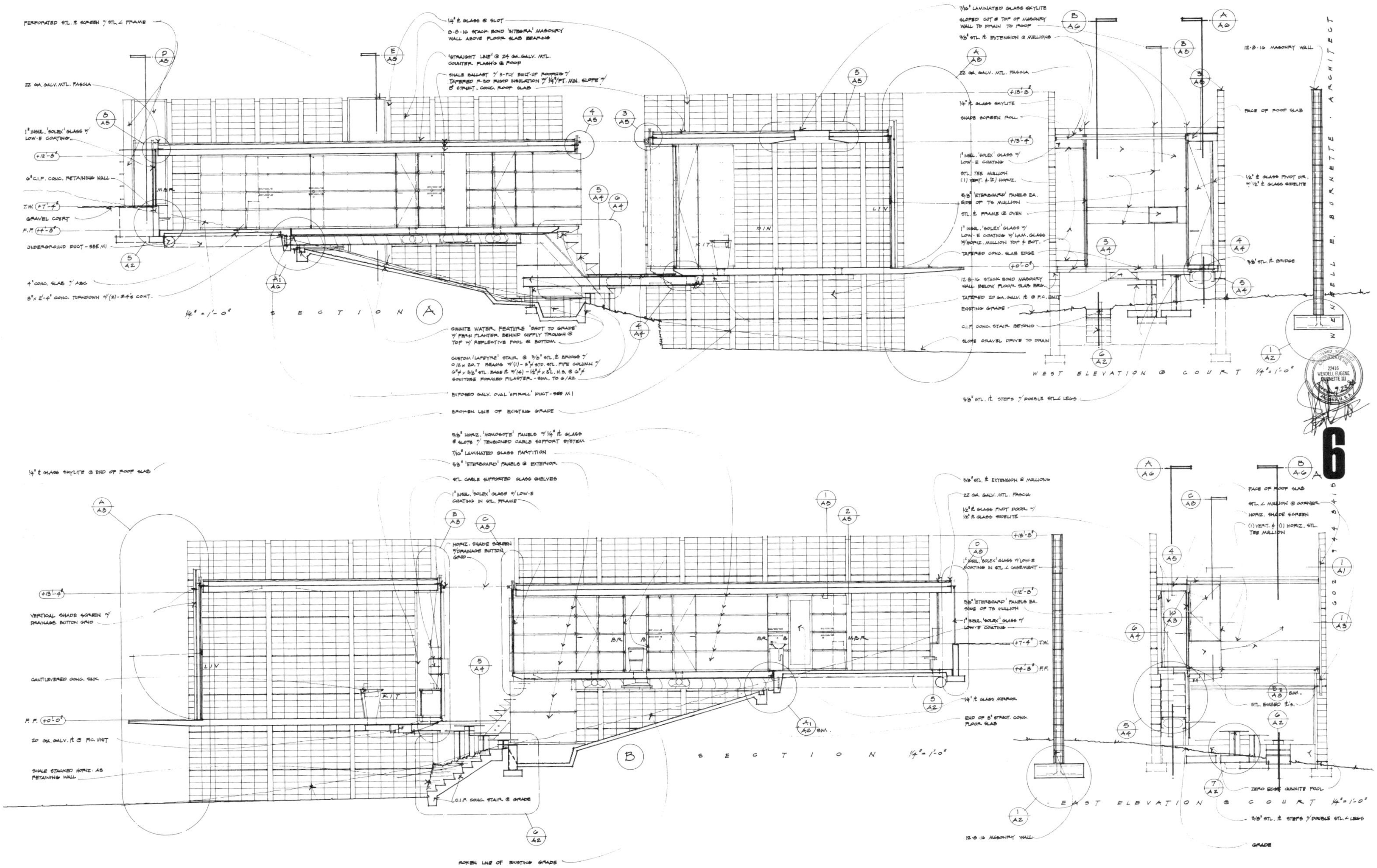

LEFT: *Carport*

Wall section details

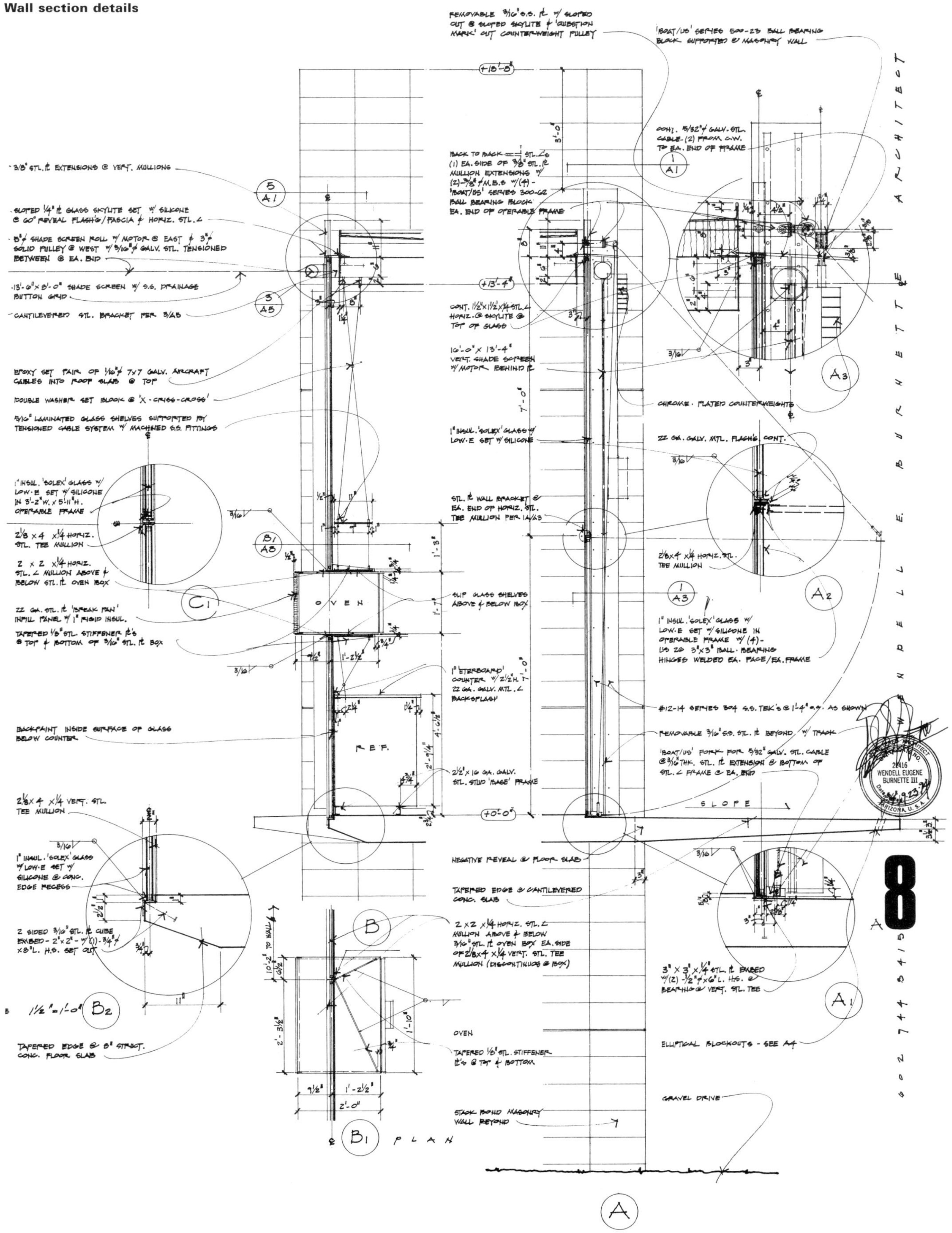

Ohlenbusch Residence *1995*
DARRYL OHLENBUSCH DESIGN

Owner: Mary Ann Ohlenbusch
Architect: Darryl Ohlenbusch
Engineer: Williams Schneider Calvetti, San Antonio,
Texas (structural)
General Contractor: Alan "Lee" Copeland, San
Antonio, Texas
Photography: Larry Pearlstone, Angela Cousins

Site: King William Historic District, San Antonio, Texas
Program: Residence for one person: living room, dining area,
kitchen, bedroom, bathroom, outdoor screened room, guest
suite. Studio apartment: living room, kitchenette, sleeping loft,
bathroom.
Square Footage: 1140 in main residence, 288 in guest suite,
640 in apartment, 456 in screened room.
Structural System: Platform wood-framing, structural steel
columns with rough cedar finish (screened room), concrete slab
foundation.
Mechanical System: RUUD Systems, heat pump
Major Exterior Materials: Cement stucco, bronze screen,
board-and-batten (rough cedar batten strips over exterior
plywood), rough cedar, limestone block.
Major Interior Materials: Sheetrock (walls), exposed and
stained framing lumber (ceilings), stained and sealed concrete
(floors).
Furnishings and Storage: Designed by Darryl Ohlenbusch
and fabricated by the following: exterior gates by Joe Ramos,
shelves and cabinets (living room) by Kevin Baker, shelves
(guest suite) by Peter Zubiate, kitchen cabinets by Cabinetry
Designs, Inc., kitchen mural by Terry Ybanez, mosaic tile tables
and pond disc by Oscar Alvarado, punched-copper light fixtures
(screened room) by Isaac Maxwell, interior reproduction lighting
fixtures by Rejuvenation, Inc., chairs and dining table by Peter
Glasford, bar chairs by Peter Zubiate, woven-back chairs by
Michael Tracey, standing lamps by Jose Solis.
Doors and Hardware: Wenco; Schlage
Windows: Wood, double-glazed by Wenco
Fixtures: American Standard (bathrooms), Kohler (kitchen)
Appliances and Equipment: Sharp (microwave/vent hood),
GE (all others)
Cost: $95 per square foot

Site

The Ohlenbusch Residence is located on a prominent
corner lot in the King William Historic District near
downtown San Antonio. The area was originally part of
the irrigated farmlands of the Mission San Antonio de
Valero (the Alamo) and was later settled by German
merchants during the boom years which followed the
arrival of the railroad in San Antonio in 1877. The large
Victorian homes built during this period form the kernel
of the King William Historic District, which was established as the first such district in Texas in 1967.

Finished in late 1995, the Ohlenbusch Residence was
built on a 6100-square-foot lot which had been vacant
for at least fifteen years. To the south and west, the site

faces a row of two-story stucco apartment buildings and to the north and east one- and two-story wood frame houses from around the turn of the century. Zoning variances were obtained to relax the setback requirements along both streets, and the design was approved by the Historic and Design Review Commission of the City of San Antonio.

Design

The design centers on a courtyard around which primary outdoor and indoor living areas are oriented. In addition to the primary residence, a separate guest suite opens to the courtyard and a second-story leasable studio with a separate entrance is located above the garage. Exterior living spaces are an integral part of the house which, due to the minimal street setbacks, has comparatively little yard area. Two long porches on the street elevations bracket a large screened room at the corner that also opens to the central courtyard.

The vertical section of the ground-level portion of the house was derived from a local pre-Civil War farmhouse type (of which there are several examples in the immediate area). It features a high gable roof oriented parallel to the street as well as full-width porches. This section was extruded to form the U-shaped primary residence, which is interrupted by the volumes of the screened room and two-story garage.

Construction

The structure is essentially a platform wood-framed house on a concrete-slab foundation. The screened room is made of a steel frame wrapped by rough cedar and is enclosed by bronze screen attached to the cedar framing. The main house materials are standing-seam galvanized steel for the roof, rough cedar trim and posts on the porches, and stucco as an exterior finish. In a reference to numerous outbuildings and carriage houses in the area, the garage volume is sheathed in board-and-batten. Uncovered on site during excavation for the foundation were limestone blocks, probably dating to 1873 and used in a house known to have been on the site at that time. These blocks now make up the limestone wall that encloses the northeast side of the courtyard. Interior finishes are sheetrock on walls, exposed and stained wood framing for ceilings, and stained and sealed concrete for floors. Exterior paving was made from concrete pavers.

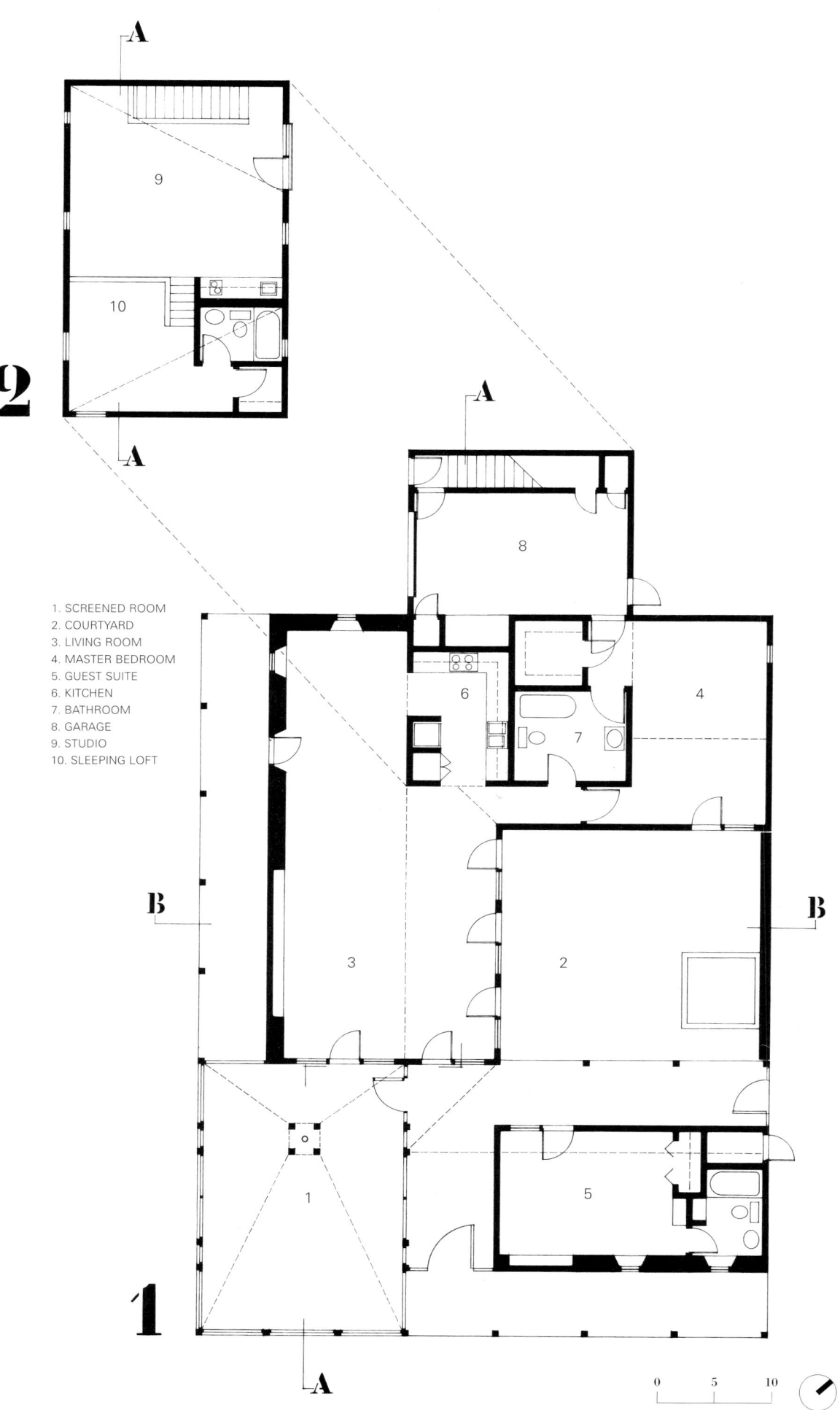

1. SCREENED ROOM
2. COURTYARD
3. LIVING ROOM
4. MASTER BEDROOM
5. GUEST SUITE
6. KITCHEN
7. BATHROOM
8. GARAGE
9. STUDIO
10. SLEEPING LOFT

Site plan

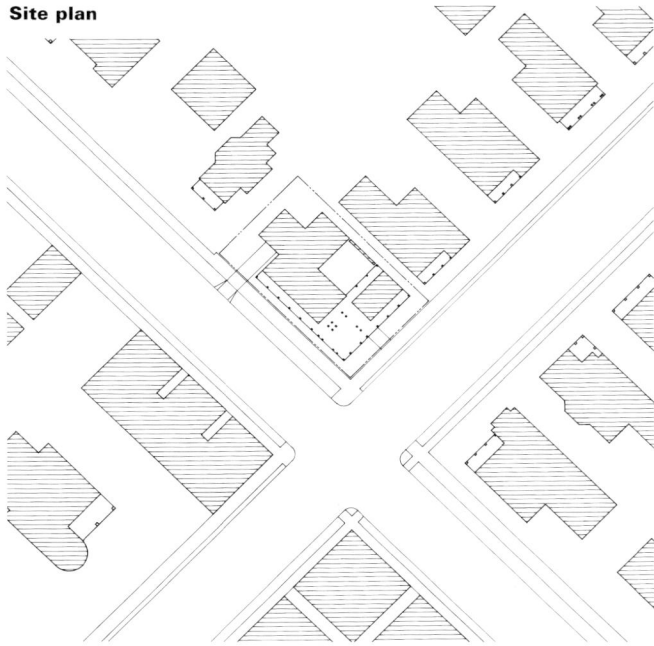

RIGHT: *Screened porch detail*
MIDDLE: *Gallery detail*
BOTTOM: *Entry detail*

Southwest elevation

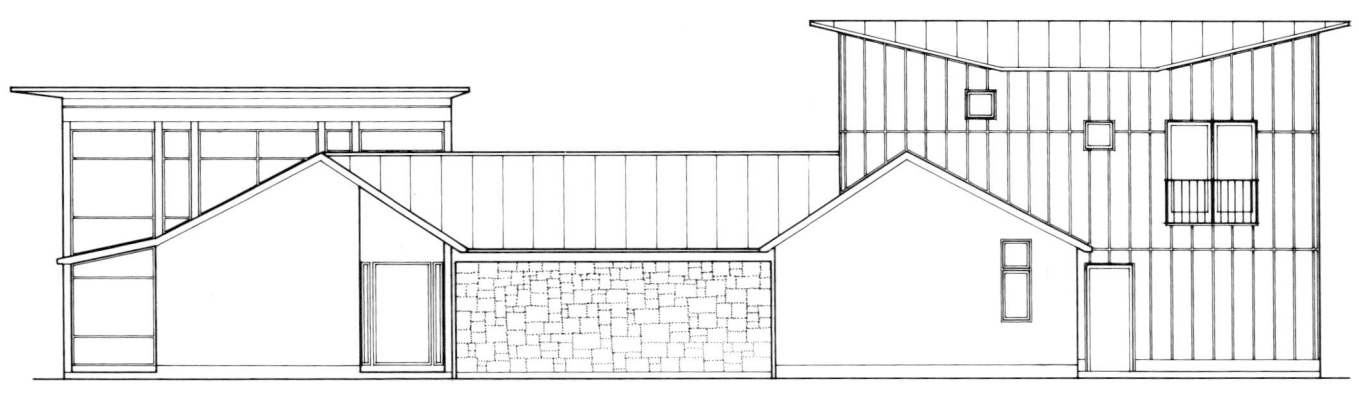

Northeast elevation

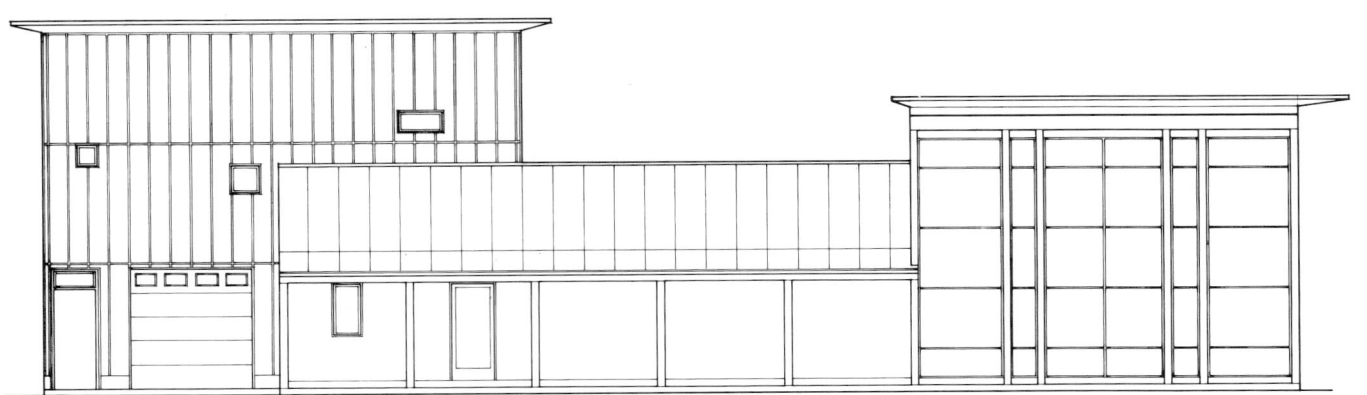

TOP: *View of dining room from living room*
ABOVE: *Living room*

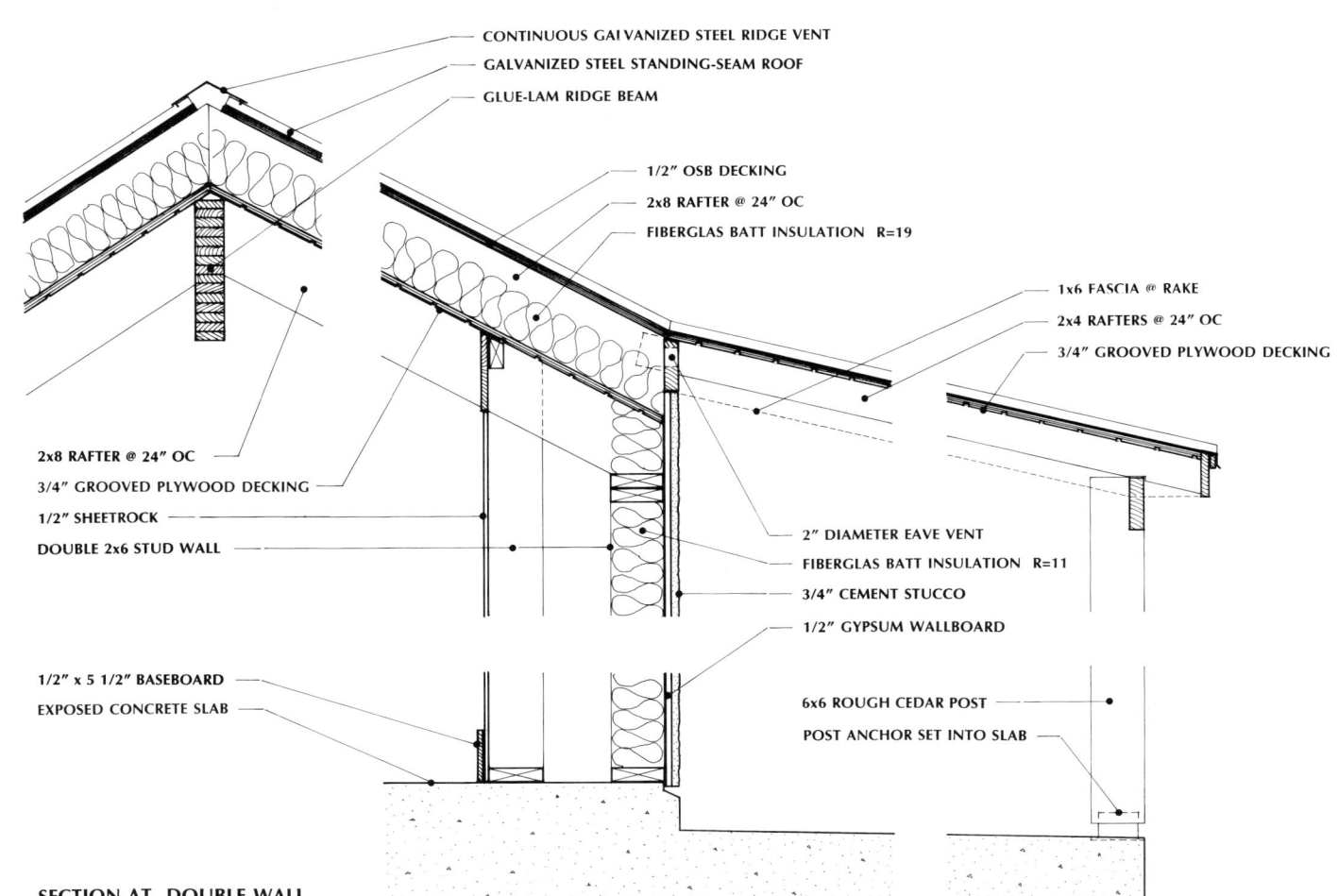

CONTINUOUS GALVANIZED STEEL RIDGE VENT
GALVANIZED STEEL STANDING-SEAM ROOF
GLUE-LAM RIDGE BEAM

1/2" OSB DECKING
2x8 RAFTER @ 24" OC
FIBERGLAS BATT INSULATION R=19

1x6 FASCIA @ RAKE
2x4 RAFTERS @ 24" OC
3/4" GROOVED PLYWOOD DECKING

2x8 RAFTER @ 24" OC
3/4" GROOVED PLYWOOD DECKING
1/2" SHEETROCK
DOUBLE 2x6 STUD WALL

2" DIAMETER EAVE VENT
FIBERGLAS BATT INSULATION R=11
3/4" CEMENT STUCCO
1/2" GYPSUM WALLBOARD

1/2" x 5 1/2" BASEBOARD
EXPOSED CONCRETE SLAB

6x6 ROUGH CEDAR POST
POST ANCHOR SET INTO SLAB

SECTION AT DOUBLE WALL

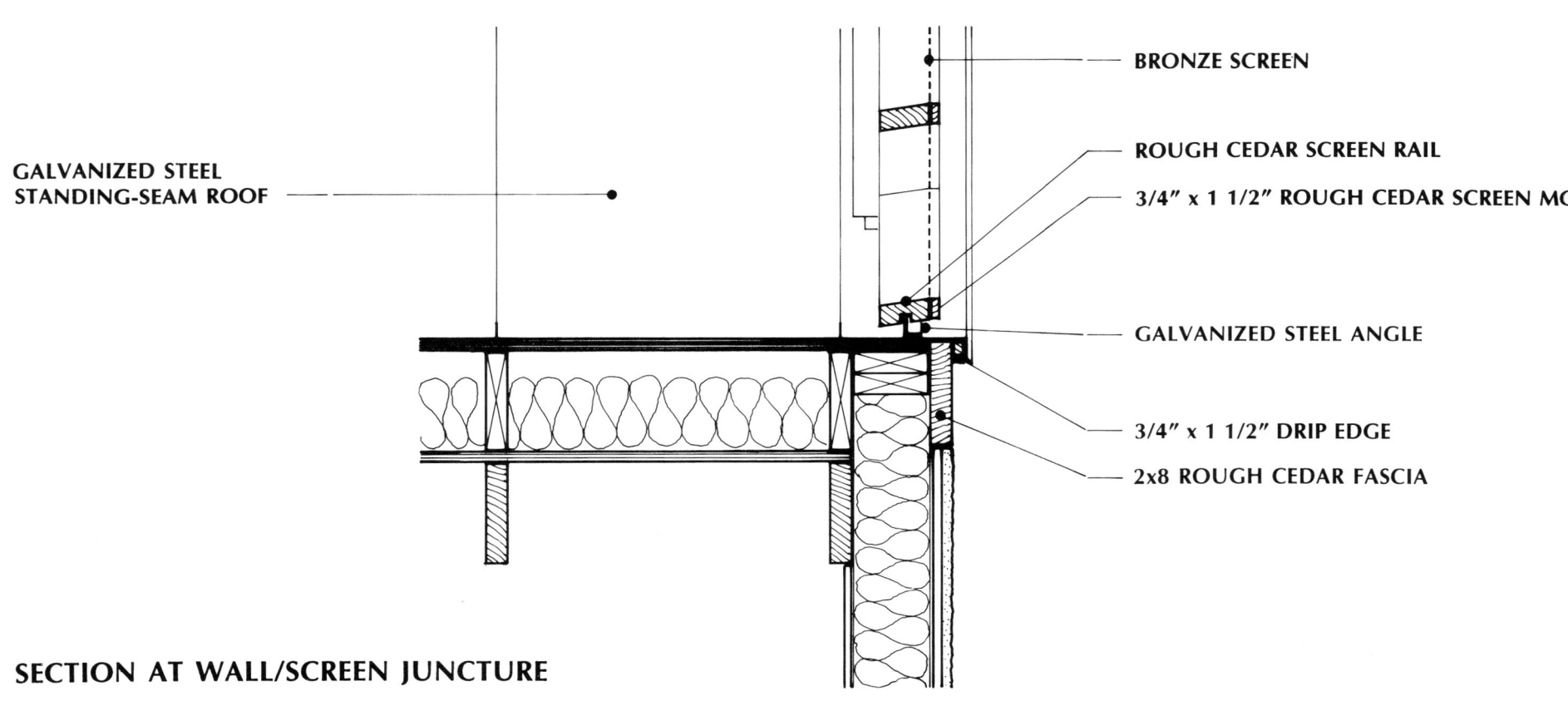

GALVANIZED STEEL STANDING-SEAM ROOF

BRONZE SCREEN

ROUGH CEDAR SCREEN RAIL

3/4" x 1 1/2" ROUGH CEDAR SCREEN MOLD

GALVANIZED STEEL ANGLE

3/4" x 1 1/2" DRIP EDGE

2x8 ROUGH CEDAR FASCIA

SECTION AT WALL/SCREEN JUNCTURE

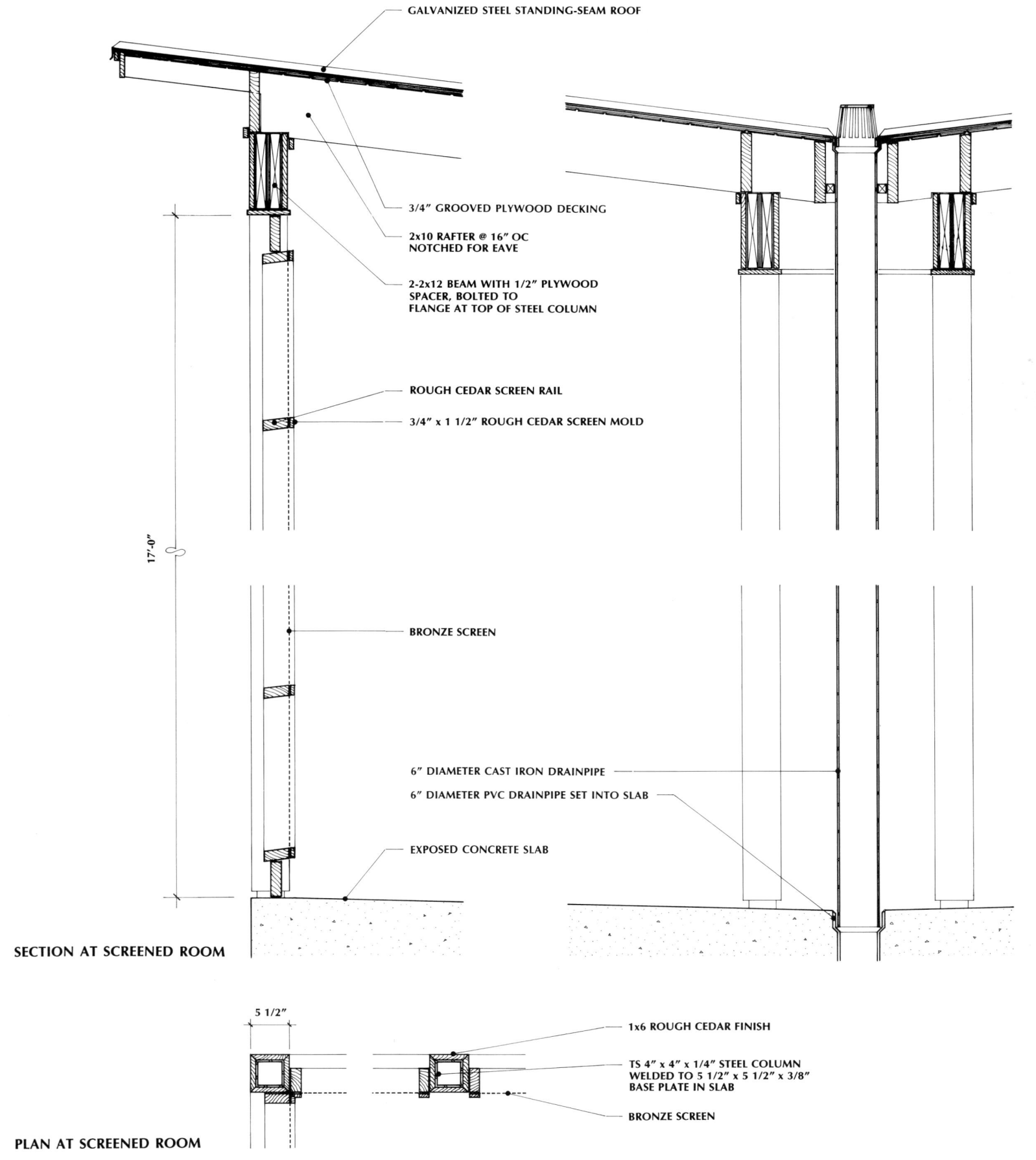

GALVANIZED STEEL STANDING-SEAM ROOF

3/4" GROOVED PLYWOOD DECKING

2x10 RAFTER @ 16" OC
NOTCHED FOR EAVE

2-2x12 BEAM WITH 1/2" PLYWOOD
SPACER, BOLTED TO
FLANGE AT TOP OF STEEL COLUMN

ROUGH CEDAR SCREEN RAIL

3/4" x 1 1/2" ROUGH CEDAR SCREEN MOLD

17'-0"

BRONZE SCREEN

6" DIAMETER CAST IRON DRAINPIPE

6" DIAMETER PVC DRAINPIPE SET INTO SLAB

EXPOSED CONCRETE SLAB

SECTION AT SCREENED ROOM

5 1/2"

1x6 ROUGH CEDAR FINISH

TS 4" x 4" x 1/4" STEEL COLUMN
WELDED TO 5 1/2" x 5 1/2" x 3/8"
BASE PLATE IN SLAB

BRONZE SCREEN

PLAN AT SCREENED ROOM

Elm Court House *1995*
LAKE/FLATO ARCHITECTS, INC.

Owner: Name withheld at owner's request.
Architect: Lake/Flato Architects, Inc., San Antonio, Texas
Interior Designer: Courtney Walker, San Antonio, Texas
Design Team: Ted Flato, David Lake, Graham Martin
Engineer: Reynolds-Schlattner-Chetter-Roll Inc., San Antonio, Texas
General Contractor: The Koehler Company, Seguin, Texas
Photography: Hester & Hardaway, Fayetteville, Texas

Site: San Antonio, Texas
Program: Master bedroom, guest kitchen/family room, dining room, living room, study, 2 studios, pool, guest quarters, garage.
Square Footage: 12,580
Structural System: Steel frame, metal studs, roof deck
Mechanical System: Fan coil, heat pump
Major Exterior Materials: "Old Yella" Texas limestone, Leuders limestone
Major Interior Materials: Painted gypsum board (walls), white oak (ceilings), exposed metal (deck ceiling), white oak and Colorado sandstone (floor).
Furnishings and Storage: Provided by owner; custom by architect (casework and cabinetry), fabricated by The Koehler Company
Doors and Hardware: Custom by architect; Russwin
Windows: Hope
Fixtures: LSI, Indy, Omega, Capri, Thomas, Prudential, Belfer, Lucifer, Modular.
Appliances and Equipment: Sub-Zero (refrigerator), Dacor (ovens), Russel (cooktop), Gaggenau (cooktop), U-line (icemaker), Marvel (wine cooler), Insinkerator (dishwasher), Waste King (disposal).
Cost: Withheld at owner's request.

Site

The Elm Court Residence is located in a densely developed suburban neighborhood in San Antonio. The house was primarily seen as a low structure that hugged the flat urban site. To maximize the connection to the outdoors and still maintain privacy, the house was pushed to the extreme edges, focusing attention away from the neighbors and toward its own private garden rooms.

Design

The client, a prominent gallery owner in San Antonio, wanted a house with a studio to work on her own sculpture, enough wall space to accommodate her large collection of contemporary art, and outdoor spaces in which to exhibit sculpture.

Bordered on one side by a row of mature oak trees and on the other by a large sculpture garden, the site was organized into a series of courtyards. At the center, a main gallery encircles a large 30' x 30' sculpture court. The gallery has large walls for art and high clerestory windows that bring in abundant natural light. More private gallery rooms receive light through cupolas.

Two steel-framed studios border a narrow, sunny pool courtyard in the backyard. The allee of trees on the west side is the central focus of a shade-loving garden. To the east, a truck access for the studios takes the form of a "green street" separating the garage from the main house and creating a contrasting exterior "sculpture room."

Construction

The materials and construction techniques used are a study in contrast; light steel lantern-like roofs rest gingerly on heavy, grounded volumes clad in monumental blocks of Texas Hill Country limestone.

To combat the severe Texas heat, the house is constructed to permit complete natural ventilation. Ventilating cupolas above the main living areas and studios work as passive thermal chimneys to draw the cool courtyard air into the house. Wide overhangs and vine-covered metal trellises shade the windows and doors from direct sunlight.

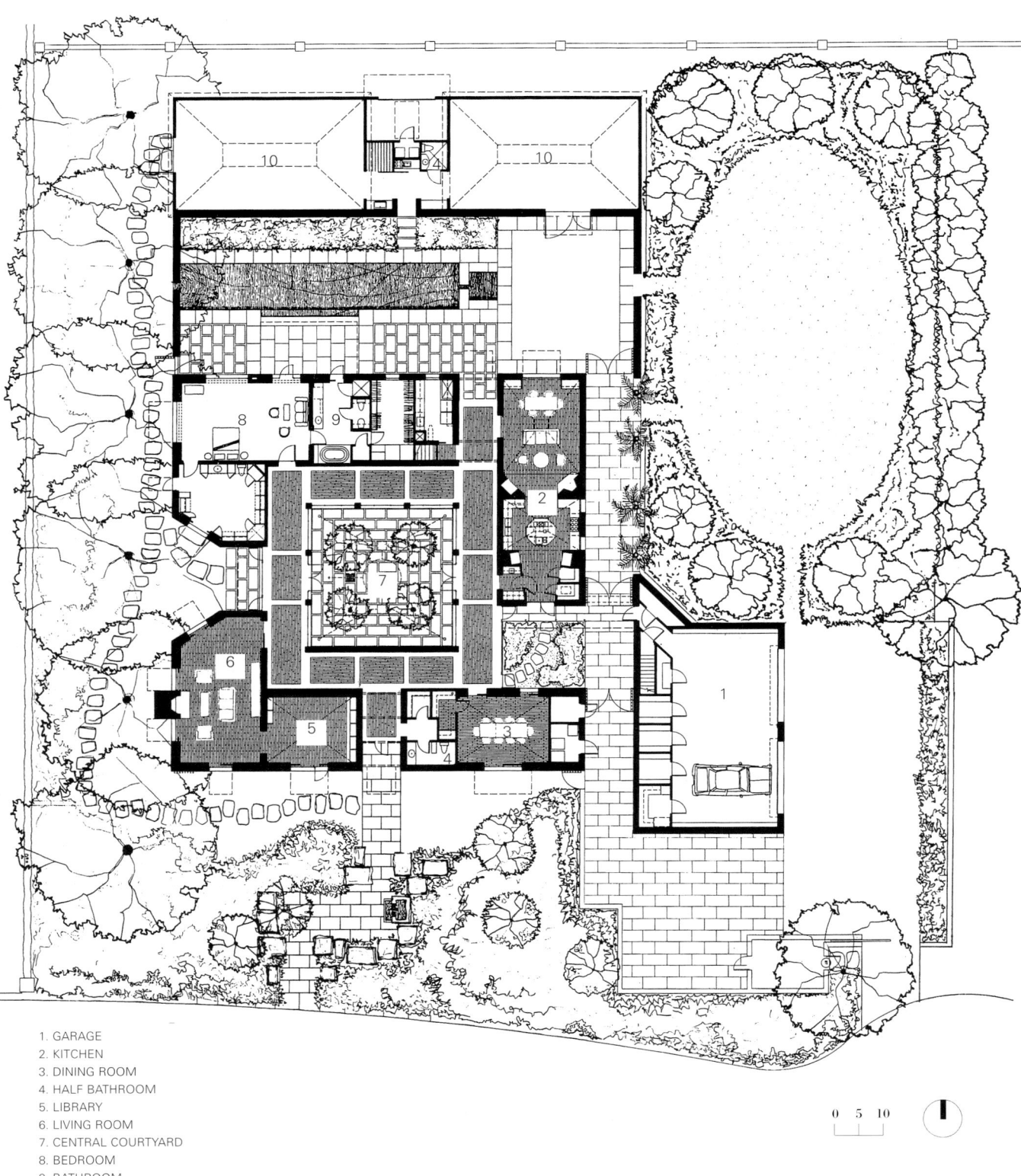

1. GARAGE
2. KITCHEN
3. DINING ROOM
4. HALF BATHROOM
5. LIBRARY
6. LIVING ROOM
7. CENTRAL COURTYARD
8. BEDROOM
9. BATHROOM
10. STUDIO

0 5 10

North elevation

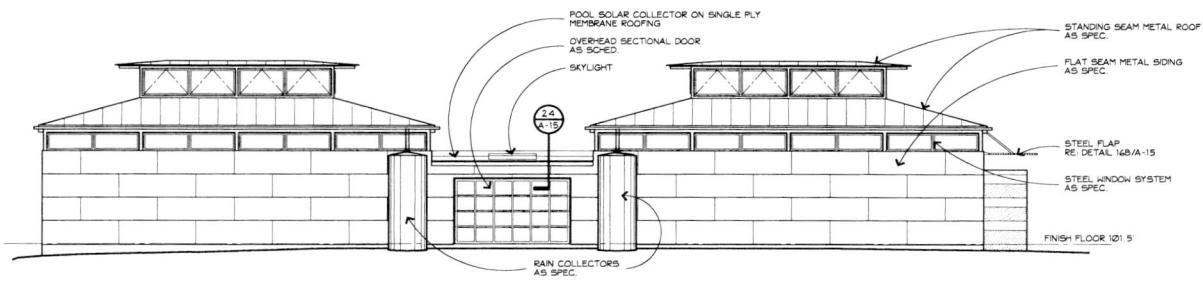

POOL SOLAR COLLECTOR ON SINGLE PLY
MEMBRANE ROOFING

OVERHEAD SECTIONAL DOOR
AS SCHED.

SKYLIGHT

STANDING SEAM METAL ROOF
AS SPEC.

FLAT SEAM METAL SIDING
AS SPEC.

STEEL FLAP
RE: DETAIL 16B/A-15

STEEL WINDOW SYSTEM
AS SPEC.

FINISH FLOOR 101.5'

RAIN COLLECTORS
AS SPEC.

West elevation

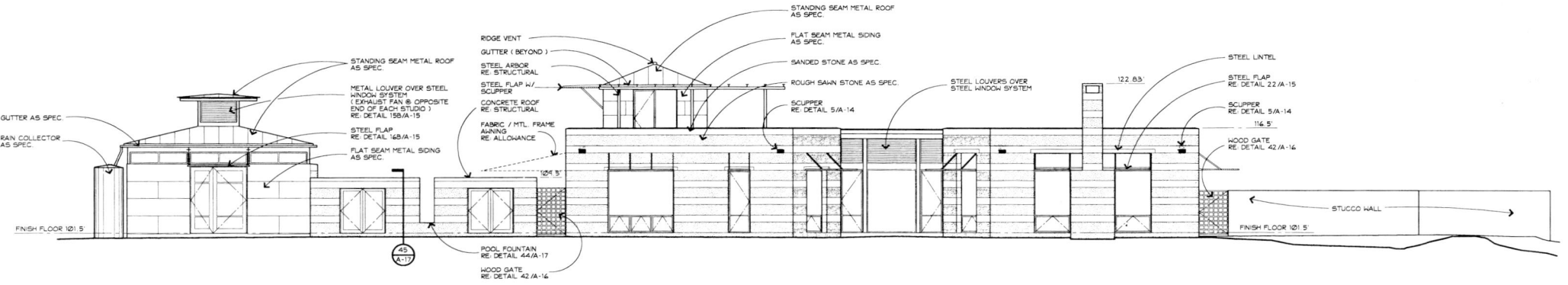

STANDING SEAM METAL ROOF
AS SPEC.

RIDGE VENT

GUTTER (BEYOND)

STEEL ARBOR
RE: STRUCTURAL

STEEL FLAP W/
SCUPPER

CONCRETE ROOF
RE: STRUCTURAL

FABRIC / MTL. FRAME
AWNING
RE: ALLOWANCE

STANDING SEAM METAL ROOF
AS SPEC.

FLAT SEAM METAL SIDING
AS SPEC.

SANDED STONE AS SPEC.

ROUGH SAWN STONE AS SPEC.

SCUPPER
RE: DETAIL 5/A-14

STEEL LOUVERS OVER
STEEL WINDOW SYSTEM

122.83'

STEEL LINTEL

STEEL FLAP
RE: DETAIL 22/A-15

SCUPPER
RE: DETAIL 5/A-14

116.5'

WOOD GATE
RE: DETAIL 42/A-16

STANDING SEAM METAL ROOF
AS SPEC.

METAL LOUVER OVER STEEL
WINDOW SYSTEM
(EXHAUST FAN @ OPPOSITE
END OF EACH STUDIO)
RE: DETAIL 15B/A-15

STEEL FLAP
RE: DETAIL 16B/A-15

FLAT SEAM METAL SIDING
AS SPEC.

GUTTER AS SPEC.

RAIN COLLECTOR
AS SPEC.

FINISH FLOOR 101.5'

104.5'

POOL FOUNTAIN
RE: DETAIL 44/A-17

WOOD GATE
RE: DETAIL 42/A-16

STUCCO WALL

FINISH FLOOR 101.5'

Elevation facing lap pool

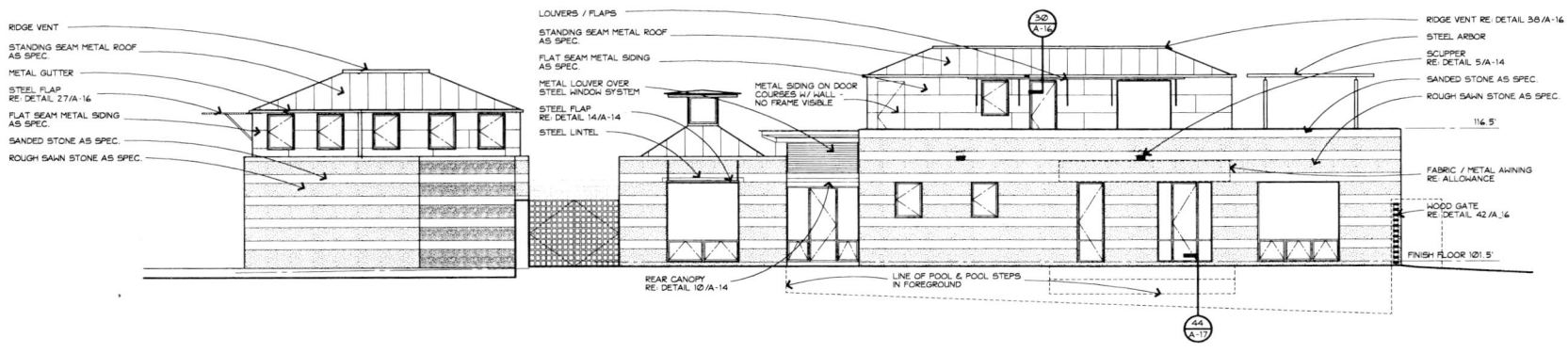

RIDGE VENT

STANDING SEAM METAL ROOF
AS SPEC.

METAL GUTTER

STEEL FLAP
RE: DETAIL 27/A-16

FLAT SEAM METAL SIDING
AS SPEC.

SANDED STONE AS SPEC.

ROUGH SAWN STONE AS SPEC.

LOUVERS / FLAPS

STANDING SEAM METAL ROOF
AS SPEC.

FLAT SEAM METAL SIDING
AS SPEC.

METAL LOUVER OVER
STEEL WINDOW SYSTEM

STEEL FLAP
RE: DETAIL 14/A-14

STEEL LINTEL

METAL SIDING ON DOOR
COURSES W/ HALL
NO FRAME VISIBLE

RIDGE VENT RE: DETAIL 38/A-16

STEEL ARBOR

SCUPPER
RE: DETAIL 5/A-14

SANDED STONE AS SPEC.

ROUGH SAWN STONE AS SPEC.

116.5'

FABRIC / METAL AWNING
RE: ALLOWANCE

WOOD GATE
RE: DETAIL 42/A-16

FINISH FLOOR 101.5'

REAR CANOPY
RE: DETAIL 10/A-14

LINE OF POOL & POOL STEPS
IN FOREGROUND

119

TOP: *Access to studio*
ABOVE: *Gallery around central courtyard*
FACING PAGE: *Lap pool with studios at right and master bedroom at left*

ANCHOR NAILERS TO DECK
W/ CARRIAGE BOLTS

TAPERED INSULATION
W/ 5/8" CDX PLYWOOD
-SCREW TO NAILERS

STANDING SEAM
MTL. ROOF

CONT. 1 1/2" x 4" ø 1/8
BENT PLATE AS
CLEAT

DECK SPAN

1 1/2"

TS 3x3 x W/CLOSURE

L 1 1/2" x 1 1/2" x 1/8

REFLECTED PLAN
1/4" = 1'-0"

MITER DECK &
CENTER BOTTOM
PAN ON BEAM
OVER WINDOWS-
& INSULATE

TS 3x2x
-INSULATE

CONTINUOUS
HIP RAFTER-
INSULATE

MITER & WELD
LINTEL BETWEEN
HIP RAFTER

2'-2"

✱ ONE WINDOW
PER CUPOLA TO
HAVE MOTORIZED
MECHANICAL
OPENER

Ⓐ

Ⓐ

WRAP ☐ COL. (2")
W/ FLASHING
& SOLDER TO
SILL FLASHING

SILL EXTENSION
BY MANUF.

FOR CHANDELIER
IN DINING ROOM:

TS 3x3

TS 5x5 x 3"

COVER PLATE
W/ 4"ø HOLE
FOR J-BOX

J-BOX DETAIL
1/2" = 1'-0"

STANDING SEAM MTL.
ROOF ON RED ROSIN
PAPER ON PLYWOOD
ON RIGID INSULATION
ON 3" MTL. DECK

BENT PLATE

PAINTED STEEL LOUVERS
1 1/2" x 1/8" BARS BETWEEN
END PLATES- BOLT
END PLATES TO TS 2x2
COL.

TS 2x2x 3/16 COL
BEYOND @ CORNERS
LIGHT STRIP AS SCHED.

METAL
DECK

3'-0" ☐

TS 10 x 2

3"

2" TS @
HIP

② CUPOLA
1 1/2"

NOTCH HIP RAFTER
@ MITERED TUBE COMPRESSION
RING - WELD TO EARS

6"

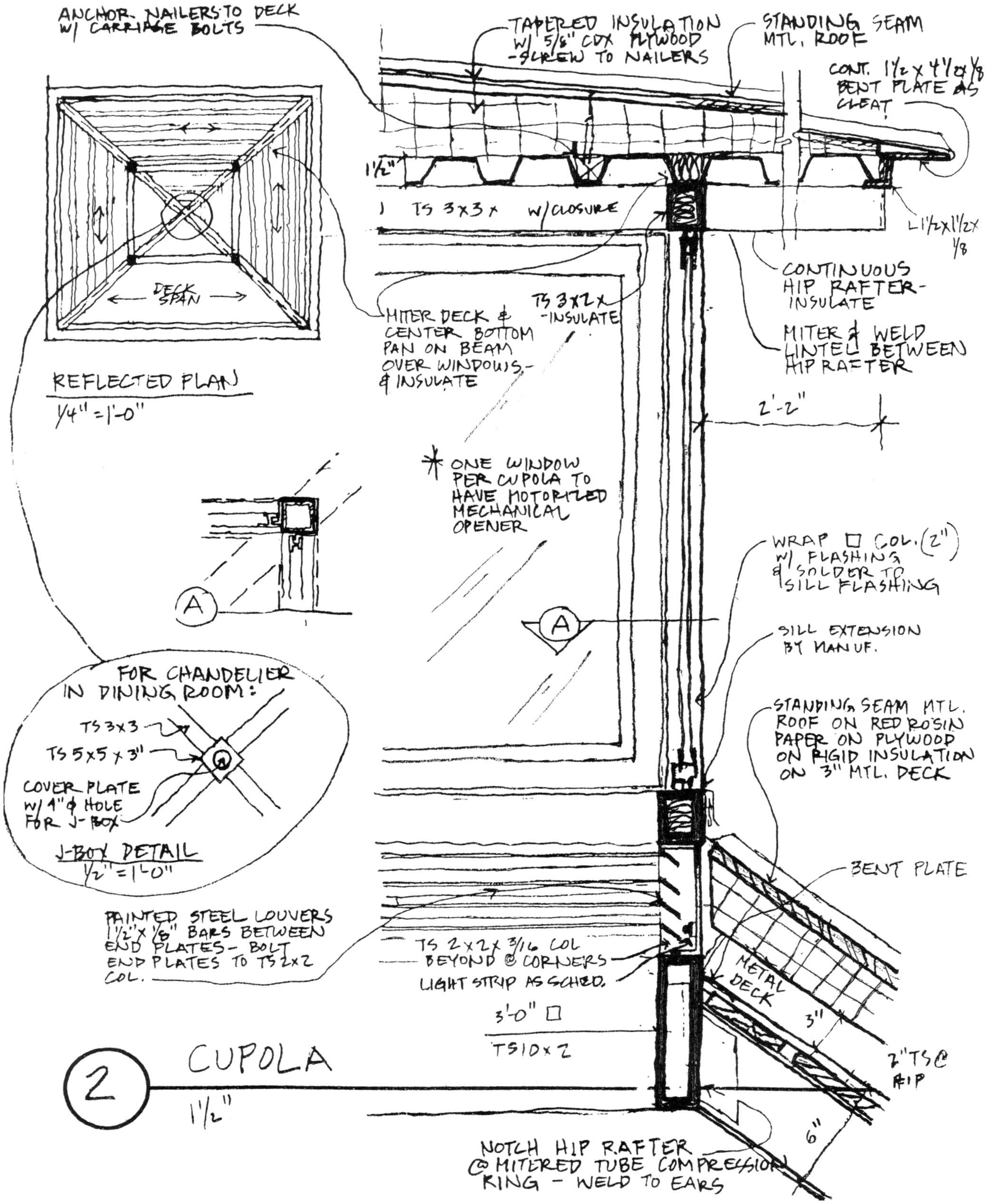

GUTTER RESTS ON
LOUVER / FLAP
& 1" x 3/16" STRAPS
AT 4'-0" O.C.

C8x

L6x3½ PLATE

:0-8½

LOUVER / FLAP
BRACKET

MTL. WINDOW
AS SCHED.

STUT BRACKET—
CENTER BETWEEN
WINDOWS & EQUALLY
AT ENDS.

GYP. BRD. ON
PLYWOOD AS
SPEC

13-6

WOOD BASE &
FLOOR AS SCHED.

RECEPTACLE IN
BASE (DASHED)

WOOD FLOOR

12-2½

2-6

MINI-VENTS
AT EACH
BAY

5'-0"

6"   EQ   EQ

4"

SCUPPER PROFILE
FOR OPPOSITE
WALL

CONTINUOUS
3/4"Ø PIN THRU
BRACKET &
LOUVER / FLAP

2"

45°

STRUT (2" x ¼")
HOT-DIP GALV.
STEEL.

SEE ALTERNATE
FOR SHEET
METAL LOUVERS

DOWN SPOUT BEYOND

FLATTEN SEAM
CLOSER AS SPEC.
IF. REQ.

RIGID INSULATION

ODEN @ 4 CENTER
BAY FOR RETURN AIR

SOUND
BATTS.

6" MTL. STUDS

12-2½"

12'-0"

⑦   GUEST ROOF / GALLERY ROOF

1½"   11-6

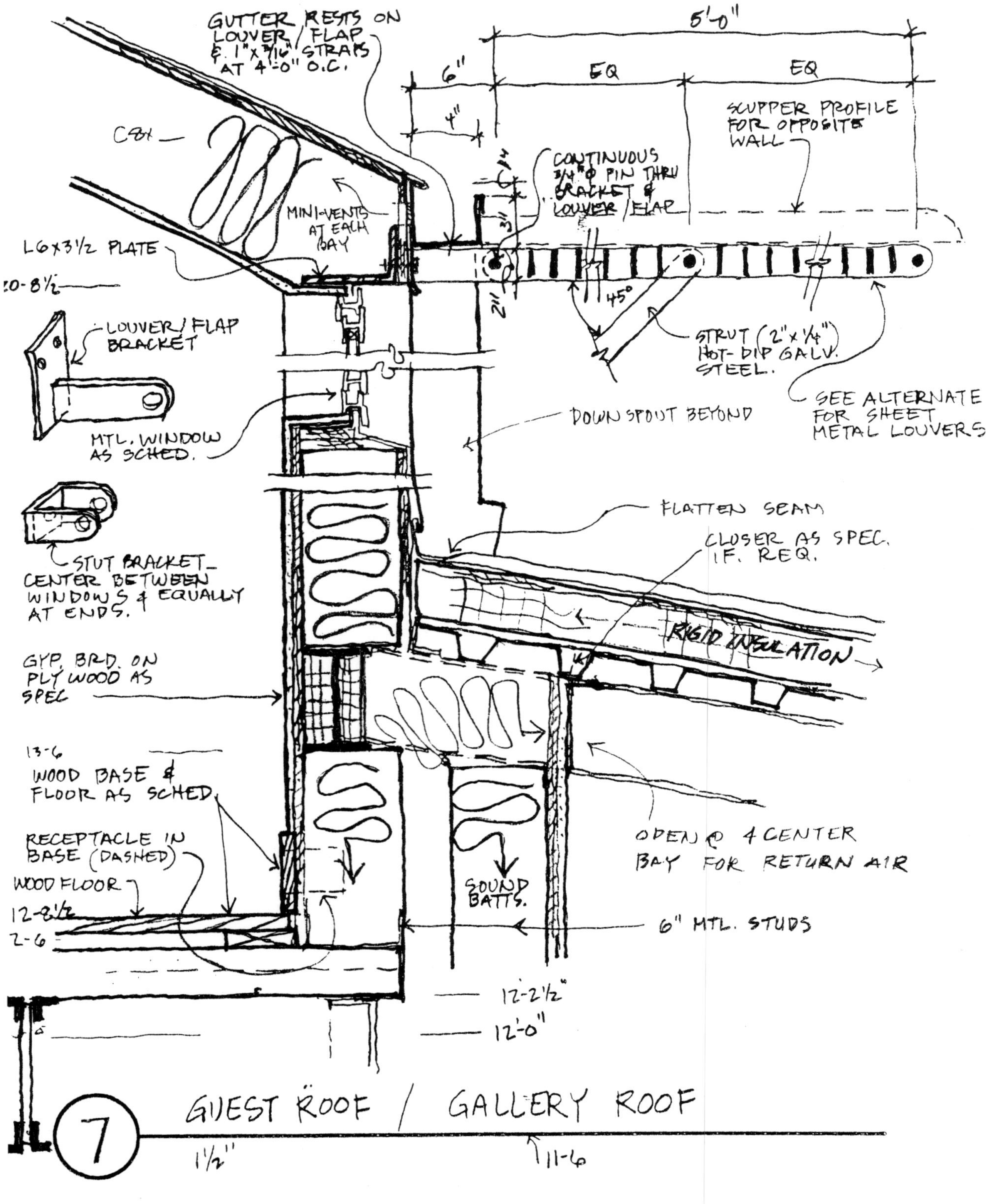

Jimenez House *1993-1994*
CARLOS JIMENEZ STUDIO

Owner: Enid and Carlos Jimenez
Architect: Carlos Jimenez Studio, Houston, Texas
Design Team: Carlos Jimenez Studio (designer); Robert Fowler, Chad Johnson (project team)
Engineer: Jon Monteith, Structural Consulting Co.
Consultant: Dennis Wright and Associates (landscape)
General Contractor: Carlos Jimenez Studio
Photography: Hester & Hardaway, Fayetteville, Texas

Site: Houston, Texas
Program: 2 bedrooms, 2 bathrooms, living room, dining room, kitchen, laundry.
Square Footage: 1600
Structural System: Concrete masonry exterior walls on reinforced concrete foundation with bell bottom piers, wood frame interior walls, floor joists, and roof trusses.
Mechanical System: Central air conditioning, electrical heat pump system
Major Exterior Materials: Stucco over C.M.U., galvanized steel (roofing), granite and flagstone (paving).
Major Interior Materials: Polished concrete (floor, first floor), oak hardwood (floor, second floor), gypsum board (walls and ceilings), exposed C.M.U. (interior walls), granite and marble (countertops).
Furnishings and Storage: Bookshelves, cabinets, and built-ins custom fabricated on site by architect.
Doors and Hardware: Exterior steel doors, solid core interior doors; Schlage handles and locks
Windows: Kawneer aluminum frame window units
Fixtures: American Standard
Appliances and Equipment: Amana (refrigerator), Thermador (cooktop/oven), Kitchen Aid (dishwasher and disposal), Whirlpool (washer and dryer), Lennox (air conditioning and furnace units).
Cost: $98,000

Site

The house is located on a 50 x 100-foot property in one of Houston's older inner-city neighborhoods. A varied mix of mostly single-story residential and light commercial units has given the neighborhood its singular character. The house occupies the lot directly across the Carlos Jimenez Studio (three small buildings interlinked by open and closed courtyards). Like the studio complex, the house introduces a new type of construction on a street of predominantly wood-framed 1930s bungalows in various stages of disrepair.

Design

The 1600-square-foot two-story house consists of a parallelepiped prism whose street elevation is essentially a high wall, reinforcing the dwelling's desired privacy. The large top window at the center of this wall infuses both interior levels with an ample quantity of north light and provides distant views of the downtown skyline and the city's profuse tapestry of trees. The

RIGHT: *View of studio across from house*
FACING PAGE: *Street façade*

architect repositioned the programmatic layout from its expected configuration by placing the public spaces on the top floor. Thus the ground floor contains two bedrooms with symmetrical views into an enclosed garden courtyard, while the upper floor is a loft-like living space where only the kitchen and a freestanding bookshelf wall subdivide the open space. The compactness and simplicity of the design, along with its economical yet highly durable construction, aim to introduce a possible prototype for the area and in turn to establish a future urban reference for the neighborhood.

Construction

The four walls that make up the main volume of the house are constructed of reinforced standard concrete block units coated on the exterior with a two-layer stucco finish and on the interior with a block filler paint. A composite wood frame system (not exceeding twenty feet in length in order to reduce lumber costs) has been inserted within the masonry shell. The roofing system is composed of on-site fabricated trusses of 2 x 8s and 2 x 6s and galvanized standing seam panels. Hinging from an inverted interior ridge, one half of this roof tapers toward the central window's top pane, expanding the living spaces' panoramic view.

Besides the substantial structure of the house, the selected interior finishes (polished concrete floors, oak hardwood floor and steps, steel railings, granite countertops, and marble vanity tops, among them) further reinforce the desire for a solid and resistant construction. Costing about the same or even less than the typical cardboard-like constructions presently sprouting in the inner city, the house presents a viable alternative for today's rampant market.

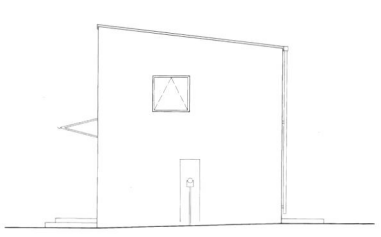

Second level floor plan

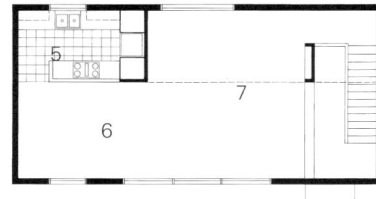

First level floor plan

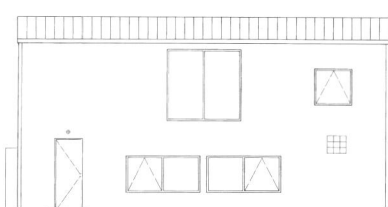

1. ENTRY
2. LAUNDRY
3. BEDROOM
4. BATHROOM
5. KITCHEN
6. DINING ROOM
7. LIVING ROOM

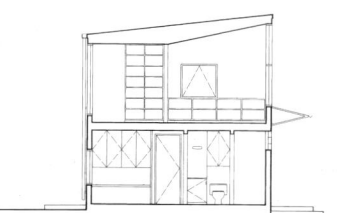

0   5   10

Site plan

Section looking west

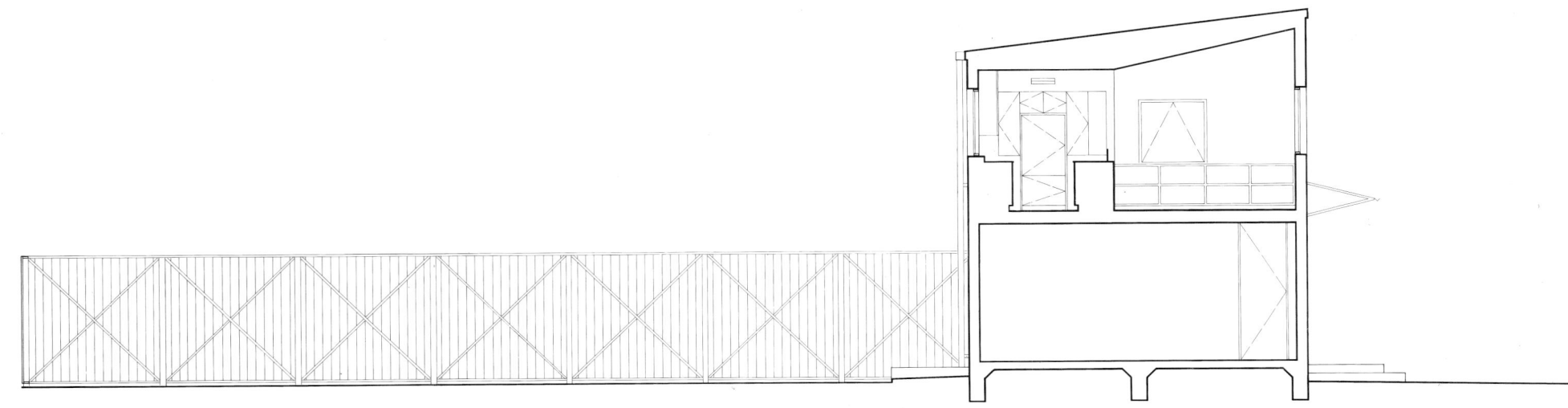

Section looking east

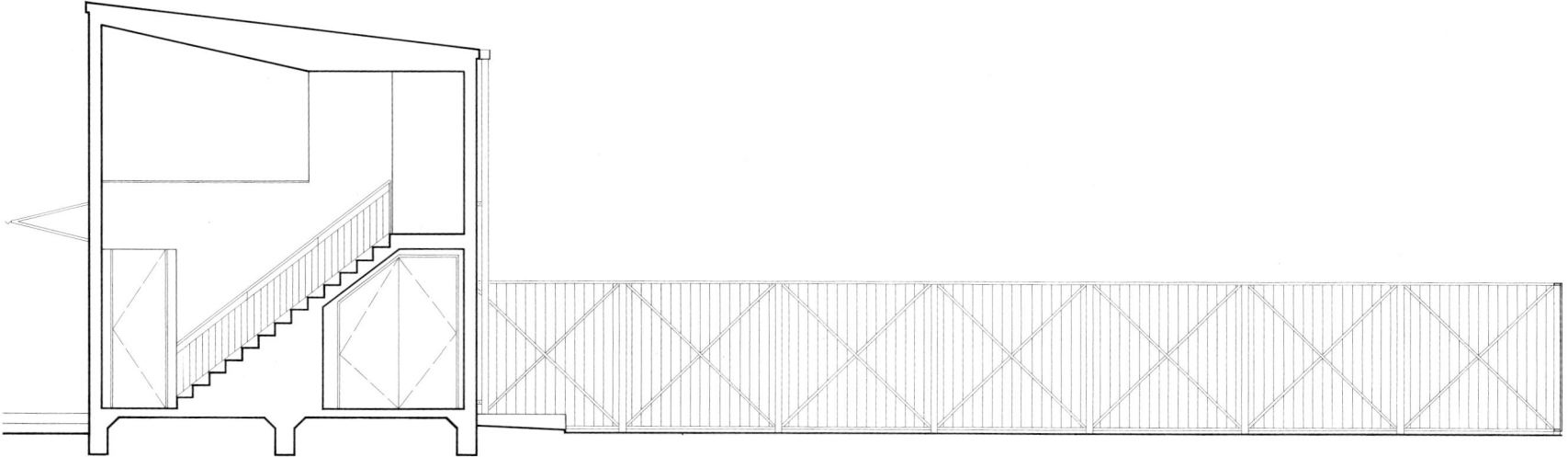

LEFT: *View of living room toward dining room*
BOTTOM: *Kitchen at left with window to backyard at right*
FACING PAGE: *View of living room from dining room*

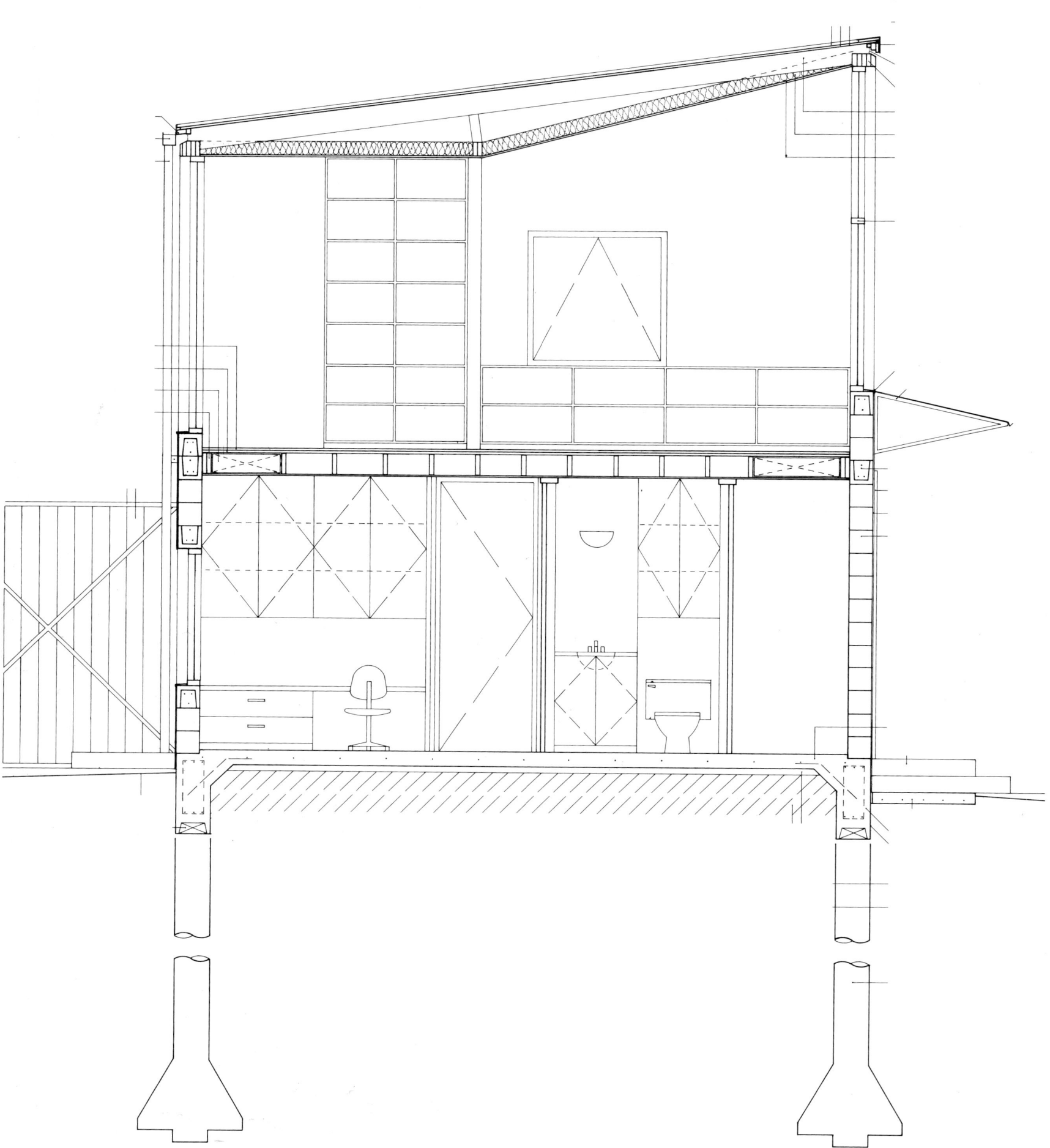

Private Estate in Montana

1992-1995

EMILIO AMBASZ & ASSOCIATES

Owner: Name withheld at owner's request
Architect: Emilio Ambasz & Associates, New York, New York
Design Team: Emilio Ambasz (designer); Daniel K. Brown (project director); Jay Kirby, James Hoffmann, James Decker (project architects); Joaquin Carter, Humberto Cordero, Merritt Bucholz, Hideotoshi Kawaguchi, Dimitris Klapsis, Hideo Tanai, Jun Tomita.
Engineers: Gordon-Prill (structural), Fussell Engineering Corporation (electrical), Western Montana Engineering (mechanical), Professional Consultants (civil).
Consultants: Philip diGiacomo (landscape rockwork); Fisher Marantz, Renfro Stone, Paul Marantz, Daina Yurkus, Kurt Wagner (lighting design); Don Reynolds USA (glass curtain wall).
General Contractor: Kevin Gordon
Photography: Daniel K. Brown, Richard Barnes, Richard Scanlan, Ryuzo Masunaga (model).

Site: Montana (Exact location withheld at owner's request.)
Program: Primary residence with separate art gallery. Residence: living room, dining room, kitchen/dining area, mud room, library, playroom, indoor pool/sauna, master bedroom/sitting room, 4 children's bedrooms, nanny's suite, family room, den, private office, 4-car garage, 7 bathrooms, 2 half bathrooms, storage rooms, laundry room, covered outdoor terrace. Art gallery: kitchen, bathroom, 2 storage rooms, gallery space, covered outdoor terrace.
Square Footage: 9300 in residence, 2300 in art gallery
Structural System: Reinforced concrete with wood and steel framing
Mechanical System: Radiant slab heating, forced air, radiator backup systems.
Major Exterior Materials: Vinyl trellis and siding, fiberglass cornice, cedar decks.
Major Interior Materials: Light green cleft slate, deep emerald polished marble, SMARG light beige medium-loop wool berber carpet, oak (floors); white painted plasterboard, oak veneer, white granite (walls); white painted plasterboard, exposed oak veneer beams (ceilings); oak veneer, deep emerald polished marble (cabinets).
Furnishings and Storage: MAC II, Chessy Rayner, Mica Winterble.
Doors and Hardware: Schlage (knobs), solid stainless D-handles, Speakman (faucets).
Windows: Andersen
Fixtures: American Standard
Appliances and Equipment: Traulsen (refrigerator), Thermador (dishwasher)
Cost: $3.5 million

Site

The house is located on a 1400-acre site along a secluded river valley surrounded only by natural wilderness.

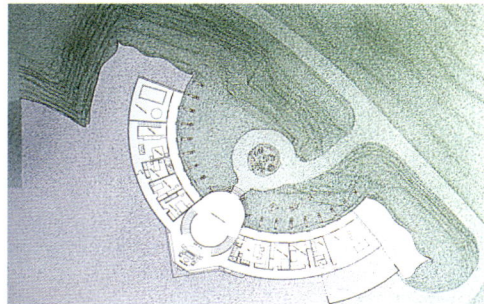
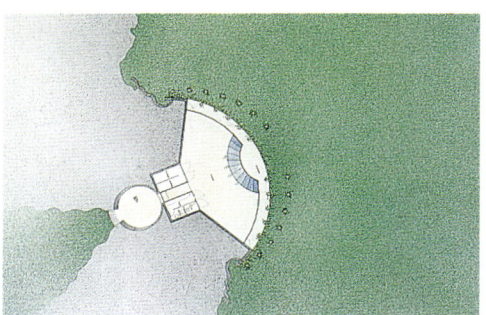

CLOCKWISE FROM TOP LEFT:
Model view; model view; floor plan; model view; section; site plan; section; model view; floor plan
FACING PAGE: *View of house*

Design

The architect was commissioned to create a complex of three buildings to house a family, a caretaker, and a private collection of contemporary art. The fourth building in the complex is a meditation pavilion, set upon a steep mountainside high above the main house. The family wanted the structures to have minimal visual impact on the natural environment, but also to reflect their love of classical architecture.

Like the buildings that epitomize the historic American Western town, each façade plane extends beyond the volume of the building it masks from view. The indigenous vegetation appears to flow down the hillside, enveloping each building mass and leaving only these bold façades exposed. Two miles from the property's entrance gateway, one is first met by the caretaker's house. Its ivy-covered trellis façade tilts forward to rest like a sturdy A-frame on a leaning colonnade of bare logs, a rustic reference to the classical articulation sought by the client. Each log is capped with a gilded capital and the façade itself terminates in a matching cornice of bronze, to capture the lingering reflections of the setting sun. Past the caretaker's house is the main residence, whose inward curve sits boldly on a promontory with breathtaking views of the natural surroundings.

Once inside the house, visitors can see the third building—the art gallery—set in a quiet meadow across the pond. Accessible only by foot, the gallery is composed of similar elements as the previous two buildings, only it curves gently outward. It is from inside the art gallery that visitors can see the fourth building—the meditation pavilion—perched enigmatically in the forest high above the main house.

Construction

Built into the face of a mountain, accessible only via steep, winding logging roads, and hampered by long winters and a short building season, construction of this project required extraordinary planning and scheduling. Existing dirt roads were continually reinforced, and additional temporary access roads plus a bridge were constructed just for the project. Due to the restricted dimensions of the clearing where the main residence is located, cut and fill was used to expand the site to accommodate the building footprint.

The U-shaped reinforced concrete retaining wall that runs along the back of the house deflects horizontal loads toward bracing at the front. Once the main slab and rear retaining wall were poured, the remainder of the house was constructed with laminated timber framing and steel reinforcing. The house is fully insulated with three separate heating systems, all tied to thermostats that proportion the heat relative to cost effectiveness and the individual requirements of each room.

The front façade was constructed in three layers: a glazing layer, a trellis layer, and a layer of log columns. Eventually, the entire façade will be completely covered in ivy, virtually disappearing and blending into the surrounding landscape.

Floor plan, gallery

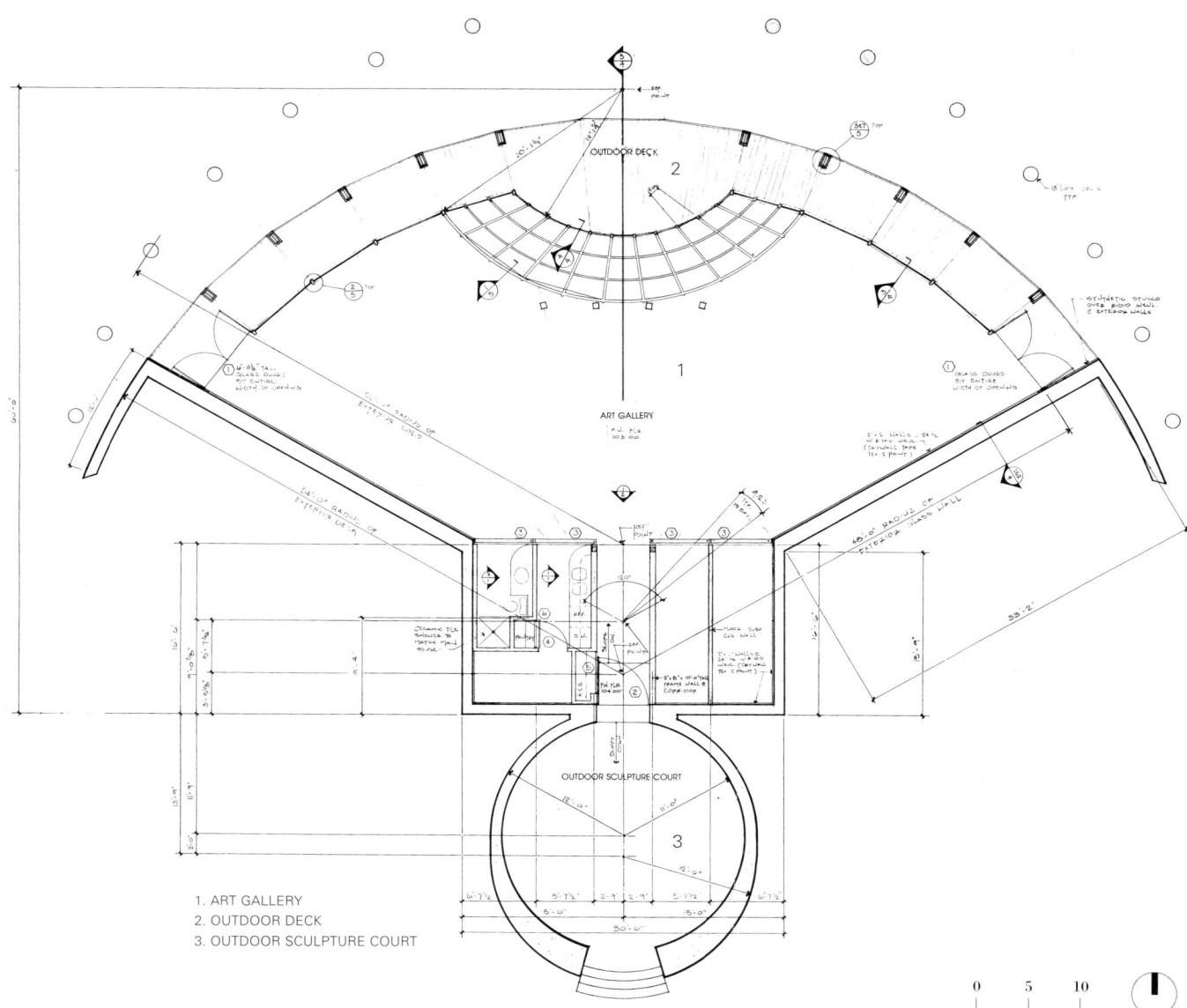

1. ART GALLERY
2. OUTDOOR DECK
3. OUTDOOR SCULPTURE COURT

Second level floor plan, house

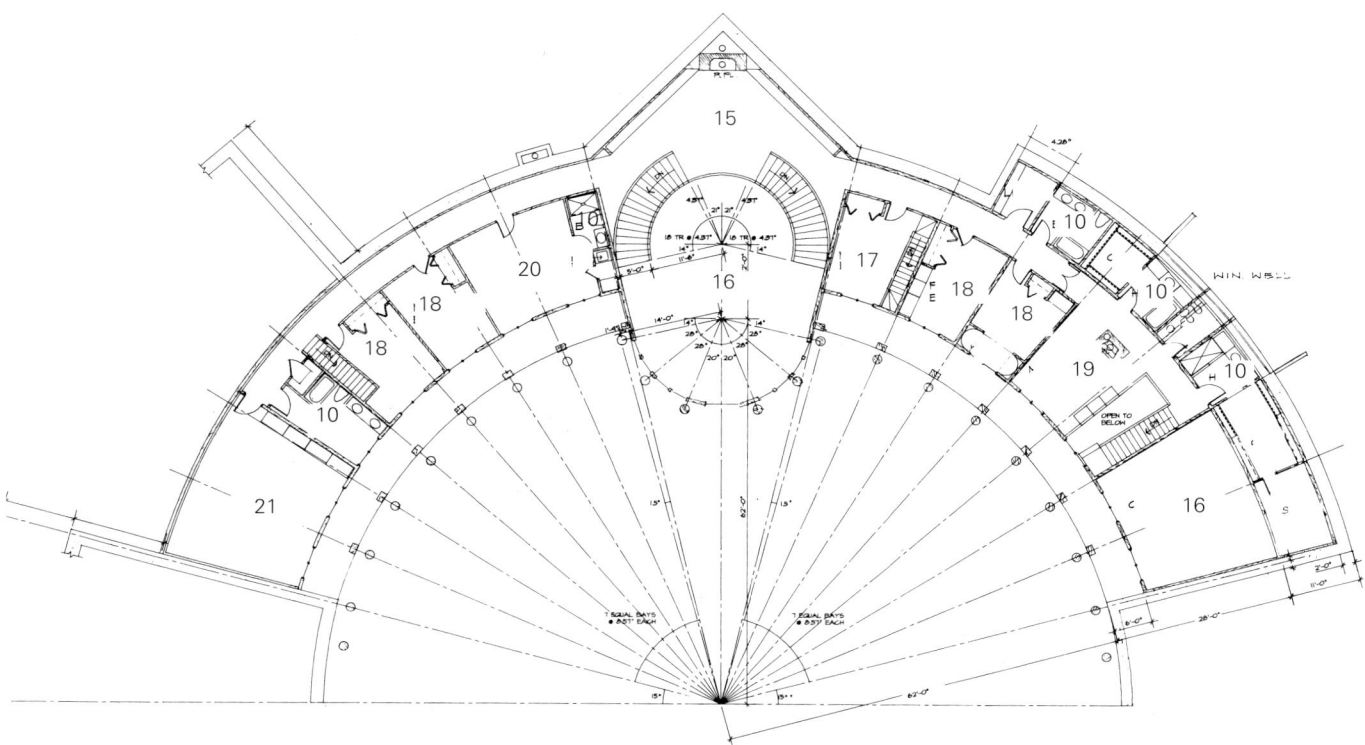

First level floor plan, house

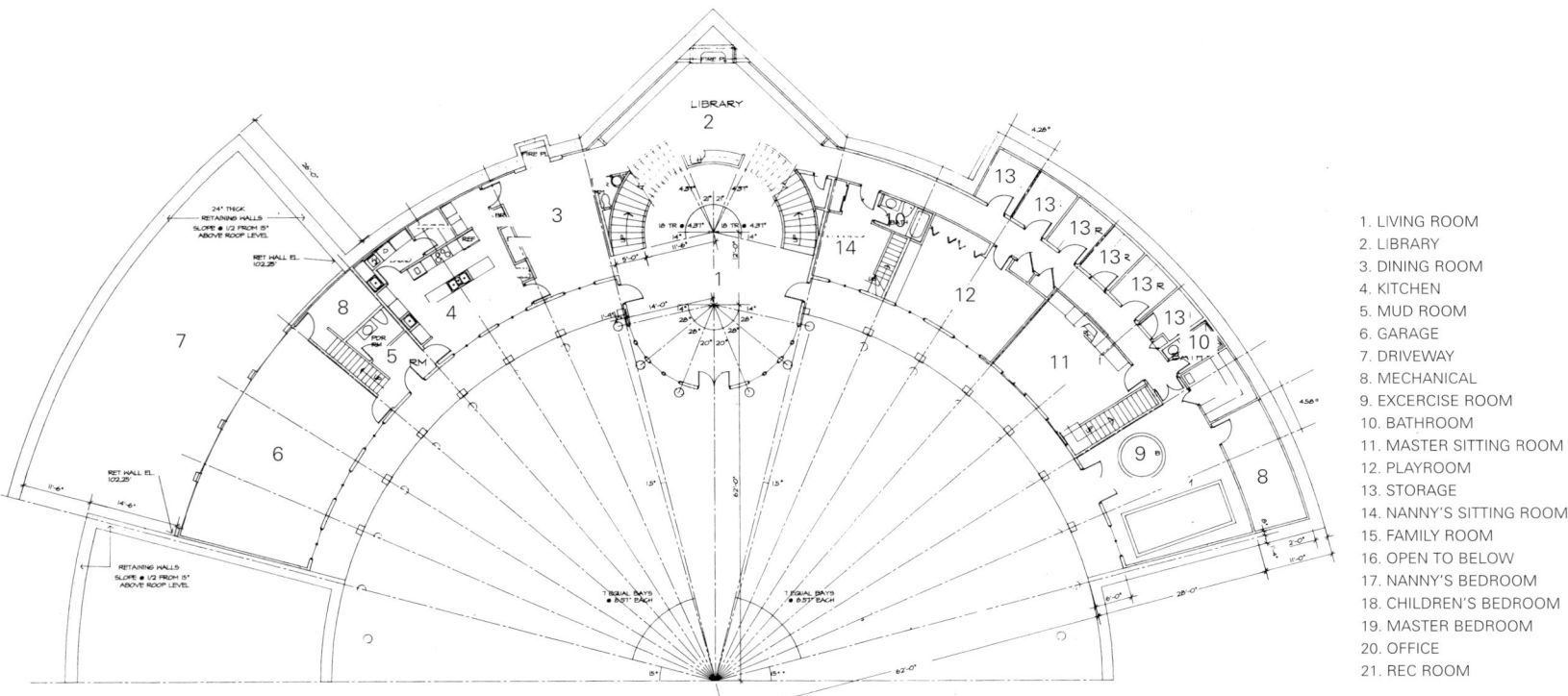

1. LIVING ROOM
2. LIBRARY
3. DINING ROOM
4. KITCHEN
5. MUD ROOM
6. GARAGE
7. DRIVEWAY
8. MECHANICAL
9. EXCERCISE ROOM
10. BATHROOM
11. MASTER SITTING ROOM
12. PLAYROOM
13. STORAGE
14. NANNY'S SITTING ROOM
15. FAMILY ROOM
16. OPEN TO BELOW
17. NANNY'S BEDROOM
18. CHILDREN'S BEDROOM
19. MASTER BEDROOM
20. OFFICE
21. REC ROOM

LEFT: *View of living room*
BOTTOM LEFT: *Library*
FACING PAGE: *Front façade of house*

LEFT: *View of family room*

Family/living room section

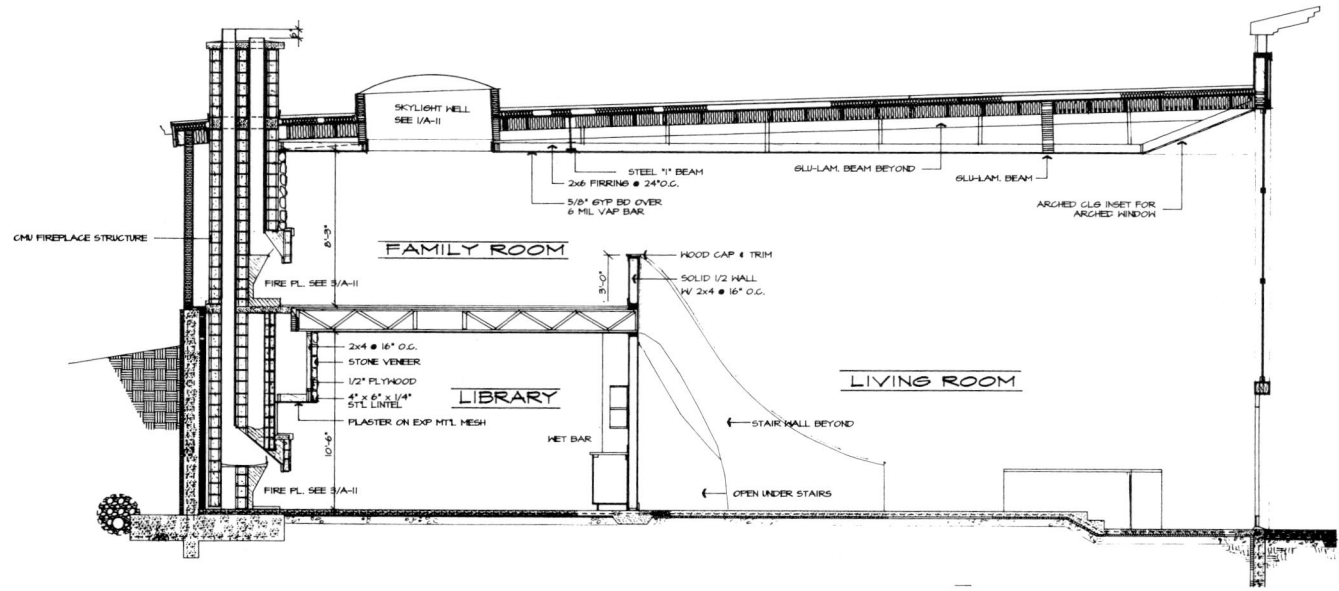

Gallery section

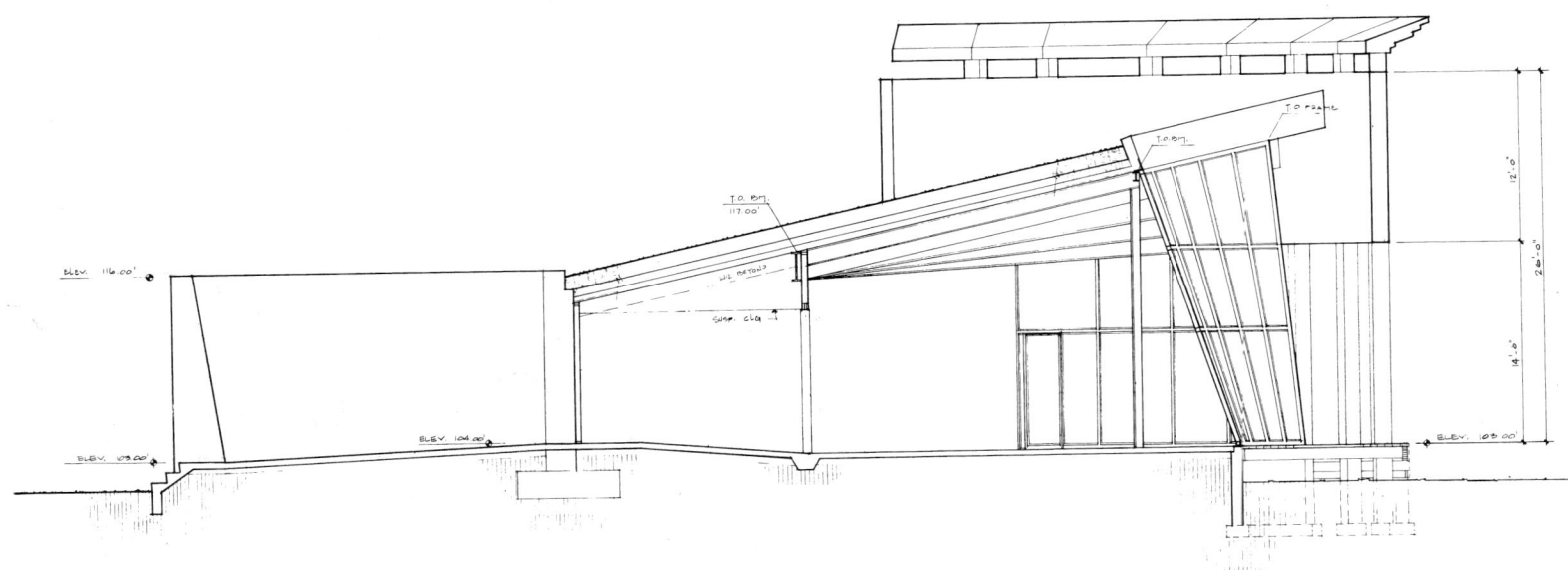

Type/Variant House

1994-1997

VINCENT JAMES ASSOCIATES

Owner: Name withheld at owner's request.
Architect: Vincent James Associates (project initiated by James/Snow Architects)
Design Team: Vincent James (principal), Paul Yaggie (project architect), Nancy Blankfard and Nathan Knutson (collaborators); Andrew Dull, Steve Lazen, Krista Scheib, Julie Snow, Taavo Somer, Kate Wyberg (project team).
Engineer: McSherry Structural
Consultant: Coen + Stumpf (landscape)
General Contractor: Yerigan Construction Company
Photography: Don F. Wong Photography, Mary Ludington

Site: Northern Wisconsin (Exact location withheld at owner's request.)
Program: Three-level house for family of seven and multiple visitors including open living room, dining room, and kitchen, master bedroom and bathroom, 7 bedrooms, 7 bathrooms, 2 semi-detached guest suites, screened porch, patio, 3 roof terraces.
Square Footage: 8000
Structural System: Wood and steel framing with laminated wood beams
Mechanical System: Forced air furnaces with air to air heat exchangers, central air conditioning, recirculating domestic water.
Major Exterior Materials: Copper (walls and roof), blue stone (foundation and paving)
Major Interior Materials: Douglas fir (cabinetry, screens, walls, ceilings and floors), blue stone (main floor with antique marble mosaic inlay in living room), slate (fireplace), stainless steel (countertops), marble mosaic tile (bathrooms).
Furnishings and Storage: Built in by architect.
Doors and Hardware: Custom Douglas fir doors; Stanley, Sugasune, Glynne-Johnson, Schlage, Ives, Hafele, Hiawatha.
Windows: Duratherm (teak exterior, Douglas fir interior)
Fixtures: Kroin (kitchen and bathrooms)
Appliances and Equipment: Sub-Zero (refrigerator/freezer), Viking (oven/cooktop), Thermador (wall ovens), Bosch (dishwasher), Viking (trash compactor), Asko (washers/dryers).
Cost: Withheld at owner's request.

Site

The five-acre site is heavily wooded with maple, oak, poplar, ash, and white pine, and is adjacent to a large lake on the east and a pond to the west. The drive approaching the house follows an abandoned logging trail, rising over a hill and then descending into a ravine before arriving at the entry court. The house is first viewed from above with the lake as a backdrop, accentuating its sculptural qualities. From this vantage point, the house is seen as a series of cubical forms resting on a plinth.

FACING PAGE: *View of living room terrace from lake*

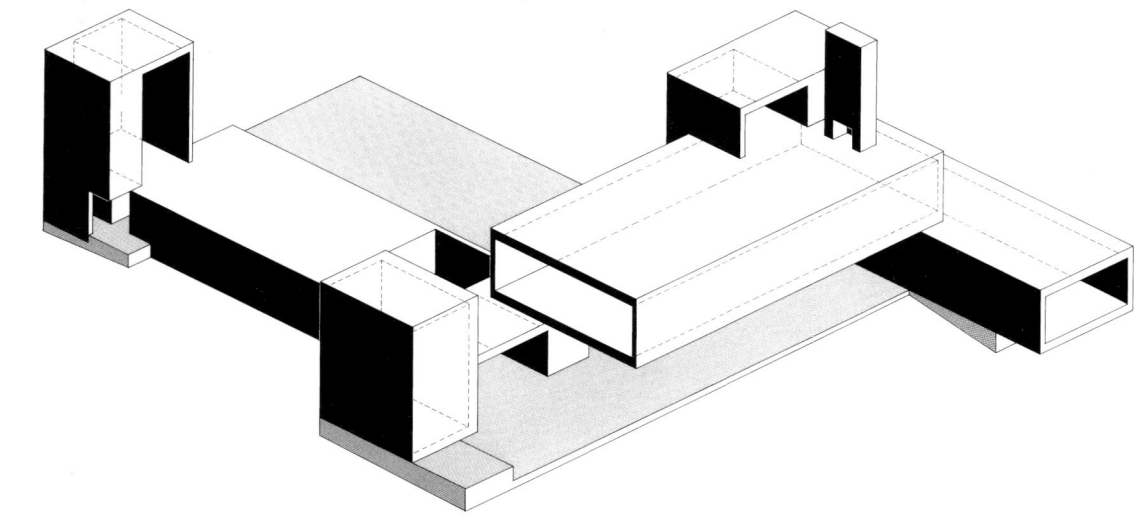

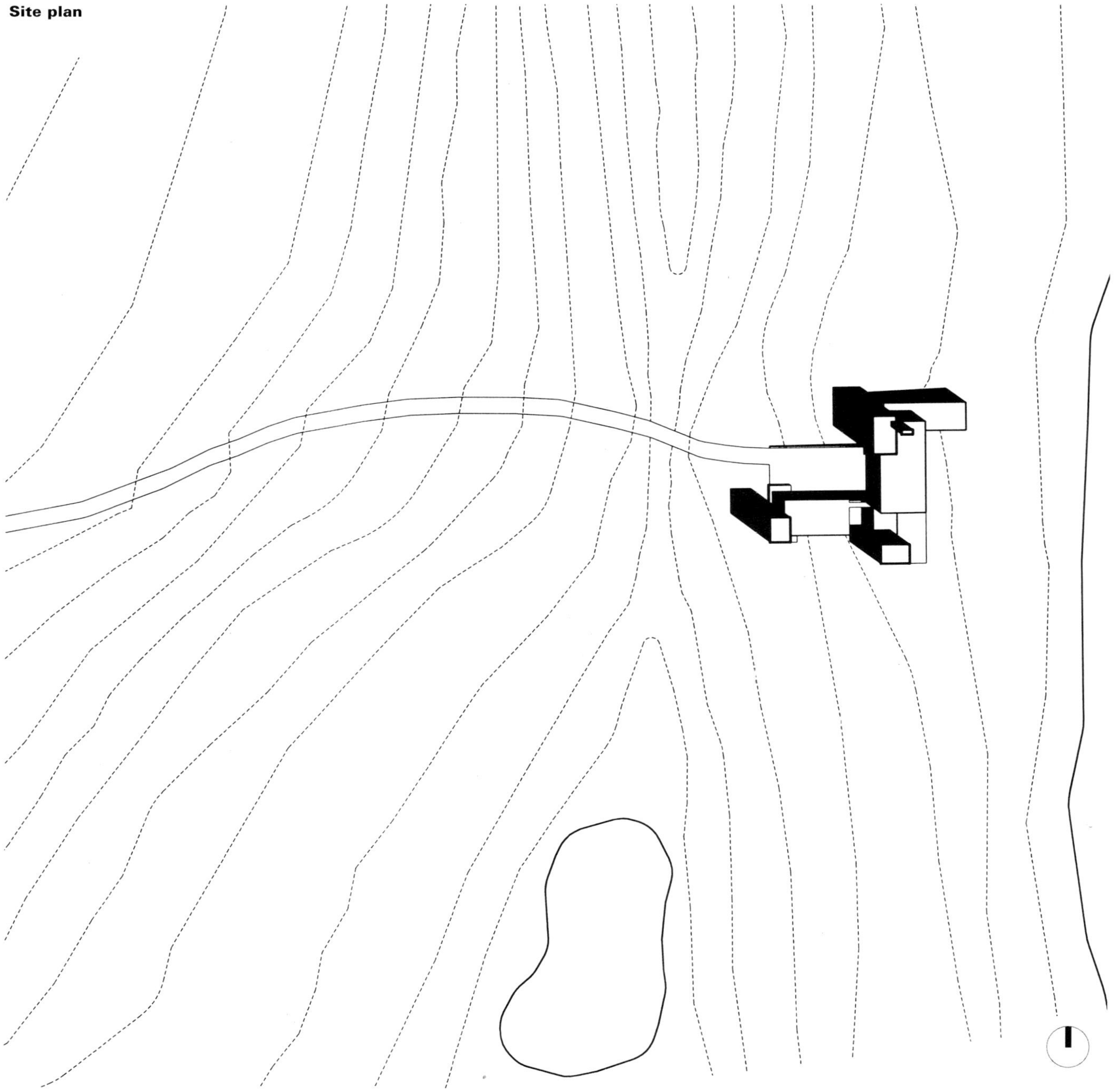

Design

The owners brought to the project a fascination for what was termed the "Type/Variant." Like a collection of butterflies in a glass case, variations within a clearly established taxonomy are made visible and amplified through classification. The play between these similarities and differences is fundamental to the aesthetic appeal of a "collection."

The Type/Variant house is a collection of like spatial conditions that responds to the rhythms and patterns of domestic life. By exclusively using wood-lined boxes, a series of interlinked architectural spaces are defined. Each has its own proportion, orientation, and natural light. The strictly orthogonal composition results in continually shifting views of the site and numerous exterior spaces. The larger living areas and terraces permit congregation while nodal spaces provide intimacy and solitude. The rooms and courtyards of the house were conceived as primal or archetypal dwelling spaces—simple in form, but animated by their use as well as the daily and seasonal cycles.

Construction

The materials of the house—primarily Douglas fir, copper, and blue stone—are assembled in a variety of rhythmic patterns. The naturally weathering materials and details were inspired by the rural industrial architecture typical of the Upper Midwest. The resulting tectonic is both familiar and abstract; compatible with the owners' desire for a rustic warmth that avoids sentimentality.

The copper siding has been left to age naturally. As the copper ages, its patina will change from the pink-orange of bright copper to blue and purple, followed by a deep brown and copper-green; at the completion of construction, a range of patinas already reflected the twelve-month installation. This natural process is considered by the owner to be one of the most important aesthetic experiences of the house, one that will be savored over the years. Blue stone was selected for the base of the house, because it contains all of these hues while echoing the texture of the bark on the surrounding hardwood trees.

Site plan

Third level floor plan

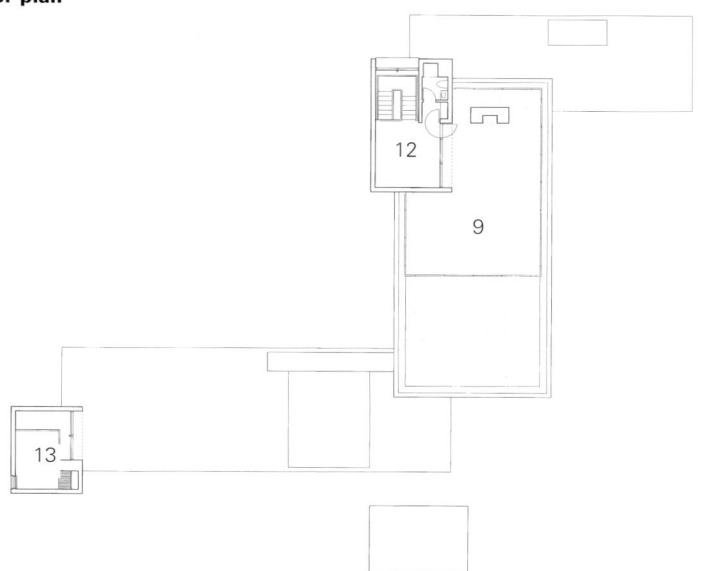

Second level floor plan

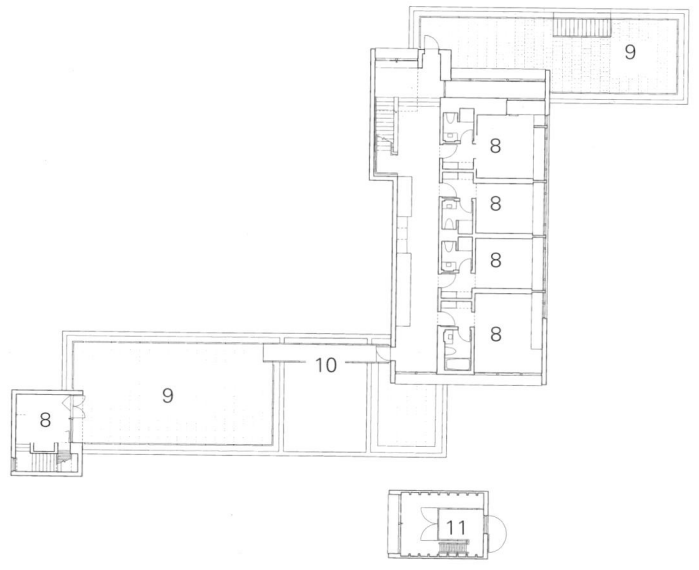

First level floor plan

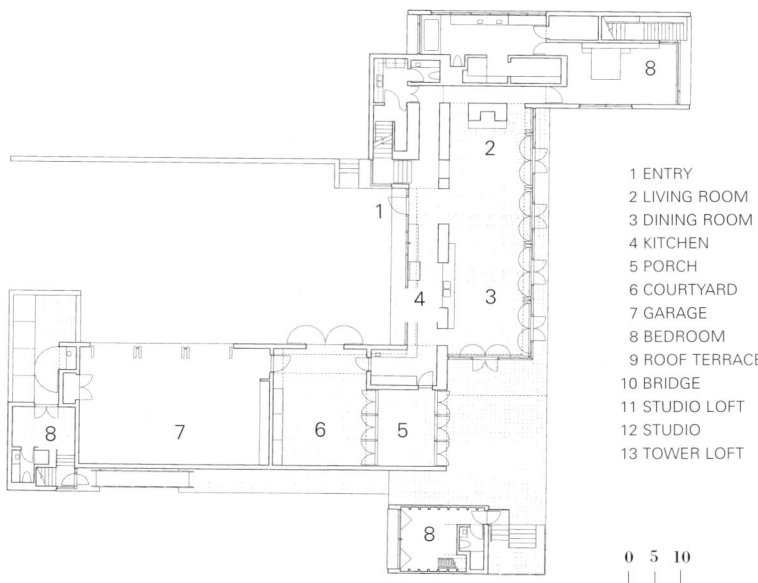

1 ENTRY
2 LIVING ROOM
3 DINING ROOM
4 KITCHEN
5 PORCH
6 COURTYARD
7 GARAGE
8 BEDROOM
9 ROOF TERRACE
10 BRIDGE
11 STUDIO LOFT
12 STUDIO
13 TOWER LOFT

0 5 10

ABOVE: *East façade*

LEFT: *View of master bedroom from north*
MIDDLE: *Studio*
BOTTOM: *East façade looking north*
FACING PAGE: *View of northwest corner*

Studio/loft section

Studio/loft screen detail

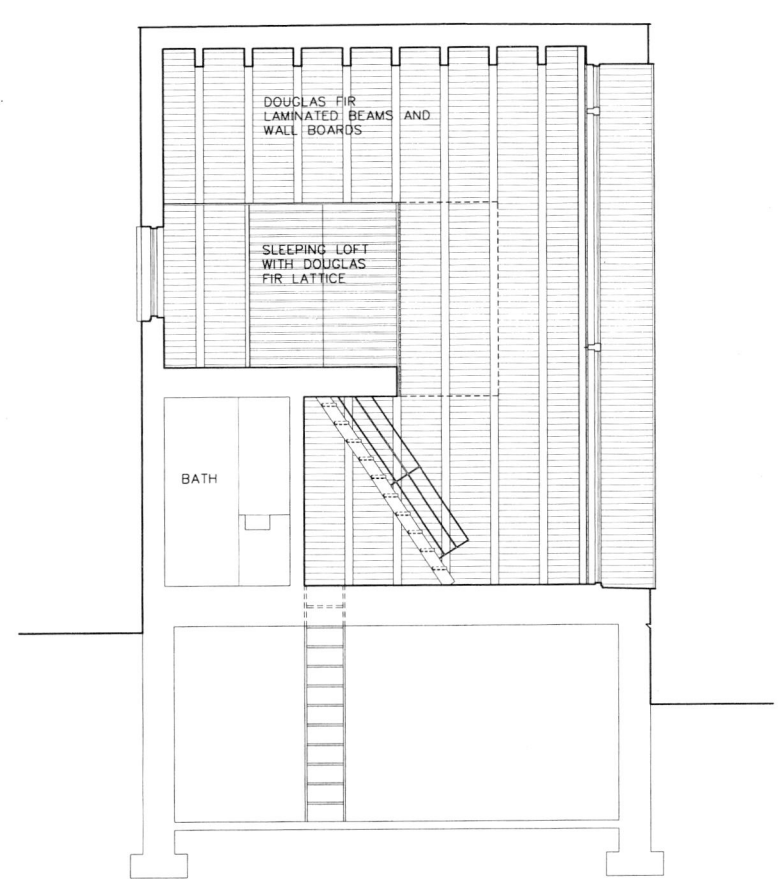

DOUGLAS FIR
LAMINATED BEAMS AND
WALL BOARDS

SLEEPING LOFT
WITH DOUGLAS
FIR LATTICE

BATH

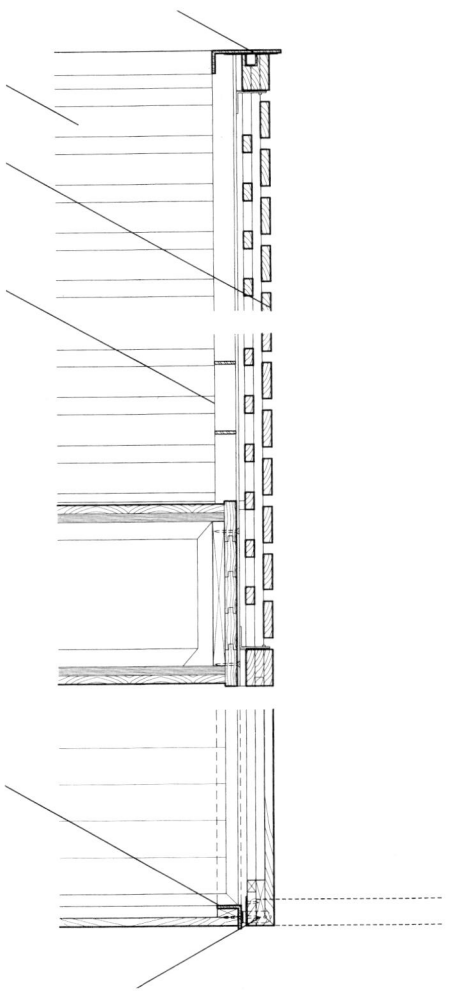

Stair to third floor detail

Wall section detail

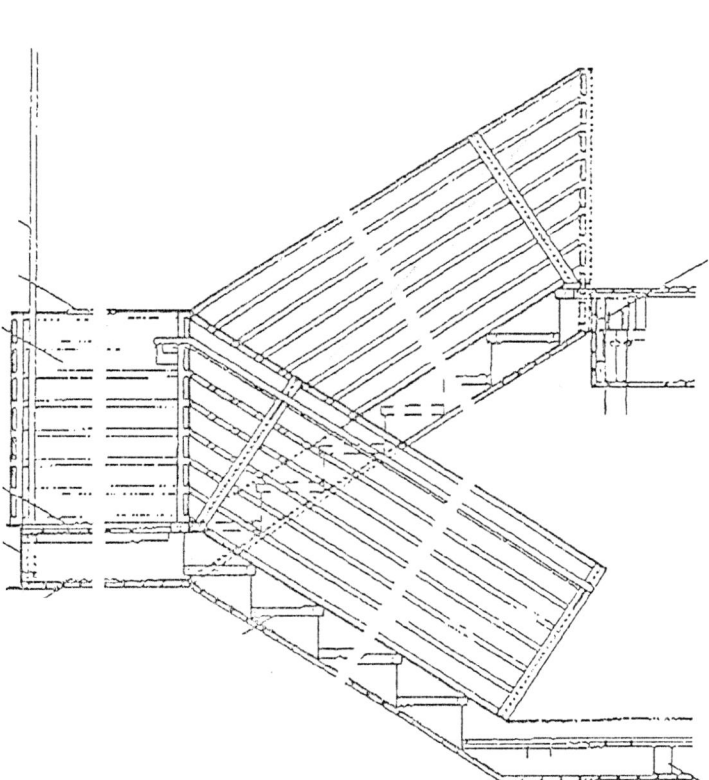

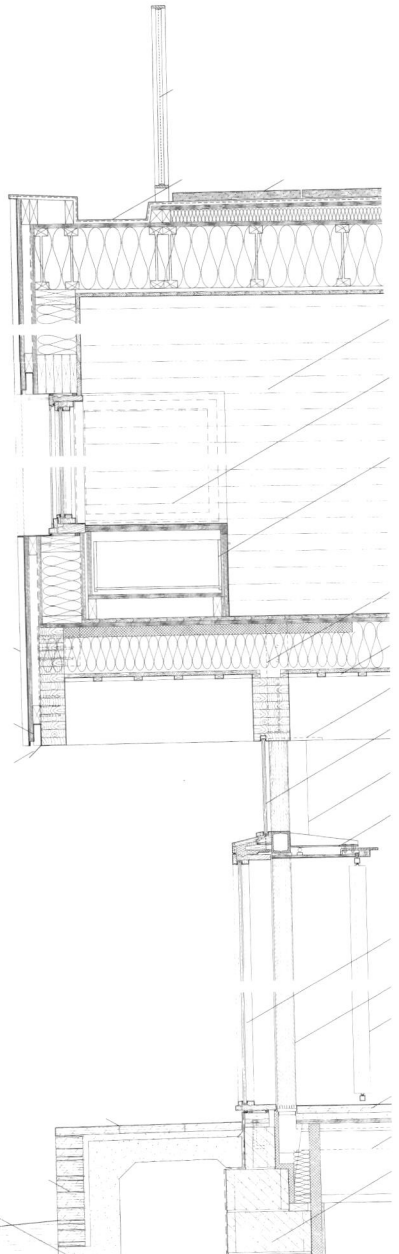

ABOVE, LEFT: *Clerestory behind fireplace*
ABOVE, RIGHT: *Bluestone stair landing at night*

CLOCKWISE FROM LEFT: *Second floor corridor toward studio; living room fireplace; view of master bedroom*

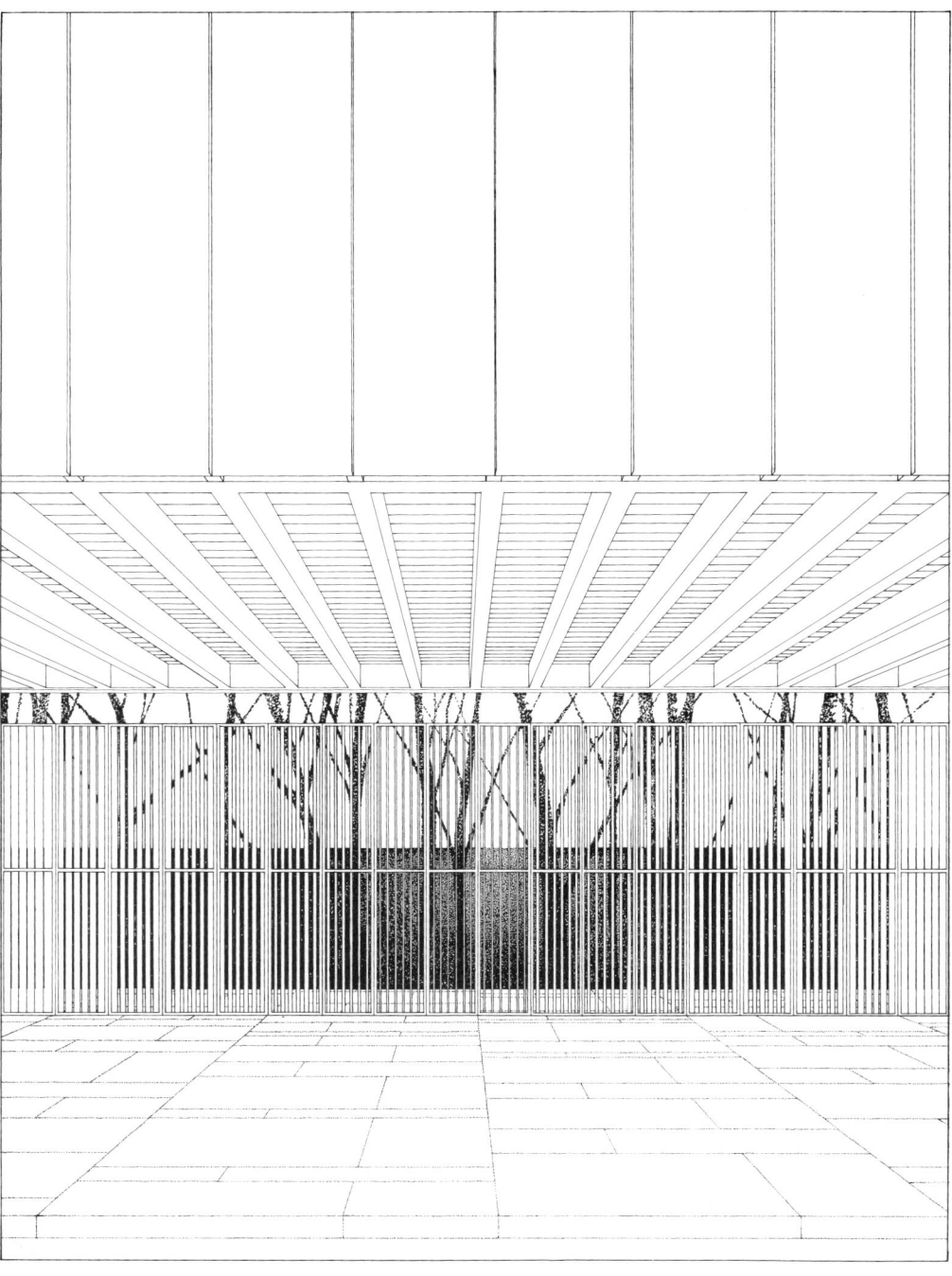

CLOCKWISE FROM TOP LEFT:
*Slate and bluestone fireplace;
perspective of living room
toward lake; view of courtyard*

ABOVE: *North façade*

Essex Live/Work Residence

1995

WHEELER KEARNS ARCHITECTS

Owner: Joseph and Nancy Essex
Architect: Wheeler Kearns Architects, Chicago, Illinois
Design Team: Daniel Wheeler, Lawrence Kearns, Mark Weber (project architect), Tom Bader, Sue Auerbach, Mark Spencer.
Engineers: LeMessurier Consultants, Spancrete Industries
General Contractor: Firehouse Construction
Photography: William H. Kildow

Site: Wicker Park, Chicago, Illinois
Program: Live/work environment for a husband and wife graphic design team. Office: reception, library, 3 offices, conference room, powder room, utility; Residence: livingroom, dining room, kitchen, pantry, 3 bedrooms, 2 bathrooms, master closet/dressing room, utility, laundry.
Square Footage: 4560
Structural System: Prefabricated composite concrete floor and wall panels with inner layer of rigid insulation, panels supported on precast insulated grade beams bearing on 43-ft. drilled concrete caissons.
Mechanical System: Gas forced air heating, electric forced air cooling
Major Exterior Materials: Precast concrete wall surface with aluminum doors, windows, copings, and downspouts.
Major Interior Materials: Precast concrete (wall and ceiling surfaces), integrally colored waxed concrete (floors), painted steel (stairs and doors), oiled medium density fiberboard (doors and window trim), aluminum (windows).
Furnishings and Storage: Designed by WKA and SX2, manufactured by Firehouse Construction.
Doors and Hardware: Steel and medium-density fiberboard interior doors, custom steel hardware manufactured by Firehouse Construction.
Fixtures: Kohler
Appliances and Equipment: GE, Whirlpool
Cost: $79 per square foot

Site

After having searched unsuccessfully for a small loft building to renovate into a combined residence and office for their graphic design firm, the owners found a vacant lot suitable for construction. It is located on a loud, busy street in Chicago's Wicker Park neighborhood amid an urban ensemble of apartment buildings, single-family residences, storefront shops, and loft buildings. The neighborhood has strived to maintain its ethnic and economic diversity while emerging as a vital urban cultural community. The 48' x 130' lot has a history of rubble, old foundations, and non-compacted soils buried beneath the topsoil. A non-combustible shell was required given the zoning and building code.

Design

It was clear from the outset that an innovative departure from standard design and construction was required. An effective solution to the issues of budget, quality, and schedule were equally important and programmed space

North elevation

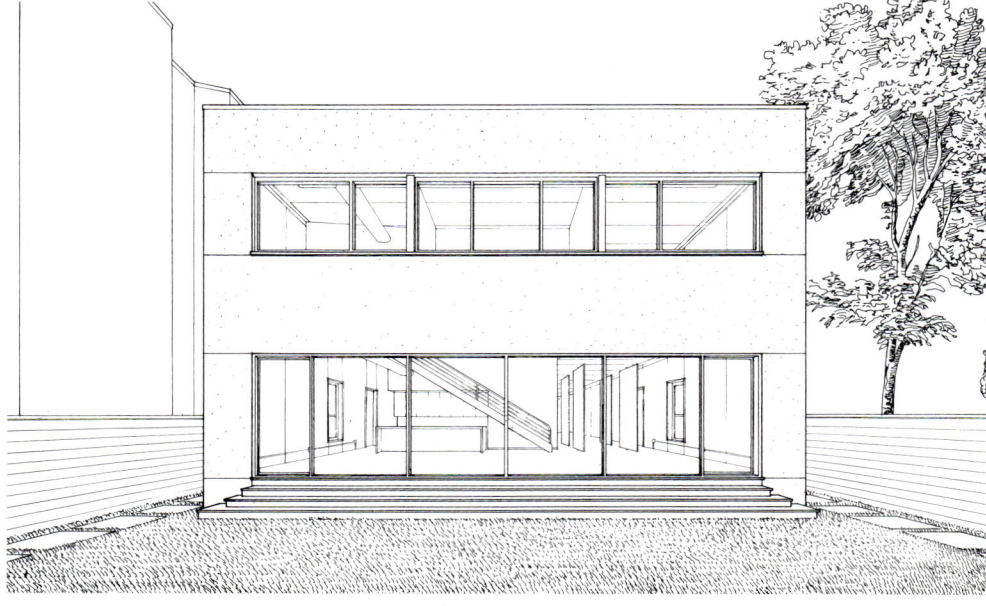

was fixed at 4500 square feet. Standard construction practices failed to meet the construction budget of roughly two-thirds the market rate in Chicago for commercial/residential construction and would have yielded marginal results at best. With the scope fixed, and understanding that approximately half the cost of construction is material and the other half labor, the only option was to limit labor on site—hence prefabrication. After pursuing several competing building systems, prefabricated concrete was the optimal choice. The building aesthetic developed as a result of the system selected.

A simple taut volume capitalizes on the reductive logic and minimalist aesthetic employed. Windows and doors are placed in cadence with the load bearing panels of the east and west walls and integrated with the structural logic of the panels. The continuous glazed opening to the garden court is an exception to the load bearing wall system and exhibits the material's spanning capabilities. A plaster core divides the spare interior volume and contains all services including bathrooms, kitchen, mechanical systems, and vertical circulation.

An unassuming entry at the midpoint of the side façade provides access to the front offices facing the street and the private living spaces facing the rear courtyard. Rotating panels, measuring 6' x 11',6" and made of oiled medium-density fiberboard set in steel frames, are positioned to direct visitors in one or the other direction, and allow free flowing passage between the two. The concrete wall panels' smooth extruded interior serves as a backdrop for warm wood panels and colorful plaster walls. The integrally colored red concrete floors add a warm glow of reflected light to the entire space. Welded steel fasteners are left exposed and exploited for their dark, contrasting color.

Construction

Subsoil foundations consist of six site-cast concrete caissons drilled through the existing subsoil debris to hardened clay. This eliminated the need for typical excavation and spoil removal costs. Insulated precast concrete grade beams were placed on the caissons, thus beginning a four-day erection process of the "kit of parts." The assemblies of wall, floor, and roof panels bear on the grade beams and transfer loads with steel angle bearing ledges welded to plates cast into the pre fabricated panels. Load bearing joints are shimmed and grouted, and others are caulked to provide weather-tight enclosure. All insulation is contained within the prefabricated panels, resulting in a one-step construction of the entire building shell for both exterior and interior finish surfaces.

Application of the roofing membrane and installation of shop-fabricated windows, doors, and stairs immediately followed the erection of the shell. Electrical distribution conduit originates from the plaster core, is distributed above the precast floor slab, and covered with a site-cast integrally colored concrete floor topping. Light switches at the entry are housed in a three-foot-tall steel pedestal with industrial push-button switches. Perimeter electrical outlets are surface mounted. Forced air HVAC ductwork is left exposed and serves as a structure for indirect fluorescent lighting.

FACING PAGE: *Views of construction process*

Roof plan

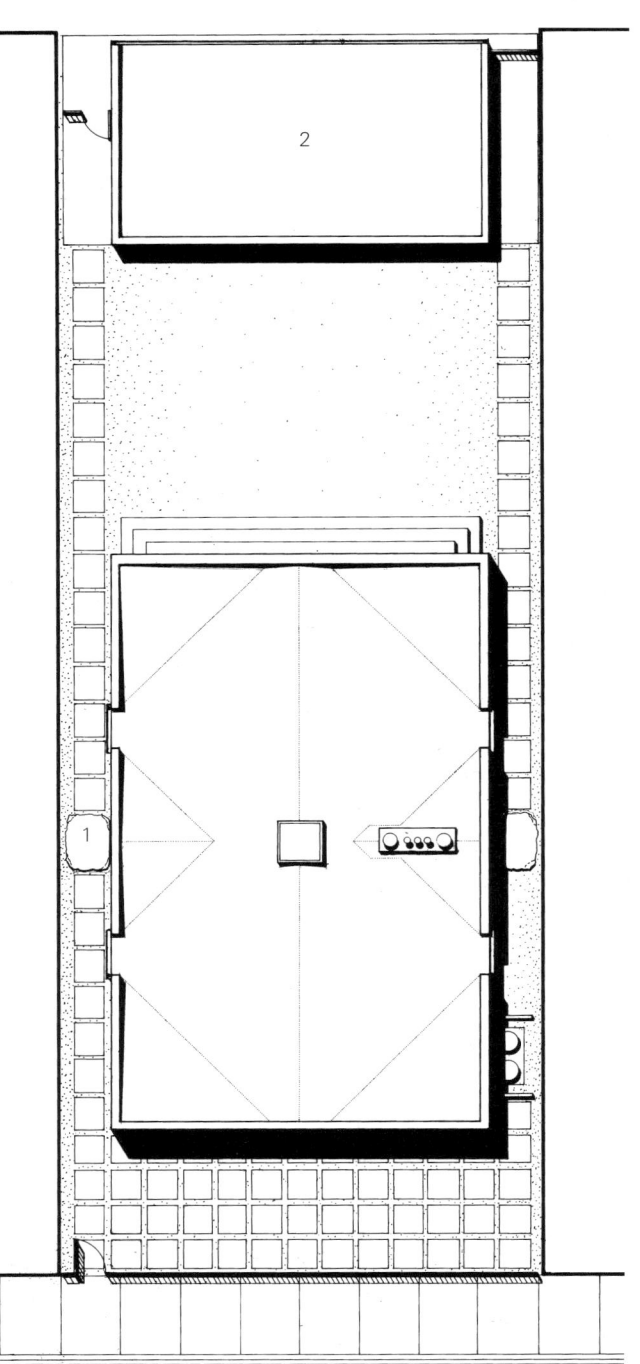

Second level floor plan

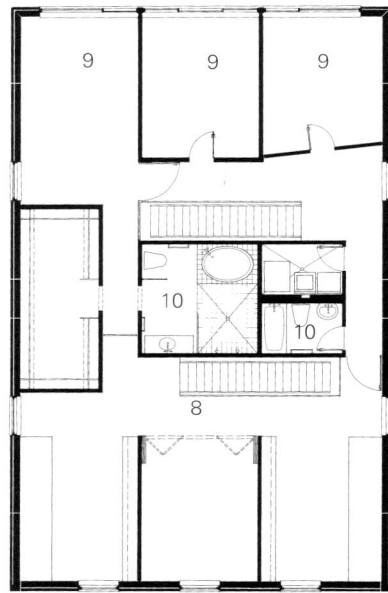

First level floor plan

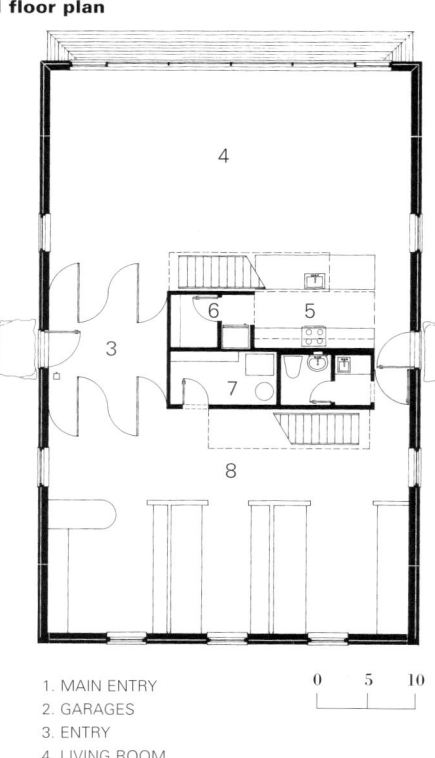

1. MAIN ENTRY
2. GARAGES
3. ENTRY
4. LIVING ROOM
5. KITCHEN
6. PANTRY
7. POWDER ROOM
8. OFFICE
9. BEDROOM
10. BATHROOM

0   5   10

LEFT: *Living room*
BOTTOM: *Entry hall*
**FACING PAGE, CLOCKWISE FROM
TOP LEFT:** *View of first floor
office space; pivoting door;
second floor hall; view of
first floor office space*

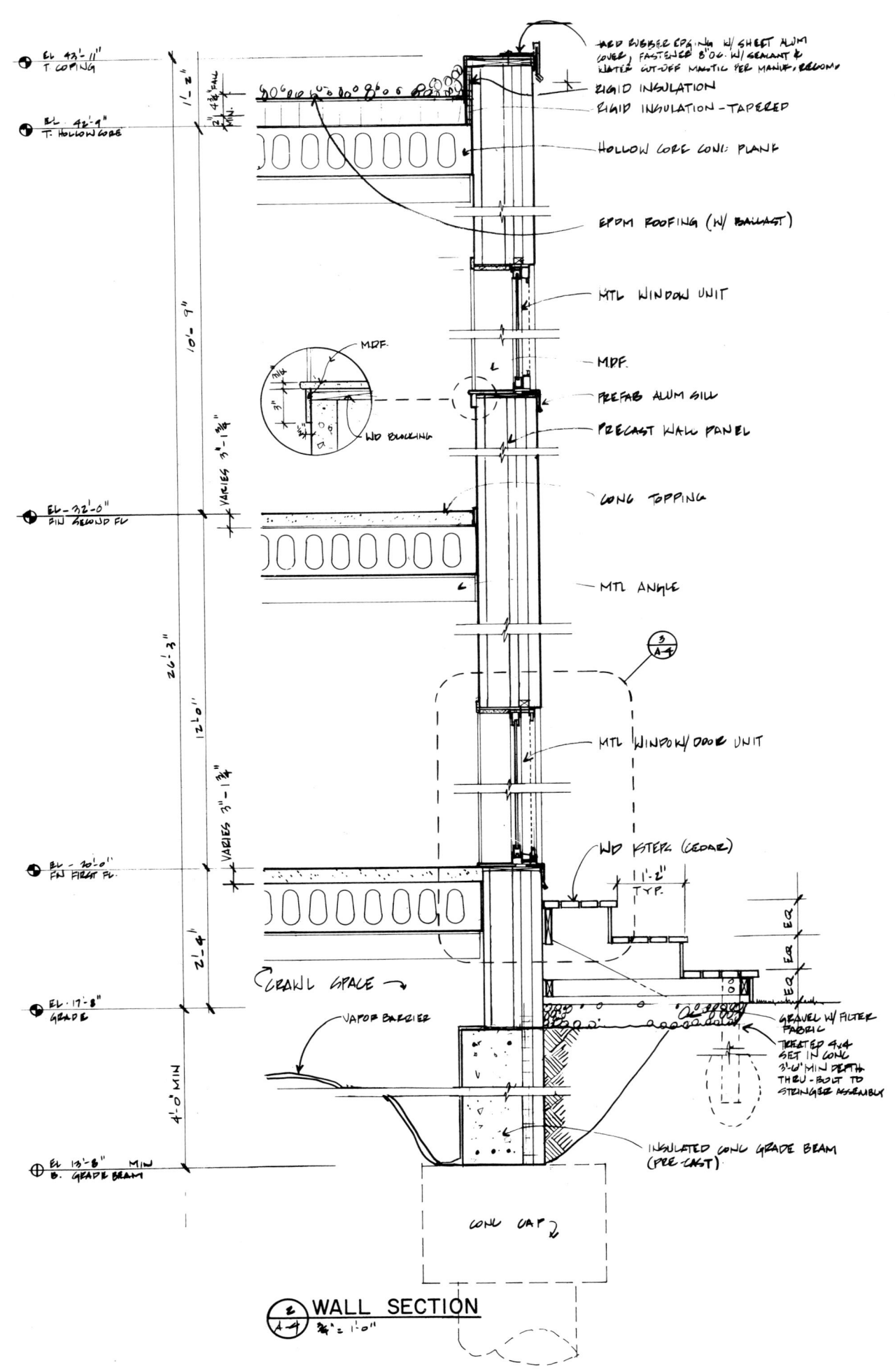

RED RUBBER EDGING W/ SHEET ALUM COVER, FASTENED 8" O.C. W/ SEALANT & WATER CUT-OFF MASTIC PER MANUF. RECOMM.

RIGID INSULATION

RIGID INSULATION - TAPERED

HOLLOW CORE CONC. PLANK

EPDM ROOFING (W/ BALLAST)

MTL WINDOW UNIT

MDF.

PREFAB ALUM SILL

PRECAST WALL PANEL

CONC TOPPING

MTL ANGLE

MTL WINDOW/DOOR UNIT

WD STEPS (CEDAR)

GRAVEL W/ FILTER FABRIC

TREATED 4x4 SET IN CONC 3'-6" MIN DEPTH THRU-BOLT TO STRINGER ASSEMBLY

INSULATED CONC GRADE BEAM (PRE-CAST)

MDF.

WD BLOCKING

EL 43'-11"
T. COPING

EL 42'-9"
T. HOLLOW CORE

EL 32'-0"
FIN SECOND FL

EL 20'-0"
FIN FIRST FL

EL 17'-8"
GRADE

EL 13'-8" MIN
B. GRADE BEAM

1'-2" WALL
2" MIN.

10'-9"

VARIES 3'-1¾"

26'-3"

12'-0"

VARIES 3'-1¾"

2'-4"

4'-0" MIN

CRAWL SPACE

VAPOR BARRIER

1'-2" TYP.

EQ   EQ   EQ

CONC CAP

3
A-4

WALL SECTION

¾" = 1'-0"

2
A-4

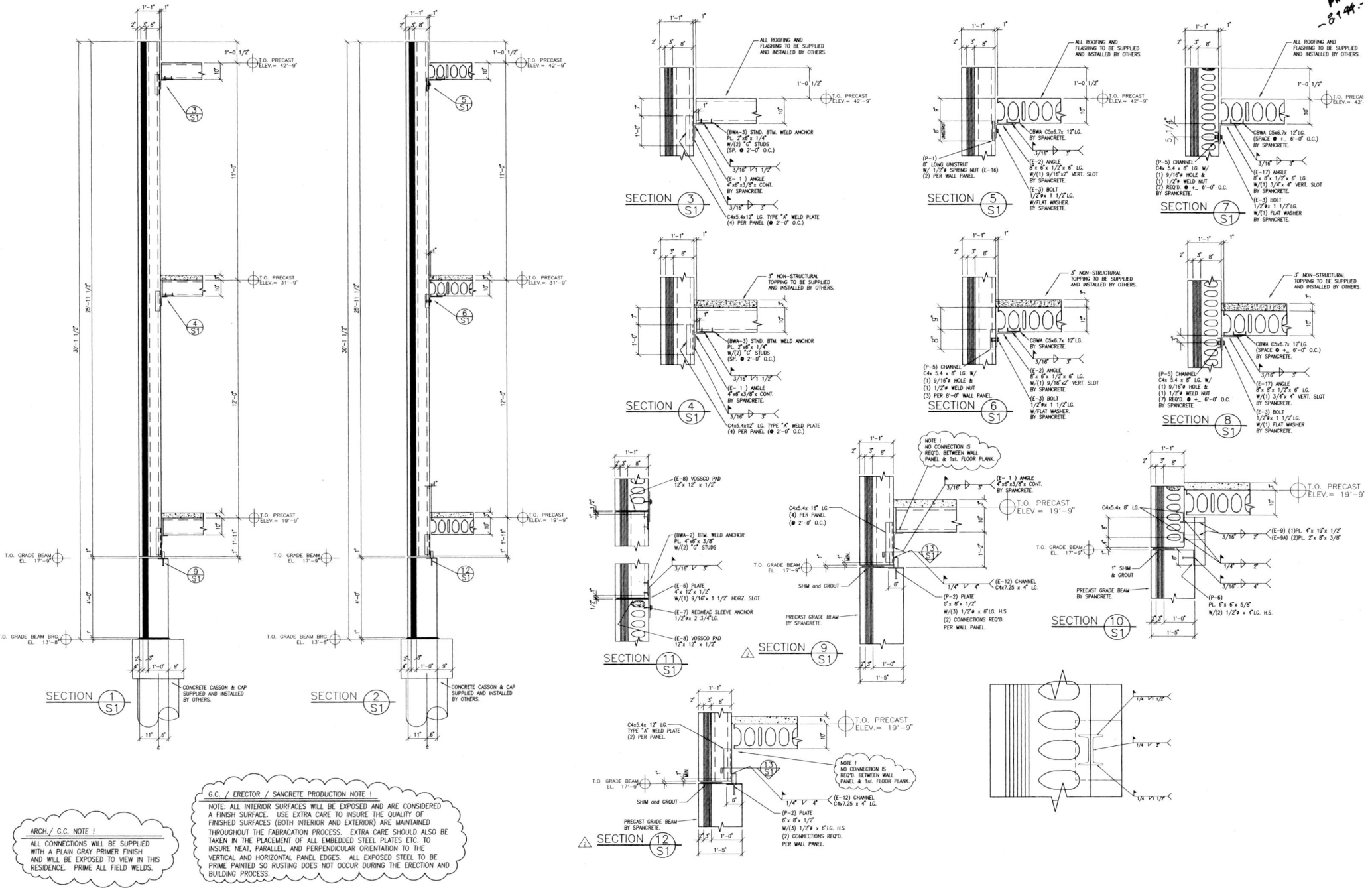

SECTION 1 / S1

SECTION 2 / S1

SECTION 3 / S1

SECTION 4 / S1

SECTION 5 / S1

SECTION 6 / S1

SECTION 7 / S1

SECTION 8 / S1

SECTION 9 / S1

SECTION 10 / S1

SECTION 11 / S1

SECTION 12 / S1

ARCH./ G.C. NOTE !
ALL CONNECTIONS WILL BE SUPPLIED
WITH A PLAIN GRAY PRIMER FINISH
AND WILL BE EXPOSED TO VIEW IN THIS
RESIDENCE. PRIME ALL FIELD WELDS.

G.C. / ERECTOR / SANCRETE PRODUCTION NOTE !
NOTE: ALL INTERIOR SURFACES WILL BE EXPOSED AND ARE CONSIDERED
A FINISH SURFACE. USE EXTRA CARE TO INSURE THE QUALITY OF
FINISHED SURFACES (BOTH INTERIOR AND EXTERIOR) ARE MAINTAINED
THROUGHOUT THE FABRICATION PROCESS. EXTRA CARE SHOULD ALSO BE
TAKEN IN THE PLACEMENT OF ALL EMBEDDED STEEL PLATES ETC. TO
INSURE NEAT, PARALLEL, AND PERPENDICULAR ORIENTATION TO THE
VERTICAL AND HORIZONTAL PANEL EDGES. ALL EXPOSED STEEL TO BE
PRIME PAINTED SO RUSTING DOES NOT OCCUR DURING THE ERECTION AND
BUILDING PROCESS.

House in Surry *1992-1994*
PETER FORBES AND ASSOCIATES, INC.

Owner: Dr. and Mrs. Earl David Nordberg
Architect: Peter Forbes and Associates, Inc., Boston, Massachusetts
Design Team: Peter Forbes, FAIA, Bradford C. Walker, AIA, Timothy Weiler, Daniel M. Hewett.
Engineers: Zaldastani Associates, Inc. (structural), Panitsas Associates, Inc. (mechanical)
General Contractor: Philip Urban Fine Homes
Photography: Nick Wheeler/Wheeler Photographics

Site: Surry, Maine
Program: Private residence with 3 discrete structures. Main house: entry, dining/living/kitchen space, master bedroom, master bathroom. Guest house: 5 bedrooms, 2 bathrooms. Studio.
Square Footage: 3800
Structural System: Reinforced concrete piers, steel floor beams and roof rafters, wood infill.
Mechanical System: Radiant heating
Major Exterior Materials: Glass, granite, cedar wall panels, fiberglass roof shingles, lead-coated copper fascias.
Major Interior Materials: Gypsum wallboard, oak strip flooring, birch veneer plywood, granite.
Furnishings and Storage: Built-ins by architect.
Doors and Hardware: Fleetwood sliding glass doors, wood doors custom by architect; Schlage
Windows: Fixed glass by architect, Kawneer aluminum double hung windows
Fixtures: Kohler, Porcher, Jacuzzi.
Appliances and Equipment: GE
Cost: Withheld at owner's request.

Site

Landscape, geometry, and light interact to define this seaside home, guest house, and studio. An open meadow punctuated by spare pine trees leads to a broad pebble beach, affording spectacular views of Blue Hill Bay and Mt. Desert Island. The site is bathed in intense, unshaded light magnified by reflection from the water barely twenty-five yards away. Light surrounds each component of the architecture, articulating the parts, "dissolving" the building, and creating an elusive, hovering form.

Design

The program called for a house and studio for a retired couple with a large extended family, all of whom would come to visit at holidays and during the summer. In addition, the owners required ample storage space for all of their belongings but preferred to leave living spaces open and uncluttered with sufficient room to display their art. Hence, the open plan needed to be served by extensive storage areas contained in a series of pods or "saddlebags" clipped onto the inland side of the house.

CLOCKWISE FROM TOP:
South façade; southwest façade; column detail; outward intersection
FACING PAGE: *Inward intersection of private and public areas*

The resulting principal living space, free of support services or structure, is a fifty-eight-foot-long room that terminates in a massive chimney wall of cut local granite. This chimney separates the owners' private area and studio from the family gathering spaces, which are contained in a large space encompassing the living room, dining room, and kitchen.

Construction

Because the site is a flood-plain area, regulations required that the house be raised off the ground with concrete piers to support the floor. These piers extend up to eave height, carry the roof, and establish an order of paired columns that bends and shifts with the land-scape. Steel beams and rafters are clipped to the columns, creating a pavilion that floats above the ground. Within this ordered structure, storage elements, enclosed sleeping areas, folding decks, bathrooms, and the kitchen are inserted as freestanding objects, wrapped or interposed with glass. A single column "hinges" the two main pavilions, forming a separate but consistent block of space under a sheltering roof.

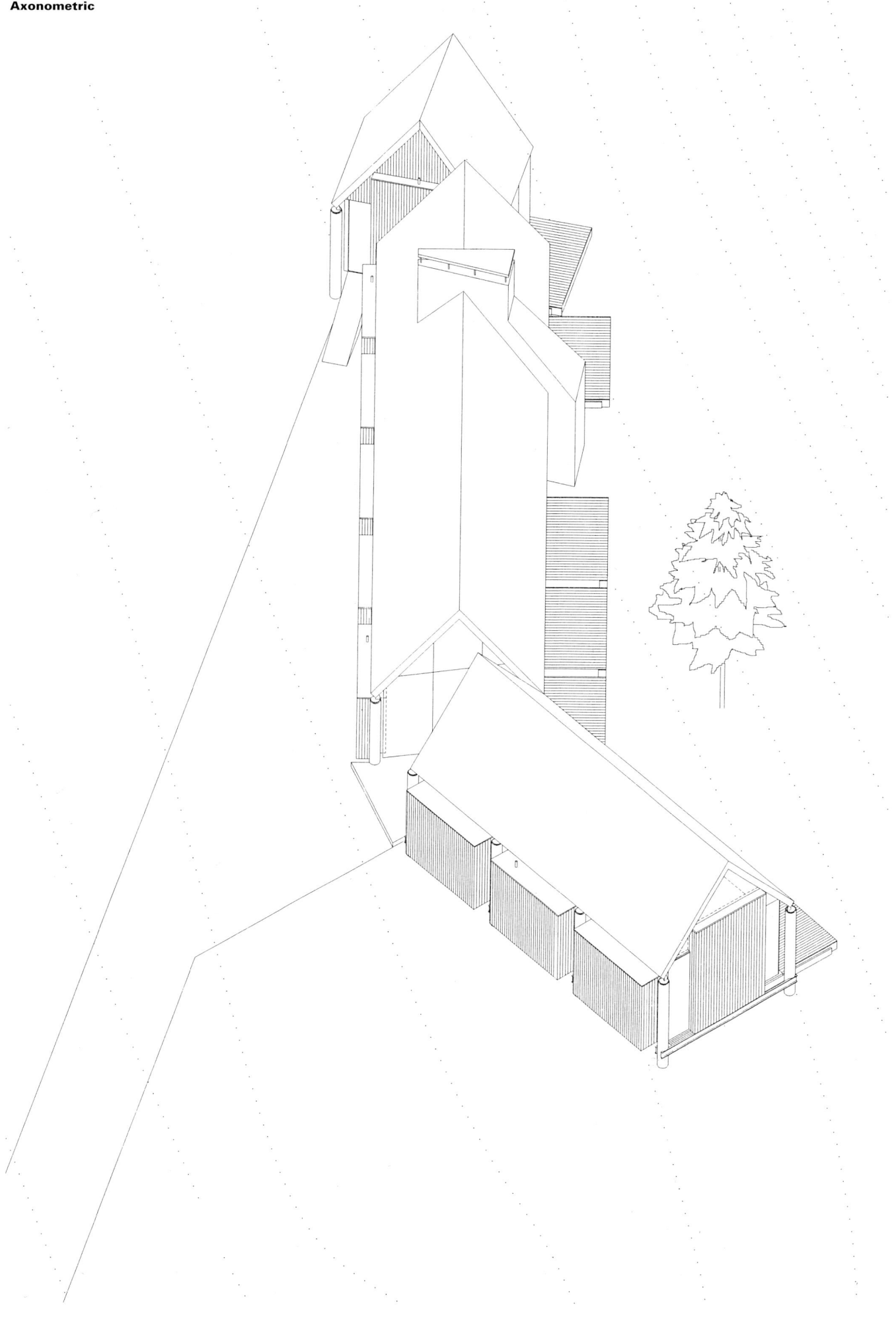

Floor plan

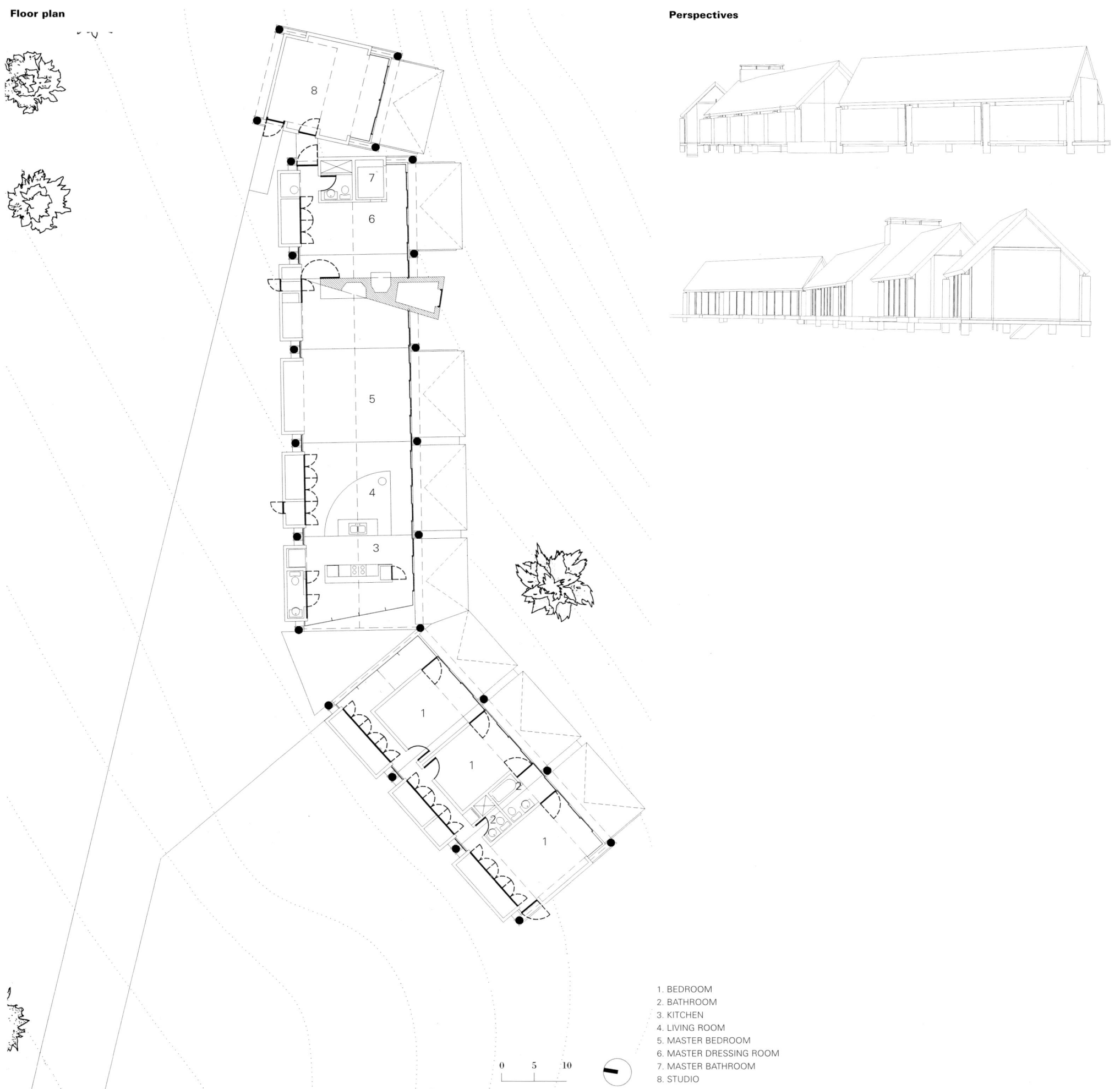

1. BEDROOM
2. BATHROOM
3. KITCHEN
4. LIVING ROOM
5. MASTER BEDROOM
6. MASTER DRESSING ROOM
7. MASTER BATHROOM
8. STUDIO

0   5   10

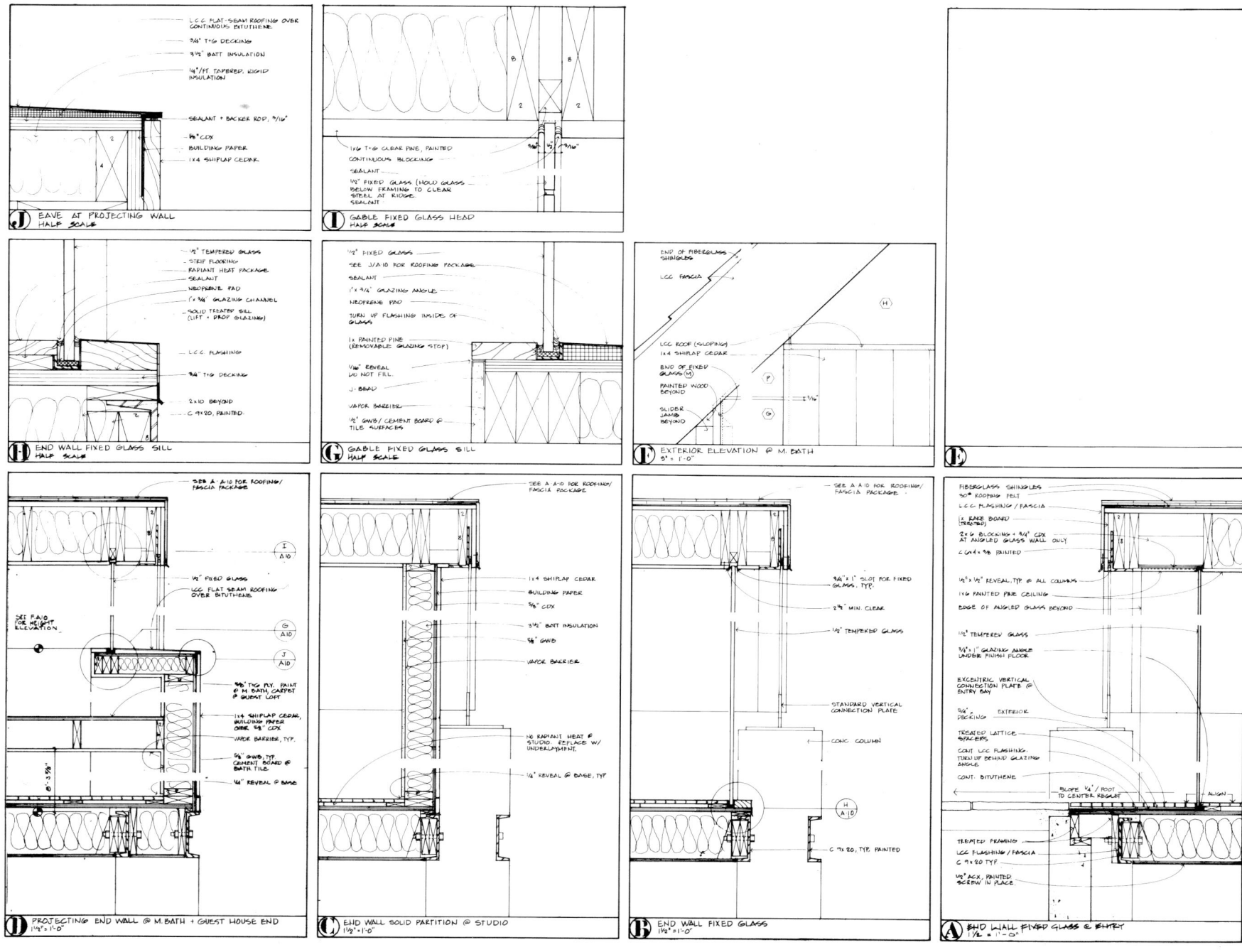

J EAVE AT PROJECTING WALL
HALF SCALE

LCC FLAT-SEAM ROOFING OVER
CONTINUOUS BITUTHENE
¾" T&G DECKING
3½" BATT INSULATION
¼"/FT. TAPERED, RIGID
INSULATION
SEALANT + BACKER ROD, ⅜"
⅝" CDX
BUILDING PAPER
1x4 SHIPLAP CEDAR

I GABLE FIXED GLASS HEAD
HALF SCALE

1x6 T&G CLEAR PINE, PAINTED
CONTINUOUS BLOCKING
SEALANT
½" FIXED GLASS (HOLD GLASS
BELOW FRAMING TO CLEAR
STILL AT RIDGE
SEALANT

H END WALL FIXED GLASS SILL
HALF SCALE

½" TEMPERED GLASS
STRIP FLOORING
RADIANT HEAT PACKAGE
SEALANT
NEOPRENE PAD
1 x ¾" GLAZING CHANNEL
SOLID TREATED SILL
(LIFT + DROP GLAZING)
LCC FLASHING
¾" T&G DECKING
2x10 BEYOND
C 9x20, PAINTED

G GABLE FIXED GLASS SILL
HALF SCALE

½" FIXED GLASS
SEE J/A10 FOR ROOFING PACKAGE
SEALANT
1" x ¾" GLAZING ANGLE
NEOPRENE PAD
TURN UP FLASHING INSIDE OF
GLASS
1x PAINTED PINE
(REMOVABLE GLAZING STOP)
⅛" REVEAL
DO NOT FILL
J-BEAD
VAPOR BARRIER
½" GWB / CEMENT BOARD @
TILE SURFACES

F EXTERIOR ELEVATION @ M. BATH
3" = 1'-0"

END OF FIBERGLASS
SHINGLES
LCC FASCIA
LCC ROOF (SLOPING)
1x4 SHIPLAP CEDAR
END OF FIXED
GLASS (M)
PAINTED WOOD
BEYOND
SLIDER
JAMB
BEYOND

D PROJECTING END WALL @ M.BATH + GUEST HOUSE END
1½" = 1'-0"

SEE A-A10 FOR ROOFING/
FASCIA PACKAGE
½" FIXED GLASS
LCC FLAT-SEAM ROOFING
OVER BITUTHENE
SEE F/A10
FOR HEIGHT
ELEVATION
¾" T&G PLY, PAINT
@ M. BATH, CARPET
@ GUEST LOFT
1x4 SHIPLAP CEDAR,
BUILDING PAPER
OVER ⅝" CDX.
VAPOR BARRIER, TYP.
½" GWB, TYP
CEMENT BOARD @
BATH TILE
¼" REVEAL @ BASE

C END WALL SOLID PARTITION @ STUDIO
1½" = 1'-0"

SEE A-A10 FOR ROOFING/
FASCIA PACKAGE
1x4 SHIPLAP CEDAR
BUILDING PAPER
⅝" CDX
3½" BATT INSULATION
½" GWB
VAPOR BARRIER
NO RADIANT HEAT @
STUDIO. REPLACE W/
UNDERLAYMENT.
¼" REVEAL @ BASE, TYP

B END WALL FIXED GLASS
1½" = 1'-0"

SEE A A10 FOR ROOFING/
FASCIA PACKAGE
¾"x 1" SLOT FOR FIXED
GLASS, TYP.
2½" MIN. CLEAR
½" TEMPERED GLASS
STANDARD VERTICAL
CONNECTION PLATE
CONC. COLUMN
C 9x20, TYP. PAINTED

A END WALL FIXED GLASS @ ENTRY
1½" = 1'-0"

FIBERGLASS SHINGLES
30# ROOFING FELT
LCC FLASHING / FASCIA
1x RAKE BOARD
(TREATED)
2x6 BLOCKING + ⅝" CDX
AT ANGLED GLASS WALL ONLY
C 6x4 x ⅜ PAINTED
1½"x½" REVEAL, TYP @ ALL COLUMNS
1x6 PAINTED PINE CEILING
EDGE OF ANGLED GLASS BEYOND
½" TEMPERED GLASS
¾"x 1" GLAZING ANGLE
UNDER FINISH FLOOR
ECCENTRIC VERTICAL
CONNECTION PLATE @
ENTRY BAY
¾" DECKING
EXTERIOR
TREATED LATTICE
SPACERS
CONT. LCC FLASHING.
TURN UP BEHIND GLAZING
ANGLE
CONT. BITUTHENE
SLOPE ¼"/ FOOT
TO CENTER RIDGE
ALIGN
TREATED FRAMING
LCC FLASHING / FASCIA
C 9x20 TYP
½" ACX, PAINTED
SCREW IN PLACE

RIGHT: *View of south façade*

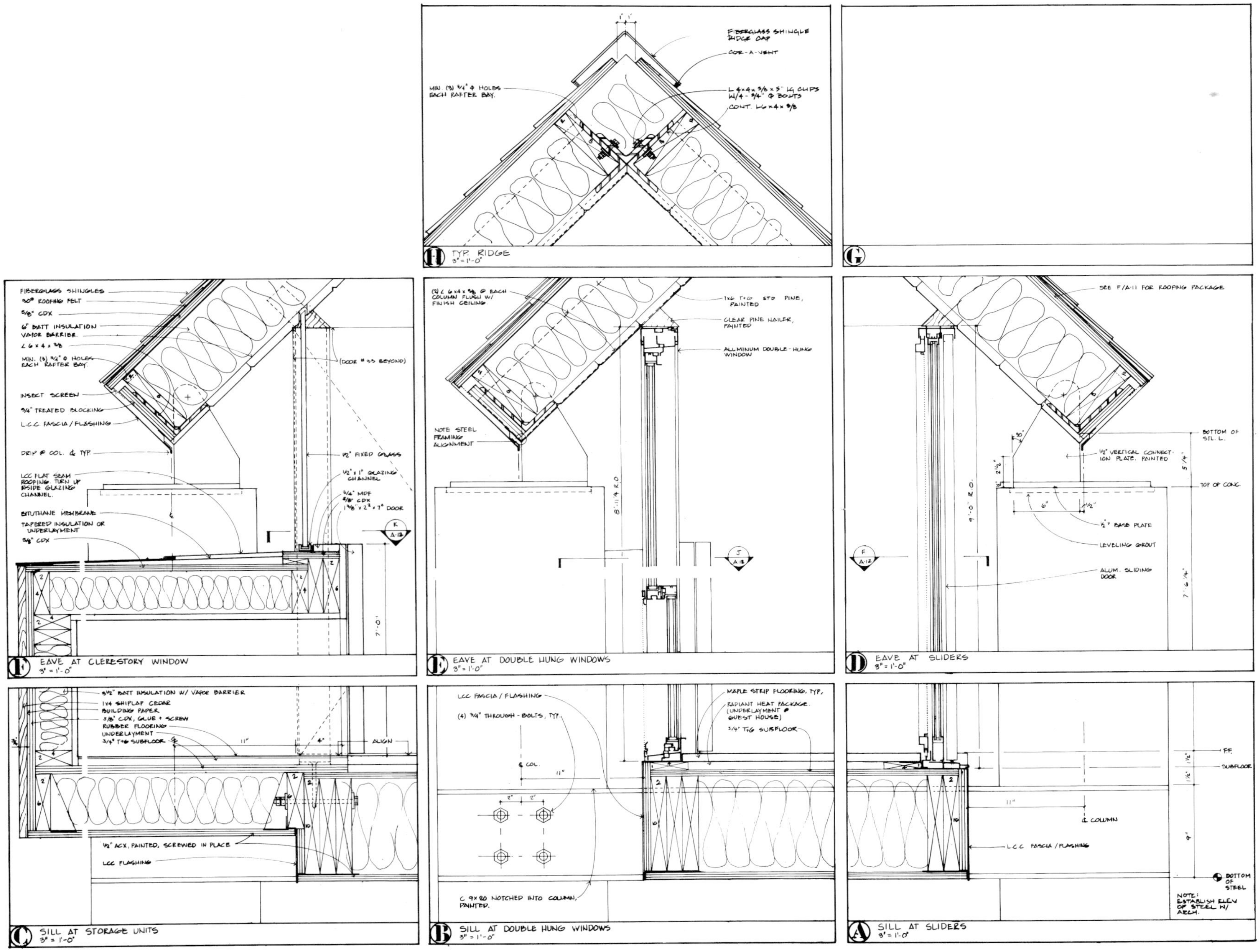

H TYP. RIDGE
3" = 1'-0"

G

I EAVE AT CLERESTORY WINDOW
3" = 1'-0"

J EAVE AT DOUBLE HUNG WINDOWS
3" = 1'-0"

D EAVE AT SLIDERS
3" = 1'-0"

C SILL AT STORAGE UNITS
3" = 1'-0"

B SILL AT DOUBLE HUNG WINDOWS
3" = 1'-0"

A SILL AT SLIDERS
3" = 1'-0"

Moore House _1986_

ALFREDO DE VIDO ARCHITECT

Owner: Richard and Noriko Moore
Architect: Alfredo De Vido Architect, New York, New York
Interior Design: Alfredo De Vido, Richard and Noriko Moore
Design Collaborators: Richard and Noriko Moore
Engineer: Paul Gossen (structural)
General Contractor: Richard Moore
Photography: Norman McGrath

Site: Lakeville, Connecticut
Program: Earth-sheltered weekend and vacation house including 2 bedrooms, 2 bathrooms, living room, dining room, kitchen, studio, and porch.
Square Footage: 2400
Structural System: Fieldstone-clad concrete retaining wall with parapet wall to support earth-covered roof.
Mechanical System: Oil-burning forced-air system and radiant heat system to warm slate floor. No air conditioning system is needed.
Major Exterior Materials: Fieldstone (walls), glass, native grasses and wildflowers.
Major Interior Materials: Oak, sandblasted concrete, slate.
Furnishings and Storage: Stickley (armchairs), Giovanni Bollini (dining room chairs); designed by architect and fabricated by Richard Moore (built-ins, cabinets, and vanities).
Doors and Hardware: Custom by architect; Baldwin
Windows: Pella Windows
Fixtures: Noriko Moore (lighting baffle)
Appliances and Equipment: GE, Sub-Zero (refrigerator)
Cost: $150 per square foot

Site

The owners preferred that the house be designed to disturb the five-acre lot as little as possible, and nestled within the land rather than on top of it. They decided on an energy efficient earth-sheltered house overlooking a pond.

Site plan

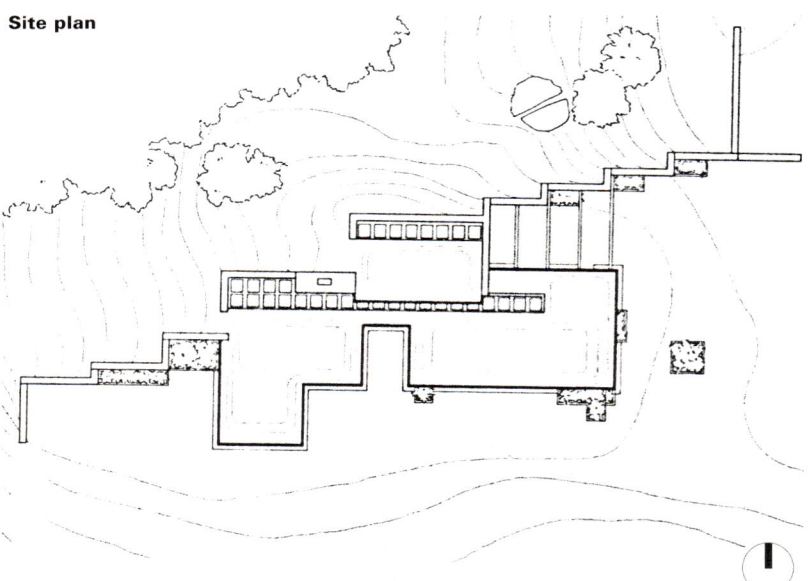

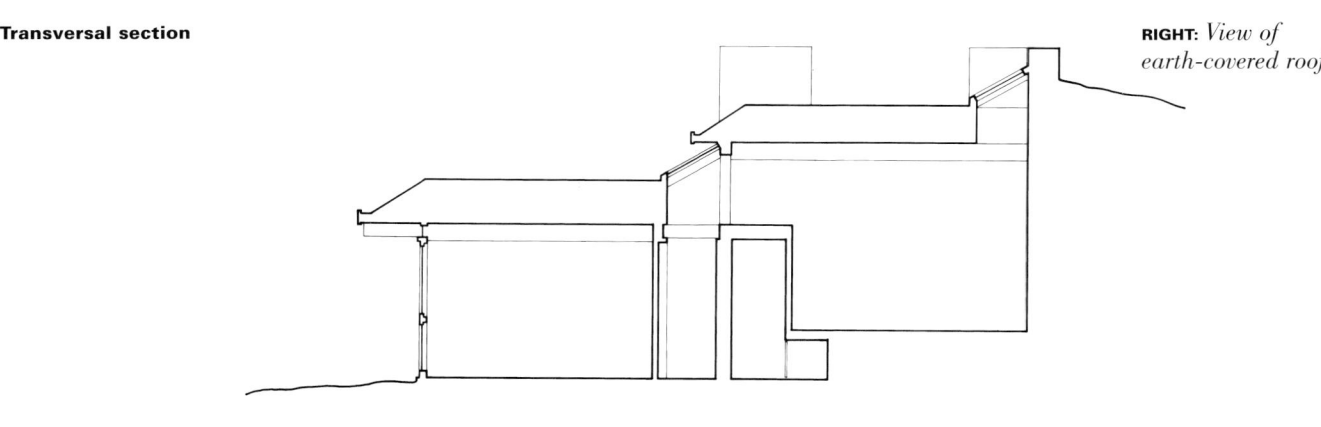

Design

The 2400-square-foot house is arranged along a sixty-foot-long east-west corridor that divides living spaces from the garage, entry court, and studio. All the rooms except the studio face south off the spine. A two-car garage occupies the northeast corner of the site.

Important design considerations were the proportion of walls and the balance between glass areas and spaces behind them. Small glass strips were fitted between beams to continue the extensive window areas below and to merge the inside of the house with the outside. The interior palette reflects the exterior as well, with its red oak posts and beams, stock pine casement windows and trim, cherry parquet floors, and ceilings and parapets surfaced with cedar and slate. Some of the materials were taken from the site itself: old fieldstone walls provided material for facing, and mature red oak trees on the property were selectively cut and seasoned to provide posts and beams.

Light along the central corridor spans was brought into the potentially dark rear of the house through a long row of skylights, thirty-three in all. The open skylights siphon warm air up and out on warm days, keeping the air circulating. Windows are sheltered from the sun by an overhang.

Construction

The structural aspects of an earth-sheltered house are important. Roof loads can get up to 250 lbs. per square foot (versus 35 lbs. per square foot for conventional construction.) Shear stresses (loads that cause a horizontal beam to break vertically) are a paramount consideration. Connections and bearing points that are commonly used in house construction are unacceptable. Ordinary nails would shear off, just as bearing plates would compress and deform, resulting in settlement cracks and ruptures in joints between materials. Because loads of this magnitude can pose a safety threat, a highly qualified structural engineer designed heavier connections, bearing points, and a roof structure. The north retaining wall was specially reinforced.

The architect's modular system was based on a three-foot, four-inch plan unit and stock material vertical unit. Half of the 3-1/4" module combines with a full module to make 5',0", and three modules make ten feet, a useful room dimension. When explained to builders, the module is readily understood as the basis for construction and can be used intuitively.

To build the roof, bentonite, polyethylene, extruded polystyrene, gravel, fabric, and earth form multiple layers over a structure of pressure-treated plywood and 2x6 tongue-and-groove pine decking.

Transversal section

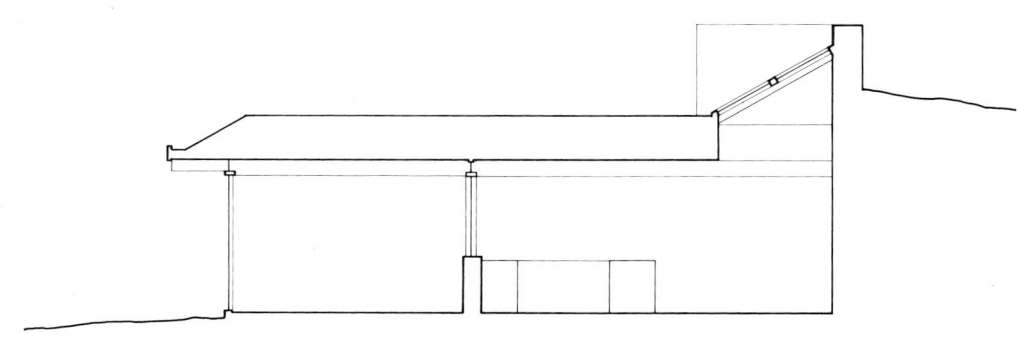

Floor plan

1. ENTRY
2. MASTER BEDROOM
3. MASTER BATHROOM
4. GUEST BEDROOM
5. GUEST BATHROOM
6. LIVING ROOM
7. KITCHEN
8. DINING ROOM
9. STUDIO
10. PORCH

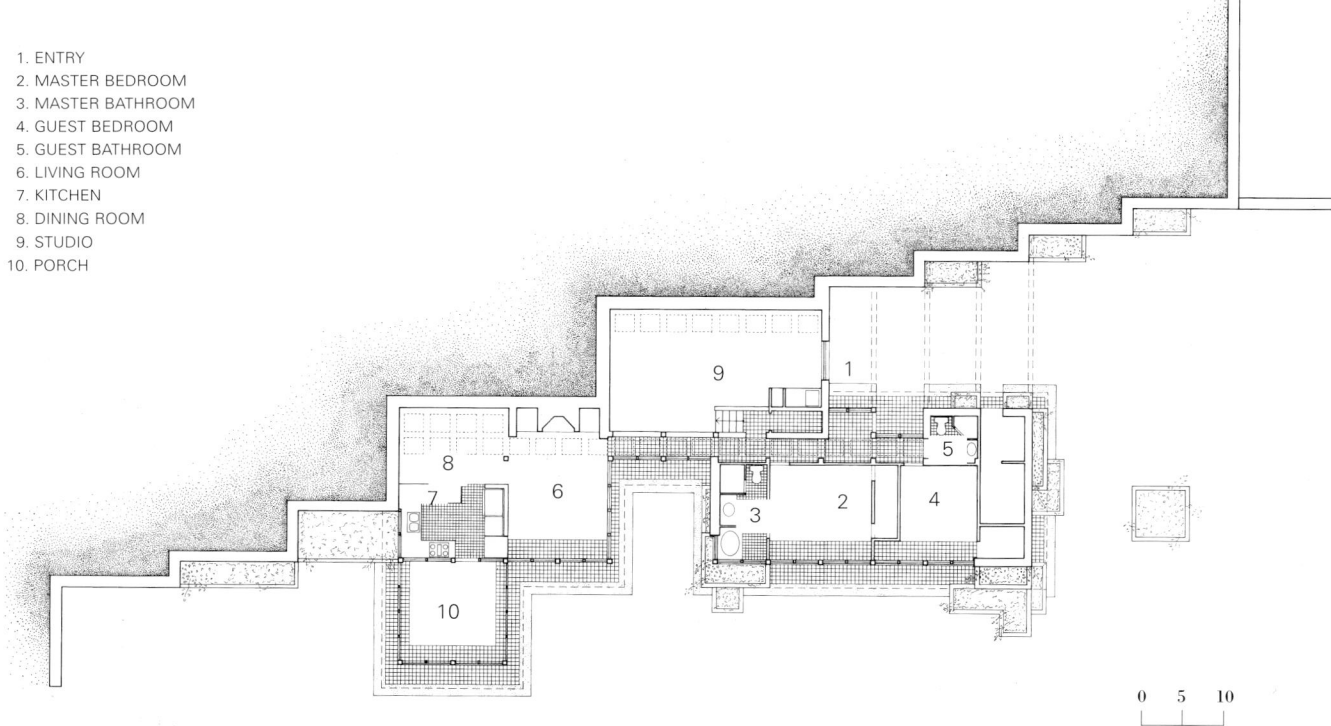

0   5   10

CLOCKWISE FROM TOP: *Living room; bedroom; view of kitchen/dining room from living room*
FACING PAGE: *View from lake*

RIGHT: *View of living room*

Wall, door, window, and screen details

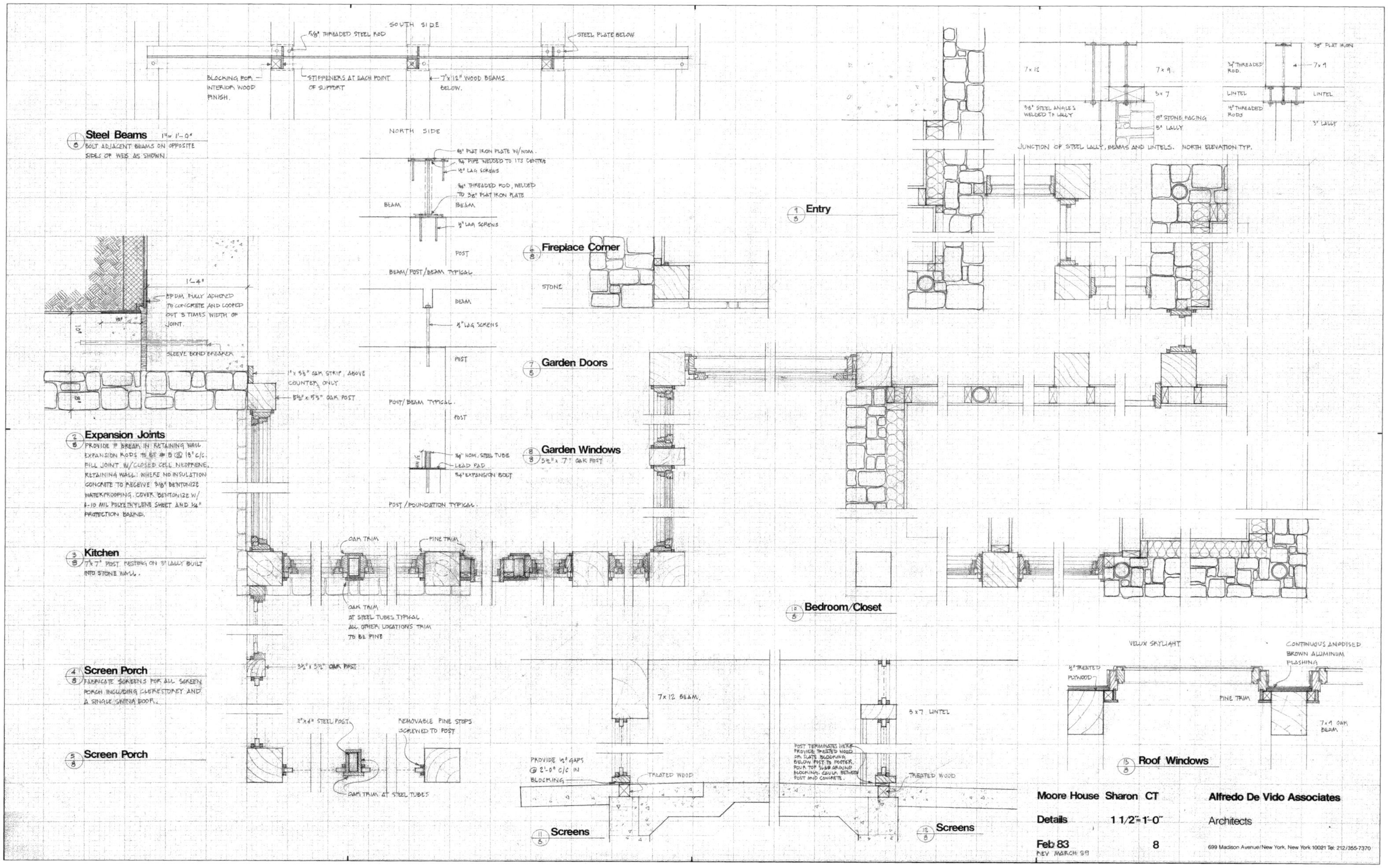

Steel Beams
Expansion Joints
Kitchen
Screen Porch
Screen Porch

Entry
Fireplace Corner
Garden Doors
Garden Windows
Bedroom/Closet
Roof Windows
Screens
Screens

Moore House Sharon, CT

Details   1 1/2"=1'-0"

Feb 83   8
REV. MARCH 8'?

Alfredo De Vido Associates

Architects

699 Madison Avenue/New York, New York 10021 Tel: 212/355-7370

RIGHT: *Hallway*

Roof, wall, and parapet details

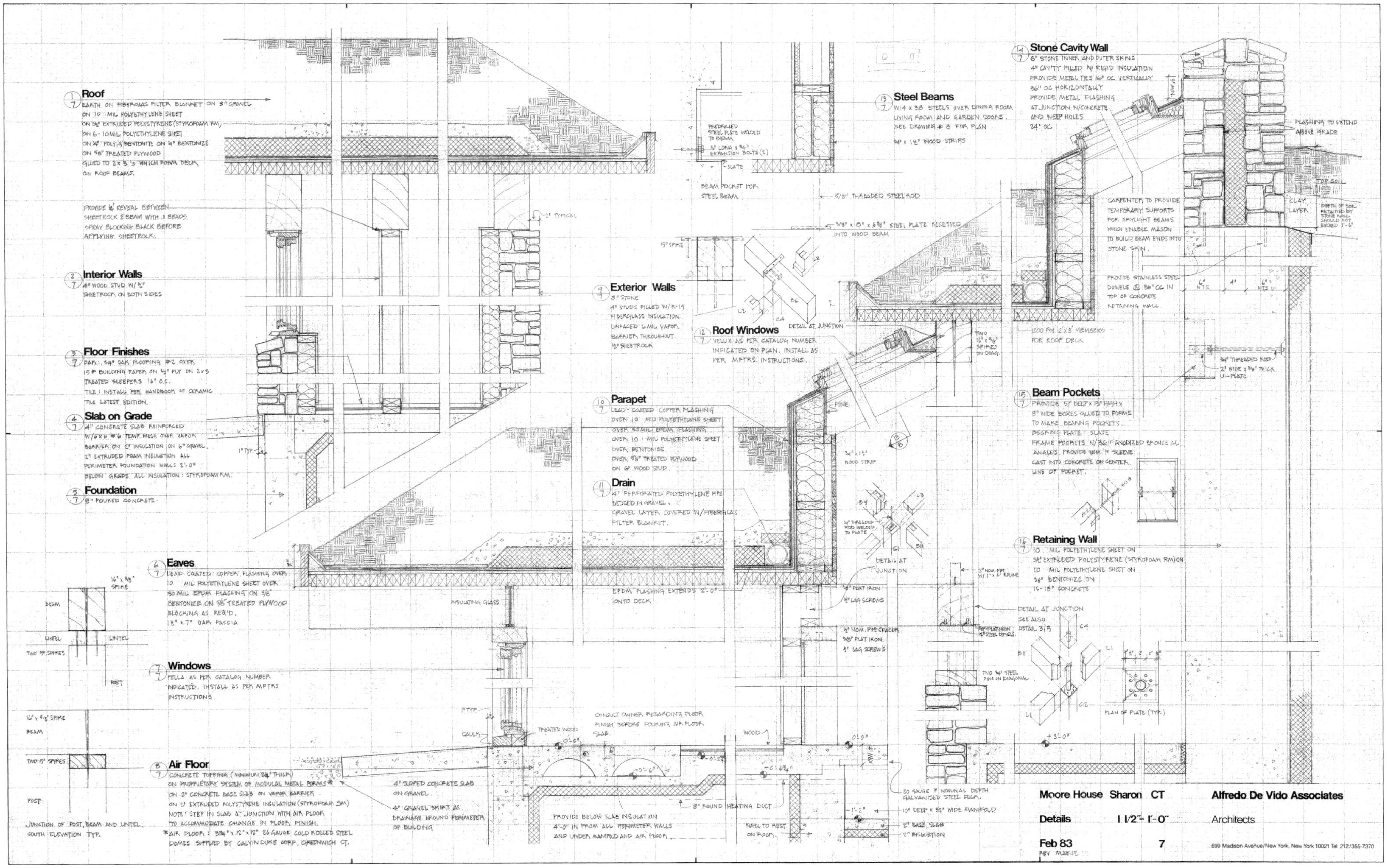

Roof

Interior Walls

Floor Finishes

Slab on Grade

Foundation

Eaves

Windows

Air Floor

Exterior Walls

Parapet

Drain

Stone Cavity Wall

Steel Beams

Roof Windows

Beam Pockets

Retaining Wall

Moore House Sharon CT	Alfredo De Vido Associates
Details 1 1/2"=1'-0"	Architects
Feb 83	7	699 Madison Avenue/New York, New York 10021 Tel. 212/355-7370

T-House 1988-1993

SIMON UNGERS AND TOM KINSLOW

Owner: Lawrence Marcelle
Architect: Simon Ungers and Tom Kinslow
Engineer: Ryan & Biggs Associates, Troy, New York
General Contractors: STS, Inc. (steel shell), Regenerative
Building Construction (interior)
Photography: ©Arch Photo, Inc. Eduard Hueber

Site: Wilton, New York
Program: Residence and 10,000-volume library including
living room, dining room, kitchen, half bathroom, bedroom,
bathroom, mezzanine.
Square Footage: 2500
Structural System: Steel frame with $1/4$" Cor-ten steel plating
(exterior), wood frame with 2' modular plywood panels (interior)
Mechanical System: Forced air
Major Exterior Materials: $1/4$" Cor-ten steel plating
(walls and roofs)
Major Interior Materials: Veneered plywood panels
(walls and ceilings), steel grating (stairs, mezzanine, shelving),
stainless steel (kitchen and bathroom fixtures).
Furnishings and Storage: Built in by architect.
Doors and Hardware: Hope hardware
Windows: Hope steel frame
Fixtures: Industrial (bathrooms)
Appliances and Equipment: Stainless steel
Cost: Withheld at owner's request.

Site
Located on a rural property adjacent to a former gravel
pit in upstate New York, the house is situated on a
southward sloping site with a view of the Berkshire
Mountains. The residential part of the house is oriented
east-west; the library north-south.

Design
The program stipulated a clear separation of living
(residence) and working (library) areas. The configuration of the building translates the programmatic
requirement into a singular, "plastic" form that
articulates the division of the two main spaces. The
perpendicular juxtaposition of the two spaces subordi-
nates the residence to the library, with the entry hall
acting as a connecting, transitional space.

Each space is developed according to specific functional
and topographic conditions. The residence, partially
imbedded in the ground, is a linear horizontal space
where individual areas are defined by core elements
(kitchen, chimney, and bathroom).

The library, a double-story space, is situated to take
advantage of the surrounding views and natural light.
Repetitive eight-foot-high openings at two-foot intervals
surround the entire reading/working area, providing a
segmented panoramic view. To protect the books from

any direct exposure to sunlight, the shelving and mezzanine are suspended within the solid upper half. The shelving system, an independent steel structure that includes a wrap-around mezzanine, is suspended from the ceiling to create a column-free reading/working space.

To further articulate the difference between spaces, the fenestration in the living quarters is conceptually and spatially the reverse of the library. Light in both spaces is controlled by an interior shutter system. The shutters are part of a two-foot modular panel system that, when shut, creates a continuous, uninterrupted interior.

Construction

The building's construction is a double shell system of steel and wood in which the materials are structurally independent of each other to account for the varying rates of expansion. The exterior shell, a steel frame clad in $1/4$-inch weathering steel plate (seam welded and ground) was pre-fabricated as six individual parts and assembled on site. The result is a seamless, monolithic structure without differentiation of vertical and horizontal surfaces. Because the shell requires no expansion joints, a homogenous, maintenance-free surface is achieved.

The interior is a wood frame with $3/4$-inch tongue and groove plywood veneer panels. Unlike the exterior, the interior deliberately emphasizes the construction. The library shelving, mezzanine, stairs, and windows are all black enamel steel. Steel grating was used for the shelving, mezzanine, and stairs to create a maximum of visual transparency. The kitchen and bathroom fixtures are stainless steel components selected from prison and commercial supplies.

Site plan

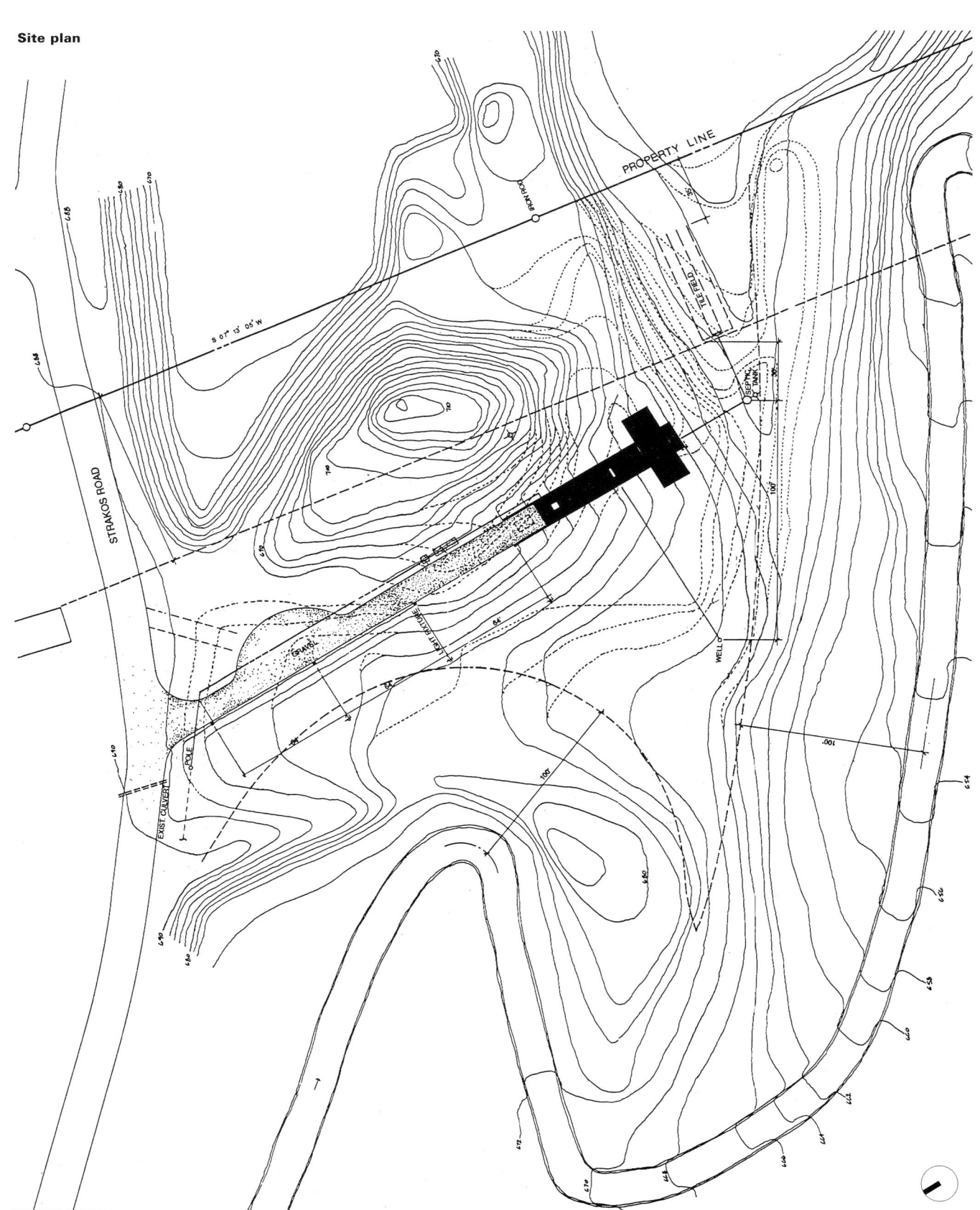

Library level floor plan

Longitudinal section

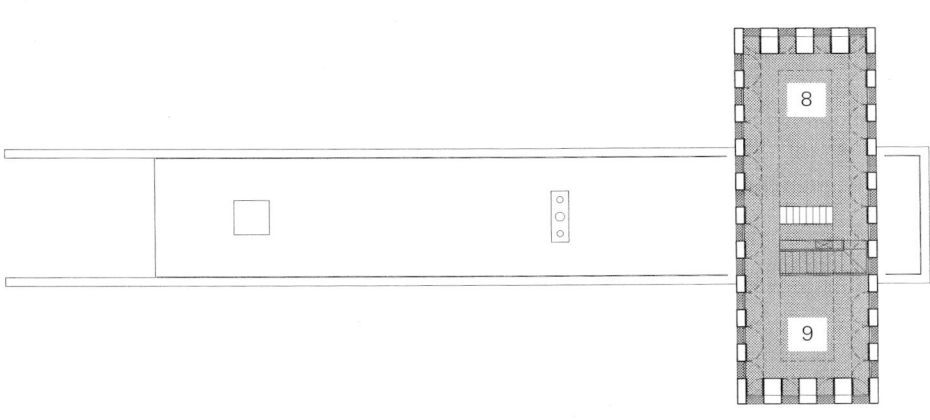
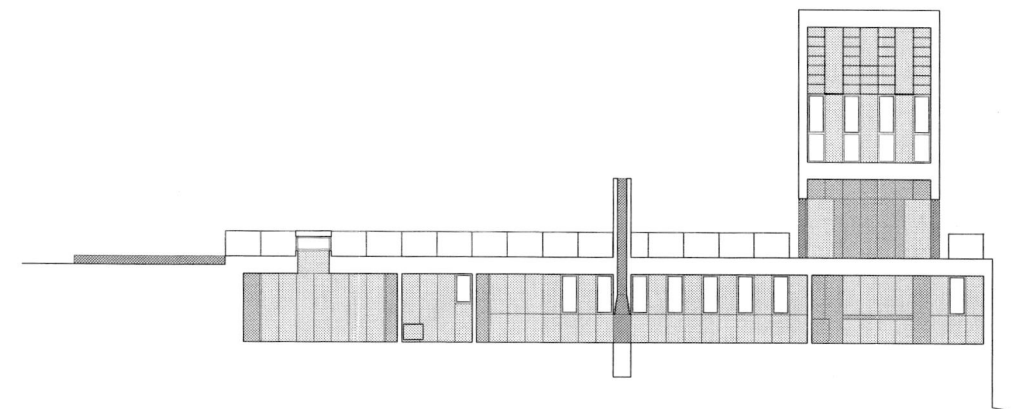

Roof/terrace level floor plan

Longitudinal section

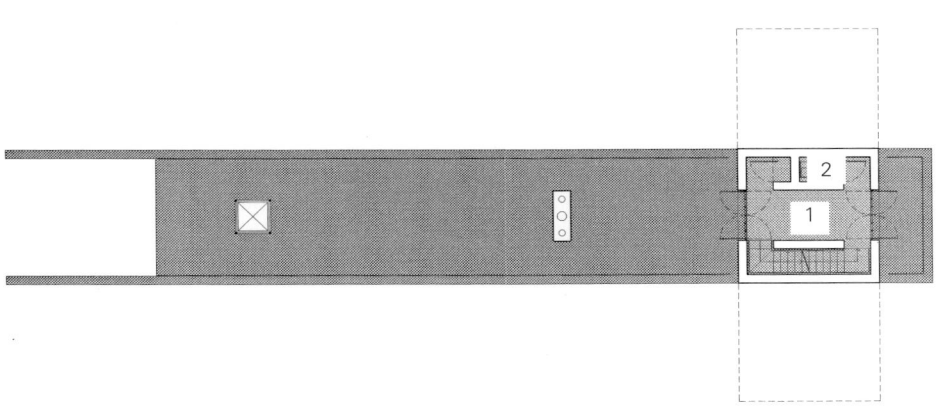
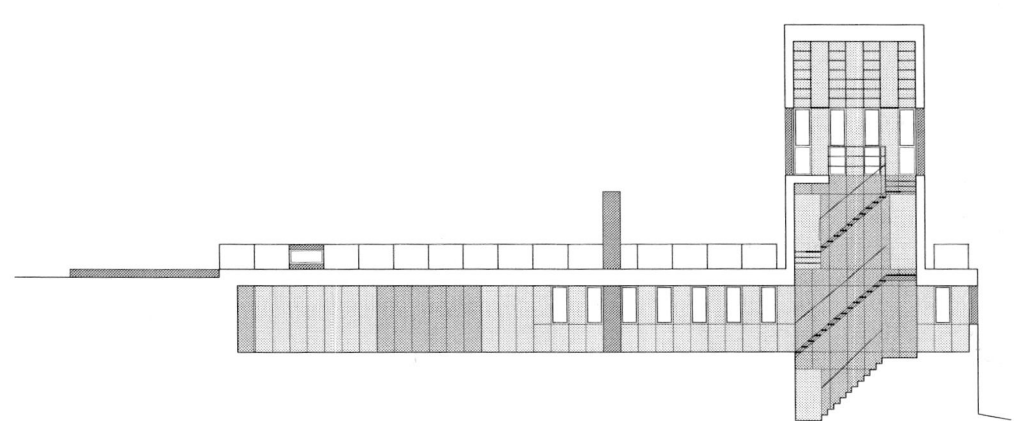

Lower level floor plan

Transversal section

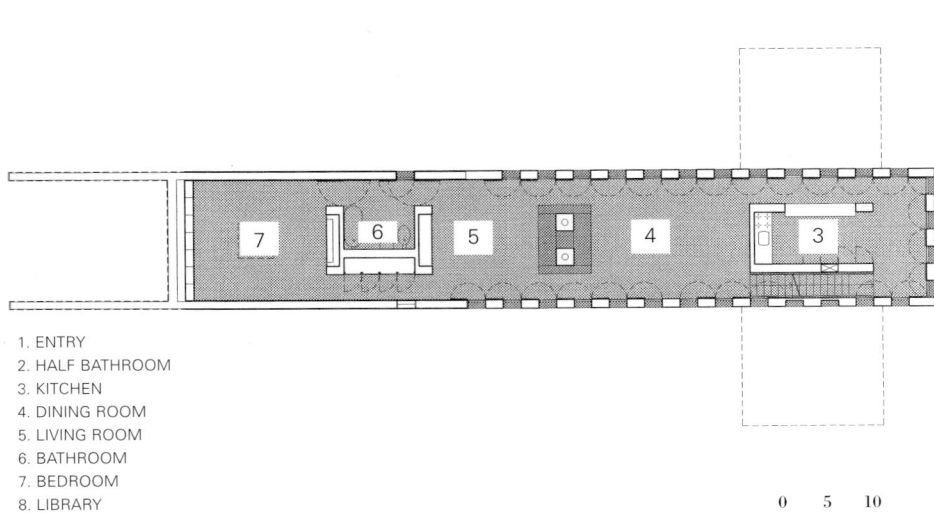

1. ENTRY
2. HALF BATHROOM
3. KITCHEN
4. DINING ROOM
5. LIVING ROOM
6. BATHROOM
7. BEDROOM
8. LIBRARY
9. MEZZANINE

0   5   10

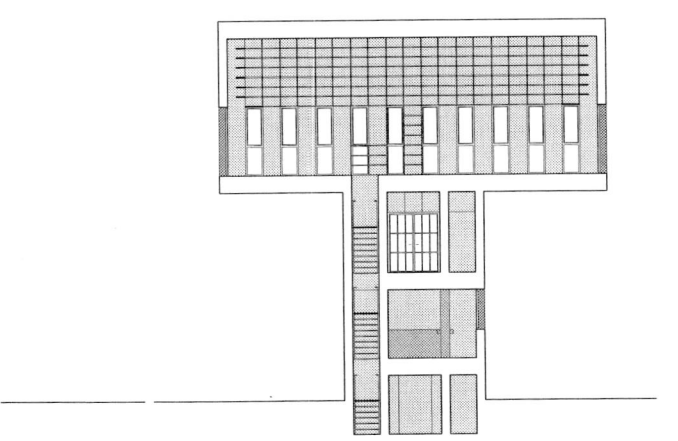

LEFT: *Living room*
MIDDLE: *Kitchen*
BOTTOM: *Bathroom*
FACING PAGE: *Bedroom*

Window detail

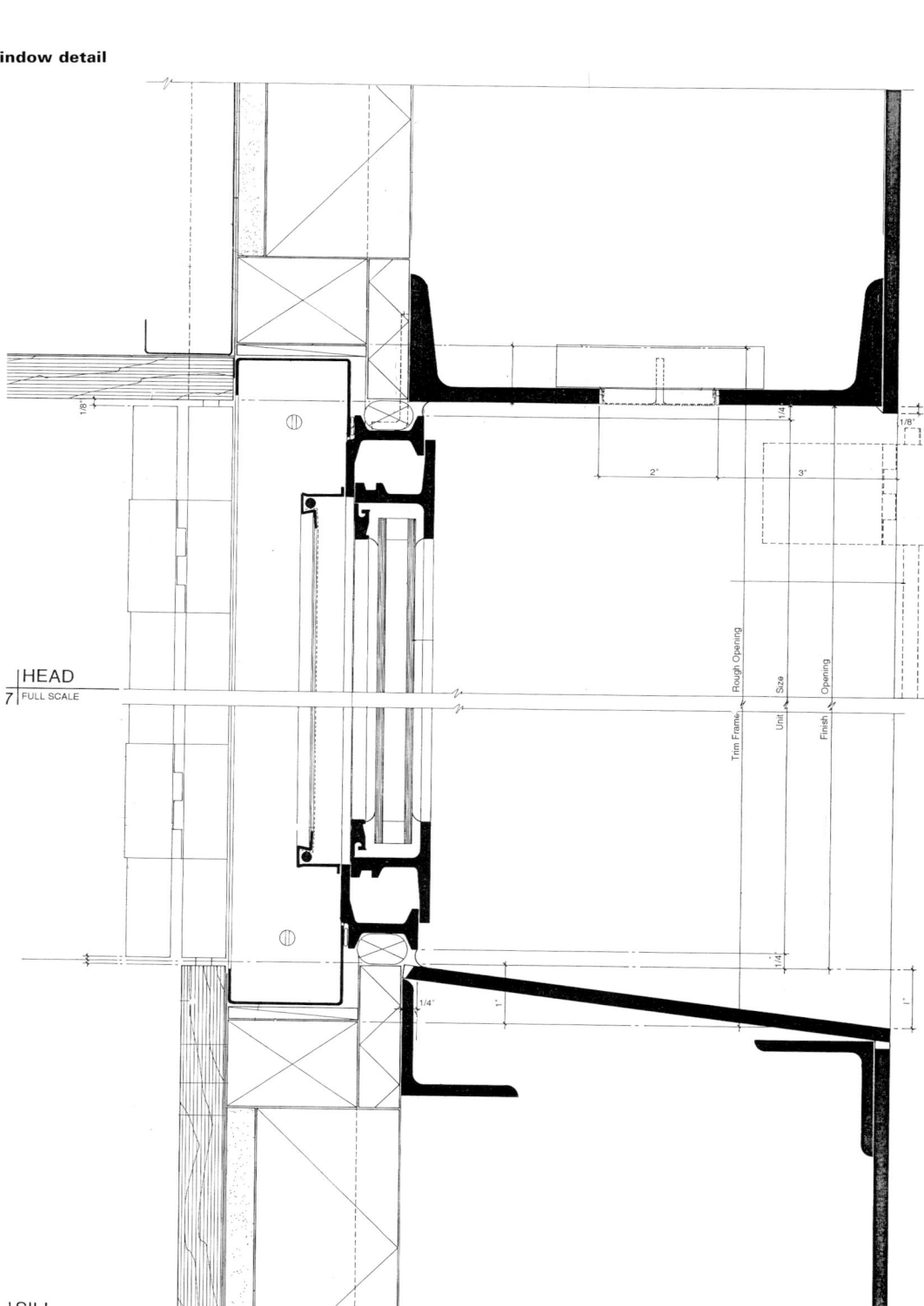

HEAD
7 | FULL SCALE

SILL
FULL SCALE

Dumb waiter details

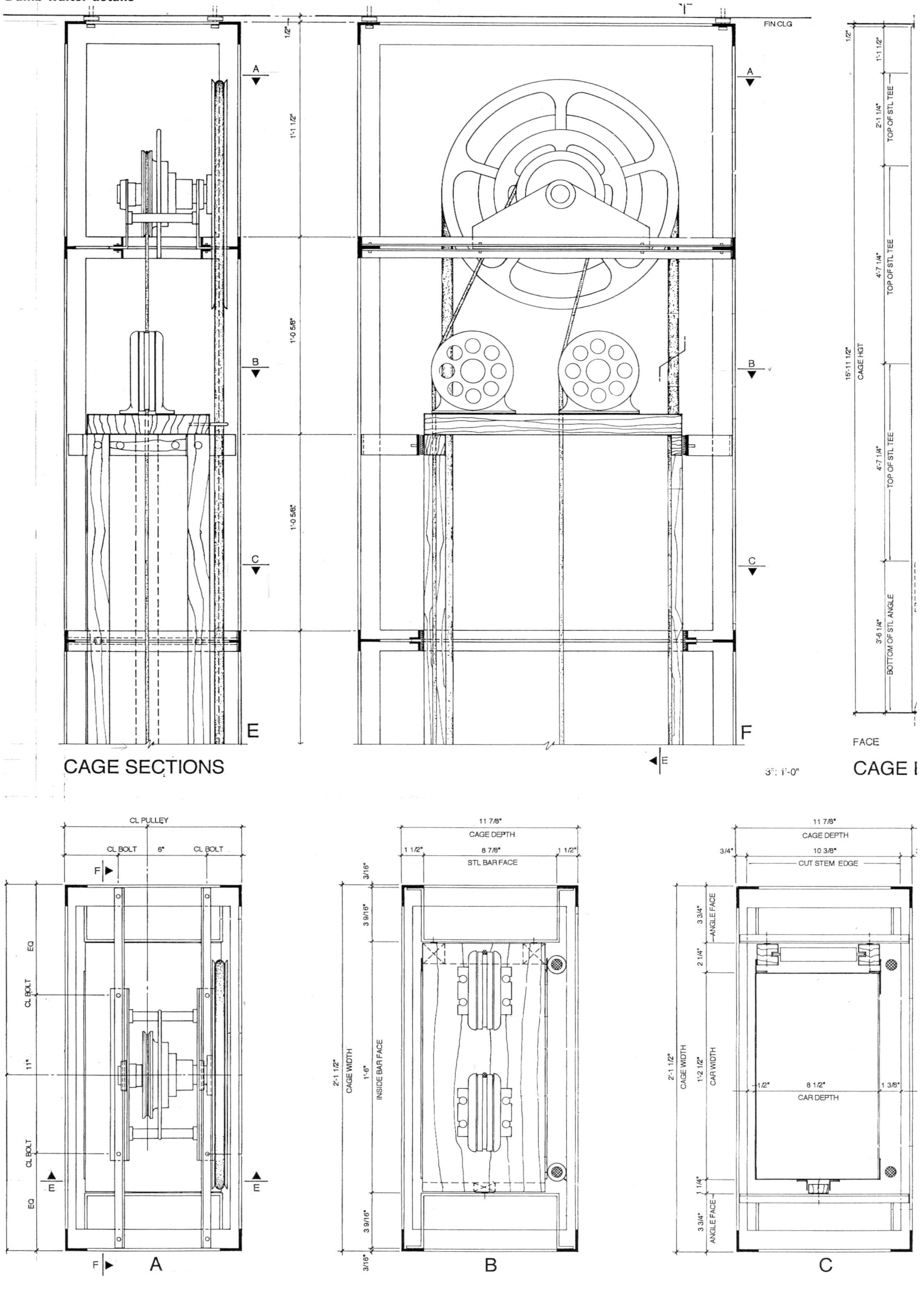

CAGE SECTIONS

CAGE [

FIN CLG

1/2"

1'-1 1/2"

1'-0 5/8"

1'-0 5/8"

A

B

C

E

A

B

C

E

F

FACE

3": 1'-0"

1/2"

1'-1 1/2"

2'-1 1/4"   TOP OF STL TEE

4'-7 1/4"   TOP OF STL TEE

4'-7 1/4"   TOP OF STL TEE

15'-11 1/2"   CAGE HGT

3'-6 1/4"   BOTTOM OF STL ANGLE

A

CL PULLEY

CL BOLT   6"   CL BOLT

F

EQ

CL BOLT

11"

CL BOLT

EQ

E

F

B

11 7/8"

CAGE DEPTH

1 1/2"   8 7/8"   1 1/2"

STL BAR FACE

3/16"

3 9/16"

2'-1 1/2"   CAGE WIDTH   1'-6"   INSIDE BAR FACE

3 9/16"

3/16"

C

11 7/8"

CAGE DEPTH

3/4"   10 3/8"

CUT STEM EDGE

3 3/4"   ANGLE FACE

2 1/4"

2'-1 1/2"   CAGE WIDTH   1 1/2"   CAR WIDTH

1/2"   8 1/2"   1 3/8"

CAR DEPTH

1 1/4"

3 3/4"   ANGLE FACE

New York City House *1994-1996*
TOD WILLIAMS BILLIE TSIEN AND ASSOCIATES

Owner: Name withheld at owner's request.
Architect: Tod Williams Billie Tsien and Associates, New York, New York
Associate Architect: Schuman Lichtenstein Claman Efron Architects, Peter Claman (partner), Richard DeMarco (project architect), Pio Graiff (job captain).
Design Team: Tod Williams (partner), Billie Tsien (partner), Vivian Wang (project architect), Peter Arnold, Christopher Haynes, Matthew Pickner, Marianne Shin.
Engineers: The Cantor Seinuk Group P.C. (structural), Cosentini Associates (mechanical)
Consultants: Cerami and Associates (acoustical), Electronic Systems Associates (security), Home Entertainment Design (A/V), Israel Berger and Associates (window wall), Plant Specialists (landscape), Richard Shaver (lighting).
General Contractor: Robert Anderson, Turner Interiors
Photography: Michael Moran

Site: New York, New York
Program: Single-family residence including pool, exercise area, play area, half bathroom laundry, dining room, gallery, kitchen, pantry, family room, library, study, living room, wet bar, 4 bedrooms, 6 bathrooms, master bedroom and bathroom, dressing area.
Square Footage: 13,760
Structural System: Steel beams spanning existing party walls
Mechanical System: Central 30-ton chilled water system, J192 J4 air handling units, circulating hot water heating system, DX system for pool.
Major Exterior Materials: Indiana limestone, Kynar painted aluminum window wall, Dryvit, bluestone paving, Jet Mist granite paving.
Major Interior Materials: Cherry (cabinetwork and floors), kirkstone (floors and countertops), Pietra del Cardoso (wall tile, hearths, and countertops), Chiampo Rosata (wall tile and hearth), Jura Beige (wall tile), glass tile, skim coat plastered gypsum wall board (walls and ceilings), glass, (rails, light shields, and light monitor).
Furnishings and Storage: Custom by architect, V'soske (custom carpets fabricator)
Doors and Hardware: Custom by architect, Modern Industries Architectural Woodworking (cherry doors fabricator), Coordinated Metals Incorporated (muntz clad doors fabricator), Omnia Industries (lever handles), SOSS (hinges).
Windows: Lynbrook Glass and Architectural Metals (fabricator front and rear kynar painted aluminum window walls)
Fixtures: American Standard (bathrooms), Kohler (bathrooms), D-Line (miscellaneous bathroom accessories), Baldwin, Dornbracht, Speakman, Newport Brass Inc., Grohe, Hansgrohe.
Appliances and Equipment: Sub-Zero (refrigerator/freezer), Wine Enthusiast (wine cellar), Kitchen Aid (dishwasher), GE (washer/dryer and microwave), Garland (range), In-Sink-Erator (hot water dispenser), Superior (prefabricated fireplace), Mr. Steam (steam unit).
Cost: Withheld at owner's request

Site
This new single-family townhouse is compressed into the 34' x 100' footprint of two demolished brownstones on a

Rendering of street façade

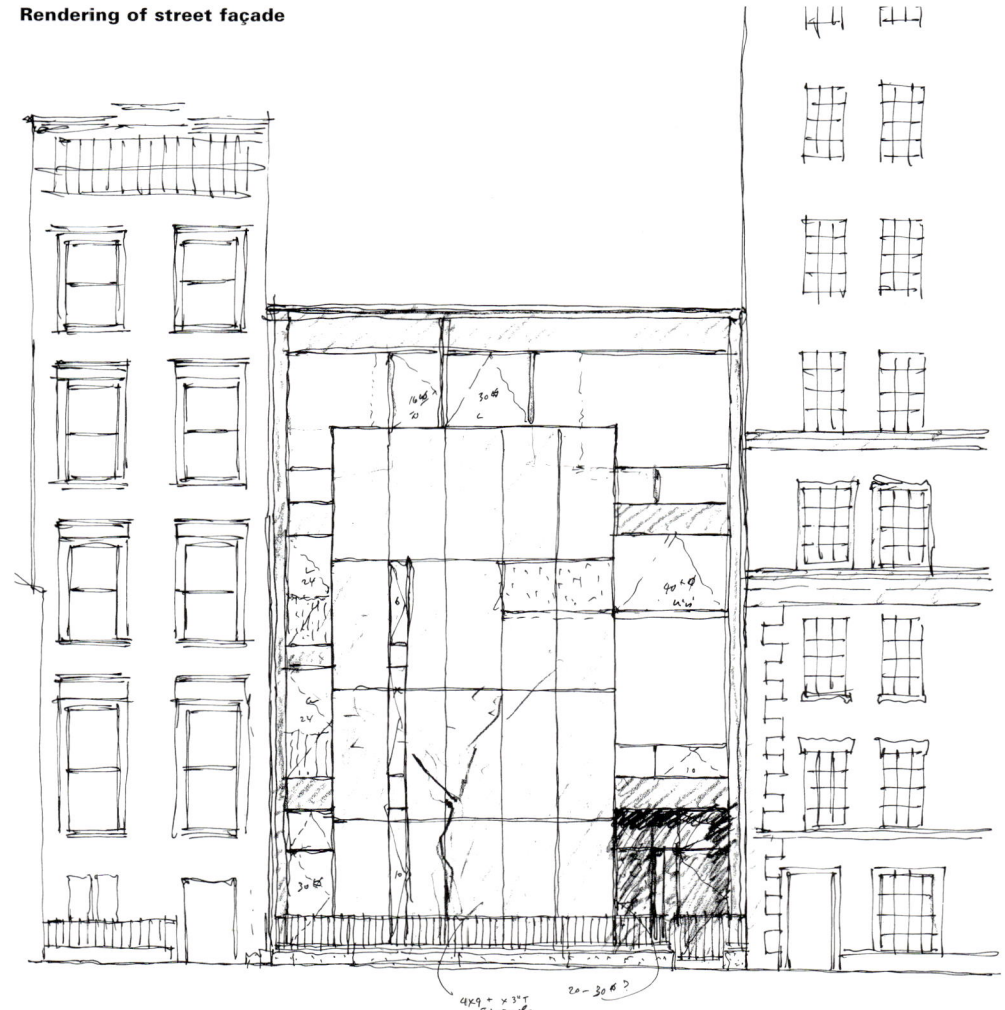

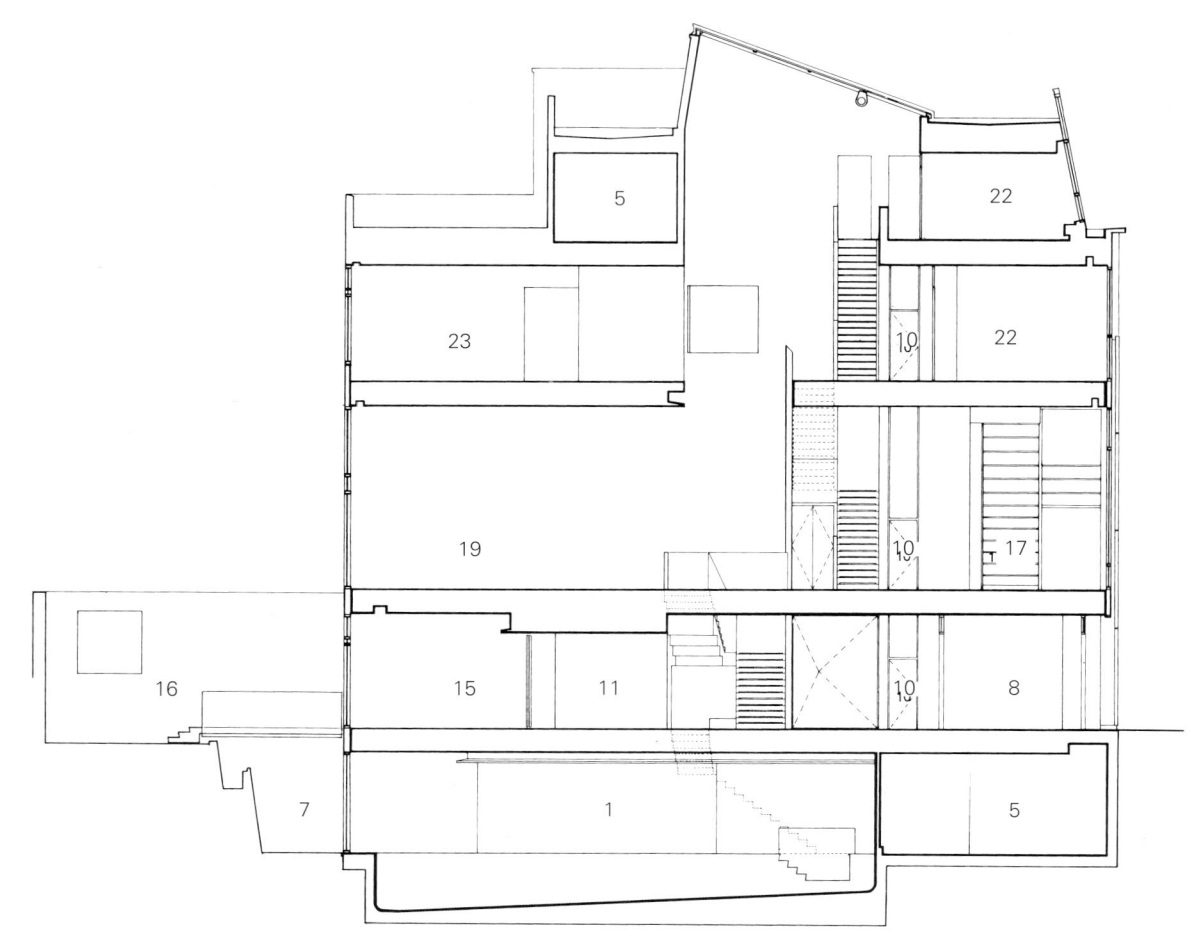

block within the dense urban fabric of Manhattan. Sandwiched between a five-story brownstone on one side and an eighteen-story apartment building on the other, the new townhouse's other neighbors are predominantly fifteen-story apartment buildings, with the occasional 19th-century brownstone and thirty-story tower.

Design

In response to the scale of the more intimate buildings and the private nature of the program, the central element in the quiet composition of the façade is a hammered limestone wall around which are composed translucent and transparent windows. The wall provides a sense of protection and privacy from the street while it also connects the structure to the surroundings through material and scale. The composition of glass surrounding this stone wall isolates and abstracts it as it brings filtered light to the rooms within. The rear façade, made mostly of glass and facing a 30' x 30' back garden, is related in its composition to the front of the house.

Inside, a monumental wall of gypsum wall board echoes the limestone façade and defines the vertical movement. Organization of spaces is clear and logical: the pool is in the cellar, family spaces, kitchen, and dining room are on the ground floor, and the living room, study, and library are on the second (double-height) floor. The guest room is located on a mezzanine level, parents' and children's rooms are on the third level, and staff rooms are on the top floor.

To encourage vertical circulation by foot rather than elevator in this six-floor house and to flood the interior with light, a large skylight illuminates the stairway from the basement level to the top floor, permitting a clear view of the sky from the pool on the lowermost level.

Construction

The construction consists of a steel frame on concrete block with poured in place concrete floor slabs. Gypsum wall board is on steel studs with full skim coat.

Transversal section

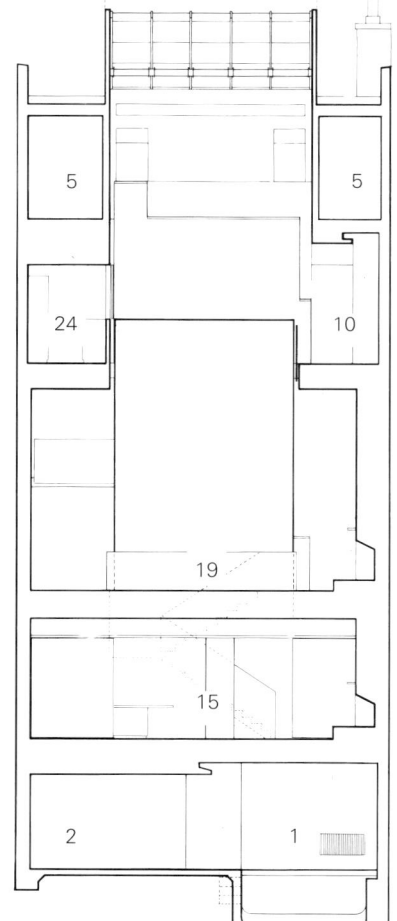

1. POOL
2. EXERCISE AREA
3. PLAY AREA
4. LAUNDRY
5. MECHANICAL
6. STORAGE
7. LOWER GARDEN
8. ENTRY VESTIBULE
9. DINING ROOM
10. GALLERY
11. HALL
12. WALK-IN CLOSET
13. KITCHEN
14. PANTRY
15. FAMILY ROOM
16. GARDEN
17. LIBRARY
18. STUDY
19. LIVING ROOM
20. WET BAR
21. BALCONY
22. BEDROOM
23. MASTER BEDROOM
24. DRESSING AREA

Second level floor plan

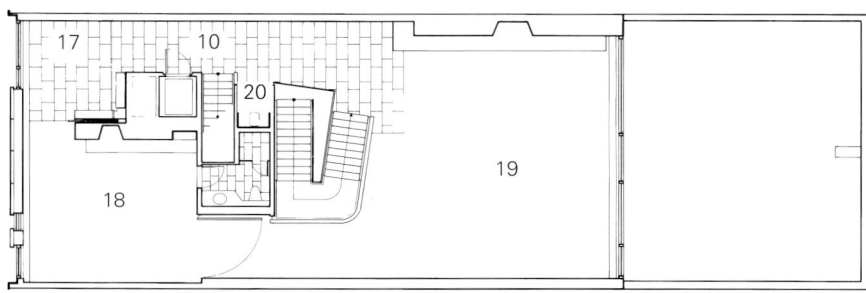

Fourth level floor plan

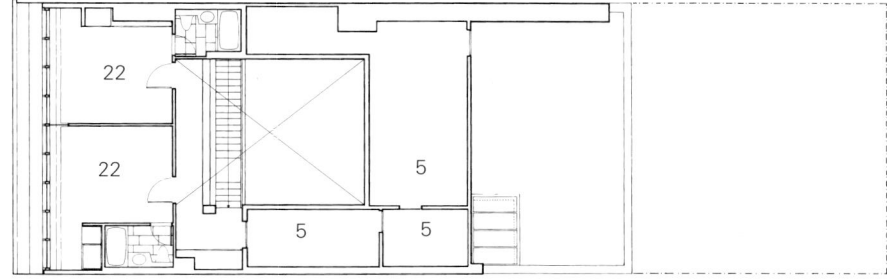

Ground level floor plan

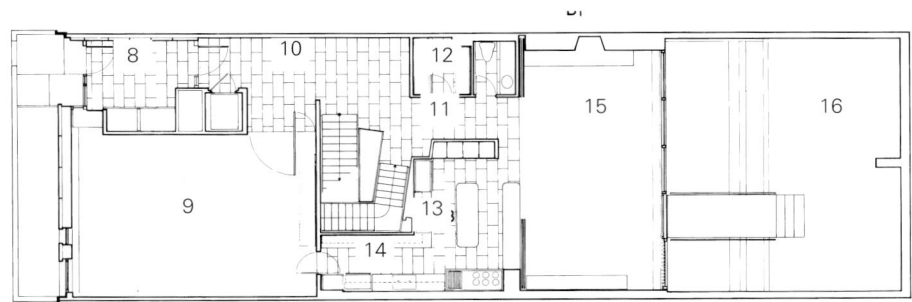

Third level floor plan

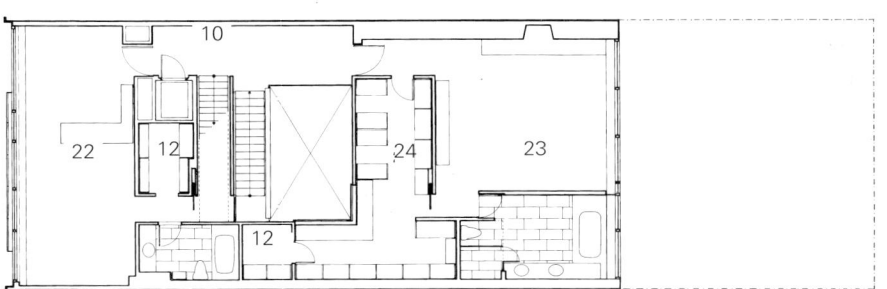

Lower level floor plan

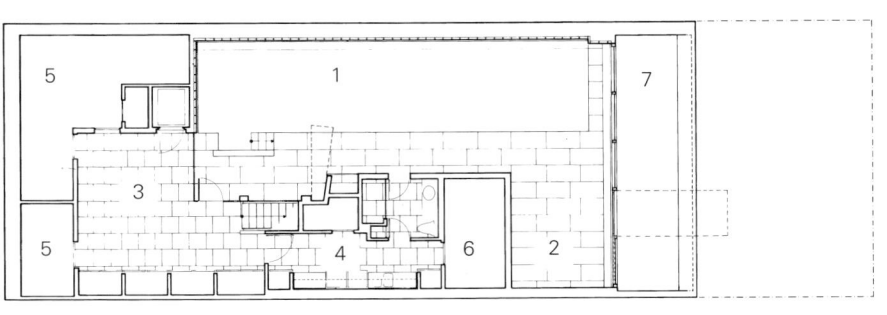

Second level mezzanine

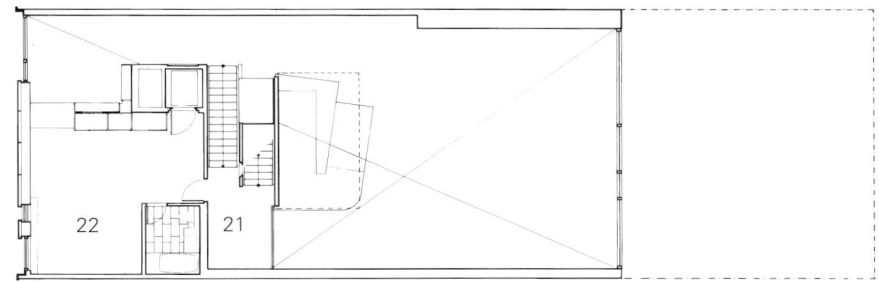

0   5   10

SOLID BLACK CHERRY, WAXED, HANDRAIL

+ 3'-0" ABOVE NOSING
T.O. RAIL

+ 2'-10" ABOVE NOSING
T.O. RAIL.

12"

1/2" DIAM.

1" DIAM.

ELEVATION AT END OF HANDRAIL, TYP.

BEAD BLASTED ST. STL., OILED, BENT THREADED STEM w/ THREADED ROD + SPANNER CAP HANDRAIL SUPPORT

1/2" THK. TEMPERED GLASS

NEOPRENE STRIP w/ COMPRESSIBLE RUBBER FILL, CONT.

1/4" THK. ST. STL. 'T' CONT. REVEAL @ STAIR TREADS + RISERS. BLK'G AS REQ'D.

STONE TREAD MUDSET ON STEEL PAN

1/16" 2"

3/8"

4"

1/4"

1"

MTL RISER PAN BEYOND

STL SUPPORTING ANGLE WELDED TO MTL. PAN + STRINGER

STL STRINGER, STL ANGLE + STL BACKPLATE, WELDED CONNECTIONS.

ST. STL. STUD, THREADED, WELDED TO STL. BACKPLATE

3"

ST. STL. COLLARED WASHER 1/4" THK, 2" DIAM., TYP.

NEOPRENE, COLOR T.B.D. TYP @ ALL GLASS CONNECTIONS.

ST. STL. SPANNER CAP., 1/2" THK 2" DIAM., TYP.

GWB TO BE FINISHED + PTD. PRIOR TO GLASS INSTALLATION

① DETAIL SECTION @ RAIL (STAIR No.2)

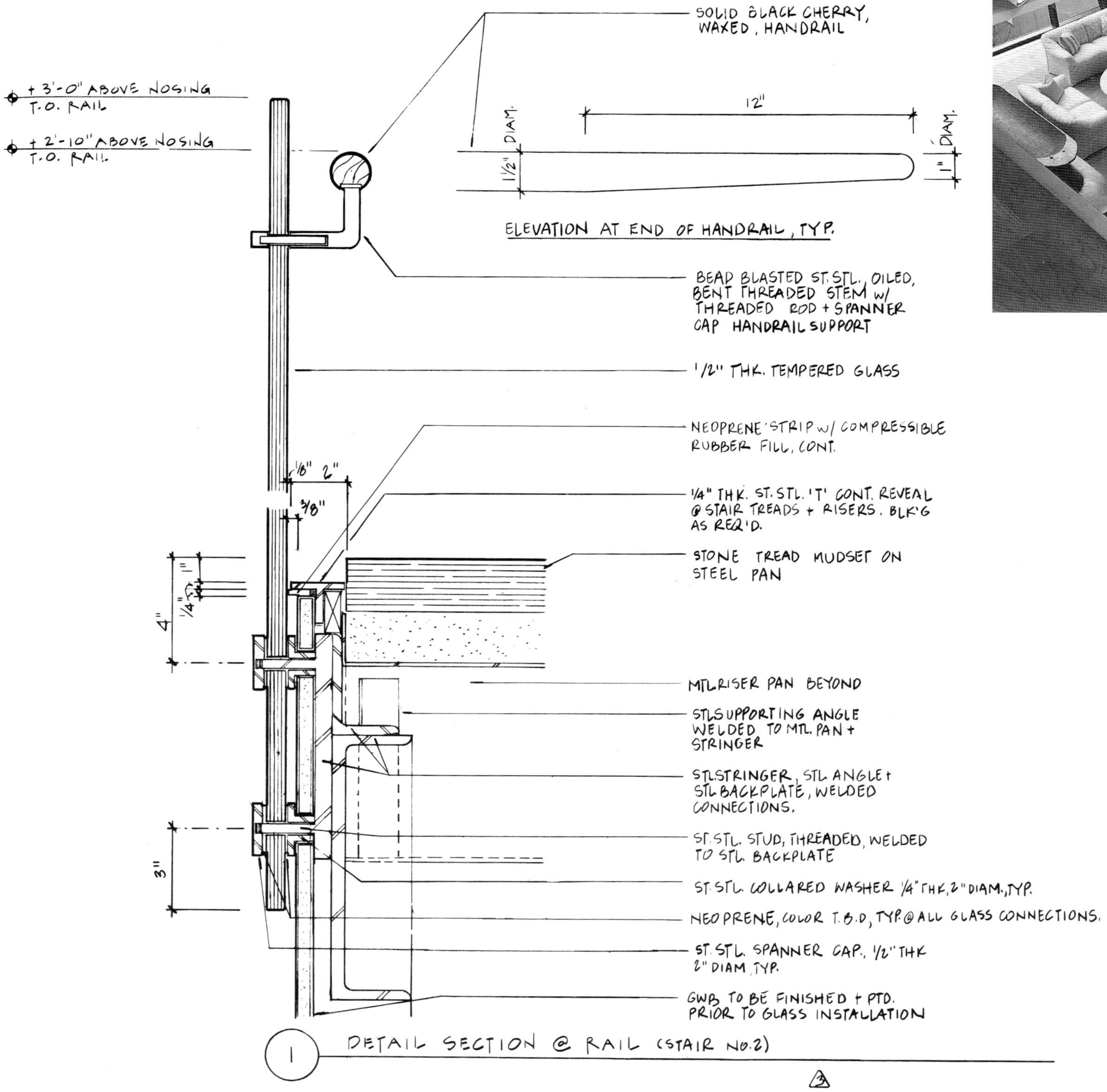

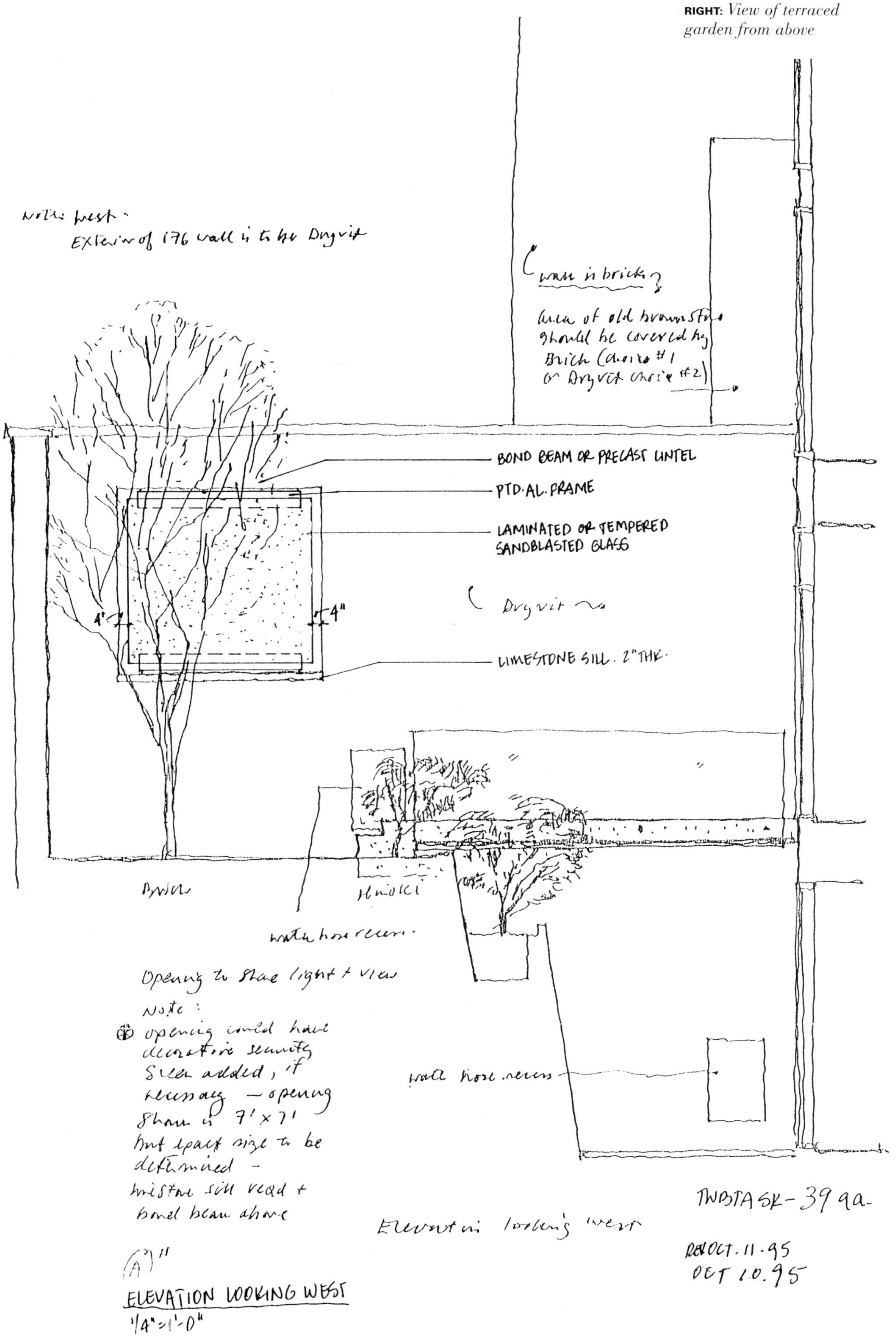

RIGHT: *View of terraced garden from above*

North West:
Exterior of 176 wall is to be Dryvit

(wall is brick)

Area of old brownstone
should be covered by
Brick (choice #1
or Dryvit choice #2)

BOND BEAM OR PRECAST LINTEL

PTD. AL. FRAME

LAMINATED OR TEMPERED
SANDBLASTED GLASS

(Dryvit)

LIMESTONE SILL. 2" THK.

4"   4"

Brick   Handrail

water hose recess

wall hose recess

Opening to share light + view

Note:
⊕ opening could have
decorative security
screen added, if
necessary — opening
shown is 7' x 7'
but exact size to be
determined —
limestone sill read +
bond beam above

(A)"

ELEVATION LOOKING WEST
1/4" = 1'-0"

Elevation looking west

TWBTA SK-39 9a-

REV OCT. 11.95
OCT 10.95

Mosley House and Studio

1987–1990

ARCHITROPE

Owner: Catherine Mosley
Architect: Architrope, New York, New York
Design Team: Andrew Bartle, Jonathan Kirschenfeld, Evans Simpson
Engineer: Ross Dalland (structural)
General Contractor: David Haust/Quadresign, Chatham, New York
Photography: Paul Warchol

Site: Canaan, New York
Program: House and studio including living room, dining room, kitchen, painting studio, graphics studio, 2 sleeping porches, guest loft, bedroom, 2 bathrooms, gallery, study.
Square Footage: 1050 in house, 800 in studio
Structural System: Concrete foundation, 2 x 6 walls and rafters
Mechanical System: Radiant heat
Major Exterior Materials: 1 x 6 tongue-and-groove cedar walls, galvalume roof
Major Interior Materials: Drywall, maple (floors)
Furnishings and Storage: Artwork by owner
Doors and Hardware: Standard doors; Baldwin
Windows: Will Parry Architectural Windows, Martha's Vineyard, Massachusetts
Fixtures: American Standard
Appliances and Equipment: GE (refrigerator and microwave), Maytag (dishwasher), Thermador (cooktop and oven).
Cost: $250,000

FACING PAGE: *View of buildings toward valley*

Site

This summer residence for an artist is built on an old hayfield overlooking the Hudson Valley, occupying an area settled in the 1840s during the heyday of Greek revival. Sited at the field's highest point, it takes advantage of summer winds and the grand prospect to the north.

Pictorial concerns were integrated into the approach to the site. The buildings first appear as one stepped form against a sloping ground. After two quick turns an oblique view reveals the two buildings as parallel forms reaching out into the distant landscape. Upon entry into the level courtyard, the buildings "disappear" as they become a frame for the magnificent view.

Design

The architects established three different scales relative to the occupation of the site: the largest scale is made by the roofs and the large north-facing porches, the second by the loggias, and the third and most intimate by the small window and door penetrations in the white volumes. The buildings themselves were conceptually modeled on the Erechtheion with a "cella," or main volume, with differently contained "porches" off each side. The

north columns between the built and natural worlds create a narrow transitional space.

The program was split into separate entities of house and studio, each placed in identical volumes across a court. This composition—an analogy to the typical New England town green—is intentionally open to allow for later building. The mirroring of the buildings is a pictorial device that frames and allows a view north.

The decision to build two nearly identical forms for different purposes speaks rhetorically to notions of type and function. Most likely, the buildings will be used in different capacities over time; one could imagine their housing a school, or even a sanatorium. No matter, the configuration of "buildings on a court" will remain.

Construction

The buildings' concrete foundations also serve as retaining walls for the court, which is one foot below grade at the south end and four feet above grade at the north. The walls and roofs are constructed of 2" x 6" wood members, and meet at what is called a "girt," or entablature. This line is continuous in both buildings and provides a visual datum to measure one's relation to the changing grade from all sides. At the end of the internal sequence on the second-story porch, for example, the girt is at waist level. The second-story porches on the north side, used as sleeping porches in the summer, are hung from the rafters like hammocks.

In order to resist the strong winds, the transverse plywood walls function as diaphragms and shear walls. The wood siding in the body of the buildings is detailed to suggest a bearing condition of the walls. At the south ends, frame and panel construction is used to suggest a direction in which the buildings would expand over time.

Site plan

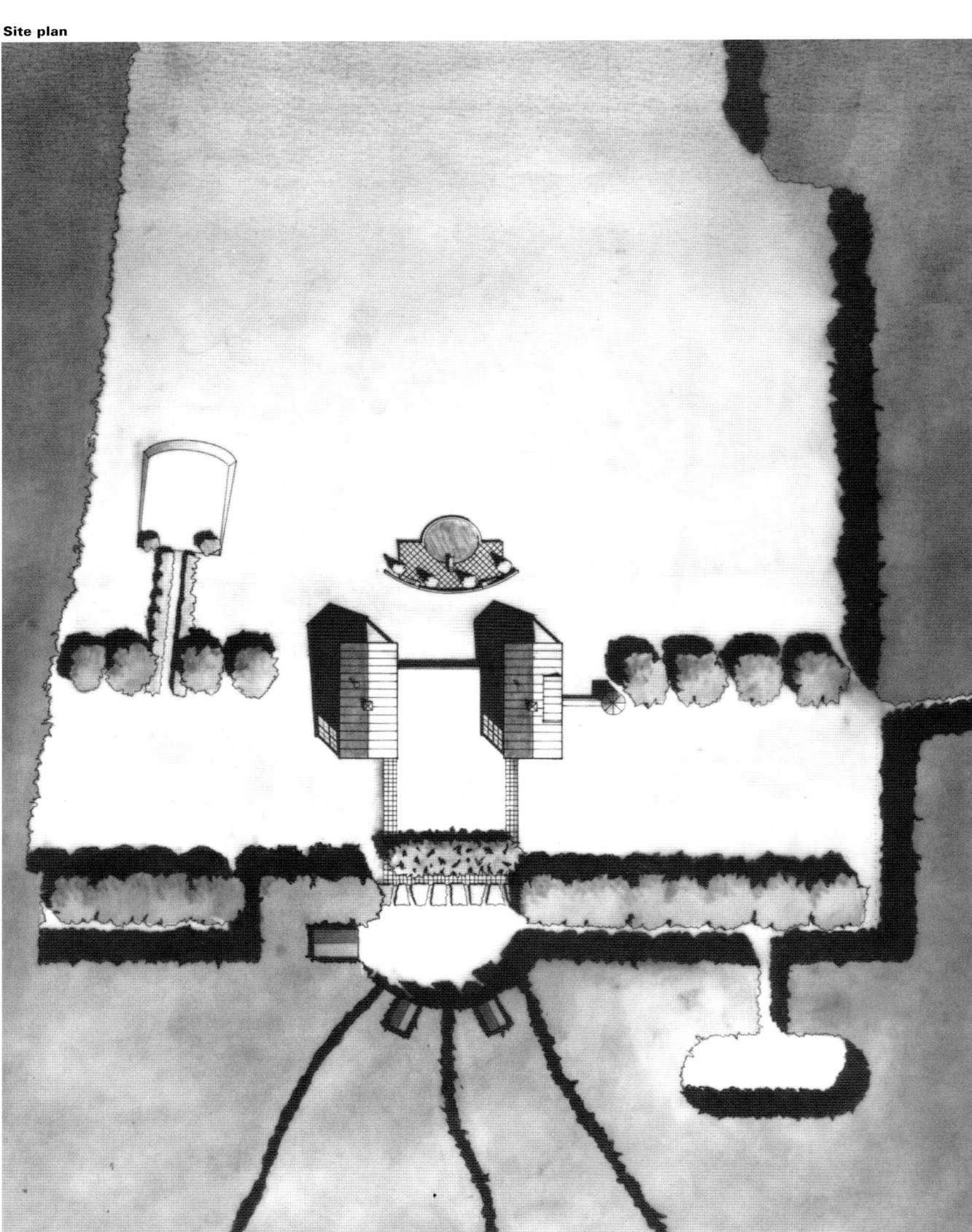

Section

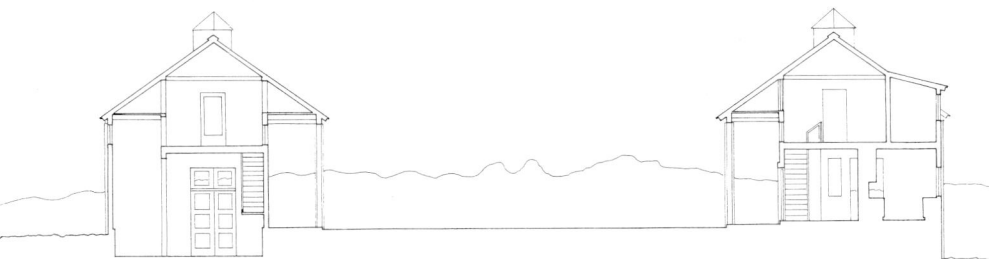

Second level floor plan

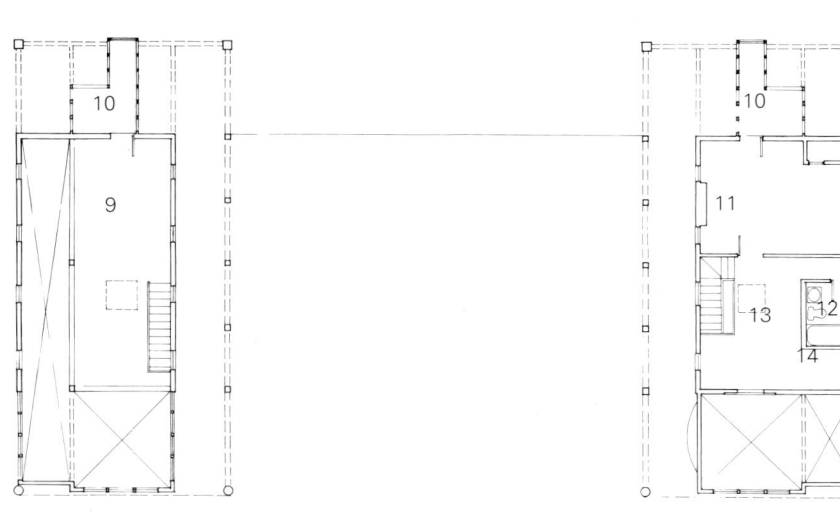

First level floor plan

1. COURTYARD
2. PAINTING STUDIO
3. GRAPHICS STUDIO
4. NORTH PORCH
5. LIVING ROOM
6. KITCHEN
7. HALF BATHROOM
8. DINING ROOM
9. GUEST LOFT
10. SLEEPING PORCH
11. BEDROOM
12. BATHROOM
13. GALLERY
14. STUDY

0   5   10

CLOCKWISE FROM LEFT:
Second story porch; view of living room; view of dining room from court

ABOVE AND RIGHT: *Views of studio*

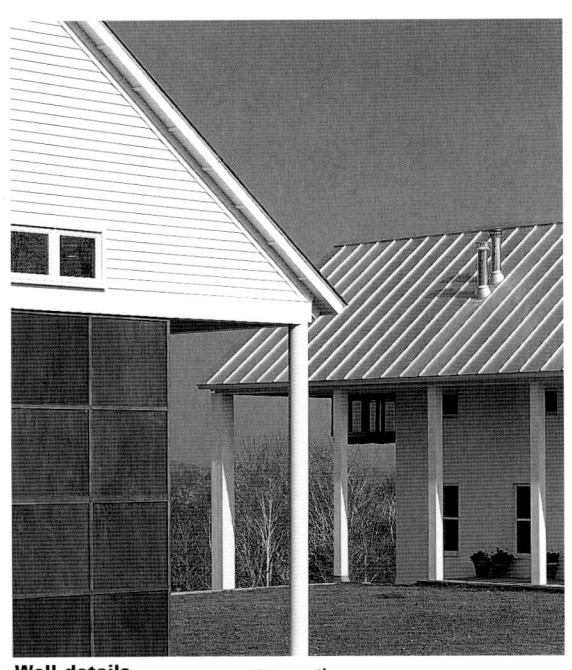

LEFT: *View from southwest*
FACING PAGE: *View from northeast*

Wall details

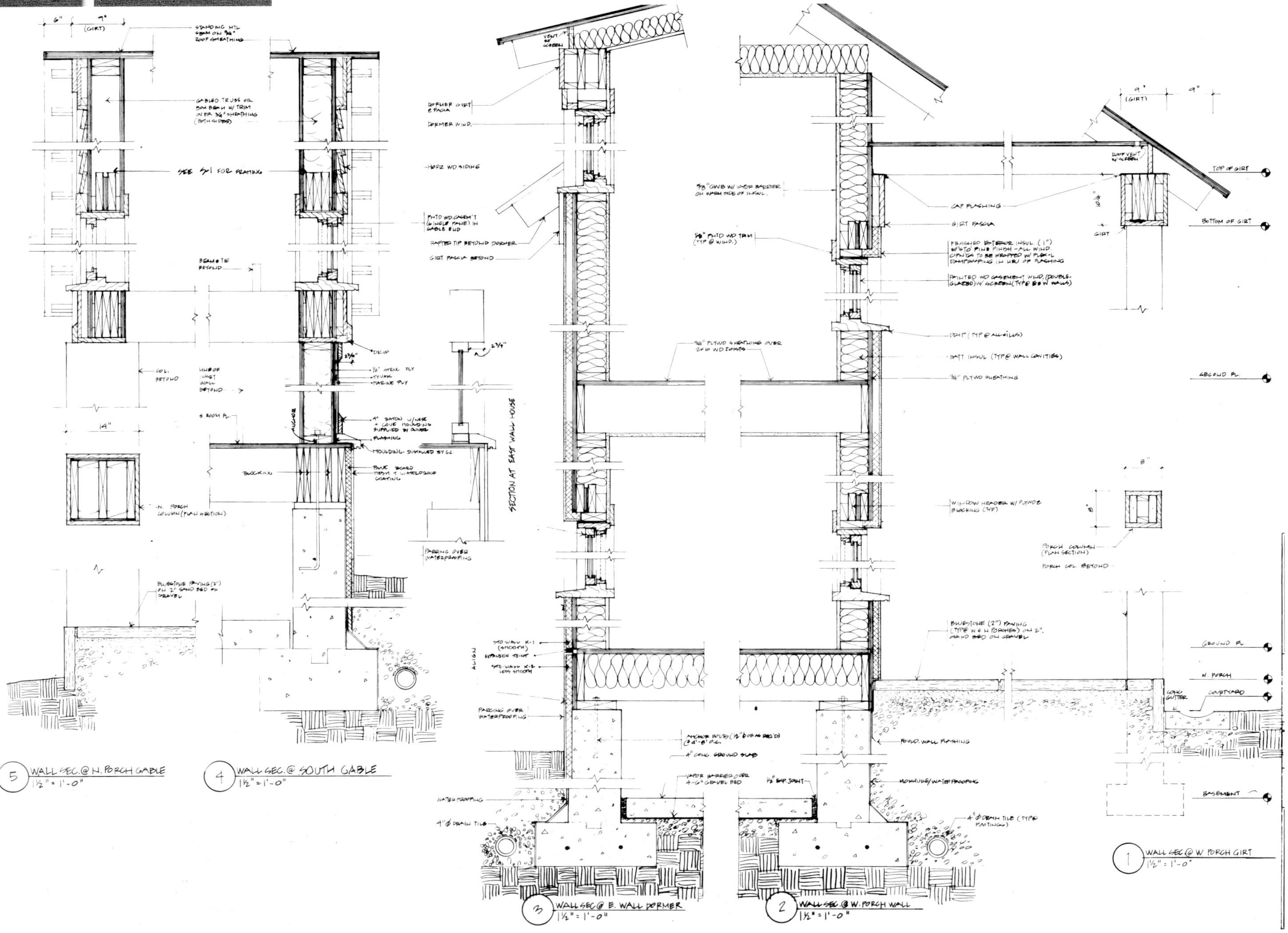
5 WALL SEC.@ N. PORCH GABLE
1½" = 1'-0"
4 WALL SEC.@ SOUTH GABLE
1½" = 1'-0"
SECTION AT EAST WALL HOUSE
3 WALL SEC.@ E. WALL DORMER
1½" = 1'-0"
2 WALL SEC.@ W. PORCH WALL
1½" = 1'-0"
1 WALL SEC.@ W. PORCH GIRT
1½" = 1'-0"

MAXmin House *1993-1994*
SMITH-MILLER + HAWKINSON ARCHITECTS

Owner: Kenneth Frampton and Sylvia Kolbowski
Architect: Smith-Miller + Hawkinson Architects, New York, New York
Design Team: Henry Smith-Miller, Laurie Hawkinson, Eric Cobb (project manager), John Conaty, Jan Greben,Eugene Harris, Lawrence Ko.
Engineer: Guy Nordenson and Caroline Fitzgerald, Ove Arup and Partners
Consultant: Nicholas Quennell, Quennell Rothschild Associates (landscape architect)
General Contractor: Tenbus Construction
Photography: Paul Warchol, Smith-Miller + Hawkinson

Site: Damascus, Wayne County, Pennsylvania
Program: Single-family weekend house including living room, kitchen, 2 bedrooms, bathroom.
Square Footage: 1100
Structural System: Steel and concrete substructure, wood structure above TJI joists and wood framing
Mechanical System: Fin-tube radiator
Major Exterior Materials: Cedar siding, galvanized sheet metal, painted steel railing, stair, and decking, siplast bitumen roofing.
Major Interior Materials: B/D plywood, galvanized sheet metal, stainless steel, ceramic tile, gypsum wall board, pine (floor).
Furnishings and Storage: Provided by owner.
Doors and Hardware: Kawneer aluminum
Windows: Kawneer aluminum
Fixtures: Speakman, Kohler, American Standard, Just, Chicago
Appliances and Equipment: Provided by owner.
Cost: Withheld at owner's request.

Site
Located on a sloping meadow in Wayne County, the house backs up against the woods with views to the Delaware River and mountains beyond.

Design
The principle behind the design of the MAXmin house lies in its name: maximize the minimum. Modernist domestic antecedents and diverse design methodologies were referred to and questioned in an effort to arrive at an idea of a contemporary rural house suited to urban dwellers. A collaboration between the architects and owners led to the design of this weekend house that ingeniously appears larger than it is, all the while testing the notion of consensus in the design process.

A simple bar begins above grade and later levels off, leaving exposed the steel columns below. The columns and grated steel entry ramp provide a sense of transparency close to the ground, so that the house nearly hovers in the environment.

The program unfolds much like that of a railroad flat, with one room following the other. The kitchen and living area are open in plan and overlook breathtaking views of the surrounding countryside. One side of the child's room is made entirely of glass, opening to the meadow and woods beyond.

Construction

The architects sought to use industrial commercial materials as much as possible, such as the windows (commercial aluminum) and entry ramp (steel grating).

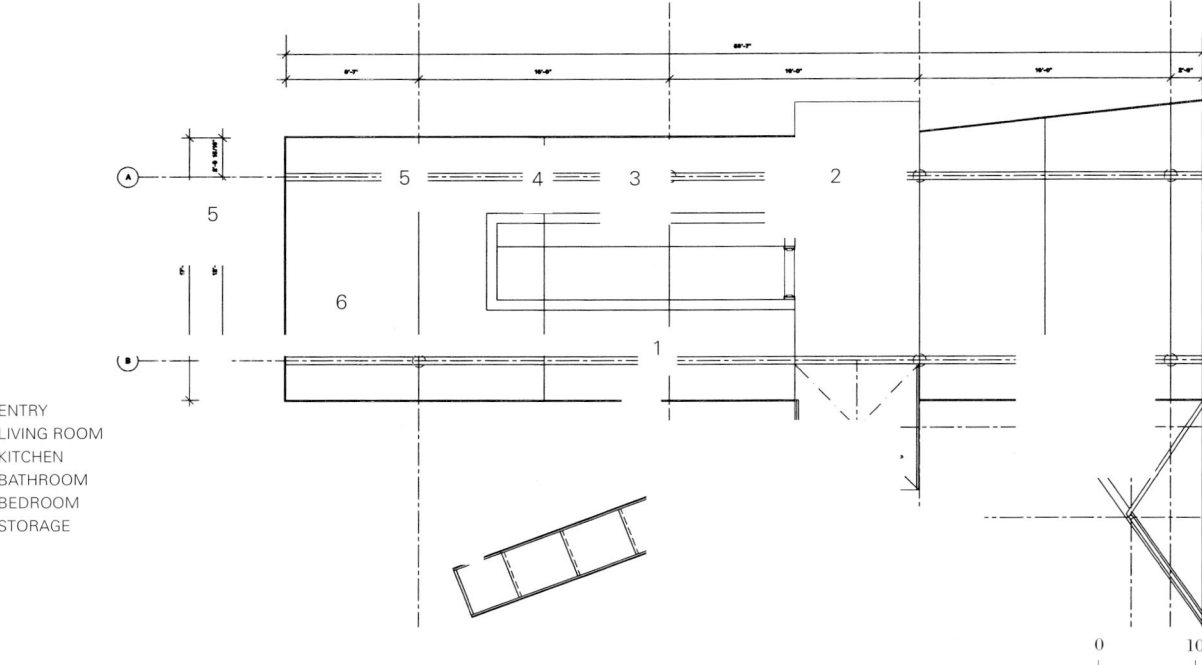

1. ENTRY
2. LIVING ROOM
3. KITCHEN
4. BATHROOM
5. BEDROOM
6. STORAGE

Site Plan

Perspective

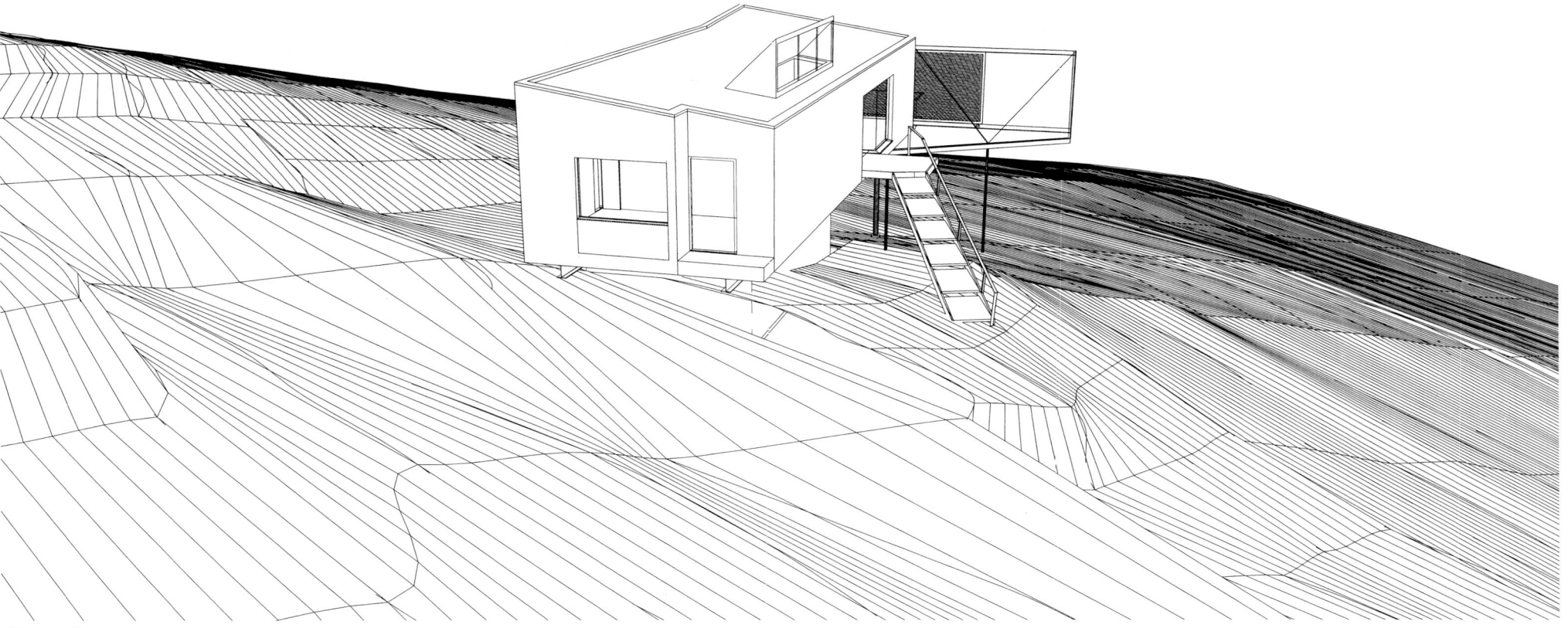

Perspective

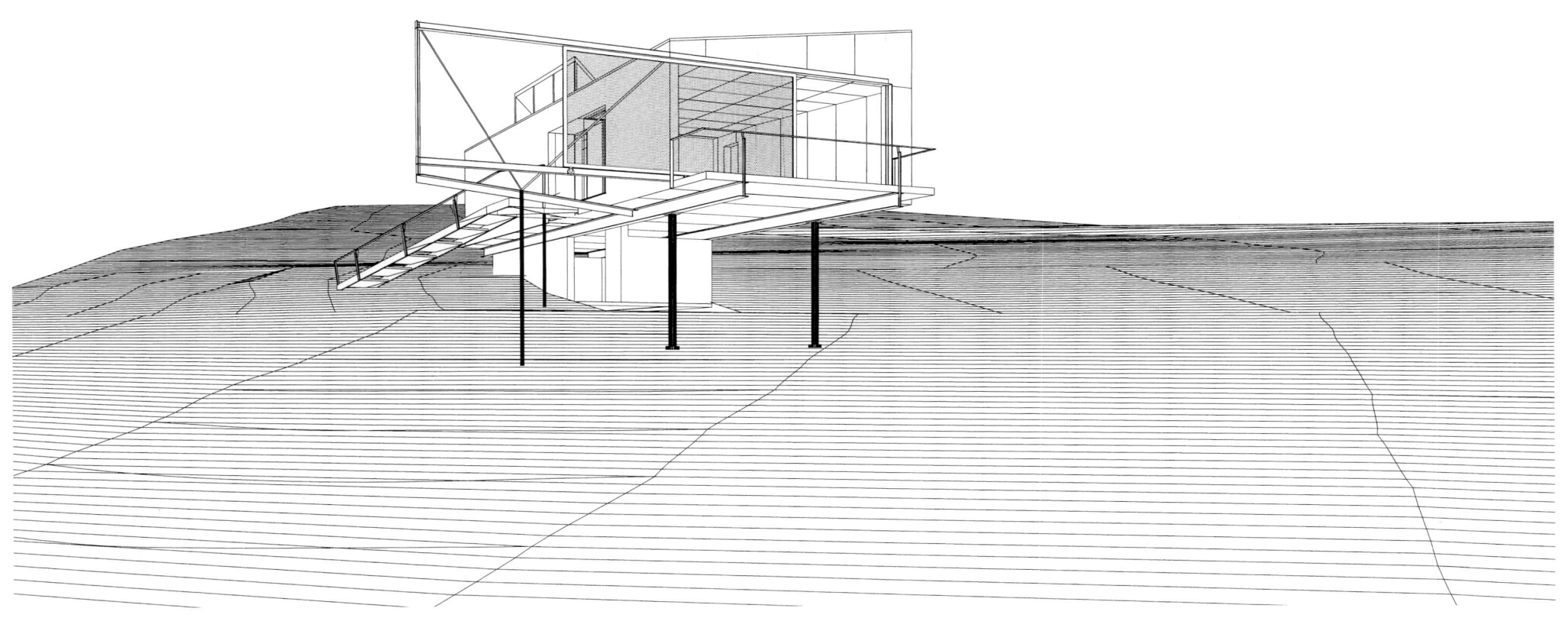

203

LEFT: *View of entry*
BOTTOM: *Entry detail*
FACING PAGE: *View of living room*

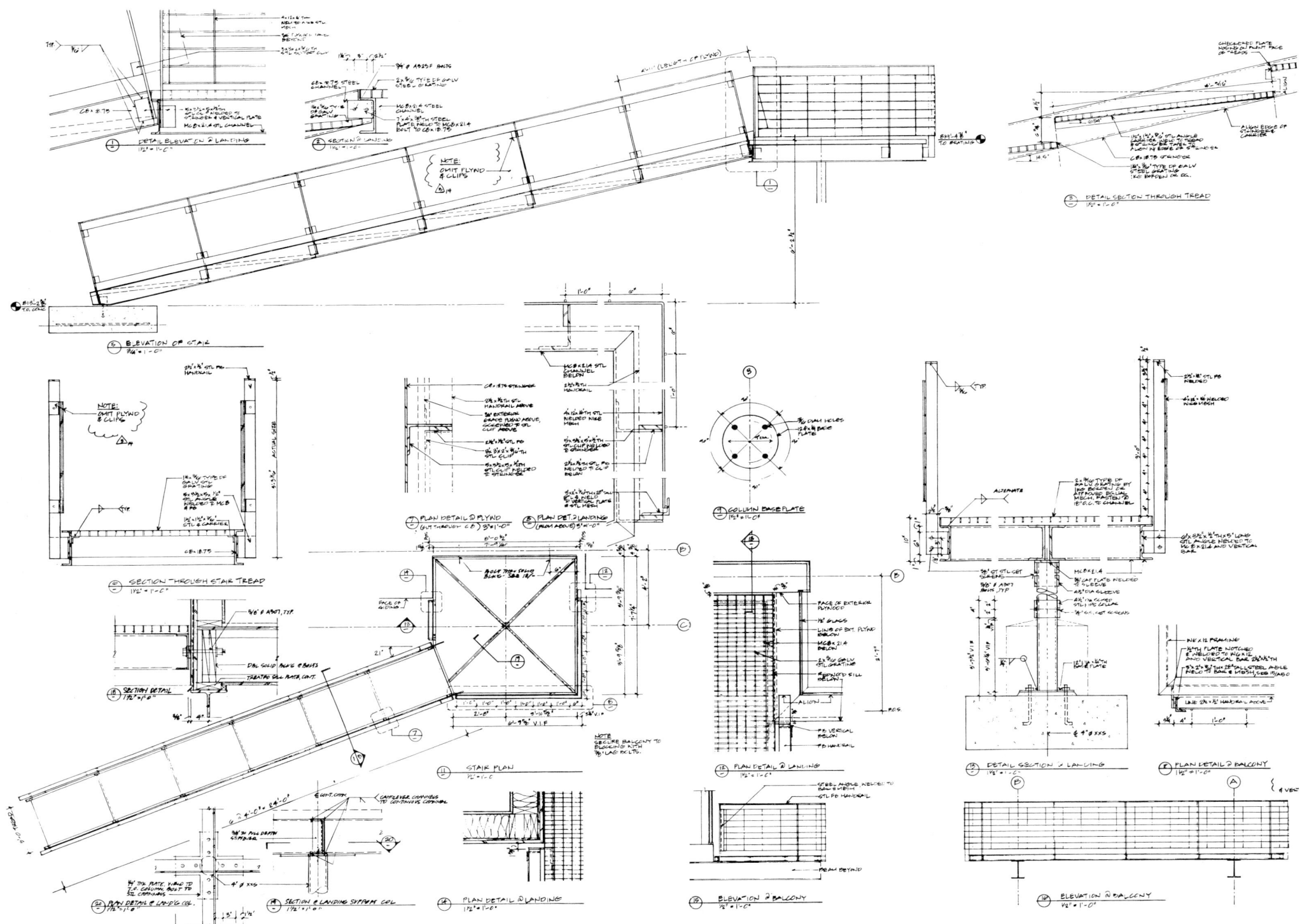

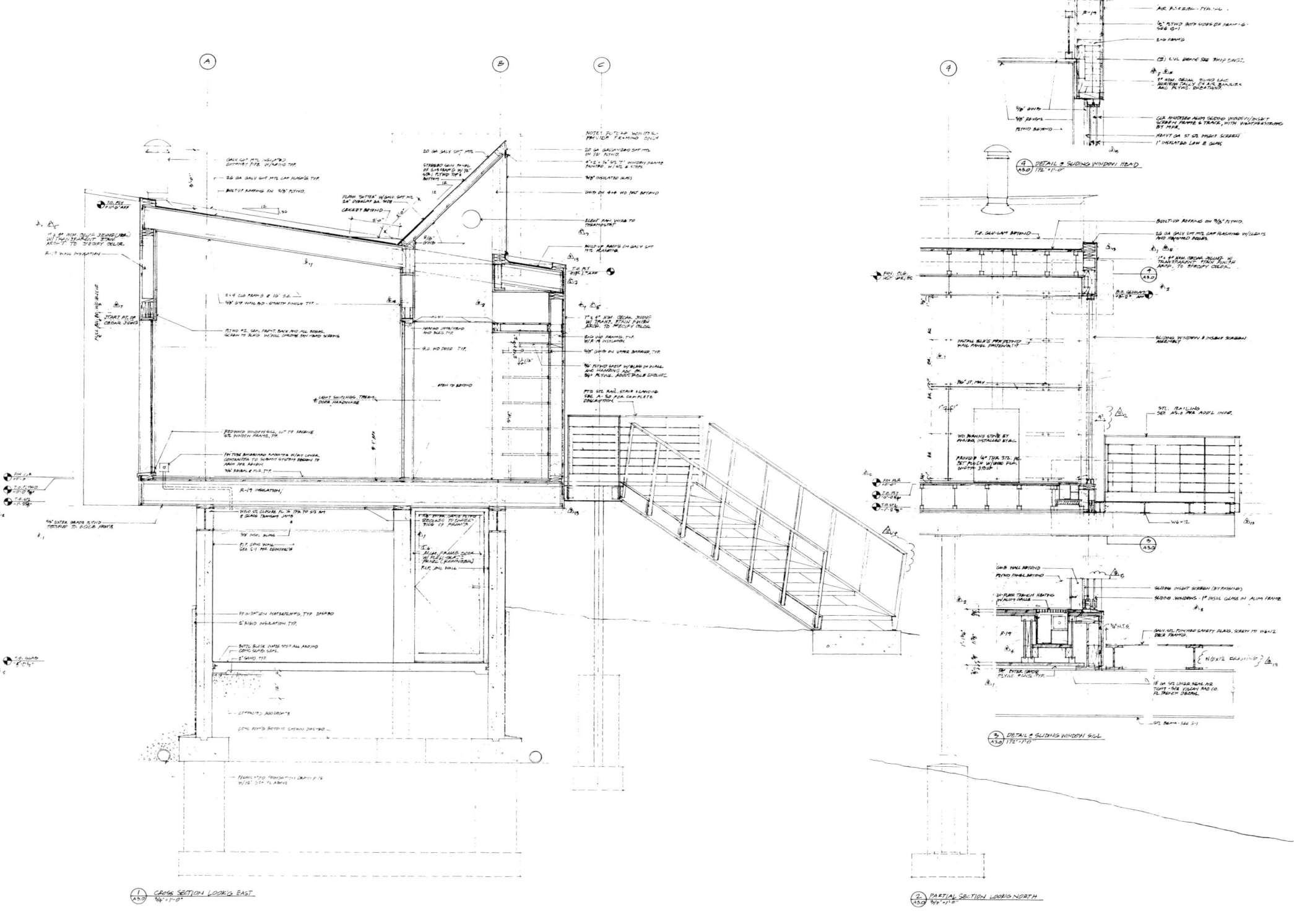

The Bach Residence

1989-1995

FRANK LUPO AND DANIEL ROWEN, ARCHITECTS

Owner: Ellen Bach and Andrew Bach
Architect: Frank Lupo and Daniel Rowen, Architects, Westchester, New York
Design Team: Frank Lupo, Daniel Rowen (partners-in-charge); Patrick Walker, Jennifer Brayer, Jenny Jaleski.
Engineer: Ove Arup and Partners (structural)
Consultants: Jerry Kugler Associates (lighting), Primo Lighting (lighting), Gazebo/Brian Beni (landscape).
General Contractor: Alternet Design Inc., Goodhill Mechanical (mechanical)
Photography: Michael Moran

Site: Pound Ridge, New York
Program: Primary residence for a single man and seasonal residence for his mother. Each house has 2 bedrooms, 2 bathrooms, kitchen, and living room. Primary residence contains a "dog" room to house 8 labradors and a cockatoo. A 6-car garage contains an automobile collection.
Square Footage: 7500
Structural System: Poured in place concrete, wood frame, steel frame, glue-laminated beams and arches.
Mechanical System: Oil fired forced air heating, radiant slab hot water heating, central air conditioning and humidity controls.
Major Exterior Materials: Lead coated copper (roof), stained vertical grain tongue and groove cedar siding (walls), quarried bluestone (paving), painted tubular steel (railings), redwood (decking).
Major Interior Materials: Edge grain maple (flooring), Vermont slate (flooring), skim coat plastered gypsum board (walls and ceilings).
Furnishings and Storage: Built-in cabinetry by architects in lacquered wood, plastic laminate, stainless steel.
Doors and Hardware: Solid core wood, glass and aluminum frame; Schlage, Grass
Windows: Commercial grade 1" insulated glass and aluminum frames with thermal breaks by Portal Windows.
Fixtures: American Standard, Speakman
Appliances and Equipment: Sub-Zero (refrigerator), Viking (gas range, range hood, wall oven, and dishwasher), Lutron (lighting control systems).
Cost: $400 dollars per square foot

Site

The houses are located in a four-acre parcel on a wooded hill overlooking a two-and-a-half acre pond. Vehicular access is available from the upper elevations of the hill. The two residences are nestled on the brow of the hill just below its top and between two major rock outcroppings. From this position looking due west, both houses enjoy a commanding view of the pond while still being accessible from the entry drive.

Design

The most unique aspect of this project is that there are two independent clients. One is a single man, the other is his mother. Two themes were described by both

RIGHT: *View toward entry terrace*
BOTTOM: *South façade*
FACING PAGE: *View from across pond*

clients as being essential to the architecture: the proximity and interdependence appropriate to a small family, and the privacy and independence appropriate to two adults. The challenge was to make these relationships concrete in built form.

The two houses sit side by side, yet each has its own axial orientation, character, and idiosyncratic detailing. The space between the houses is shared and connects views from the upper entry drive down to the pond below.

The barrel vaulted cubic volume of the mother's house is located at a slightly higher level than that of her son's. By contrast, the son's house is more directional as it extends down the hillside toward the pond.

The two houses are joined by a stone terrace that is sheltered by the cantilevered roof of the mother's house. The natural materials and openness of this terrace allow the site to remain as a continuous element, with views and the surrounding environment "moving through" the composition. Appropriately, this shared space is both a buffer and a bond mediating between the mother and the son as well as between the landscape and the architecture. It embodies the tension found where separation and connection coexist.

Construction

The houses are built on a steep rock outcropping that required both concrete foundations and concrete piers, some of which were poured into cavities blasted into the rock formations. The construction of the main volumes of the houses is a hybrid of traditional wood framing, glue laminated beams, steel beams, and steel columns. The mechanical systems include multi-zoned heating, cooling, humidification, and dehumidification. The mother's house includes a hydraulic elevator connecting the first and second floors.

Exterior wall surfaces are comprised of tongue-and-groove vertical cedar siding with aluminum windows and doors. The cantilevered roof forms are made of glue-lam beams which are skinned with bent plywood and sheathed with standing-seam stainless steel roofing. The cantilevered redwood decks are supported by a continuous steel edge beam which is triangulated back to vertical supports in the walls by means of custom steel brackets.

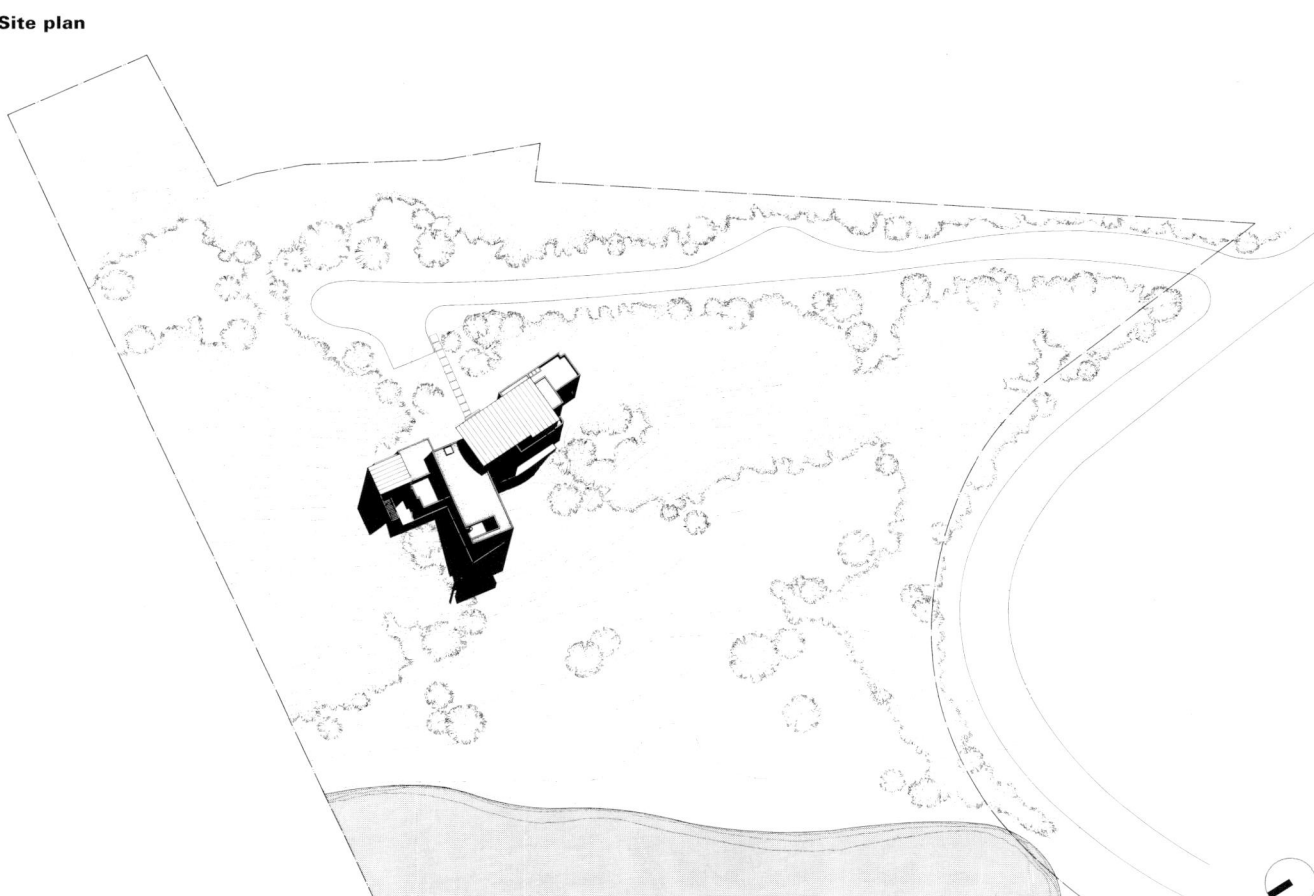

FAR LEFT: *View of son's house with mother's house behind*
LEFT: *View of entry terrace to both houses from northeast*

Southwest elevation

Northeast elevation

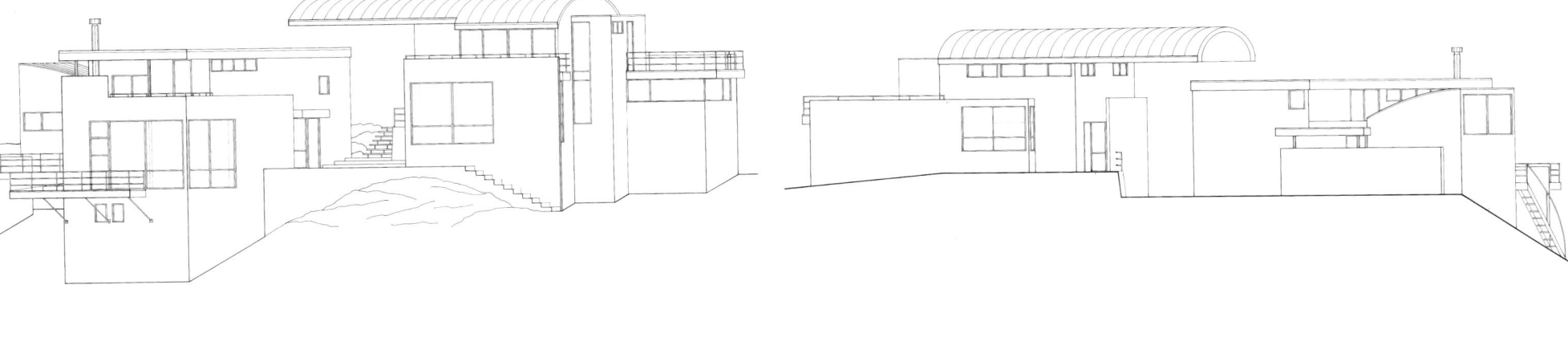

First level floor plan

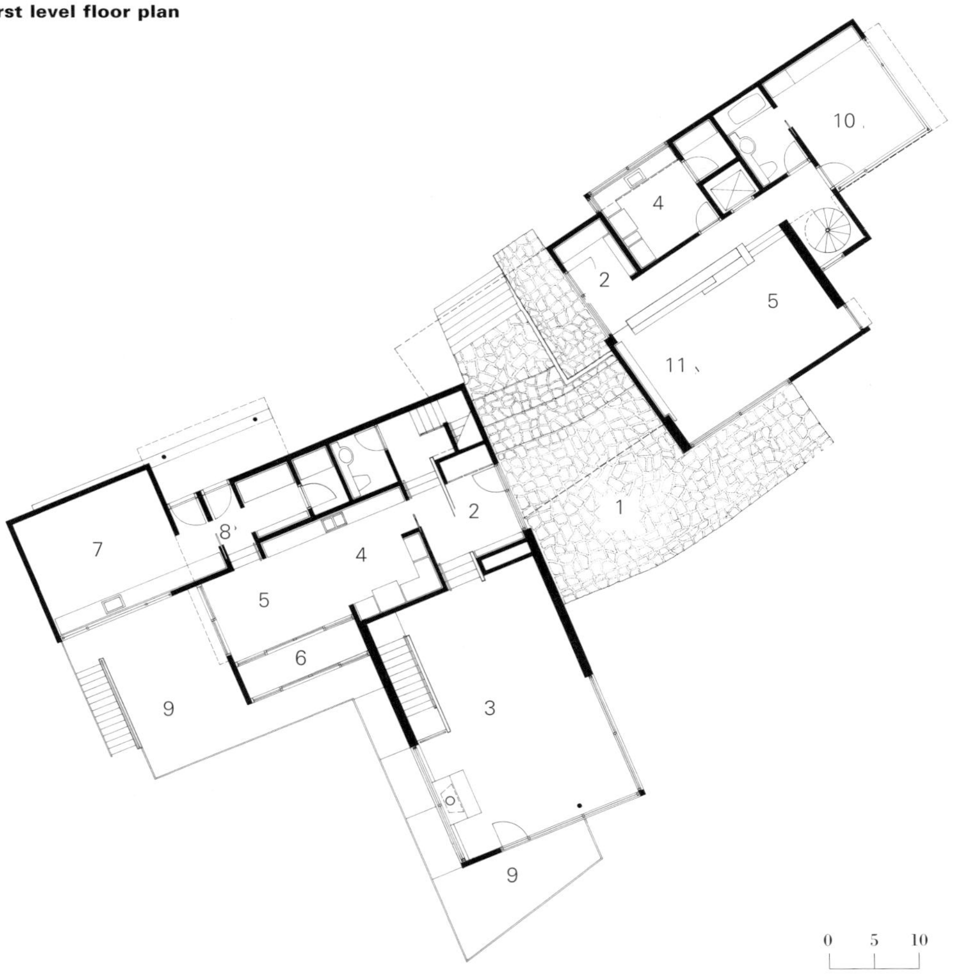

Second level floor plan

0   5   10

1. TERRACE
2. ENTRY
3. LIVING ROOM
4. KITCHEN
5. DINING ROOM
6. AVIARY
7. STUDIO
8. MUD ROOM
9. DECK
10. GUEST BEDROOM
11. SITTING ROOM
12. MASTER BEDROOM
13. MASTER BATHROOM
14. GUEST BATHROOM
15. CLOSET/STORAGE
16. DECK
17. STUDIO BELOW
18. ROOF

TOP: *Son's living room*
ABOVE: *Son's kitchen*
FACING PAGE: *Mother's living room*

RIGHT: *View of mother's house*

Wall section

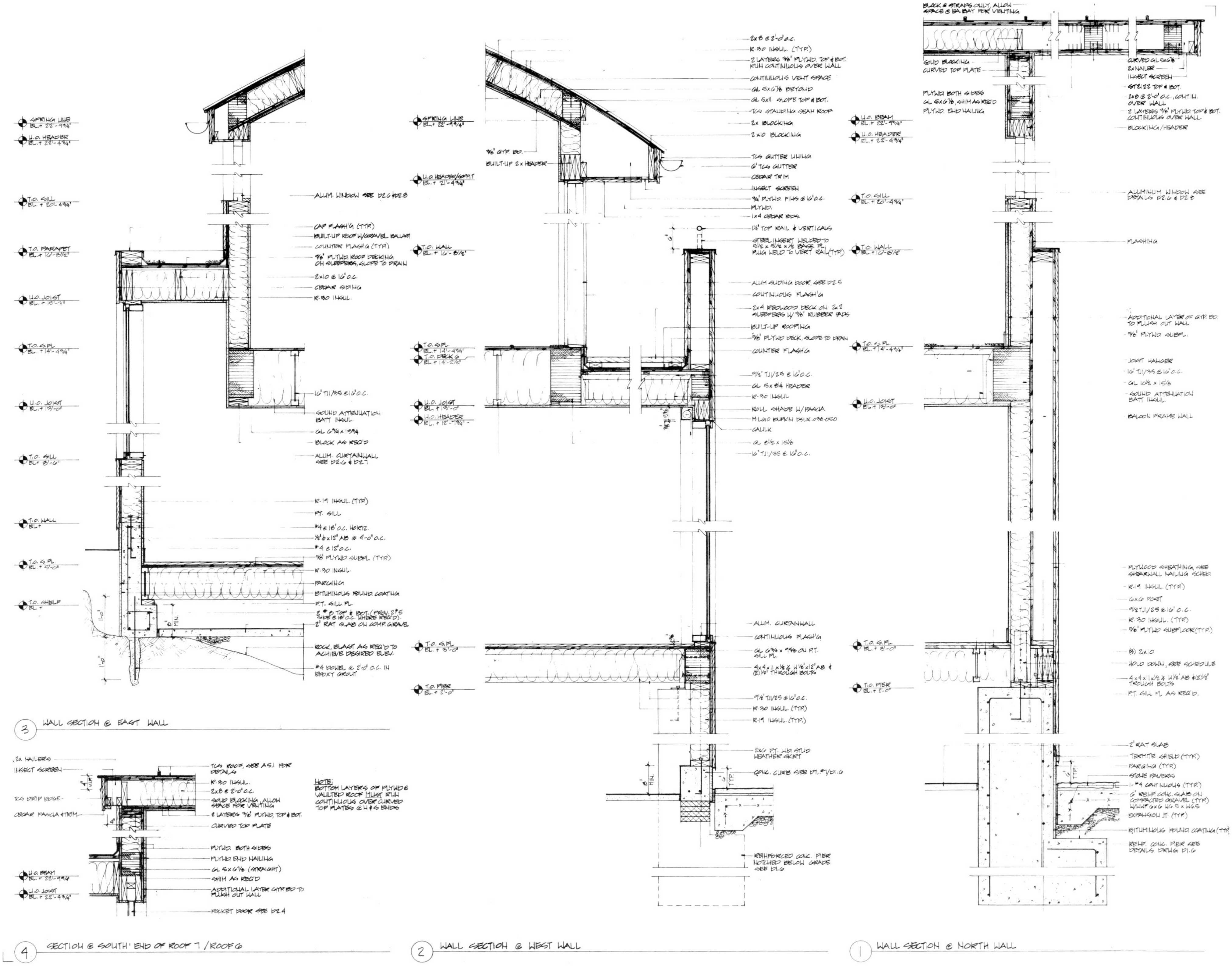

③ WALL SECTION @ EAST WALL

④ SECTION @ SOUTH END OF ROOF T/ROOF G

② WALL SECTION @ WEST WALL

① WALL SECTION @ NORTH WALL

South elevation, son's house

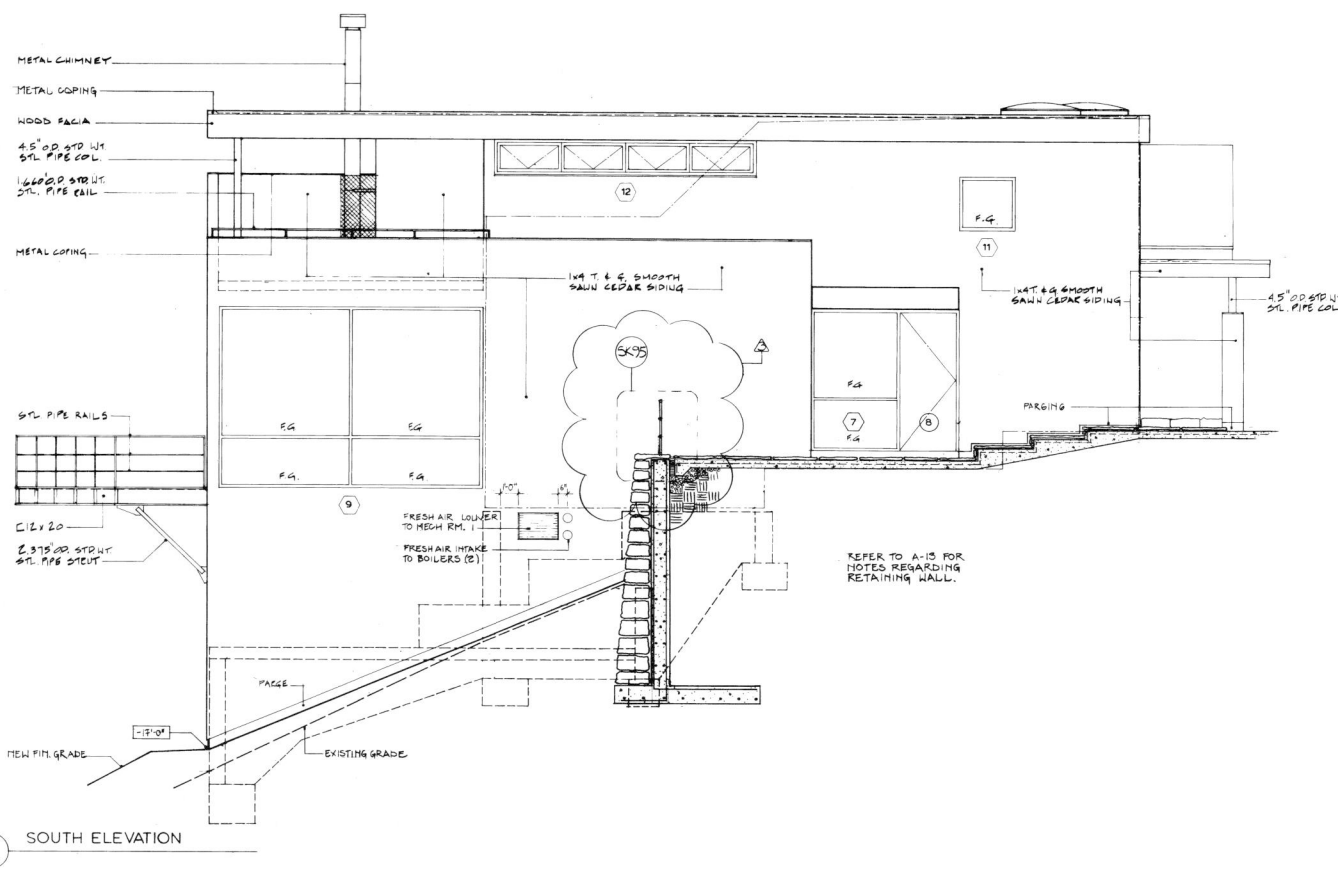

West elevation, son's house

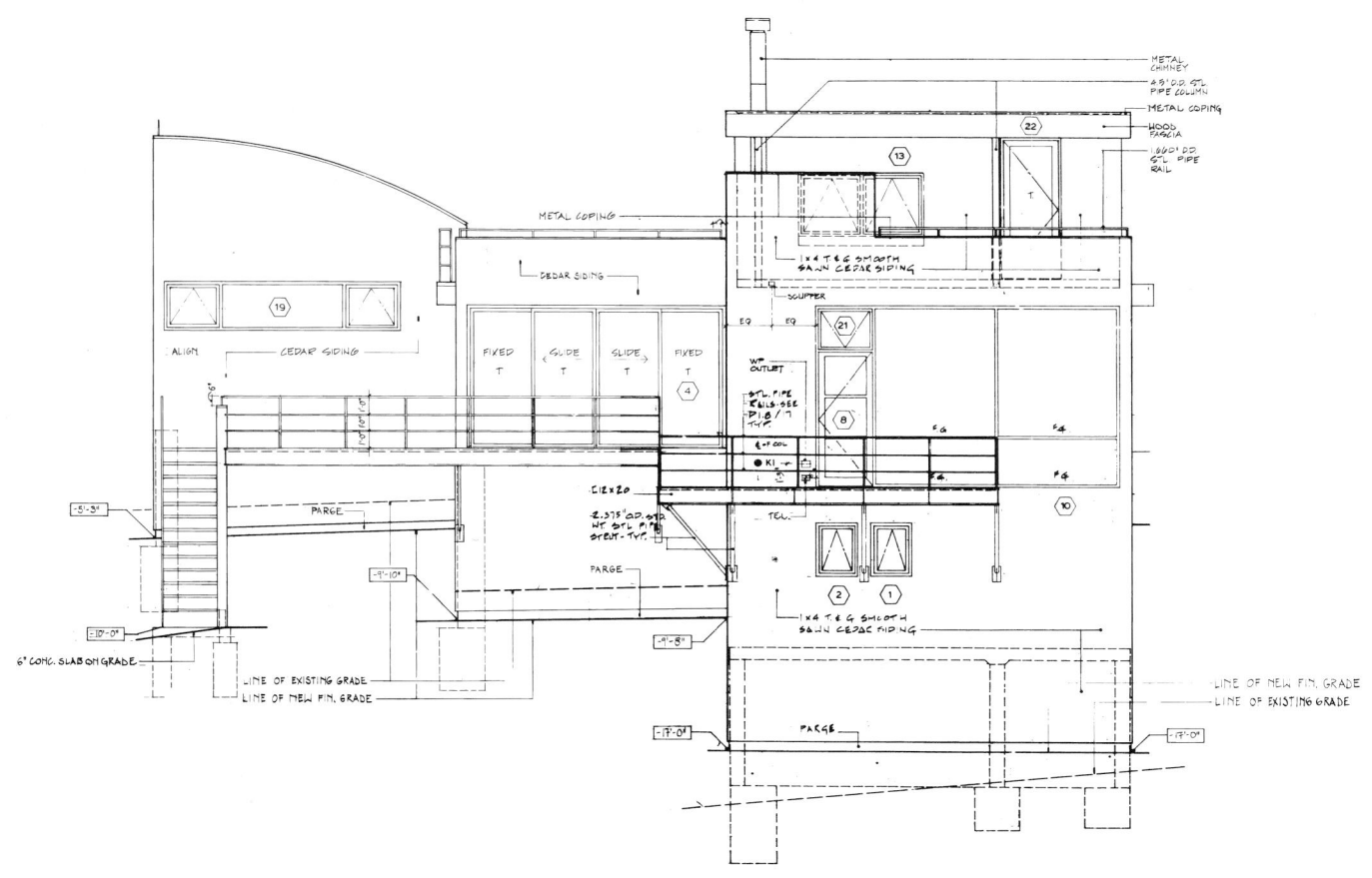

Spiral House

1991-1994

DEAN/WOLF ARCHITECTS

Owner: Andrew and Lisa Greenberg
Architect: Dean/Wolf Architects, New York, New York
Design Team: Kathryn Dean (project designer), Charles Wolf (project architect)
Engineer: Anchor Consulting (structural)
Consultants: Land-Tech Consultants, Inc. (civil)
General Contractor: Dowko Development Inc.; Einor Moi (site work and foundations)
Photography: Peter Aaron/Esto

Site: Armonk, New York
Program: Single-family house including living room, dining room, eat-in kitchen, 6 bedrooms, 5 ½ bathrooms, playroom, guest room, 3-car garage, walk-out basement.
Square Footage: 5800
Structural System: Reinforced concrete anchored into rock at foundations and lower level; structural steel with wood infill for upper level and roof.
Mechanical System: 5 Zone forced air heating and central air conditioning
Major Exterior Materials: Exposed architectural concrete, stone, cedar siding (walls), single-ply membrane (roof), lead-coated copper and precast concrete (copings and drip caps), bluestone (paving).
Major Interior Materials: Ash (cabinets and window trim), white oak and Normandie limestone (floors), granite (counter tops), skim coated plaster on gypsum board (walls and ceiling).
Furnishings and Storage: Built in by architect.
Doors and Hardware: Brushed stainless by Schlage
Windows: Duratherm (teak exterior/ash interior)
Fixtures: Halo
Cost: Withheld at owner's request

Site

The site of this house is a prominent rock outcropping overlooking a forest stream. To preserve the summit and shield the house from a golf course located behind the site, the house was carved into the perimeter of the rock formation. This carving created a courtyard centered on the rock formation itself. A landscape wall that emerges from the ground encircles this summit and defines the perimeter of the courtyard. This wall steadily rises, continuing the spiraling motion of approach, and culminates at the entry court. This wall, the house's primary structural and grounding element, binds the house to its site.

Design

The contradictions found in the inherent qualities of the site established the design characteristics of grounded/floating and dynamic/static.

Grounded/floating describes the contradiction of weighted rock floating above a delicate stream. From this situation two realms were developed in which shared spaces merge into the rock and float into the

CLOCKWISE FROM TOP: *Entry court; entry; stair to terrace; view of cantilevered living room; view from north*
FACING PAGE: *View from west*

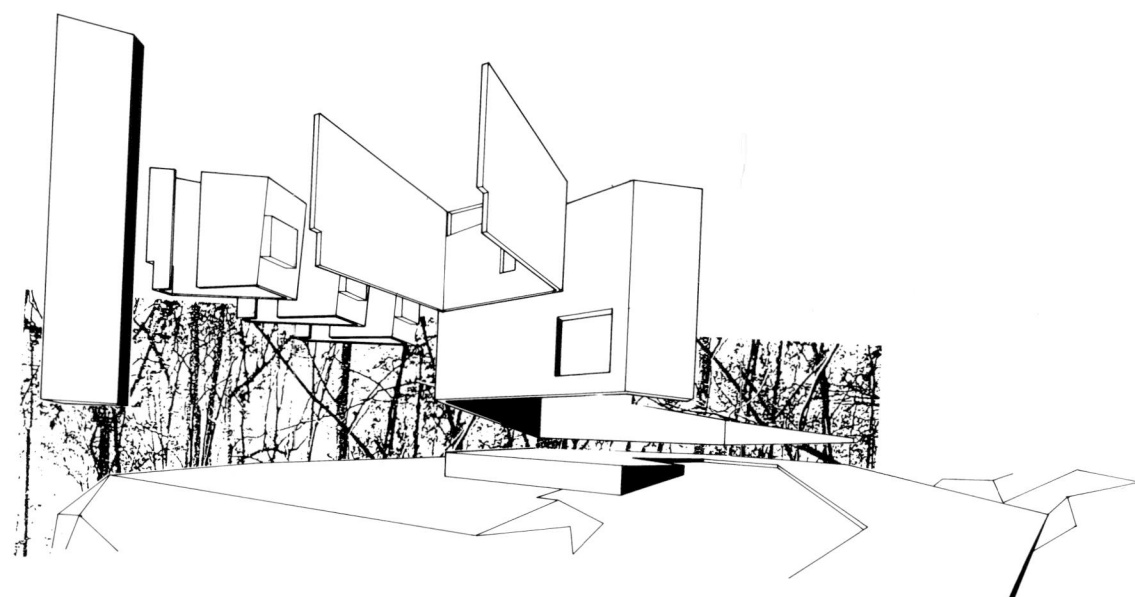

forest edge. Individual spaces float above the shared spaces and are bound to them spatially by the light voids that connect the two.

Dynamic/static is a contradiction created from the spiraling movement of the site: upward to the rock summit and again downward to the forest stream. Continuous expansion and compression develop here in the graduated geometry of both plan and section, reinforcing the dynamic component of the site. Stasis is created at the moment just before the spiral releases, and is achieved by the floating voids of light overhead that connect the ground floor to the sky.

Construction

Grounded/floating and dynamic/static are themes that are expressed tectonically as well. The concrete emerges from the rock formation and cantilevers itself over the forest edge, thereby becoming the weighted aspect of the house imprinted on the site. The steel superstructure is always suppressed. Woven into the wood structure and cladding of the house, it allows the upper story to magically float over the forest edge. The courtyard wall becomes a planar mapping of the zones of grounded and floating spaces beyond. The concrete system, lined with stone quarried from the site, creates a tactile scale for the entry courtyard and links it to the rock formation. The wood framing of the floating zone interlocks with the concrete and stone system and is clad in cedar.

Site plan

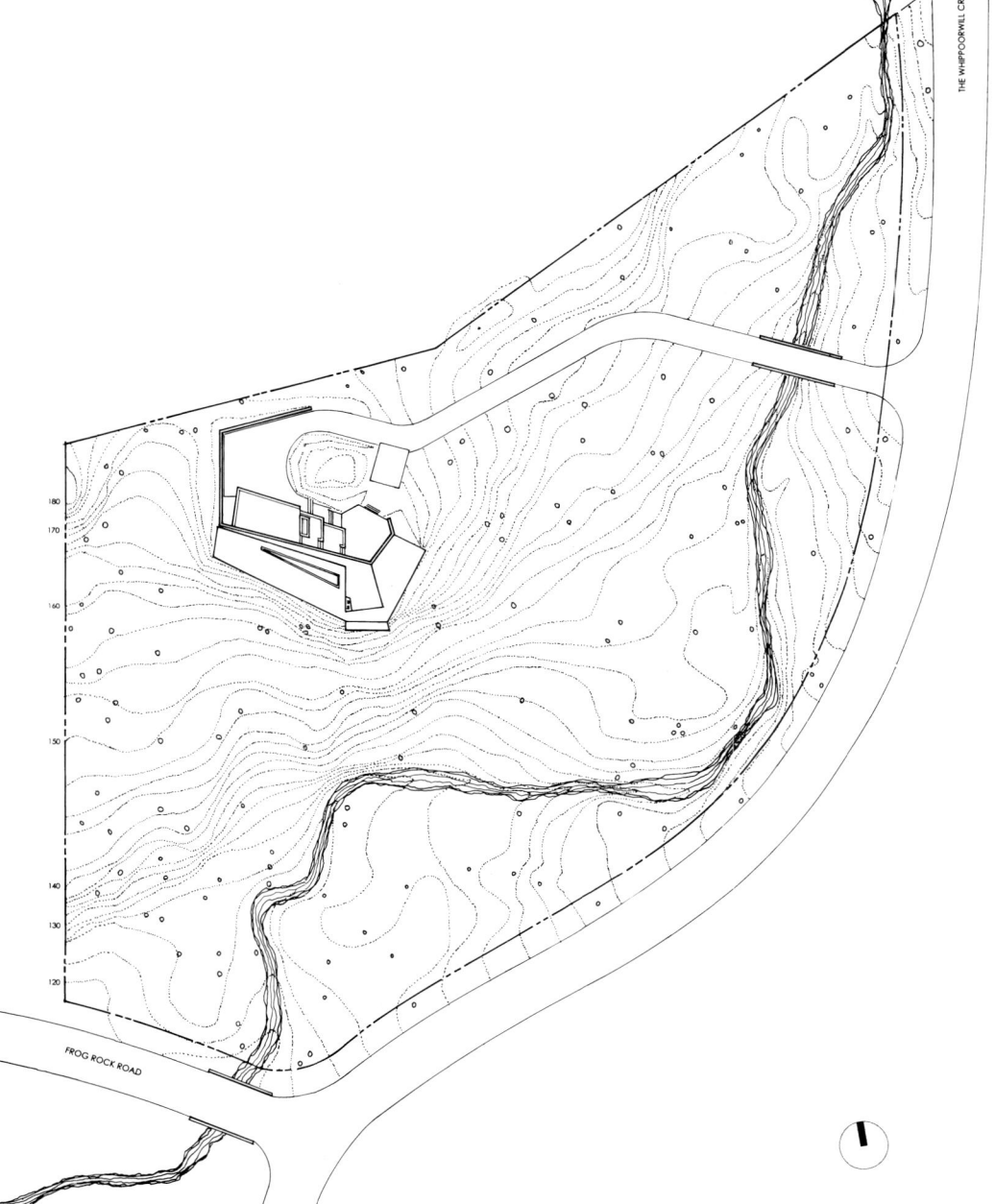

Spatial study

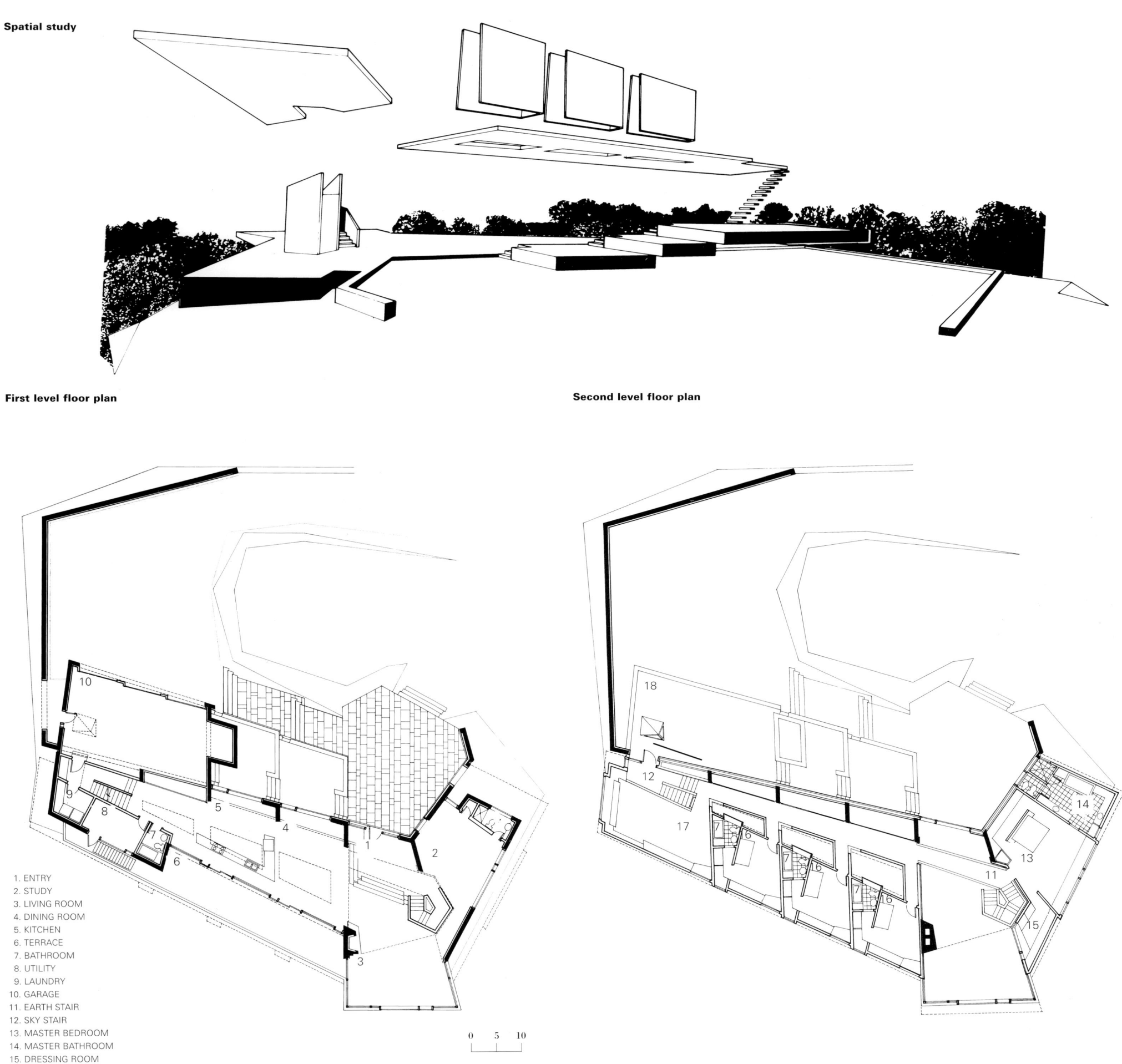

First level floor plan

Second level floor plan

1. ENTRY
2. STUDY
3. LIVING ROOM
4. DINING ROOM
5. KITCHEN
6. TERRACE
7. BATHROOM
8. UTILITY
9. LAUNDRY
10. GARAGE
11. EARTH STAIR
12. SKY STAIR
13. MASTER BEDROOM
14. MASTER BATHROOM
15. DRESSING ROOM
16. BEDROOM
17. PLAYROOM
18. TERRACE

0   5   10

LEFT: *Bridge with living room below*
BOTTOM: *Second floor hallway*
FACING PAGE: *Dining room*

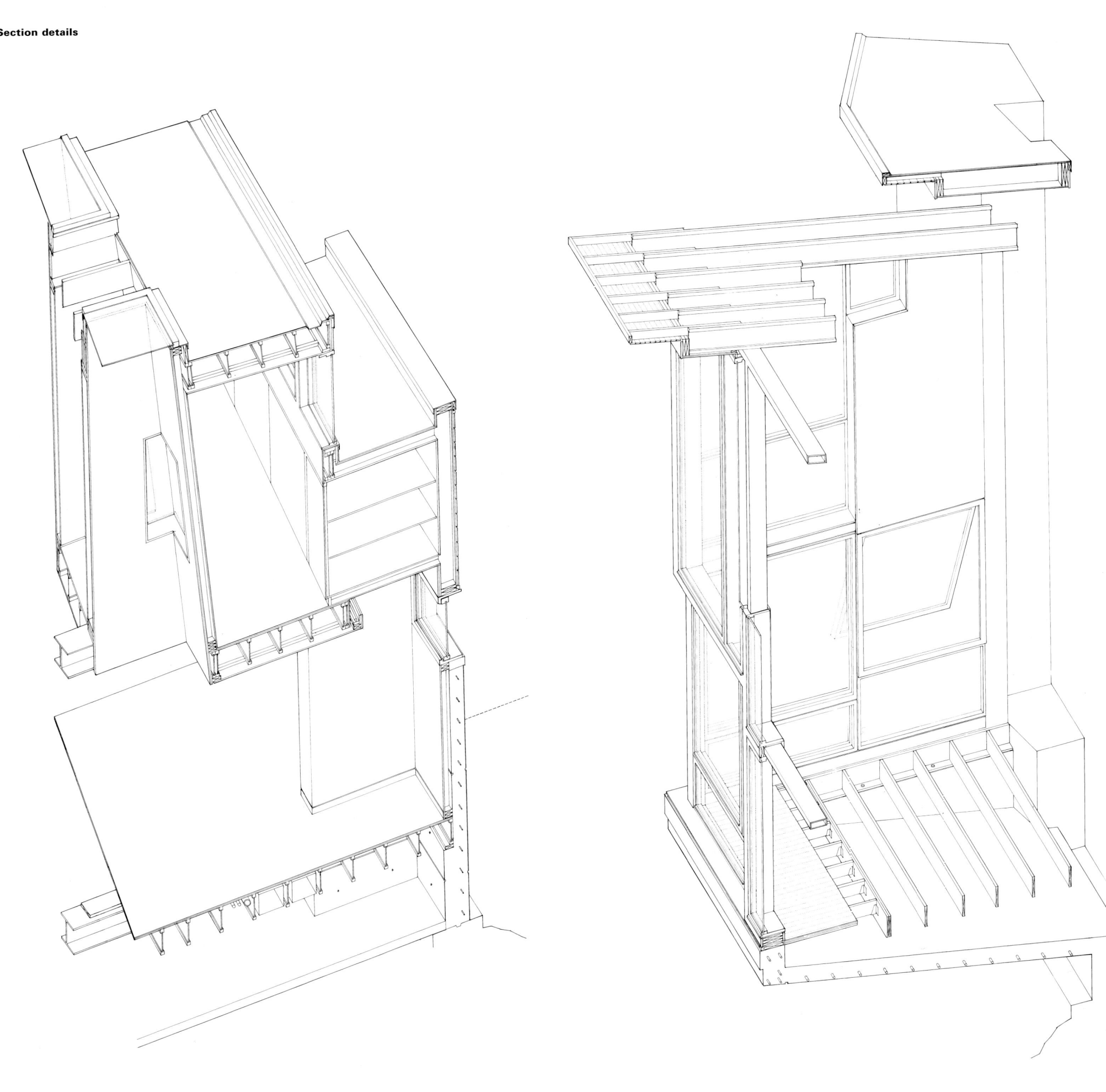

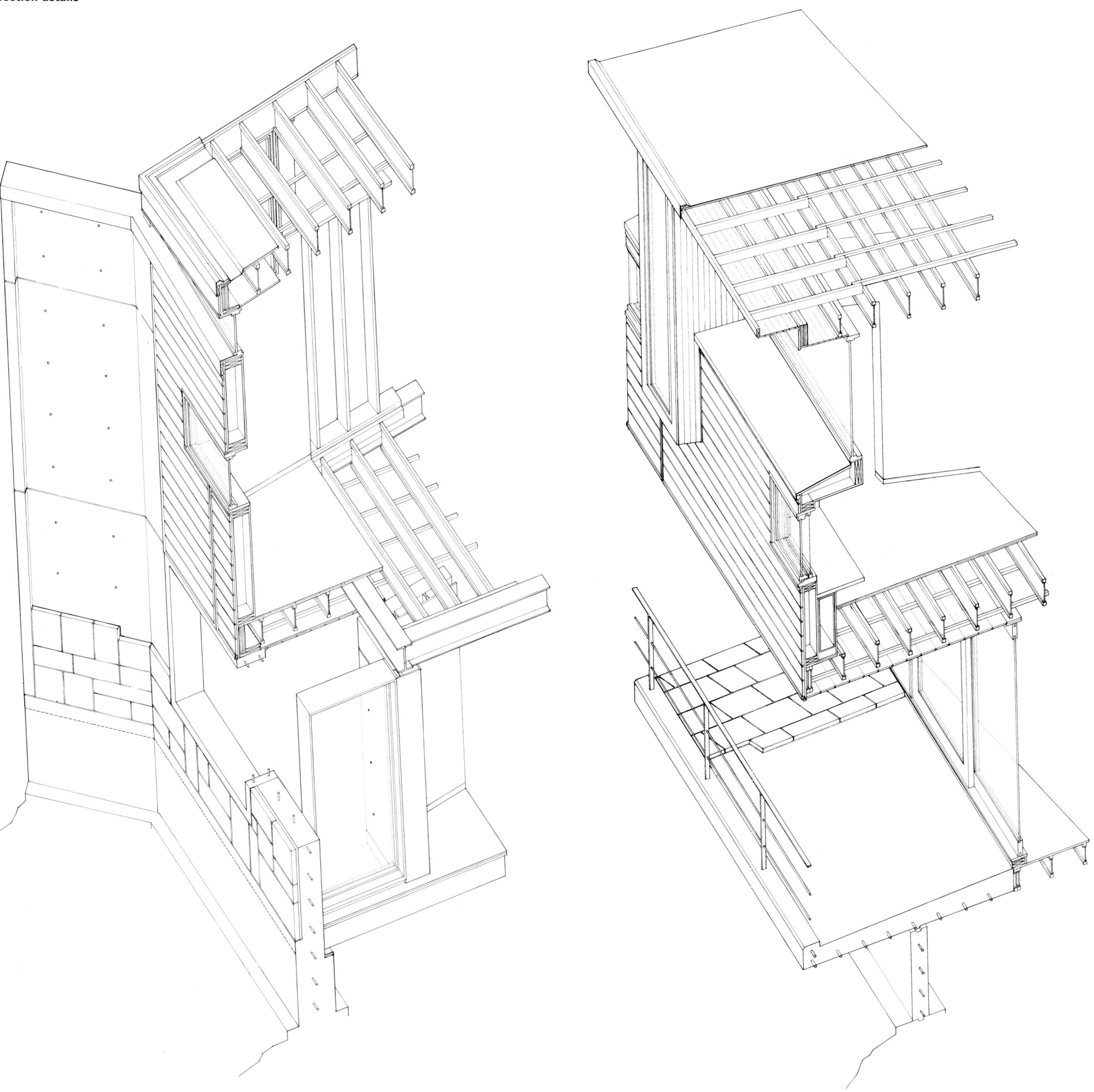

Residence on the Tennessee River *1994-1996*

MOCKBEE/COKER ARCHITECTS

Owner: Name withheld at owner's request.
Architect: Mockbee/Coker Architects, Memphis, Tennessee
Interior Design: Schecter Flom
Design Team: Coleman Coker, Agrippa Spence Kellum
Patrick Johnson, Samuel Mockbee
Engineer: Mark Askew (structural)
Consultant: Tom Pillett & Associates (landscape architect)
General Contractor: L.D. Briley Construction Co.
Photography: Timothy Hursley

Site: Shiloh Falls, Tennessee
Program: Weekend house including gallery, sitting room, kitchen, dining room, living room, half bathroom, garage, 3 bedrooms, 3 bathrooms, reading room.
Square Footage: 3200
Structural System: Slab on grade, wood framing walls and roof structure, glulam beams and steel column supported roof system.
Mechanical System: Electric heat pumps for heating and cooling
Major Exterior Materials: Brick veneer (walls), aluminum (window wall), galvalume panels ASC-Pacific (roof), EPDM by Carlisle Syntec Roofing (roof).
Major Interior Materials: End grain Douglas fir and edge grain birch (floor), Indiana limestone (floor, stair treads and vanity tops), exposed concrete (floor), painted gypsum board (walls and ceilings), exposed painted structural roof members, patinated copper foil circuit board (fireplace), aluminum, steel, stainless steel.
Furnishings and Storage: Donald Judd (bench), Paul Frankl (coffee table), T.H. Robsjohn-Gibbings (console), Alain Richard (dining table), Mathieu Mategot (bar cart), Paul McCobb (headboard), Charlotte Perriand (sconces), Joe Adkinson (swivel desk), Edward Wermley (interlocking tables).
Doors and Hardware: Kawneer, Sargent (exterior), custom by interior designer and fabricated by Nanz Custom Hardware (interior); Sargent, Rixon
Windows: Kawneer framing System with low-E glass by PPG Industries.
Fixtures: Kroin, Kohler, Laufen
Appliances and Equipment: Sub-Zero (refrigerator/freezer), Gaggenau (oven and cooktop), Jenn-Air (range), Bosch (dishwasher).
Cost: Withheld at owner's request.

Site

Making its way down a steeply sloping site overlooking the Tennessee River is an uncharacteristic weekend house for two brothers designed by Mockbee/Coker. The house is sited south with Mississippi to the west and Alabama to the east.

Design

One of the clients' primary conditions was that while they wanted a comfortable second home with river views, the space should also accomodate their extensive collection of contemporary photography and pre-Columbian

RIGHT: *View of house from Tennessee River*
BOTTOM: *Exterior deck*
FACING PAGE: *West façade*

art. "Stepping" down the topography of the hillside, the house is divided into three floor-level changes of five feet each.

On the main level, the narrow sixty-foot-long entry/gallery displays artworks and leads to the main public space. Here, in the living/dining area, is a two-story glass window wall through which one looks south to the river; to the west are an enclosed inglenook and fireplace.

There is an overwhelming sense of spatial continuity as the rooms "unfold," and one descends to the ground level directly below the living area. Two bedrooms and bathrooms occupy this space, with a third bedroom and bathroom situated over the dining room and kitchen. Adjacent to this and above the inglenook is the reading area, which opens to the living area below. While views of the river can be had from this private reading area, the windows are designed in such a way that the viewer must be seated (and—the thinking goes—relaxed) to enjoy them.

Construction

Both inventive and spontaneous, the construction process involved a great deal of collaboration between the architects and building professionals. Masons used commercial grade brick to form their very own two-color, random design. The secondary brick turned on its edge and projected an inch beyond the primary wall face offers support and creates a change of shadows throughout the day. Constructed of steel tubing welded in branch-like patterns, the sculptural qualities of the house's north end and chimney comfortably coexist with the surrounding trees. Ribbed industrial panels of galvalume sheathe the roof and portions of the exterior walls, while tangled groupings of steel rods configured by the steelworkers serve as deck rails.

Ground level floor plan　　　　　　　　　　**First level floor plan**　　　　　　　　　　**Second level floor plan**

1. ENTRY
2. GALLERY
3. SITTING ROOM
4. KITCHEN
5. UTILITY
6. DINING ROOM
7. LIVING ROOM
8. FIREPLACE
9. TOILET
10. EXTERIOR DECK
11. GARAGE
12. STORAGE
13. BEDROOM
14. BATHROOM
15. READING ROOM
16. OPEN TO BELOW
17. OUTDOOR TERRACE

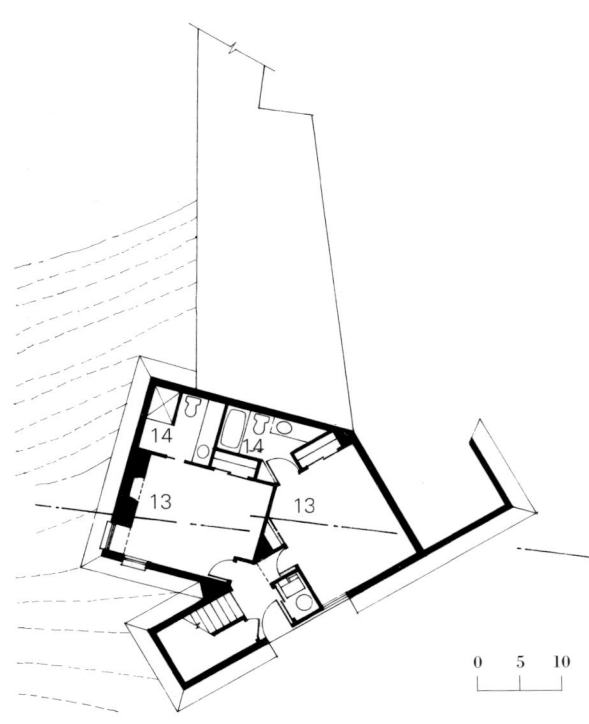

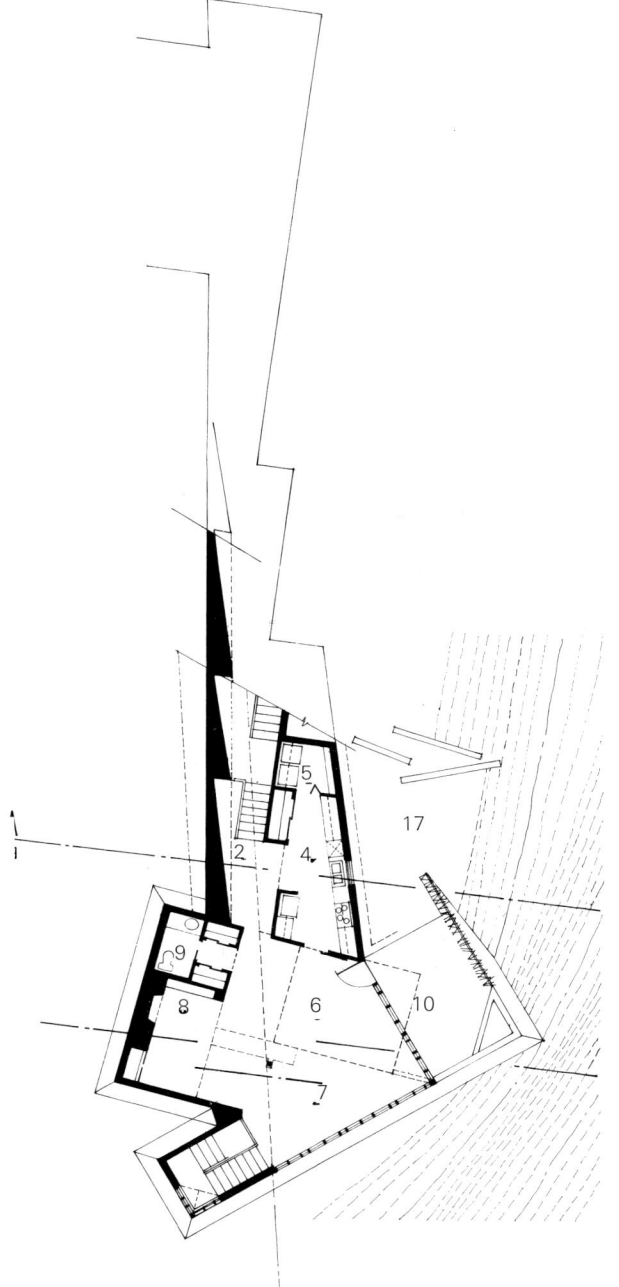

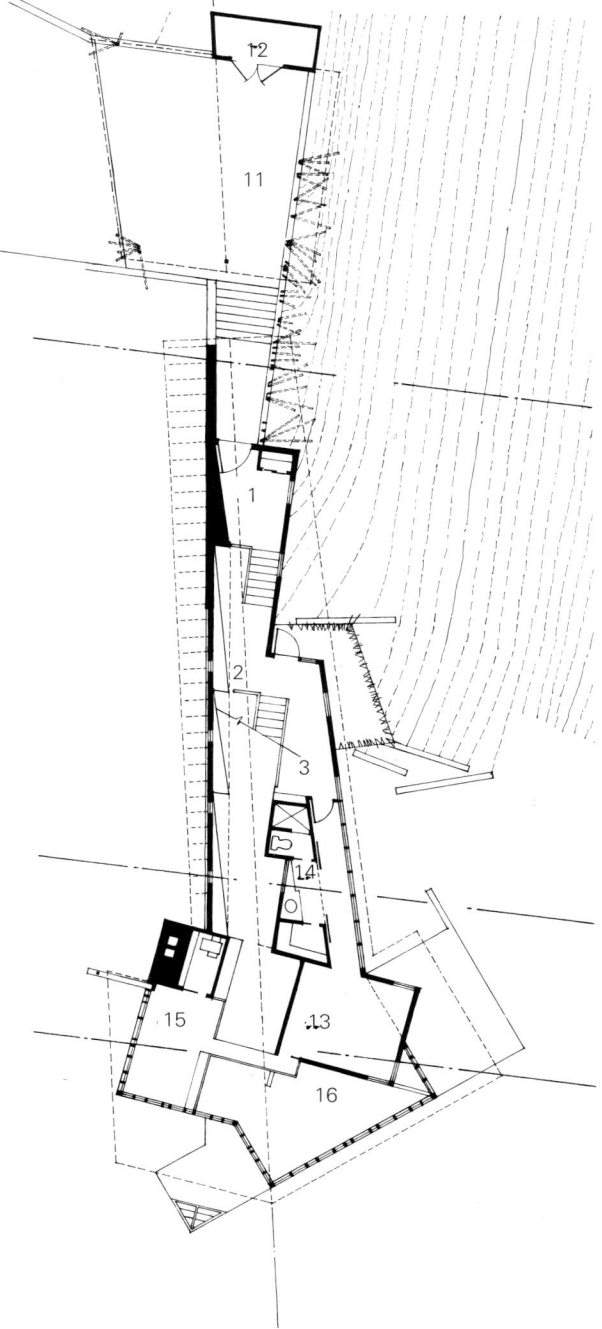

RIGHT: *View of study*
FACING PAGE, CLOCKWISE FROM LEFT: *Study with living room below; gallery; ship ladder to sleeping loft with gallery at right*

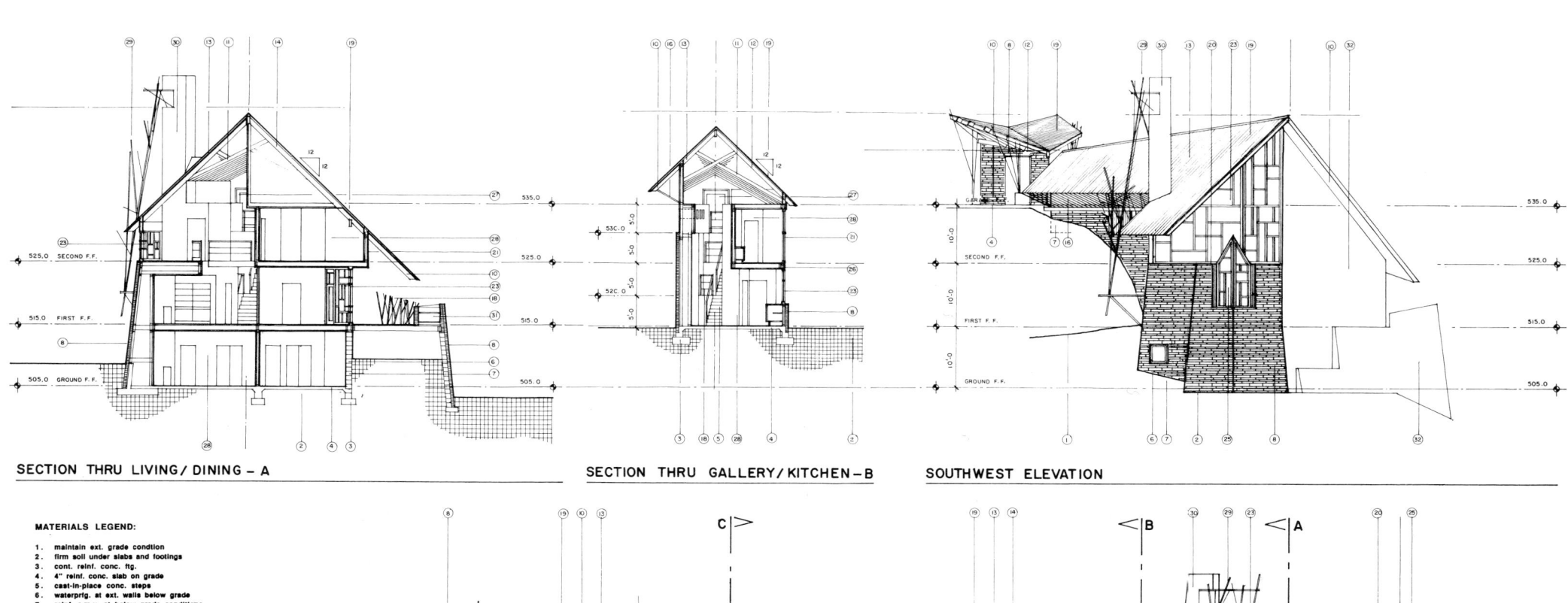

SECTION THRU LIVING/DINING – A

SECTION THRU GALLERY/KITCHEN – B

SOUTHWEST ELEVATION

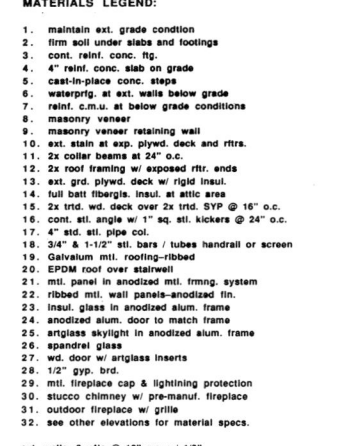

MATERIALS LEGEND:

1. maintain ext. grade condtion
2. firm soil under slabs and footings
3. cont. reinf. conc. ftg.
4. 4" reinf. conc. slab on grade
5. cast-in-place conc. steps
6. waterprfg. at ext. walls below grade
7. reinf. c.m.u. at below grade conditions
8. masonry veneer
9. masonry veneer retaining wall
10. ext. stain at exp. plywd. deck and rftrs.
11. 2x collar beams at 24" o.c.
12. 2x roof framing w/ exposed rftr. ends
13. ext. grd. plywd. deck w/ rigid insul.
14. full batt fibergls. insul. at attic area
15. 2x trtd. wd. deck over 2x trtd. SYP @ 16" o.c.
16. cont. stl. angle w/ 1" sq. stl. kickers @ 24" o.c.
17. 4" std. stl. pipe col.
18. 3/4" & 1-1/2" stl. bars / tubes handrail or screen
19. Galvalum mtl. roofing-ribbed
20. EPDM roof over stairwell
21. mtl. panel in anodized mtl. frmng. system
22. ribbed mtl. wall panels-anodized fin.
23. insul. glass in anodized alum. frame
24. anodized alum. door to match frame
25. artglass skylight in anodized alum. frame
26. spandrel glass
27. wd. door w/ artglass inserts
28. 1/2" gyp. brd.
29. mtl. fireplace cap & lightning protection
30. stucco chimney w/ pre-manuf. fireplace
31. outdoor fireplace w/ grille
32. see other elevations for material specs.

ext. walls: 2 x 4's @ 16" o.c. w/ 1/2"
wd. sheathing & full batt fiberglass insul.

int. walls: 2 x 4's @ 16" o.c. w/ 1/2"
gyp. brd. ea. side

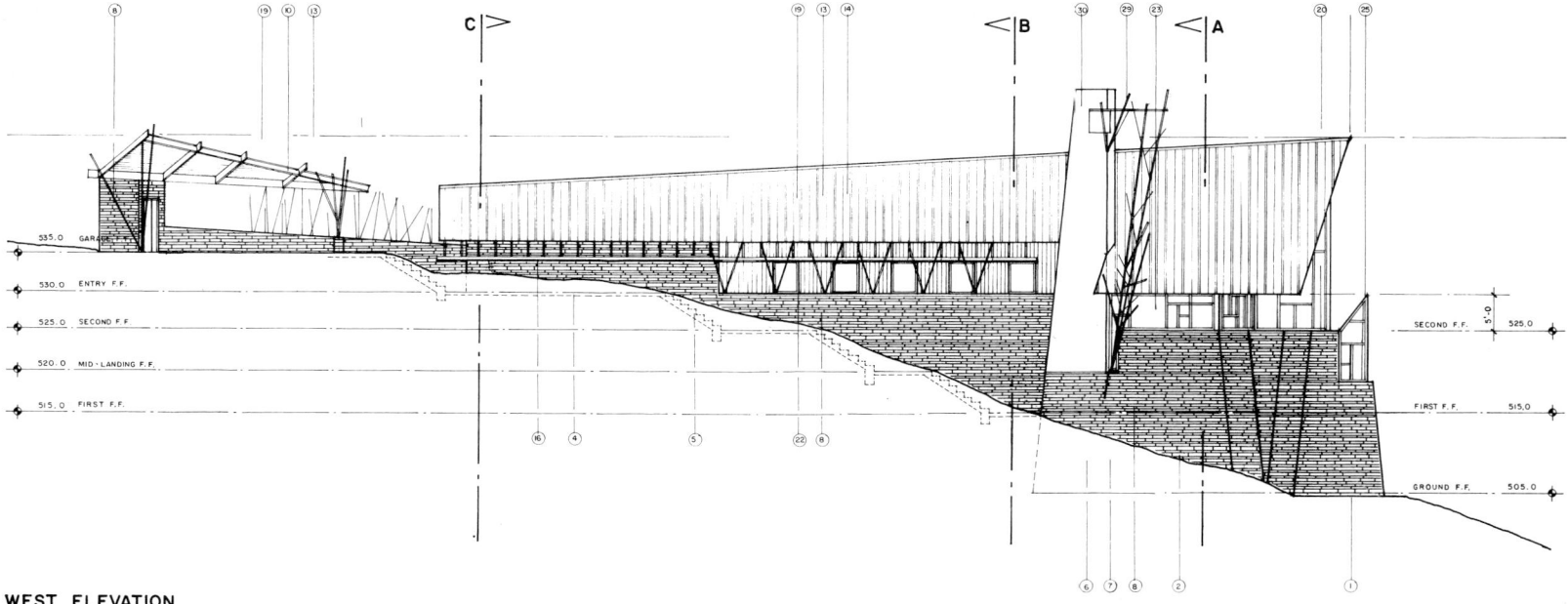

WEST ELEVATION

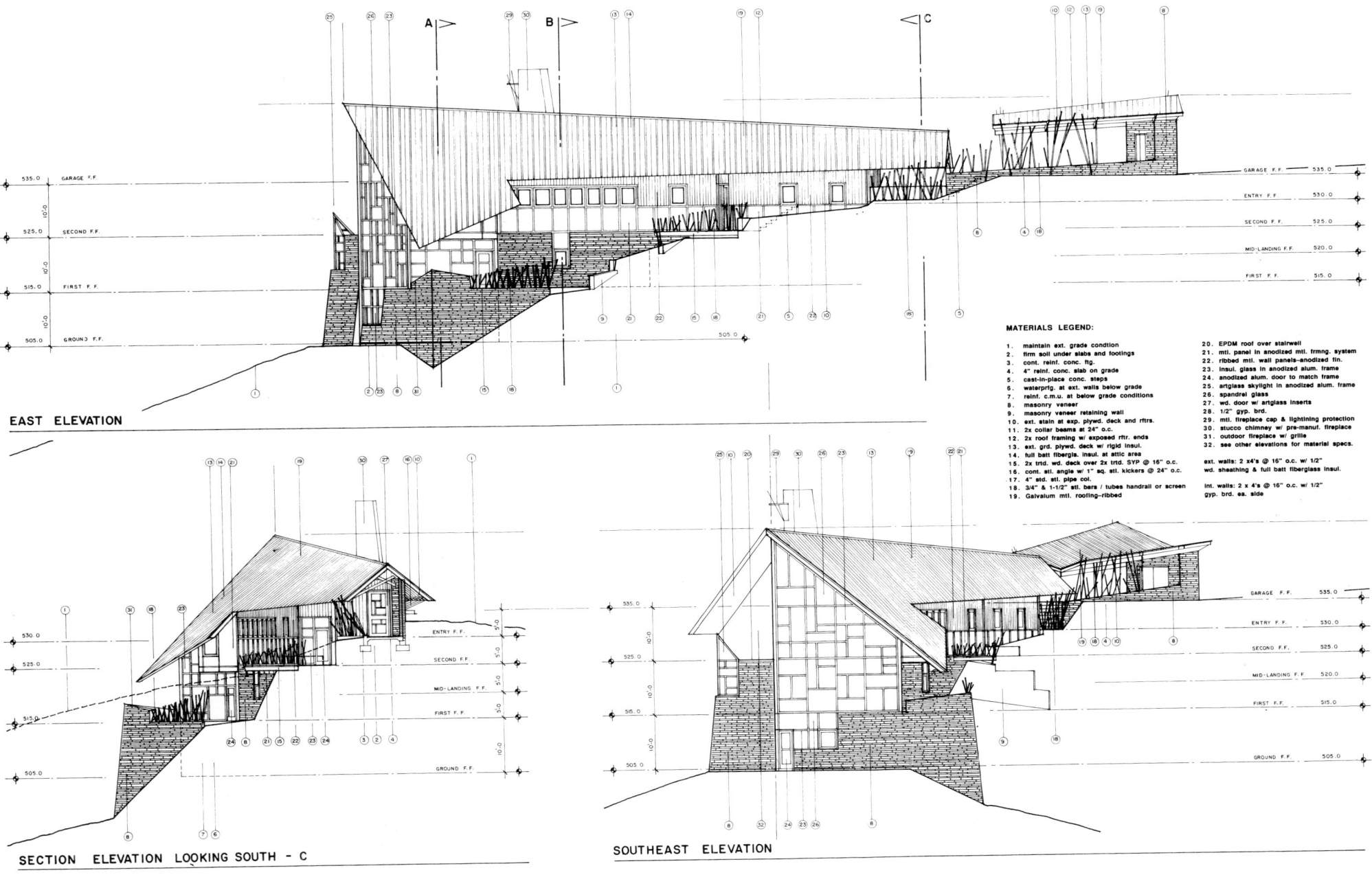

EAST ELEVATION

SECTION ELEVATION LOOKING SOUTH - C

SOUTHEAST ELEVATION

MATERIALS LEGEND:

1. maintain ext. grade condtion
2. firm soil under slabs and footings
3. cont. reinf. conc. ftg.
4. 4" reinf. conc. slab on grade
5. cast-in-place conc. steps
6. waterprfg. at ext. walls below grade
7. reinf. c.m.u. at below grade conditions
8. masonry veneer
9. masonry veneer retaining wall
10. ext. stain at exp. plywd. deck and rftrs.
11. 2x collar beams at 24" o.c.
12. 2x roof framing w/ exposed rftr. ends
13. ext. grd. plywd. deck w/ rigid insul.
14. full batt fibergls. insul. at attic area
15. 2x trtd. wd. deck over 2x trtd. SYP @ 16" o.c.
16. cont. stl. angle w/ 1" sq. stl. kickers @ 24" o.c.
17. 4" std. stl. pipe col.
18. 3/4" & 1-1/2" stl. bars / tubes handrail or screen
19. Galvalum mtl. roofing-ribbed

20. EPDM roof over stairwell
21. mtl. panel in anodized mtl. trmng. system
22. ribbed mtl. wall panels-anodized fin.
23. insul. glass in anodized alum. frame
24. anodized alum. door to match frame
25. artglass skylight in anodized alum. frame
26. spandrel glass
27. wd. door w/ artglass inserts
28. 1/2" gyp. brd.
29. mtl. fireplace cap & lightning protection
30. stucco chimney w/ pre-manuf. fireplace
31. outdoor fireplace w/ grille
32. see other elevations for material specs.

ext. walls: 2 x4's @ 16" o.c. w/ 1/2"
wd. sheathing & full batt fiberglass insul.

int. walls: 2 x 4's @ 16" o.c. w/ 1/2"
gyp. brd. ea. side

Root House Interior *1990-1995*

PASANELLA KLEIN STOLZMAN BERG ARCHITECTS

Owner: Chapman J. Root II
Interior Architect: Pasanella Klein Stolzman Berg Architects, PC, New York, New York
Design Team: Wayne Berg, FAIA (design principal), Albert Ho, AIA (project architect)
Consultants: Jerry Kugler Associates (lighting design), Tse-Yun Chu Studio (materials and finishes), Fu-Teng Cheng (kitchen design)
General Contractor: Owner, with Foley & Associates, Construction Co., Inc.
Photography: Paul Warchol

Site: Ormond Beach, Florida
Program: Main residence including refectory, kitchen, pantry, 2 changing rooms, living room, library, maid's room, guest room, master bedroom, master bathroom, office/study, observatory/crow's nest.
Square Footage: 6500 in three floors
Structural System: Auger pile foundations, reinforced Demaco fluted concrete masonry unit bearing walls and pilasters, open web truss joists for spans exceeding 12', laminated timber beams, steel framing at stairs, landings, and specialty areas.
Mechanical System: Carrier split system, air coded heat pumps in multiple zones with indoor fan units
Major Exterior Materials: Fluted concrete block, glass (William Morgan, FAIA, exterior architect)
Major Interior Materials: Aluminum and copper mesh (bridge screen panels), shellstone and grassy green slate (refectory floor), maple burl with hand-rubbed finish (fireplace), quarter saw ash (library canopy), black granite (library ledge/banquette), teak with ebony insets (library floor), flat-cut maple with checkerboard pattern veneer (kitchen screen partition), stainless steel with random orbital finish (kitchen partition frame), maple (kitchen floor), milk-white onyx (third floor translucent corner partition and kitchen workshelf), Carrara glass with brass reveal (bathroom walls), Idaho quartzite (bathroom floors), cast concrete with integral metal and colored powders and colored glass insets (kitchen island base).
Furnishings and Storage: Custom by architect (kitchen island/counter and onyx workshelf, kitchen cabinetry, library exhibit shelves, stainless steel magazine rack), Florence Knoll (dining table with marble top), Warren Platner (dining chairs), Jean-Michel Frank through Palazzetti (love seat and sofa), Mies van der Rohe through Palazzetti (day bed), Kessler through Palazzetti (coffee table), Kevin Walz (lamp), ready-made furniture selected by Steven Harris, Architect, Florida; Eric Bauer, Fayston Iron and Steel (custom metalwork), Jeff Vaida, JFV Design (millwork).
Doors and Hardware: Blumcraft (entry); custom by architect, fabricated by Eric Bauer, Fayston Iron & Steel
Windows: Aluminum framed by Kawneer, structural glass and fins by Tempglass Eastern, Inc.
Fixtures: Kroin (bathroom and kitchen faucets, bathroom towel bars)
Appliances and Equipment: Custom by architect (stainless steel commercial-type range hood), Speakman (shower)
Cost: $400 per square foot

RIGHT: *View of gallery and bridge*
BOTTOM: *Third floor ramp*
FACING PAGE: *Bridge*

Site

The house, designed by William Morgan, FAIA, and constructed of fluted concrete block, is situated at the edge of the Atlantic Ocean. While its sides are mostly solid, the house's ocean-facing façade is almost entirely made of glass. When viewed through the windowed wall the surrounding buildings and even much of the beach seem to disappear, so that only the sea and sky are present.

The house is made up of three main volumes: a triple-height void (the refectory) flanked by three stories of rooms on either side. (One houses entry, stair, and observatory/crow's nest; the other houses living spaces.) Pasanella Klein Stolzman Berg's design maintains the house's volumetric organization and relationship with the ocean, but the interior architecture's use of light planar and linear elements forms a counterpoint to the massiveness of the structure.

Design

Throughout the interior, screens, pivot panels, linear banquettes, and other light planar elements were inserted to reinforce the house's inherent spatial sequences and accommodate the programmatic requirements.

The main intervention consists of two three-story aluminum and copper mesh screens supporting a cantilevered wood bridge that spans the refectory. This assembly brackets the edges of the refectory and mediates the grand scale of the triple-volume space and the residential scale of the single-volume open floors overlooking the refectory. The maple screen in the first-floor kitchen, the maple burl fireplace screen in the second-floor library, and the translucent aluminum screen in the third-floor master bedroom are proportioned to the scales of their respective spaces.

The triple-height refectory/gallery and bridge are used for formal gatherings. The refectory serves as a dining hall, while the kitchen—screened from view—supports a catering staff. Changing rooms are mainly for guests.

The kitchen, designed and scaled primarily for the client's own use, precedes a casual living room that looks out over the ocean. On the third floor is the client's private retreat, with simple, intimately scaled, and serene bedroom, bathrooms, and office/study. The observation deck has four windows offering panoramic views of the ocean.

Construction

Insertions, and particularly points where they meet, are carefully detailed and crafted, celebrating the intricate joinery of disparate materials. Semitransparent copper mesh is juxtaposed with its tough, sandblasted steel supporting frame; raw cast concrete at the kitchen island base is set against a polished, antique countertop carved from a single plank of teak wood; Idaho quartzite is left rough where it clads the master bathroom's walls, but polished smooth on the floor.

Third level floor plan

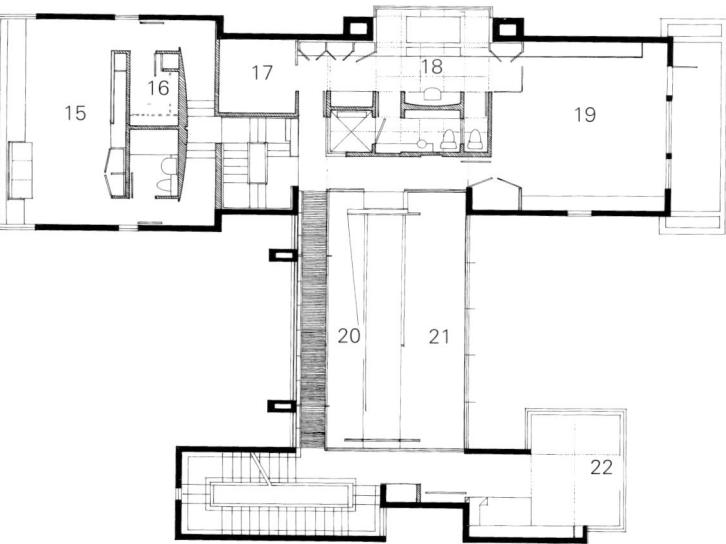

Second level floor plan

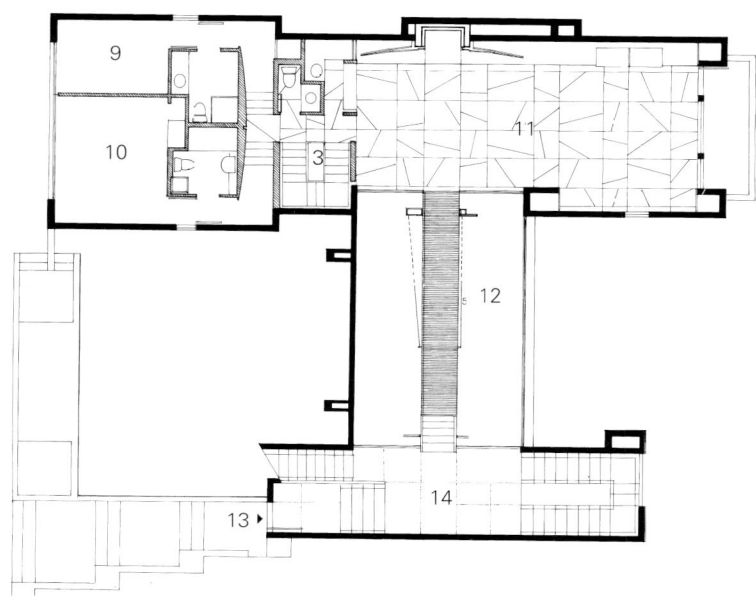

First level floor plan

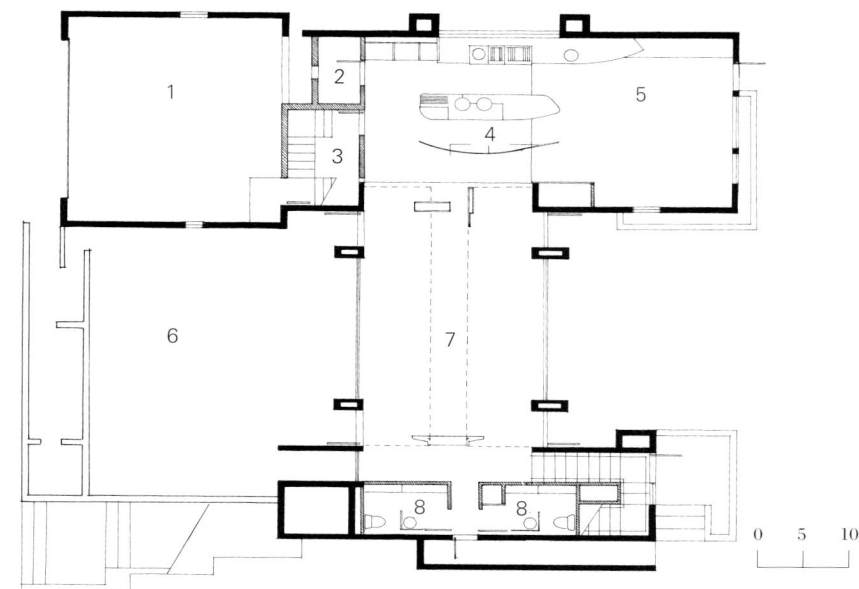

1. GARAGE
2. PANTRY
3. PRIVATE STAIR
4. KITCHEN
5. LIVING ROOM
6. GARDEN
7. GALLERY
8. CHANGING ROOM
9. MAID'S ROOM
10. GUEST ROOM
11. LIBRARY
12. BRIDGE
13. ENTRY
14. FOYER
15. PRIVATE OFFICE
16. CLOSET
17. WALK-IN CLOSET
18. MASTER BATHROOM
19. MASTER BEDROOM
20. RAMP
21. GALLERY BELOW
22. CROW'S NEST/
OBSERVATION DECK

0   5   10

Section

Site plan

Bridge axonometric

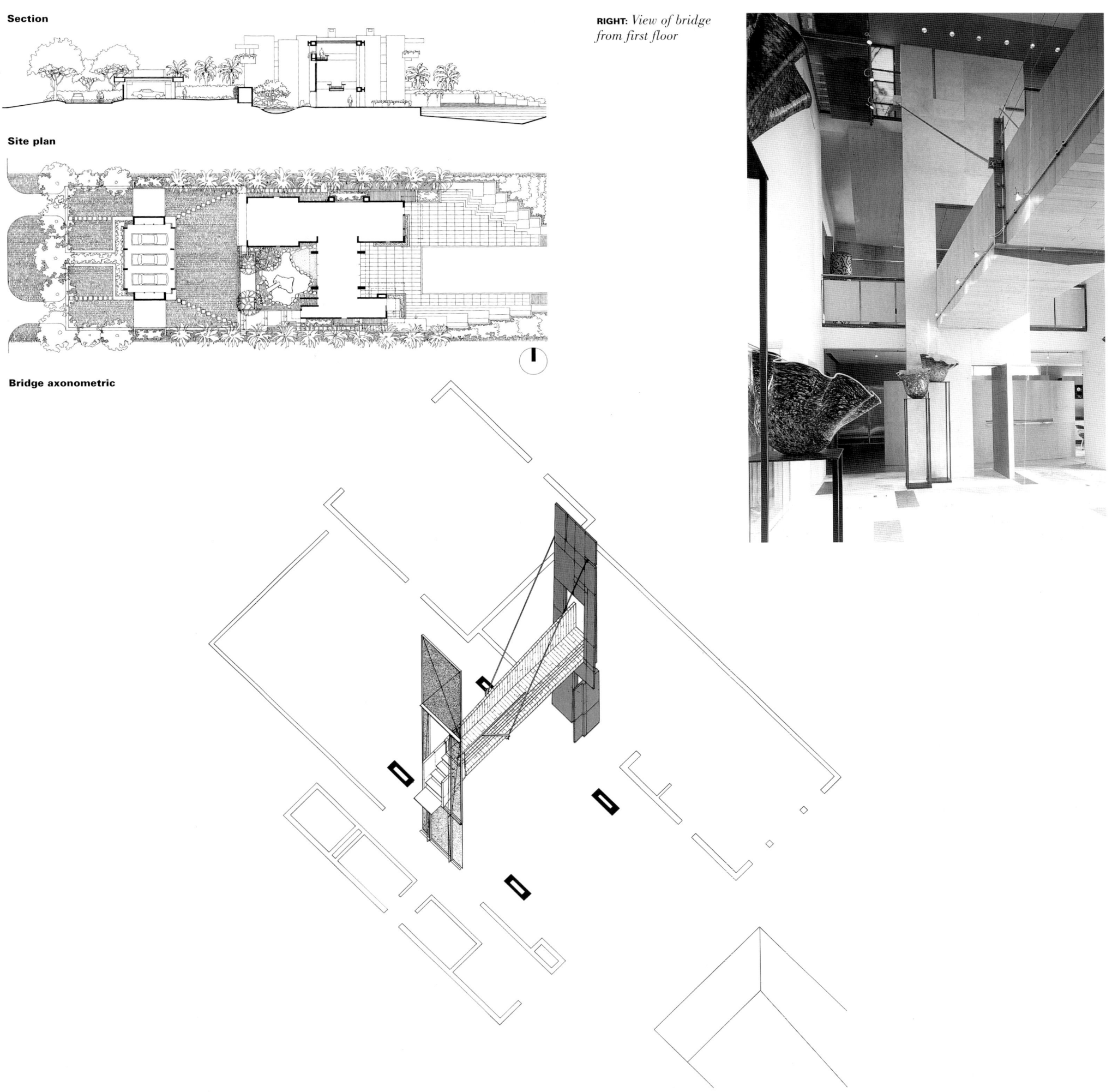

CLOCKWISE FROM TOP LEFT:
Main façade; hand rail details; views of master bathroom; living room
FACING PAGE: *View of gallery on left and kitchen on right*

Section at bridge support

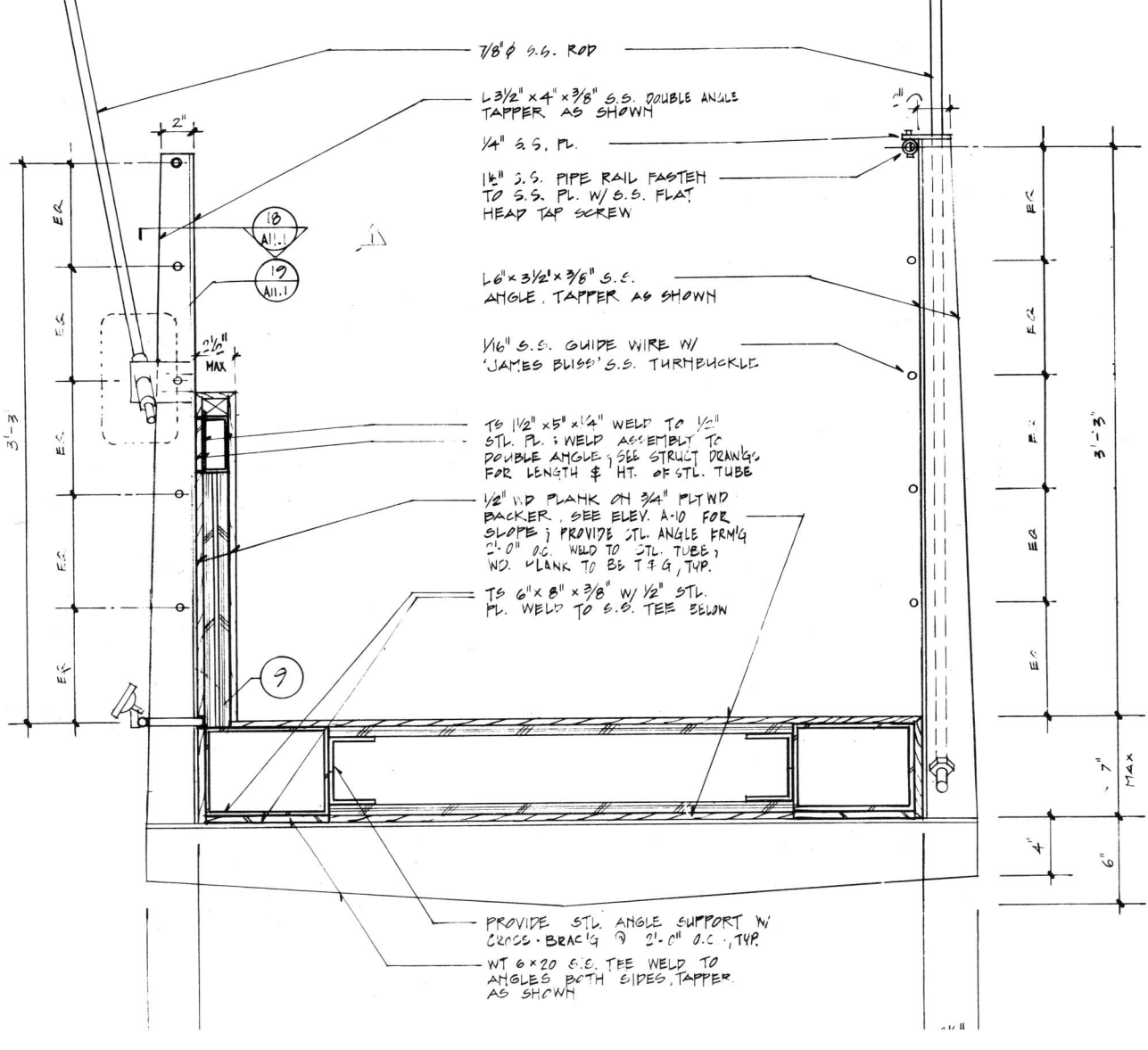

7/8"φ S.S. ROD

L 3½" x 4" x 3/8" S.S. DOUBLE ANGLE
TAPPER AS SHOWN

¼" S.S. PL.

1½" S.S. PIPE RAIL FASTEN
TO S.S. PL. W/ S.S. FLAT
HEAD TAP SCREW

L 6" x 3½" x 3/8" S.S.
ANGLE, TAPPER AS SHOWN

1/16" S.S. GUIDE WIRE W/
'JAMES BLISS' S.S. TURNBUCKLE

TS 1½" x 5" x ¼" WELD TO ½"
STL. PL. ; WELD ASSEMBLY TO
DOUBLE ANGLE ; SEE STRUCT DRAWG.
FOR LENGTH & HT. OF STL. TUBE

½" WD PLANK ON ¾" PLYWD
BACKER , SEE ELEV. A-10 FOR
SLOPE ; PROVIDE STL. ANGLE FRM'G
2'-0" OC. WELD TO STL. TUBE ;
WD. PLANK TO BE T & G , TYP.

TS 6" x 8" x 3/8" W/ ½" STL.
PL. WELD TO S.S. TEE BELOW

PROVIDE STL. ANGLE SUPPORT W/
CROSS-BRAC'G @ 2'-0" O.C., TYP.

WT 6x20 S.S. TEE WELD TO
ANGLES BOTH SIDES, TAPPER
AS SHOWN

RIGHT: *View of bridge*

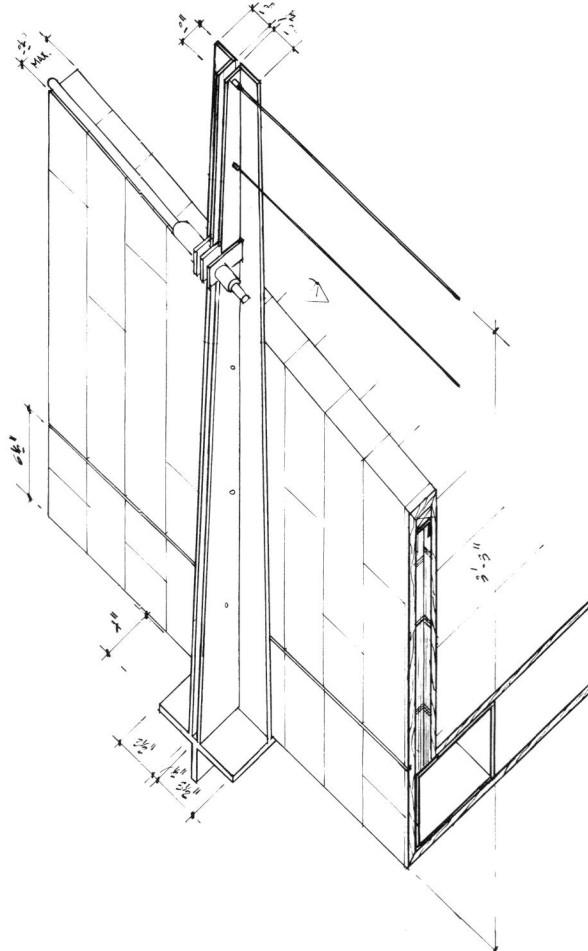

Axonometric

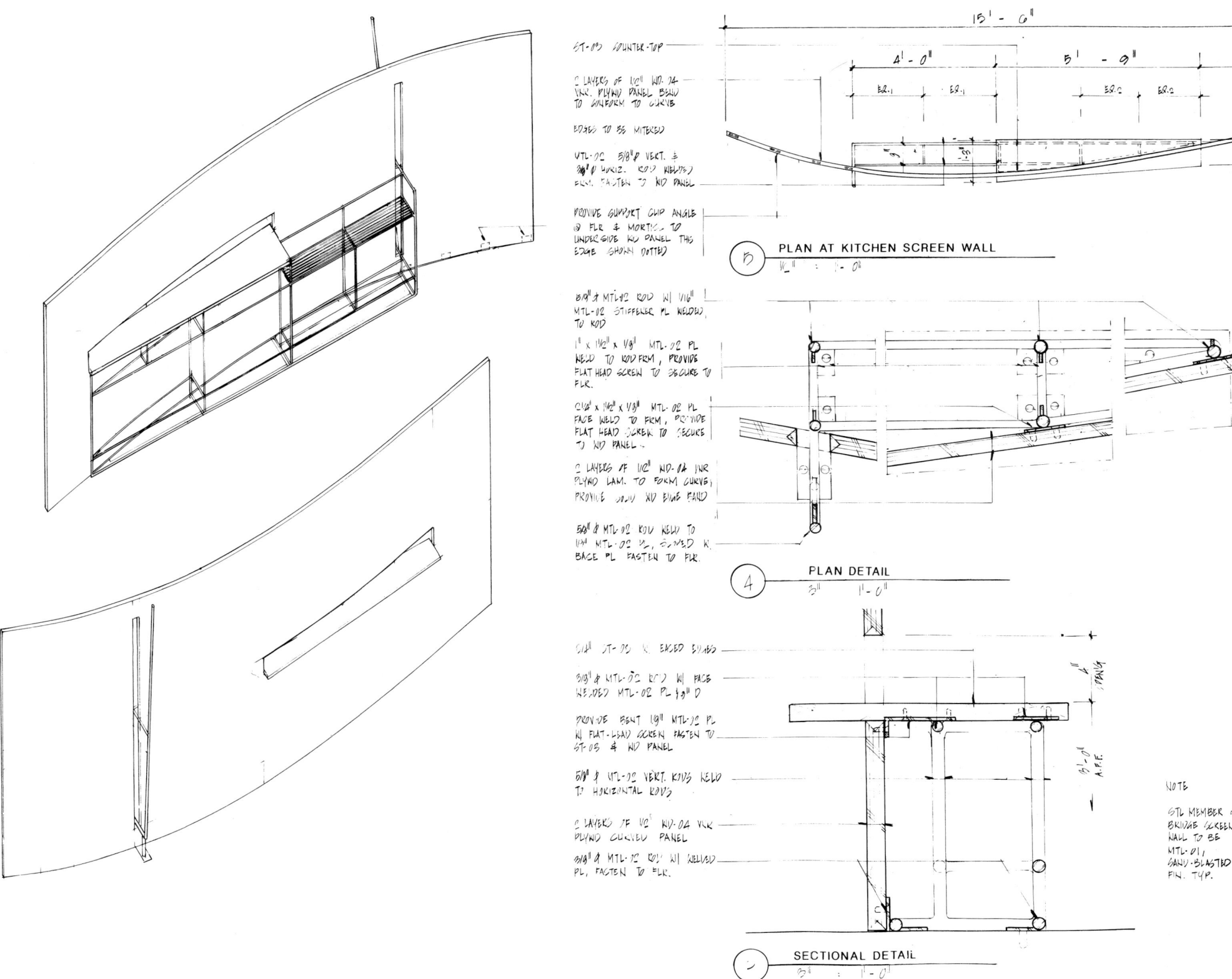

ST-03 COUNTER-TOP

2 LAYERS OF 1/2" WD-04
VNR. PLYWD PANEL BENT
TO CONFORM TO CURVE

EDGES TO BE MITERED

MTL-02 5/8"⌀ VERT. &
3/8"⌀ HORIZ. ROD WELDED
FLM. FASTEN TO WD PANEL

PROVIDE SUPPORT CLIP ANGLE
@ FLR & MORTISE TO
UNDERSIDE WD PANEL THIS
EDGE SHOWN DOTTED

15' - 0"

4' - 0"   5' - 9"

ER-1   ER-1   ER-2   ER-2

PLAN AT KITCHEN SCREEN WALL
1/2" : 1' - 0"   (5)

3/8"⌀ MTL-02 ROD W/ 1/16"
MTL-02 STIFFENER PL WELDED
TO ROD

1" X 1 1/2" X 1/8" MTL-02 PL
WELD TO ROD FRM, PROVIDE
FLAT HEAD SCREW TO SECURE TO
FLR.

1 1/2" X 1 1/2" X 1/8" MTL-02 PL
FACE WELD TO FRM, PROVIDE
FLAT HEAD SCREW TO SECURE
TO WD PANEL

2 LAYERS OF 1/2" WD-04 VNR
PLYWD LAM. TO FORM CURVE,
PROVIDE SOLID WD EDGE BAND

5/8"⌀ MTL-02 ROD WELD TO
1/4" MTL-02 PL, SCREWED W.
BASE PL FASTEN TO FLR.

PLAN DETAIL
(4)   3" : 1' - 0"

5/8" ST-03 W. EASED EDGES

3/8"⌀ MTL-02 ROD W/ FACE
WELDED MTL-02 PL 1/8" D

PROVIDE BENT 1/8" MTL-02 PL
W/ FLAT-HEAD SCREW FASTEN TO
ST-03 & WD PANEL

5/8"⌀ MTL-02 VERT. RODS WELD
TO HORIZONTAL RODS

2 LAYERS OF 1/2" WD-04 VNR
PLYWD CURVED PANEL

3/8"⌀ MTL-02 RODS W/ WELDED
PL, FASTEN TO FLR.

3'-0"
A.F.F.

NOTE

STL MEMBER @
BRIDGE SCREEN
WALL TO BE
MTL-01,
SAND-BLASTED
FIN. TYP.

SECTIONAL DETAIL
3" : 1' - 0"

Golden Beach Residence

1991-1994

CARLOS ZAPATA DESIGN STUDIO

Owner: Nicolas and Catalina Landes
Interior Architect: Carlos Zapata Design Studio, Boston, Massachusetts and Miami Beach, Florida
Design Team: Una Idea (associate architect); Carlos Zapata, John West, Catalina Landes (design direction); Eduardo Calma, Maria Wilthew, Frank Gonzalez, Jose Rodriguez, Claudia Busch; Melissa Koff (project coordinator).
Engineers: William Faschan, Leslie E. Robertson Associates (structural), Lauredo Engineers (mechanical/electrical)
Consultant: Raymond Jungles Inc. (landscape architect)
General Contractor: Cruz R. Rodriguez
Photography: Peter Aaron/Esto

Site: Golden Beach, Florida
Program: Single-family residence including master bedroom, bathroom, gym, and terrace, family room, 3 bedrooms, 3 bathrooms, laundry, kitchen, dining room with outdoor terrace, living room, study, projection room, guest house, pool.
Square Footage: 6200 main house, 630 in guest house
Structural System: Steel, wood, concrete.
Mechanical System: Central heat and air conditioning
Major Exterior Materials: Poured-in-place concrete, structural steel, wood, reinforced concrete block.
Major Interior Materials: Custom green-tinted insulated glass, stainless steel, exposed concrete, stucco, copper, onyx, Verde Serpentino, Swiss pearwood, maple, mahogany (studio only), sisal carpet.
Furnishings and Storage: Custom by architect, ICF, Rosenthal, Luminaire.
Doors and Hardware: Custom by architect; Hafele, D Line, custom by architect.
Windows: Custom by architect.
Fixtures: Kroin, Hans Groin, Villeroy-Boche.
Appliances and Equipment: Gaggenau, Sub-Zero
Cost: Withheld at owner's request.

RIGHT: *West façade detail*
BOTTOM: *Guest quarters at left and main house at right*
FACING PAGE: *Entry*

Site

This new house sits on the foundations of a 1930s beachfront residence of approximately 6200 square feet, with a guest house of approximately 630 square feet. The original perimeter has been strategically altered to accommodate a more dynamic expression, though the original massing distribution is still reflected in the final realization.

Design

The house has uninterrupted views of the Atlantic Ocean to the east of the property, therefore most of its rooms face east and are characterized by large spans of glass. Because the east façade faces the street, its magnificent onyx, stainless steel, and glass wall permit privacy while allowing the passage of afternoon light.

The center space has been transformed into an area where both wings merge. It contains the entry, family

room, and living areas. The south wing houses the master suite, gym, and study, and the north wing contains the children's bedrooms, dining room, kitchen, and laundry.

The guest house/studio, situated next to the pool and beach, is equipped with an operable copper shield that opens the second floor of the house entirely to the beach and ocean.

Construction

The copper shield is supported by two stainless steel arms that hydraulically pivot the shield upward. The remainder of the guest house's east façade is floor-to-ceiling tempered glass supported by stainless steel mullions.

The east façade of the main house is composed of a collage of materials: stucco, glass, and concrete. Its structure is of steel and wood clad with copper.

Second level floor plan

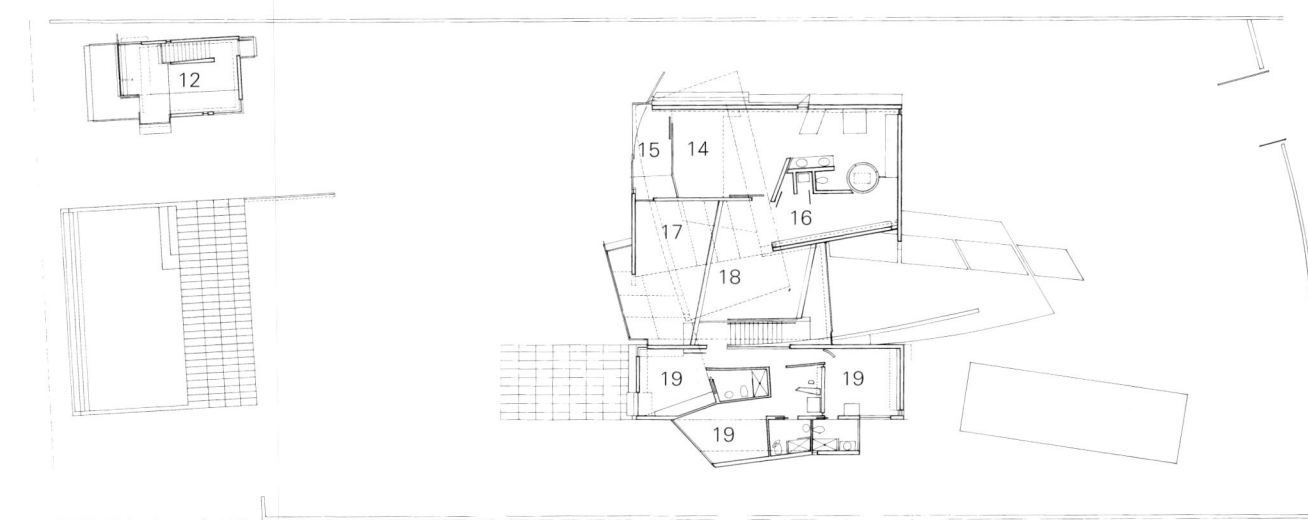

First level floor plan

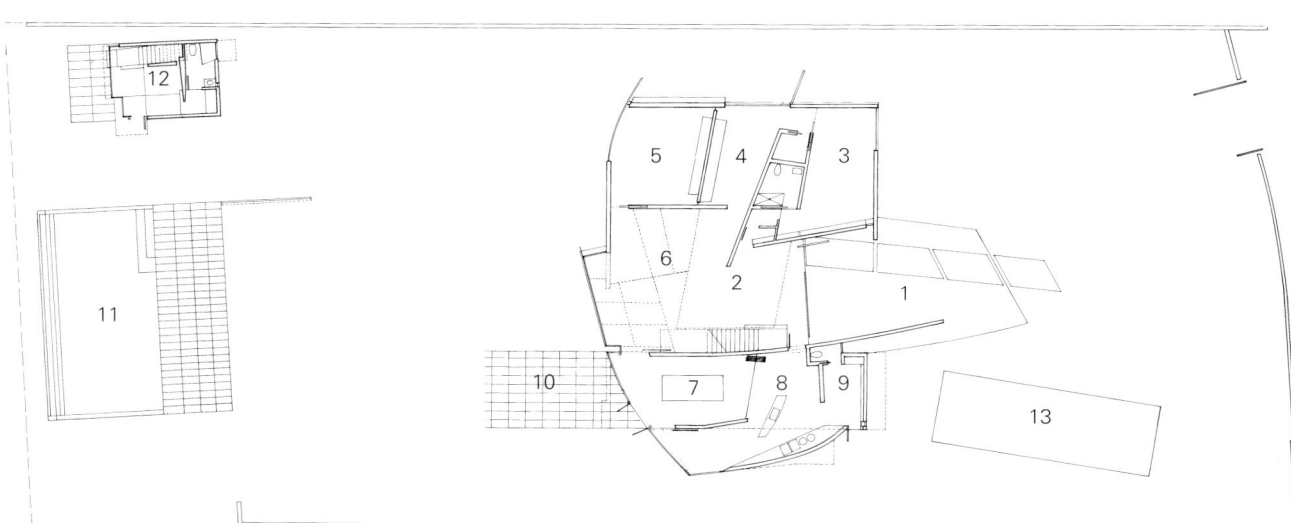

1. LILY POND
2. FOYER
3. DEN/GUEST ROOM
4. GARDEN ROOM
5. STUDY
6. LIVING ROOM
7. DINING ROOM
8. KITCHEN
9. LAUNDRY
10. OUTDOOR DINING
11. POOL
12. GUEST HOUSE
13. PROPOSED GARAGE
14. MASTER BEDROOM
15. TERRACE
16. GYM
17. OPEN
18. FAMILY ROOM
19. BEDROOM

0   10

Section looking north

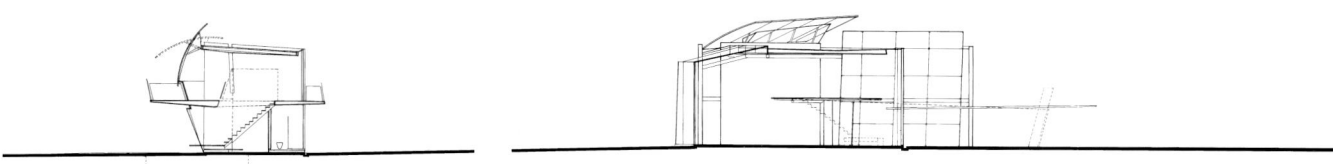

Roof plan

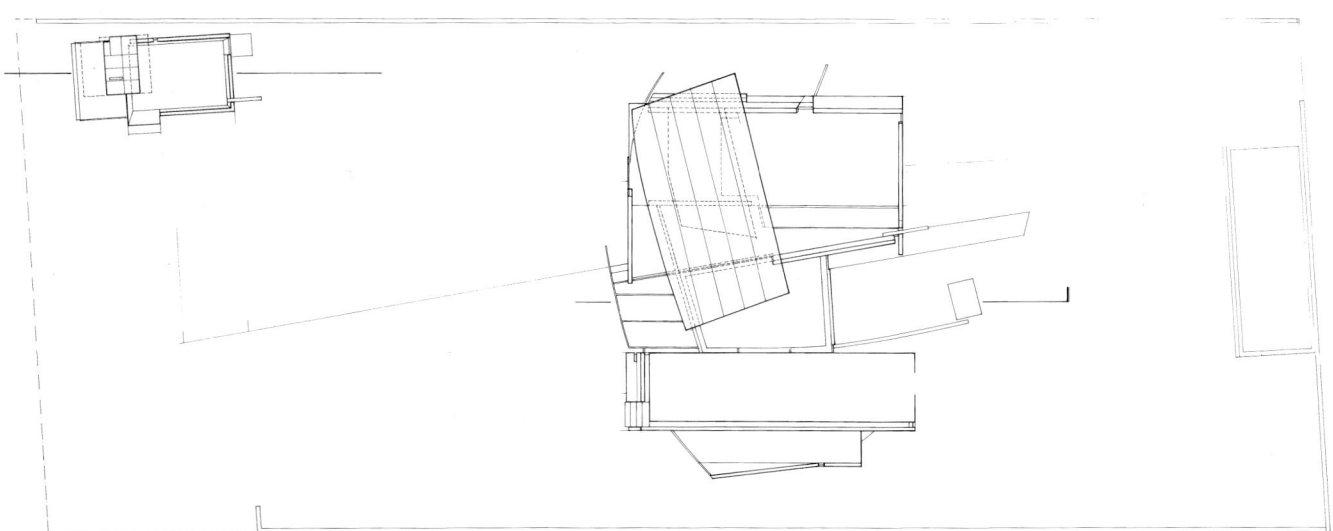

ABOVE: *View of second floor*
ABOVE RIGHT: *View of living room toward foyer*

ABOVE: *View of hallway toward living room*
ABOVE RIGHT: *Entry*

Roof detail

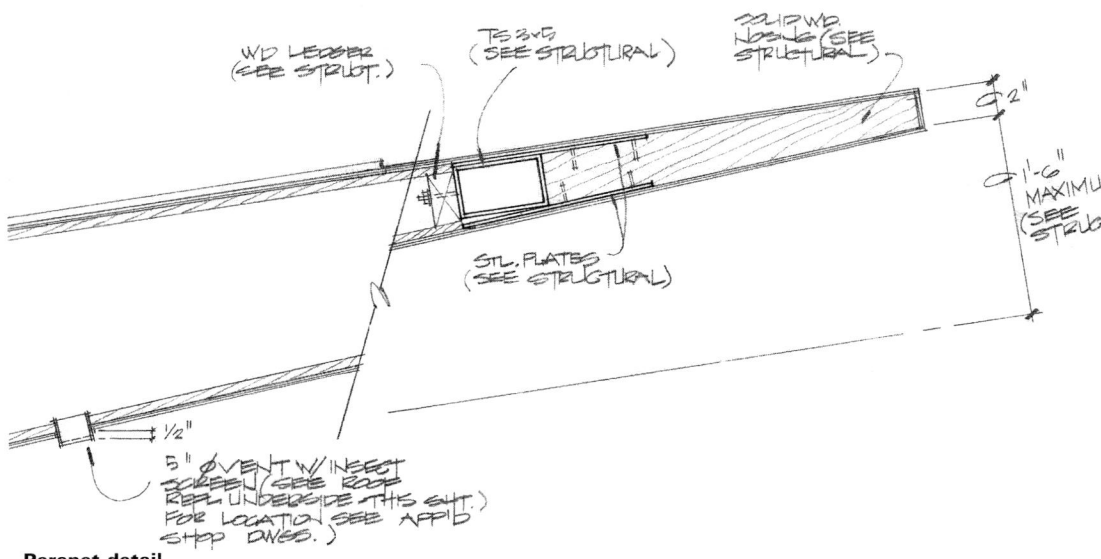

WD. LEDGER (SEE STRUCT.)

TS 3x5 (SEE STRUCTURAL)

SOLID WD. NOSING (SEE STRUCTURAL)

⌀2"

1'-6" MAXIMUM (SEE STRUCTURAL)

STL. PLATES (SEE STRUCTURAL)

½"

5" ⌀ VENT W/INSECT SCREEN (SEE ROOF REFL UNDERSIDE THIS SHT.) FOR LOCATION SEE APP'D SHOP DWGS.)

Parapet detail

RIGHT: *View of guest house/studio*

T.O. ST. STL.

6" x ⅛" CON'T. FORMED ST. STL. (BRUSH FINISH)

WELDING

#10 F.H. TEX SCREW @ 12" O.C.

3/8" ⌀ ST. STUD ANCHOR

ST. ANGLE CLIP 1/4" x 5" x 1/4" 8" LONG. (2) PER OPENING

TOP OF CONCRETE BEAM

SHIM AS REQ'D.

1¾" x 1¾" TYP. ALUMINUM CHANNEL

ST. STL. CLADDING 16 GA. (BY OTHERS)

2½"

UNIT HEIGHT

1" INSULATED GLASS

BOTTOM OF CONCRETE BEAM

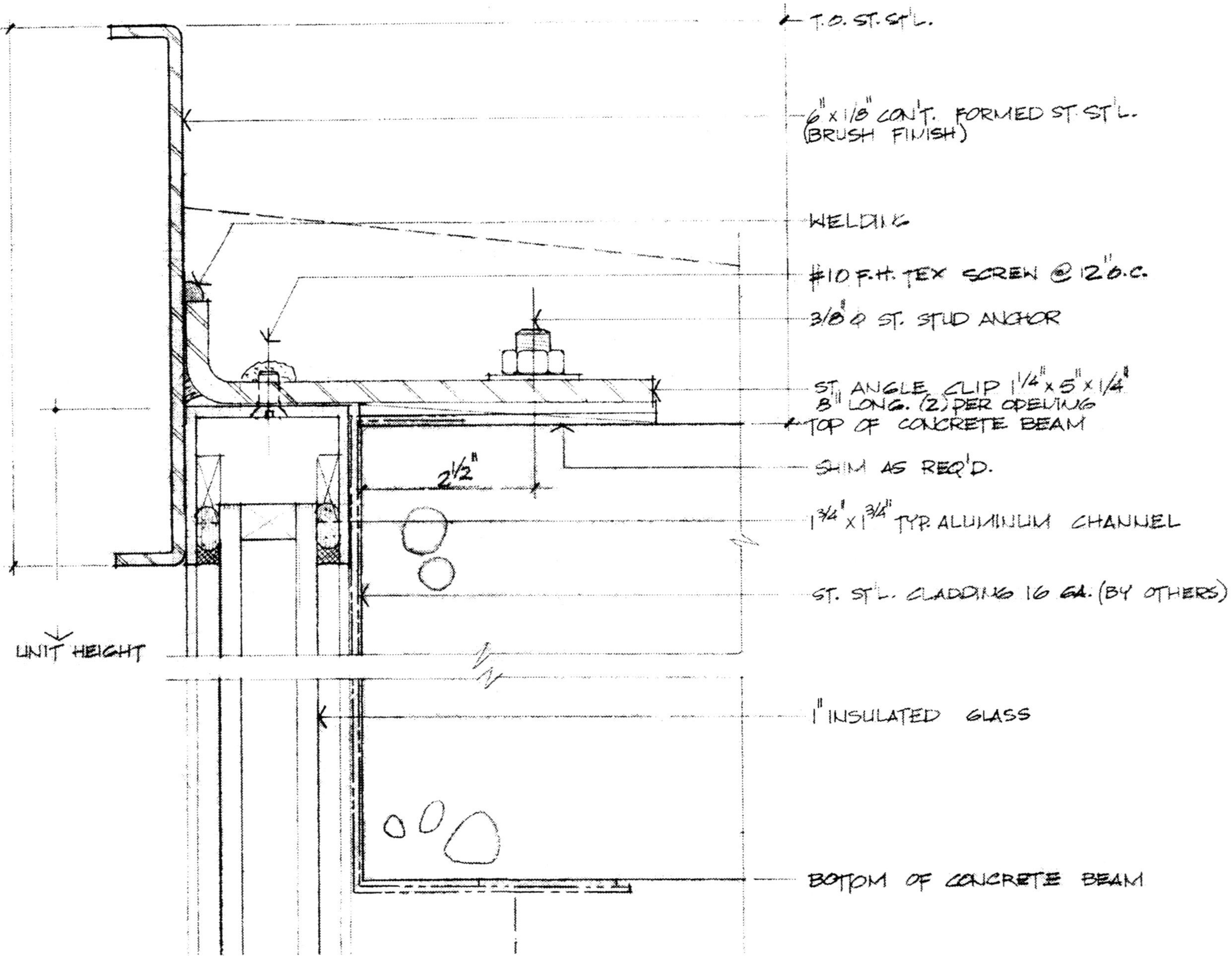

RIGHT: *View of stair*

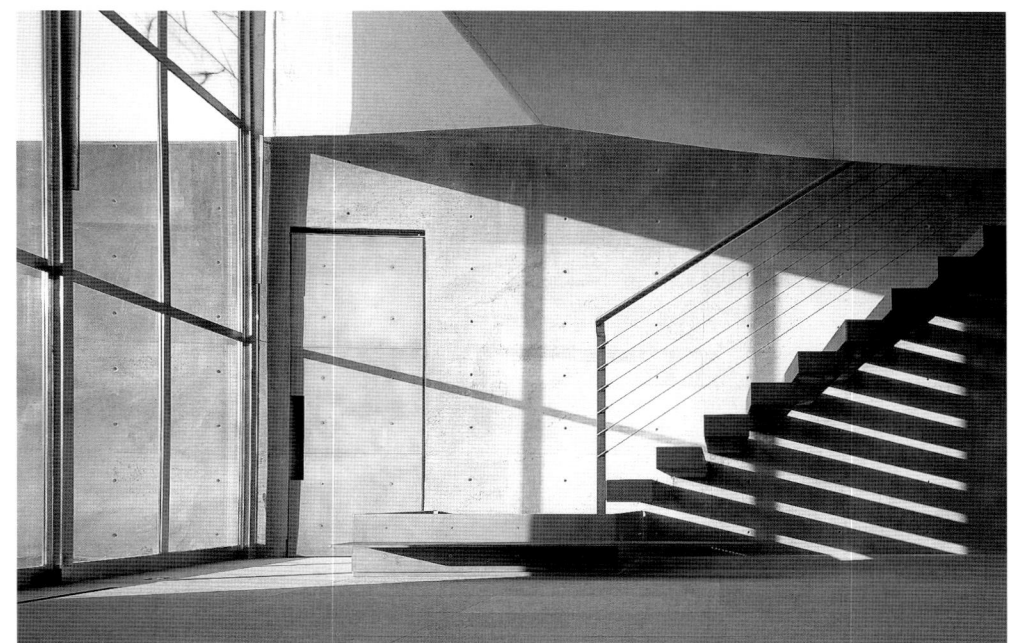

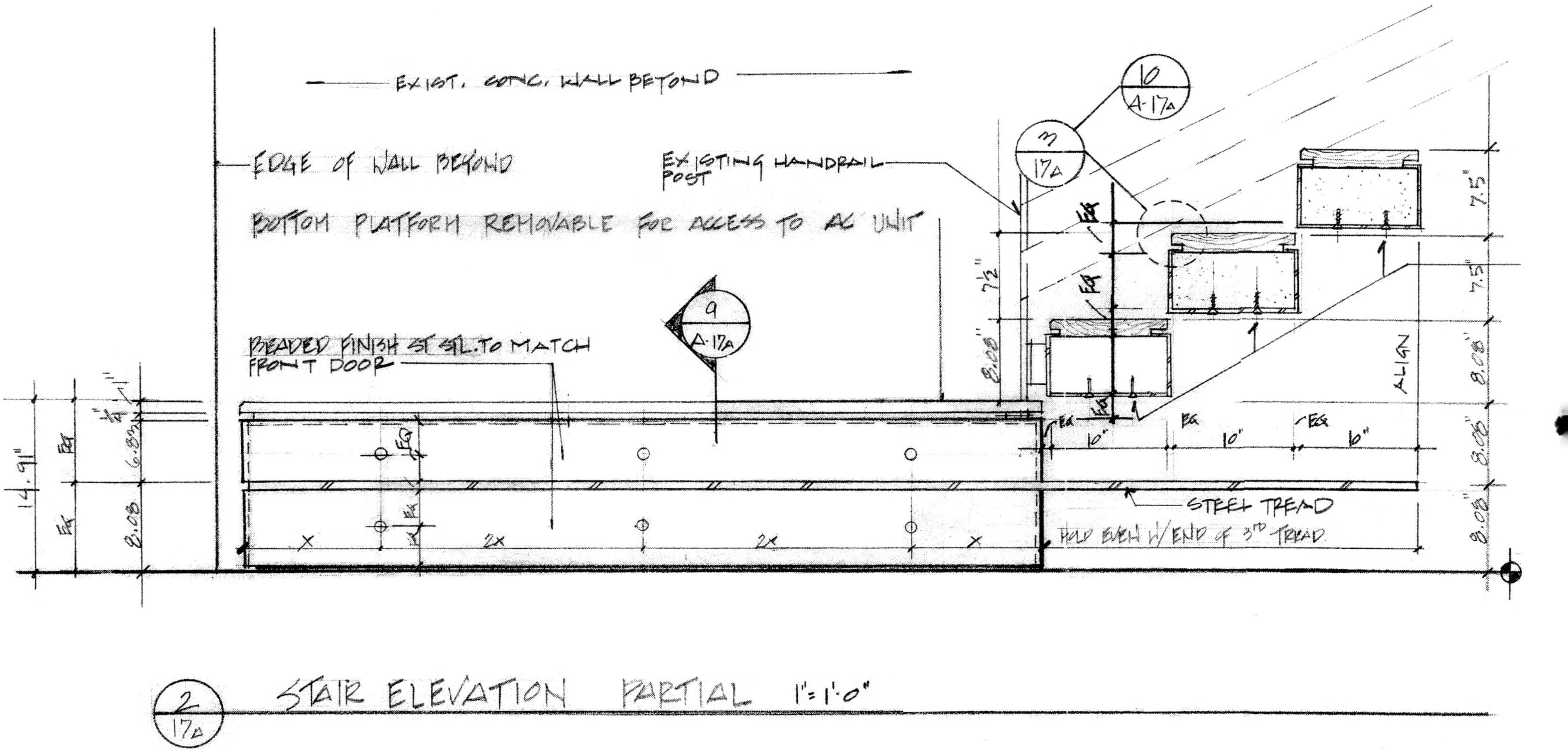
EXIST. CONC. WALL BEYOND
EDGE OF WALL BEYOND
EXISTING HANDRAIL POST
BOTTOM PLATFORM REMOVABLE FOR ACCESS TO AC UNIT
BEADED FINISH ST STL. TO MATCH FRONT DOOR
STEEL TREAD
HOLD EVEN W/ END OF 3RD TREAD
ALIGN
10
A-17A
3
17A
9
A-17A
14.91"
6.83"
8.08"
7.5"
10"
2x
EQ
2
17A
STAIR ELEVATION PARTIAL 1"=1'-0"

Mies House Pavilions and Second Addition

1985-1989

PETER L. GLUCK AND PARTNERS

FACING PAGE, TOP:
First addition pavilions
FACING PAGE, BOTTOM:
Existing house by Mies van der Rohe

Owner: Richard and Jane Wolf
Architect: Peter L. Gluck and Partners, New York, New York
Design Team: Pavilions: Peter L. Gluck, Kent Larson, Louis Turpin. Second addition: Peter L. Gluck, Kent Larson, Cary Davis.
Engineers: Pavilions: DeSimone & Chaplin, Michael Theiss (structural). Second addition: Thune Associates, P.C. (structural), Thomas A. Polise (mechanical), Frank Scandale (mechanical).
General Contractor: W.R.T. Smith
Photography: Paul Warchol (pavilions), Norman McGrath (second addition)

Site: Weston, Connecticut
Program: Pavilions: 2 bedrooms, bathroom/Japanese bath, sauna, kitchen, entertainment pavilion. Second addition: Master bedroom suite, kitchen, dining room, storage/playroom/laundry.
Square Footage: 2050 in pavilions, 1500 in new second addition plus original
Structural System: Steel frame-concrete slab on grade (pavilions), steel frame and concrete basement (second addition).
Mechanical System: Forced hot air/air conditioning, oil fired
Major Exterior Materials: Kawneer aluminum siding (pavilion doors), Hope's steel (second addition windows), glass, brick.
Major Interior Materials: Pavilions: Oak veneer paneling, bluestone flooring, wool carpeting, mosaic 1" x 1" ceramic tile. Second addition: Travertine marble floors
Furnishings and Storage: Kitchen custom by architect.
Doors and Hardware: Kawneer aluminum siding doors (pavilions)
Windows: Hope's steel windows (second addition)
Fixtures: Litolier
Cost: $275 per square foot

Site

In 1952-53, Mies van der Rohe was asked to design a house in Weston, Connecticut for the brother of Herbert Greenwald, the developer for whom he had just finished construction of the Lake Shore Drive apartments in Chicago. After rejecting the original site chosen by his new client, Mies selected a slightly elevated location, set back some three hundred feet from a slow-moving river. Facing southeast, the rectangular house would look out across natural field grasses to the river and a cliff on its opposite side. One of only three Mies houses extant in the United States, it would be occupied by the Greenwald family for almost thirty years and generally unknown to the architectural community. Unpublished and perhaps not of the same caliber as the Farnsworth House, its siting is conceptually similar to that earlier project of 1945-50 in Plano, Illinois.

Design

Finished in 1955, the Greenwald house design was based on Mies's row house prototype for workers' housing and had elements similar to his Lake Shore

Site plan

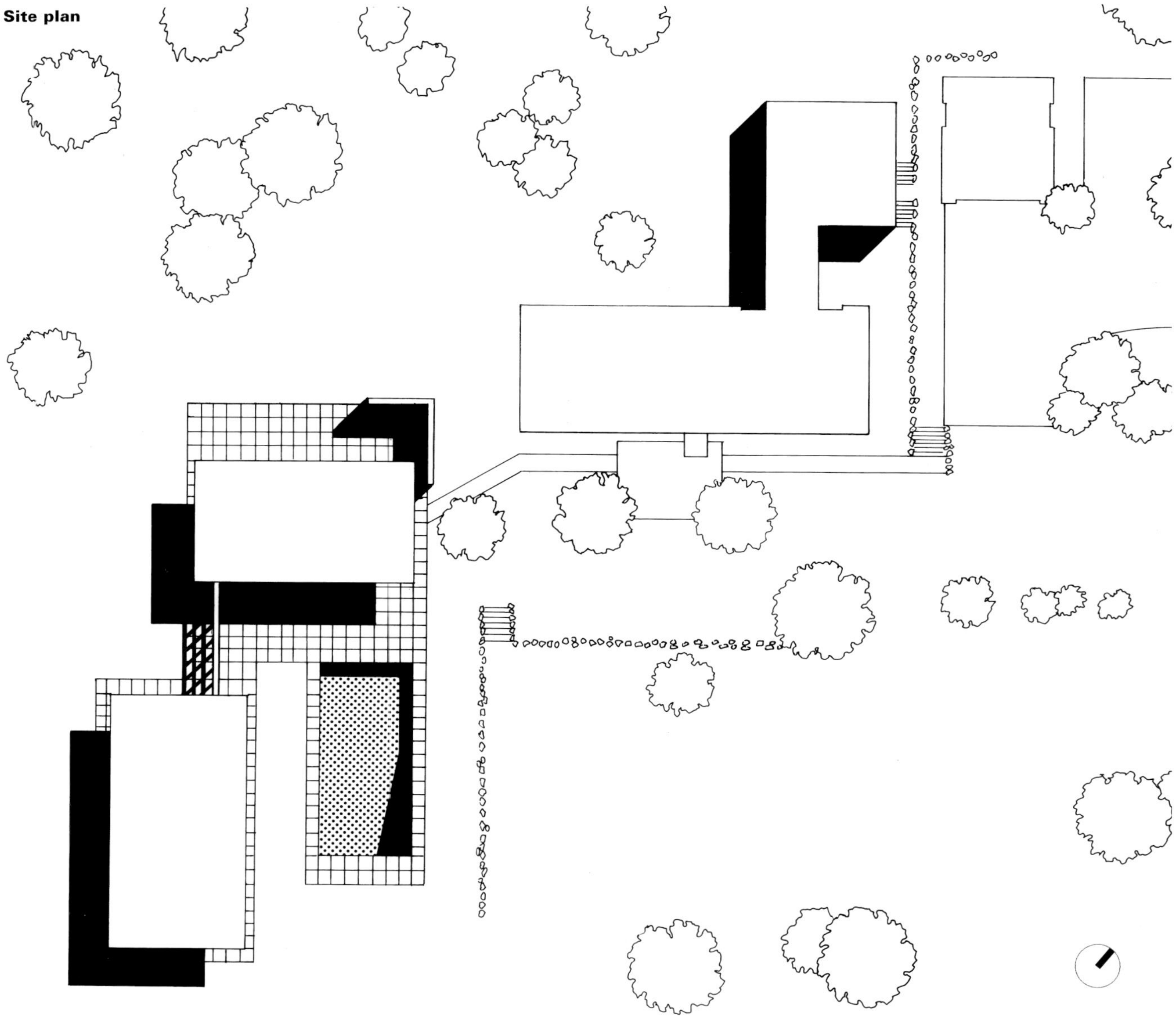

Diagram of additions

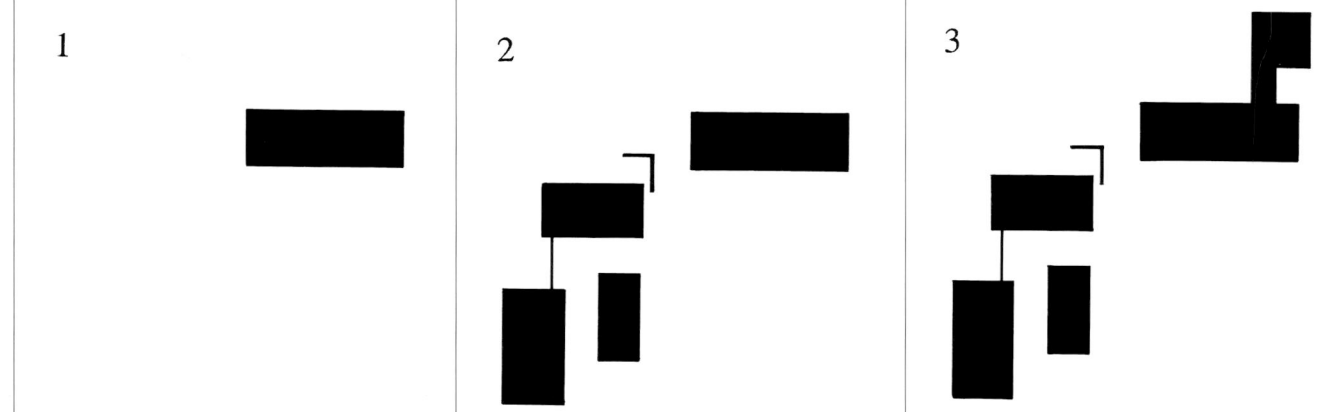

Drive apartment project. Its distinctive window wall is in fact identical to that of the finished Chicago apartments. Left-over window sash from that project was actually shipped to Connecticut for use in construction of the house.

The new owner wanted a weekend retreat for his family and for his corporate executives. The idea of "adding to Mies" was daunting. The challenge was to respect this icon of high modernism without mimicking the original. With respect to Mies and history the design had to be "contextual"; with respect to the new owners, it had to meet their needs better than the original.

Left intact as an icon, the original house became part of a composition of buildings, which now includes two discrete but linked pavilions inspired by the plan of Mies's Barcelona Pavilion of 1929. One pavilion contains two guest rooms, a sauna, and a Japanese bath; the other, a large common room, complete with kitchen, for meetings and entertaining. The two are joined by a perforated steel screen that also marks the precinct of the outdoor swimming pool. The alterations focused on provision of privacy and sound separation, both of which Mies found unnecessary.

Construction

Glass and steel are materials that bear reference to Mies's work and the International Style. But beyond specific allusion to Miesian architecture runs a recognition of the influence of Japan on the development of the modern movement. Elements such as raised platform floors, deep interior storage walls, light exterior walls that disappear into pockets, and horizontal roof planes supported on a seemingly unbraced columnar structure invoke Japan as well as the high modern.

Both pavilions have walls of insulated glass and aluminum insect screens that move on ceiling and floor tracks into fixed glass storage pockets. Miesian cross columns fabricated from rolled structural angles support the "floating" roof planes. "Murphy" beds pull down from storage walls, allowing unencumbered use of space during the day.

The transparency of the second addition is achieved with a light horizontal steel curtain wall that contrasts with the vertical rolled "H" sections of the Mies building. End walls of matching brick provide comparable closure to the openness of the glass walls.

Floor plan

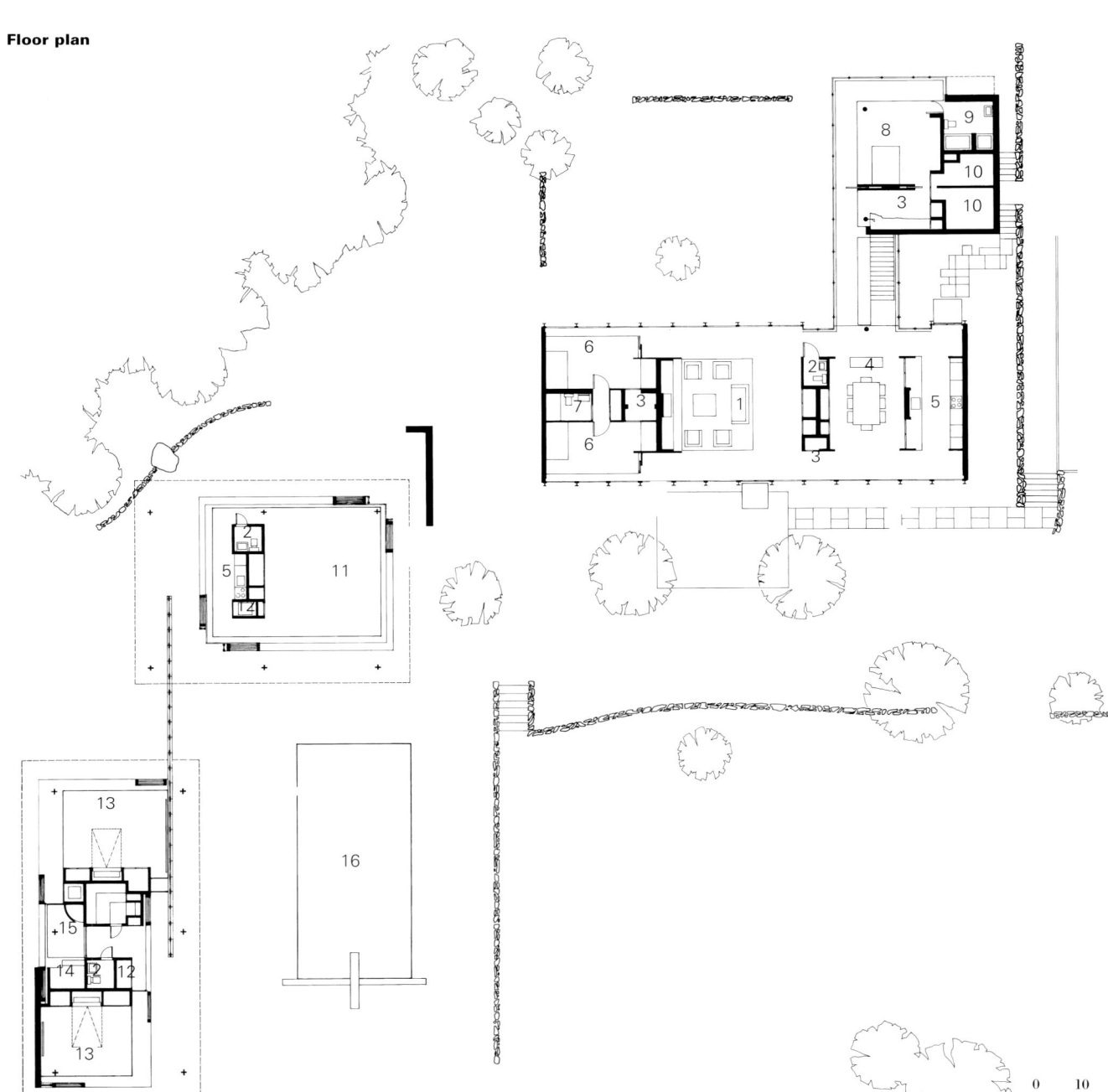

1. LIVING ROOM
2. HALF BATHROOM
3. STORAGE
4. DINING ROOM
5. KITCHEN
6. BEDROOM
7. BATHROOM
8. MASTER BEDROOM
9. MASTER BATHROOM
10. DRESSING ROOM
11. PAVILION
12. MECHANICAL
13. GUEST BEDROOM
14. JAPANESE BATH
15. SHOWER
16. POOL

0   10

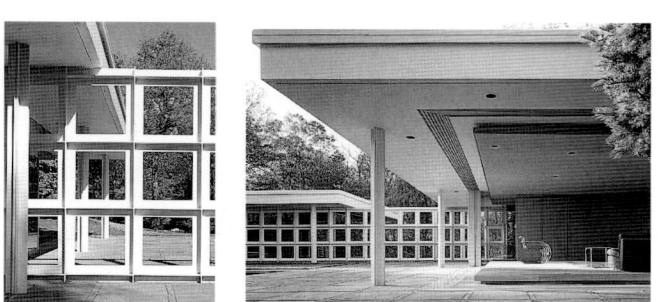

FAR LEFT: *Steel wall detail*
LEFT: *Pavilion lounge*

Steel wall detail

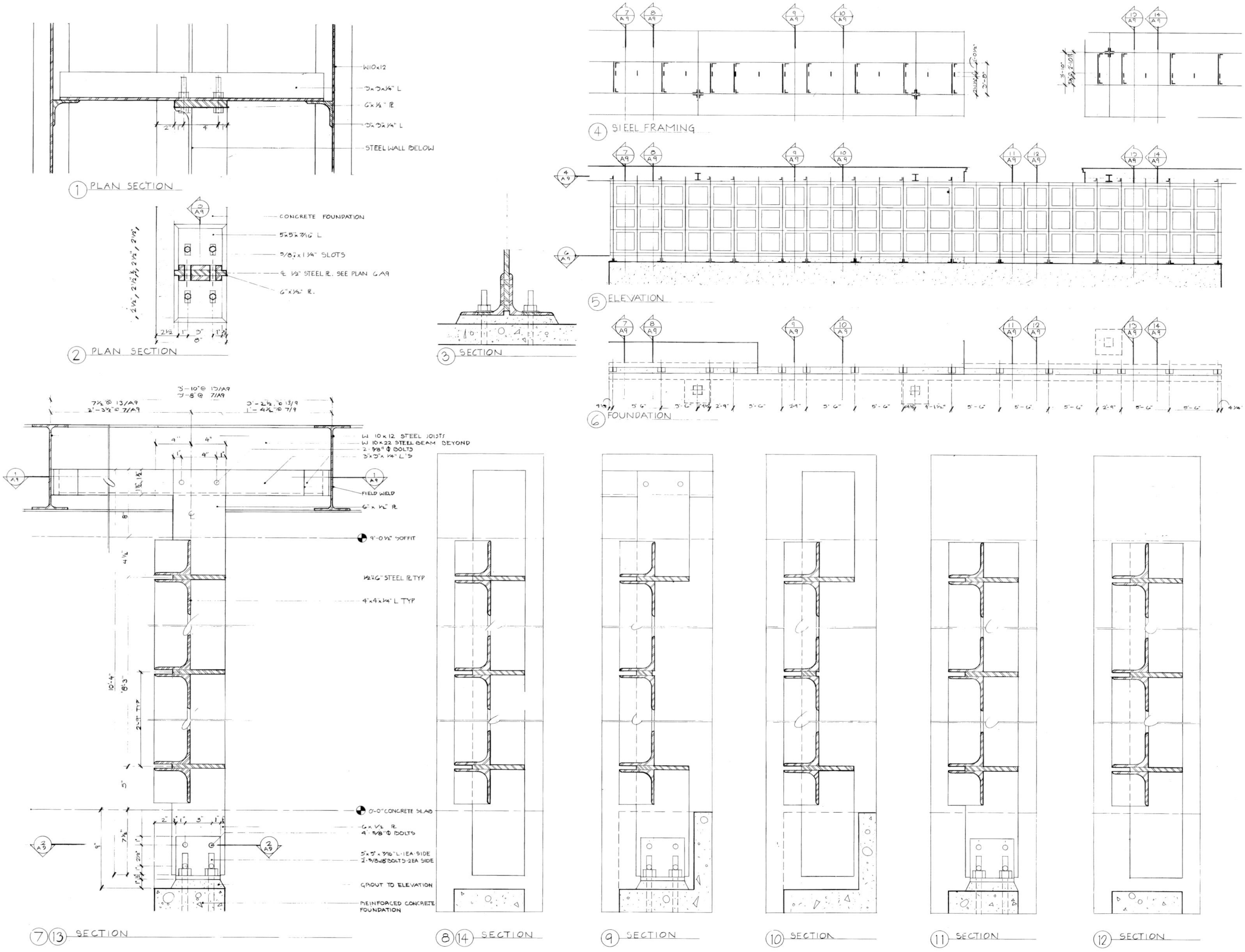

1 PLAN SECTION
2 PLAN SECTION
3 SECTION
4 STEEL FRAMING
5 ELEVATION
6 FOUNDATION
7 13 SECTION
8 14 SECTION
9 SECTION
10 SECTION
11 SECTION
12 SECTION
W10x12
STEEL WALL BELOW
CONCRETE FOUNDATION
5/8"x1 1/4" SLOTS
W 10x12 STEEL JOISTS
W 10x22 STEEL BEAM BEYOND
FIELD WELD
9'-0 1/2" SOFFIT
1/2"x6" STEEL PL TYP
4"x4"x1/4" L TYP
0'-0" CONCRETE SLAB
GROUT TO ELEVATION
REINFORCED CONCRETE FOUNDATION

Pavilion wall section

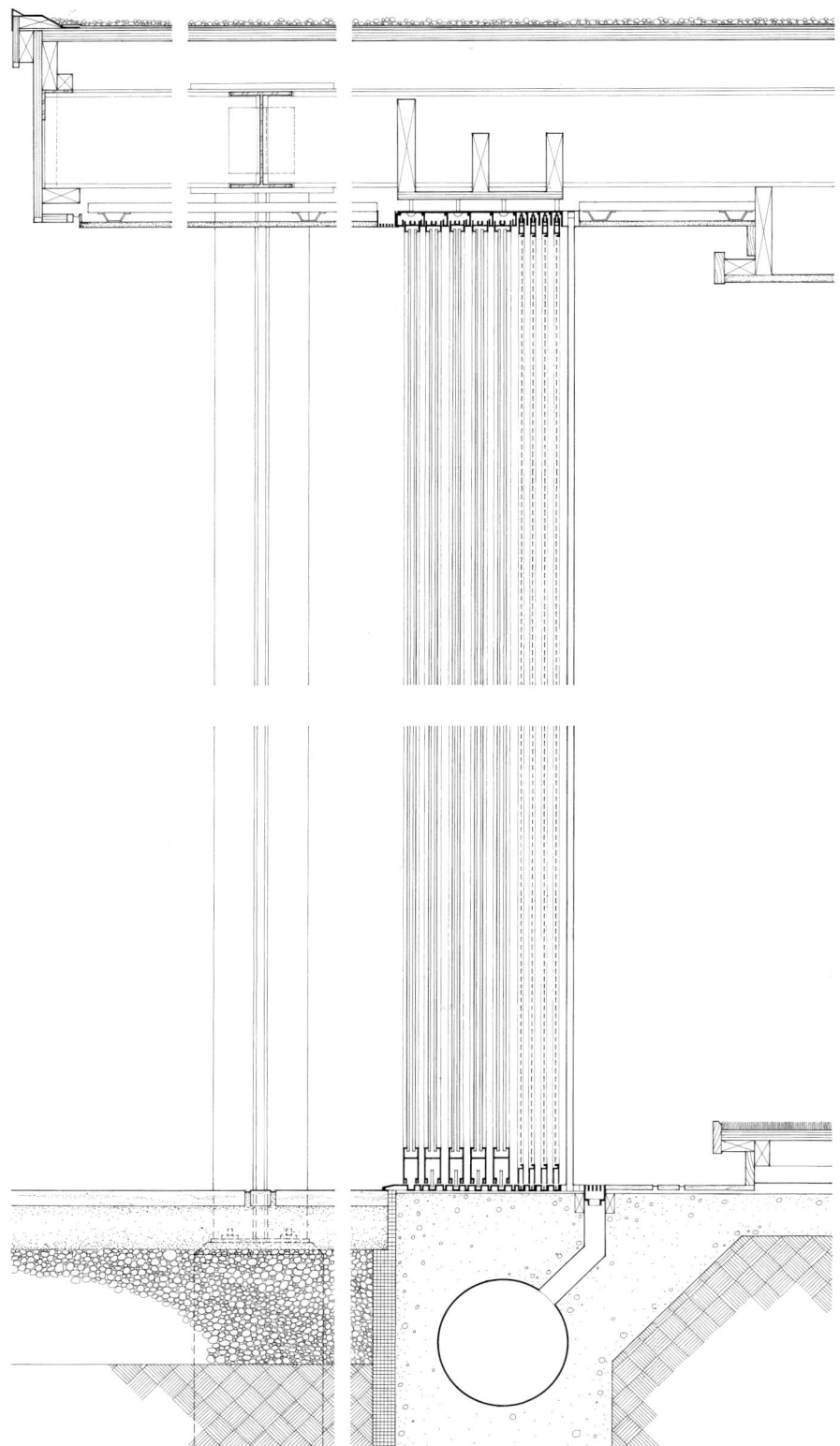

Plan of tracks for sliding glass panels

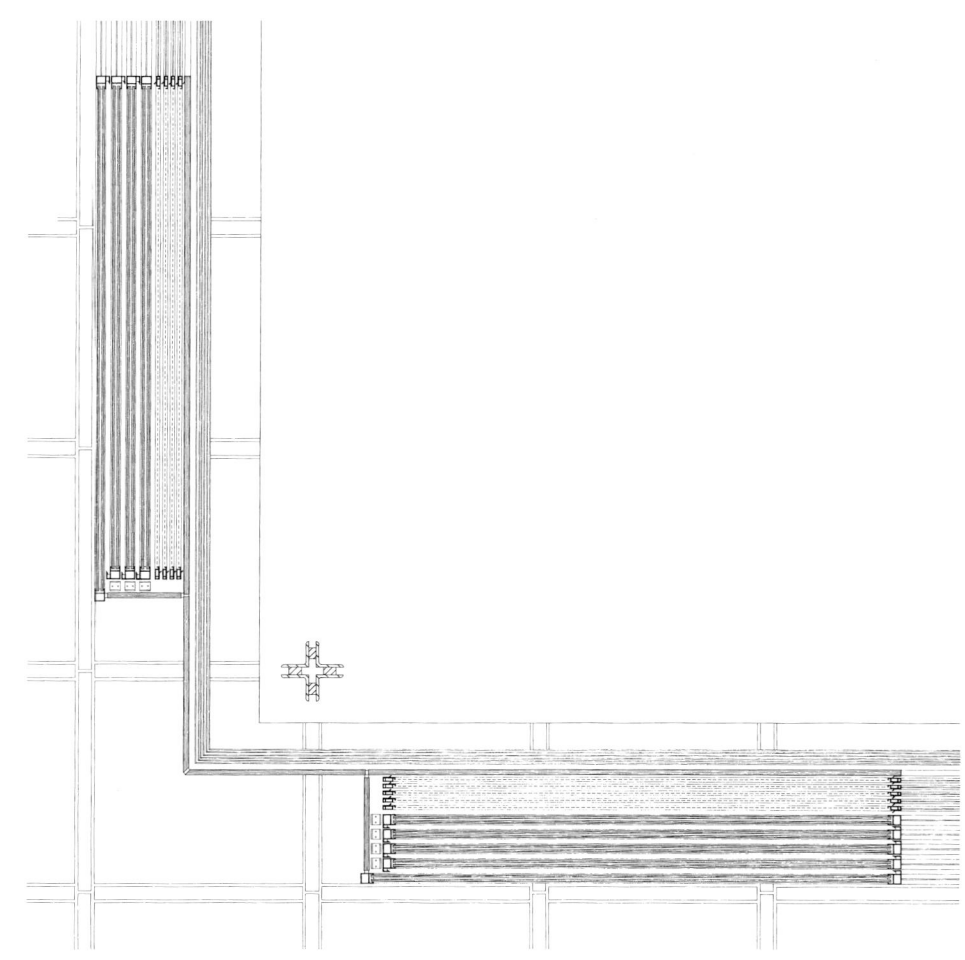

Wall section detail

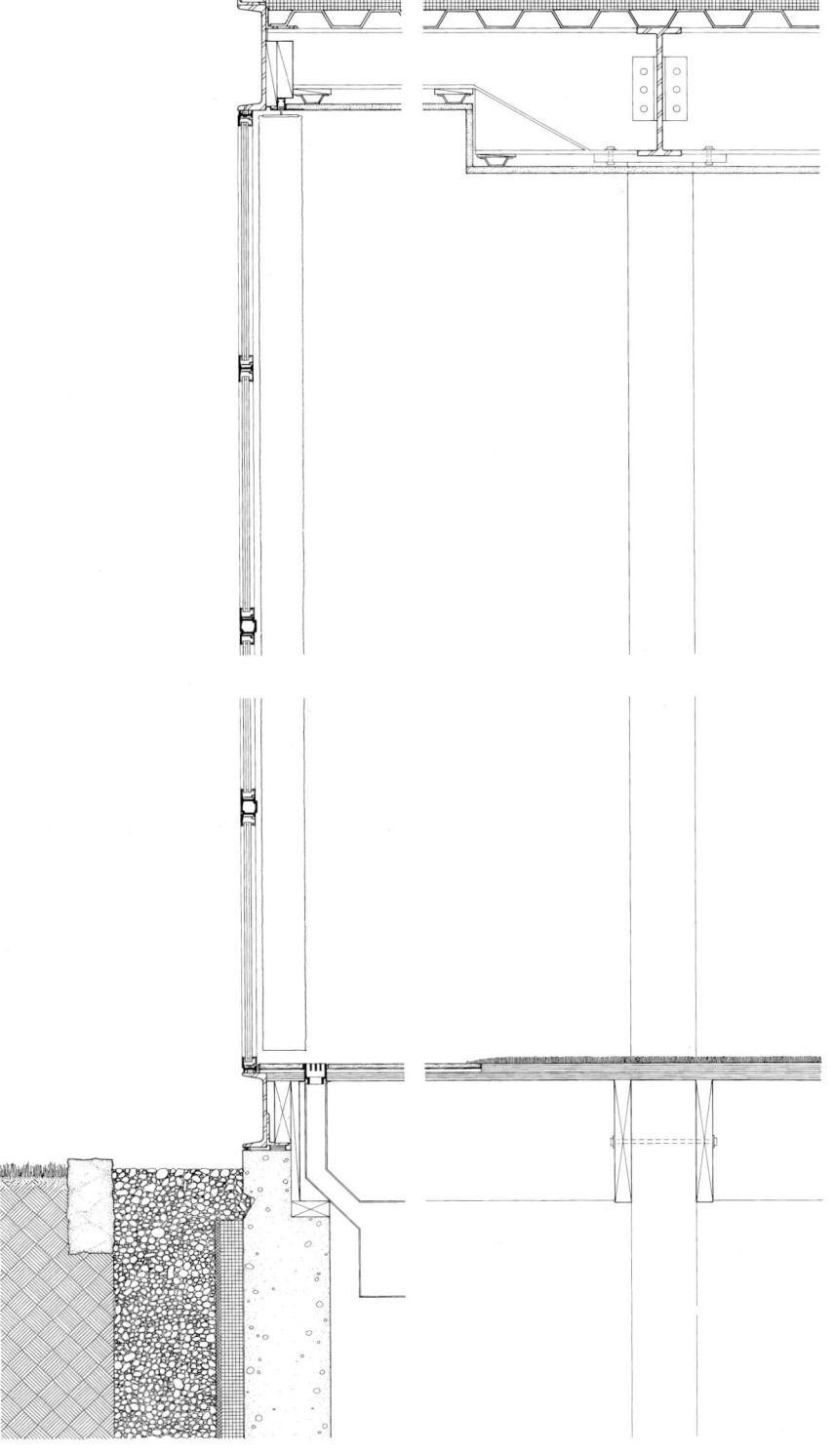

Second addition detail

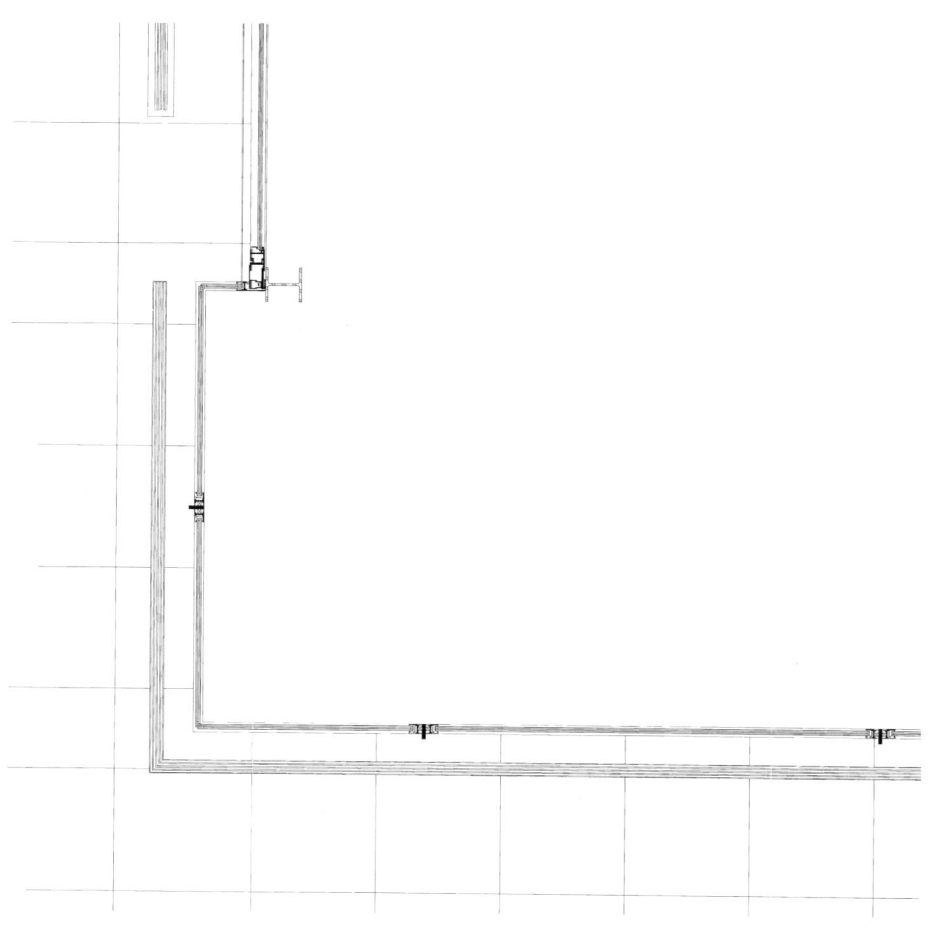

CLOCKWISE FROM TOP LEFT:
Dining room; second addition bathroom; new living room in existing house; second addition bedroom
FACING PAGE: *Hall connecting second addition with existing house*

Index